"This world is like a vestibule before the world to
come; prepare yourself in the vestibule, so that you
may enter the banqueting hall."

RABBI JACOB B. TAL. ABOTH 4.16

Since I am come to that holy room,
Where with thy choir of saints for evermore,
I shall be made thy music; as I come
I tune the instrument here at the door,
And what I must do then, think here before.

JOHN DONNE HYMN TO GOD MY GOD, IN MY SICKNESS

"The yearning for an afterlife is the opposite of
selfish: it is love and praise for the world that we are
privileged, in this complex interval of light,
to witness and experience. Though some believers
may think of the afterlife as a place of retribution,
where lives of poverty, distress, and illness will be
compensated for, and where renunciations will be
rewarded—where the last shall be first . . . the basic
desire, as Unamuno says in his *Tragic Sense of Life,* is
not for some *other*world but for *this* world, for life
more or less as we know it to go on forever."

JOHN UPDIKE SELF-CONSCIOUSNESS

"But I wonder whether people who ask God
to intervene openly and directly in our world quite
realise what it will be like when He does.
When that happens it is the end of the world.
When the author walks on the stage the play is over. . . .
It will be too late then to choose your side.
There is no use saying you choose to lie down when
it has become impossible to stand up."

C. S. LEWIS MERE CHRISTIANITY

JESUS, PAUL
AND THE END
WORLD *OF THE*

BEN WITHERINGTON III

A Comparative Study
in New Testament Eschatology

INTERVARSITY PRESS
DOWNERS GROVE, ILLINOIS 60515

InterVarsity Press
P.O. Box 1400, Downers Grove, IL 60515-1426
World Wide Web: www.ivpress.com
E-mail: mail@ivpress.com

InterVarsity Press® is the book-publishing division of InterVarsity Christian Fellowship/USA®, a student movement active on campus at hundreds of universities, colleges and schools of nursing in the United States of America, and a member movement of the International Fellowship of Evangelical Students. For information about local and regional activities, write Public Relations Dept., InterVarsity Christian Fellowship/USA, 6400 Schroeder Rd., P.O. Box 7895, Madison, WI 53707-7895, or visit the IVCF website at <www.intervarsity.org>.

ISBN 0-8308-1759-X

Printed in the United States of America ∞

Library of Congress Cataloging-in-Publication Data

Witherington, Ben, 1951-
    Jesus, Paul, and the end of the world: a comparative study in New
    Testament eschatology / Ben Witherington.
      p. cm.
    Includes bibliographical references.
    ISBN 0-8308-1759-X
    1. Eschatology—Biblical teaching.   2. Bible. N.T.—Criticism,
    interpretation, etc. I. Title.
    BS2545.E7W58   1992

236'.9'09015—dc20   91-39616
                                               CIP

P	21	20	19	18	17	16	15	14	13	12	11	10	9	8	7	6
Y	19	18	17	16	15	14	13	12	11	10	09	08	07	06		

Dedication

This book is dedicated to two groups of people, without whom I would not be who and where I am today. First, to the numerous godly master teachers of the New Testament that I have had over the years—Bernard Boyd (in memoriam), David Scholer, Gordon Fee, Andrew Lincoln, Ramsey Michaels, Bruce Metzger, Krister Stendahl, C. E. B. Cranfield and especially C. K. Barrett. Second, I must dedicate this work to those friends who in my formative years helped lead me to a fully formed Christian faith and commitment both within and outside of InterVarsity Christian Fellowship at the University of North Carolina—Chapel Hill: Rick Sanders, Bill Brafford, Don and Kathy Tyndall, Spencer Tilley, Clyde and Val Godwin, Tom Morris, Andy Dearman, Tom Sweets, Scott and Nancy Sunquist, Richard and Pam Haney, Richard Carriker, John and Nora Sherrill, Sarah Batchelor, Lisa Blank, Mary Ellen Johnson and Al Thorne to mention but a few. Last, special thanks and dedication must be given to James David Kline, my previous *shaliach,* who has faithfully helped me prepare indexes and read endless pages of my work as my teaching assistant, and to Rick Ravine, my current teaching assistant, for his aid in the production of this book. Blessings on all their houses.

Introduction

One of the more abiding contributions of the Judaeo-Christian tradition to human understanding and development is the idea that human history has a purpose, a direction and a goal. In the Western world, this linear view of human life and development challenged and eventually replaced earlier notions of fatalism, or of human life simply following the repeated pattern of the seasons or the crop cycle. This sense of human purpose, direction and goal also has spawned such diverse theories as Darwinian evolution on the one hand and Heideggerian dialectical thought on the other. Today, however, the teleological approach to human life and history is being challenged in the West by a resurgence of various Oriental ideas, such as reincarnation. These ideas are being represented to Western culture in many forms, notably as part of the religious phenomenon known as the New Age movement.

Even apart from such movements, in the scholarly discussion of the Judaeo-Christian tradition many are challenging the idea that human history has a purpose, direction and goal. We are constantly being told that the eschatological language of the Bible, the language that discusses what will happen at the close of human history, must be demythologized since it can no longer be held to correspond with historical reality. Some are bold enough to say that this language, insofar as it speaks of the ultimate future of humanity at all, is simply mistaken since the world did not come to an end in the first century A.D. or shortly thereafter. Other scholars insist that this eschatological language is meant to comfort distressed early Jews or Christians, not to explain the purpose, direction or goal of human history. We are confronted with the suggestions *either* that early Jews and Christians were wrong, at least in regard to the timing of the ultimate future (which raises the very real possibility that they were wrong in regard to the character of that future as well), *or* that eschatological language does not intend to comment on the historical human future in any concrete way.

It is my contention that both views are in error, at least as they apply to the eschatological teaching of two notable early Jews who have rightly been called the founders of Christianity: Jesus and Paul. While some early Jews and Christians did believe that the world would definitely end in the first century A.D., and this belief colored their eschatological thinking and language, I do not think Jesus or Paul were among them.

I also maintain that the eschatological teachings of these two figures, while certainly requiring interpretation within the context of early Jewish and Christian eschatological and apocalyptic thinking, do not require demythologizing, if by demythologizing one means evacuating the eschatological symbols of any possible future historical reference. It is one thing to claim that Jesus and Paul spoke with great certainty about ultimate human destiny as a historical reality; it is another to insist that they thought this reality would come to pass within a few years or generations. I contend that their beliefs about the *certainty* and the *character* of the end of human history, not some belief about its *timing,* account for the way Jesus and Paul speak.

In this book I will compare and contrast what Jesus and Paul are reported to have said about "the end things"—the final resurrection, the coming of the Son of Man, the future of Israel and the world, and the kingdom of God among other topics. We will examine those traditions which suggest that either Jesus or Paul commented not only on the nature but also on the timing of these end things. This requires paying special attention to the thoughts of the person who more than any other led (or misled) scholars to conclude that both Jesus and Paul definitely and wrongly expected the imminent end of human history—Albert Schweitzer. I hope that by studying what Jesus and Paul said about our human future we may be in a position to reassess whether or not these teachings have any relevance for the current discussion about the goal and direction of human history.

As we approach the year 2000 such a discussion should be pertinent, not least because such dates seem to prompt apocalyptic or eschatological or millenarian thinking of various sorts. J. B. Lightfoot once noted: "In the tenth century . . . the expectation of the approaching end of the world in or about the year 1,000 A.D. was almost universal. This event was to usher in the seventh sabbatical period of a thousand years, the preceding six millenia being calculated as five between Adam and Christ, and one after the Nativity."[1] Despite the fact that in the last two thousand years such forecasts of an imminent end to the world have all been wrong, this has not deterred many from continuing to speculate. As I write this introduction, apocalyptic speculations are being fueled not only by the war in the Persian Gulf, but also by various popular treatments of eschatology from a Dispensational perspective, such as J. F. Walvoord's reissued and updated version of his 1974 book, *Armageddon, Oil, and the Middle East Crisis.* At last report Walvoord's book had sold over one million copies in its 1990 edition. This shows the great interest in things eschatological among the general population, especially in a time of crisis, but it may also serve as a reminder to the scholarly community that it has too long neglected such subjects.

In examining the material in the Gospels and Paul's letters I will be using the method most widely accepted in the scholarly community—the historical-critical method. By its nature this method is cautious in its approach to historical data. It does not assume the historicity of any given piece of biblical data but rather requires that one argue for such a conclusion. I attempt to provide such arguments where they are necessary. One could often say much more on many of the subjects treated in this book but because of the constraints of the historical-critical method I shall not be doing so. This does not necessarily cast aspersions on the historicity of the material not included in this study. It must be kept in mind that by using the historical-critical method we are only able to demonstrate the probability, not the certainty, that Jesus or Paul said this or that. This may say more about the limitations of the historical-critical method than about the historical authenticity of any text. However, I have taken this approach because I intend to address the widest possible audience within the Christian community. I hope that this book will provide a means for people on all points of the theological spectrum to discuss eschatological matters meaningfully.

This study deals selectively with certain key aspects of the future hope of Jesus and Paul since the issues involved are too large to be given adequate treatment in one book. I hope that it will give these old eschatological issues the serious attention they deserve, especially in quarters where they have been too long ignored, neglected, misunderstood or too lightly and easily dismissed.

PART ONE

The Language
of
Imminence

—1—

Paul, Jesus
and the
Language
of Imminence

As any study that involves comparing and contrasting the thoughts of Jesus and Paul will show, the scholarly community is divided on the question of whether and to what degree there *is* any continuity between these two figures. Some scholars, such as J. Jeremias, F. F. Bruce or, to a lesser degree, J. D. G. Dunn, have stressed the continuity between Jesus and Paul.[1] By contrast, E. Käsemann sees only a minimal connection between the two major figures that influenced early Christianity, and Rudolf Bultmann rejected the search for continuity outright.[2] Various other scholars have taken more mediating positions.[3]

However, Jesus and Paul do seem to share common beliefs in some of their eschatological convictions and in the early Jewish eschatological framework of their thought.[4] Yet a battle over terminology recently has been waged on these matters, and at least in Paul's case the growing trend is to speak of his *apocalyptic* rather than eschatological gospel.[5] Thus, I must explain why I choose to refer to Jesus' and Paul's world views as eschatological rather than apocalyptic in character.

Jesus' and Paul's Teachings—Eschatological or Apocalyptic?

The term *apocalyptic,* like the term *eschatology,* has been notoriously difficult to define. If we use the former term to refer to a specific genre of literature (apocalypses), then it is apparent that neither Jesus nor Paul, so far as we know, produced any apocalyptic literature. However, some elements in both Jesus' and Paul's thought seem apocalyptic in character, such as the saying of Jesus about Satan falling from heaven (Lk 10:18), or Paul's account of being carried up to the third heaven (2 Cor 12:1-5). By and large, however, neither Jesus' nor Paul's presentations of the gospel are like what we find in Daniel or in the Animal Apocalypse in the Enoch literature or in Revelation.[6] C. K. Barrett was right when he remarked of Paul:

> His epistles are almost as different from apocalypses in content as they are in form. The sense of expectancy with which Paul looked for a future consummation is combined in his epistles with an intense spiritual life lived in the present, and with a concentrated attention focused upon events in the past— the life, death and resurrection of Jesus regarded as the fulfillment of prophecy and the completion of the OT.[7]

For this reason, J. J. Collins has stressed that one of the basic problems in the study of things apocalyptic is that various scholars tend to select some features of apocalypticism and see them as the essence of apocalypticism.[8] These features usually are (1) some form of dualism, perhaps including a two-age schema; (2) the proclamation of the imminent end of the world, or the end of some aspect of the world; and (3) the use of apocalyptic symbols and metaphors to comfort the afflicted or persecuted and reassure them that God is in control and that the forces of evil both natural and supernatural will finally lose their battle against the righteous and be punished. However, only (1) in some form (sometimes moral dualism, sometimes cosmic dualism, sometimes both)[9] and (3) in part (the use of symbols to speak of final judgment) are characteristic of *all* apocalypses. There is, in fact, no apocalyptic orthodoxy on the matter of the timing of things eschatological. Some apocalypses of the heavenly ascent type do not address eschatological matters, such as the end of human history, at all.

These three characteristics are generalizations based on some historical apocalypses (usually the biblical ones). For example, Revelation and 4 Ezra have end-of-the-world language, but this is otherwise atypical of apocalypses, especially those of the heavenly ascent type.[10] No two apocalypses express their vision of the future in the same way. Also striking is that the examples of clearly apocalyptic language cited above from Jesus and Paul are more like the material found in heavenly ascent rather than in historical apocalypses (though some apocalypses mix the two types).

While some have based generalizations on the genre apocalypse, others have looked more specifically at a Jewish (or Jewish-Christian) apocalyptic world view. A recurring element in the relevant literature is a belief in and reliance on supernatural revelation, usually in the form of visions or dreams, that comes from the heavenly world mediated by an angel or some sort of otherworldly being in order to help a believer deal with some sort of problem. This revelation comes at least usually in the form of images and metaphors, and judgment/destruction of the wicked is characteristically part of its message. It entails a belief that

there is a hidden world of angels and demons that is directly relevant to human destiny; and this destiny is finally determined by a definitive eschatological judgment. In short, human life is bounded in the present by the supernatural world of angels and demons and in the future by the inevitability of a final judgment.[11]

A person with an apocalyptic world view believes that the revelation of what lies both behind and beyond the tapestry of human life and history provides a key to understanding one's situation and dealing with one's dilemma.

In this regard, neither Jesus' nor Paul's teachings contain much that could be said to manifest the characteristic apocalyptic *forms*—visions and dreams or the use of bizarre symbols.[12] To be sure, both Jesus and Paul believed in angels and demons, but their teaching is not about such beings. Nor is it about what is happening behind or beyond the tapestry of human history, for it focuses on happenings *in* human history. Neither Jesus nor Paul concentrate on revealing heavenly battles, scenarios or journeys. Nor is there any indication that they saw themselves as reliant on angel visitations to provide them with the substance of their revelations. Both Jesus and Paul, insofar as they talk of cosmological change at all, do not focus on this matter, but rather focus on salvation/redemption, either of the individual or of God's people.

Nor do we have any sort of detailed reflection from either Jesus or Paul on the causes or nature of suffering or the problem of evil in the world. Both Jesus and Paul focus on the positive new thing that God is already doing in human history—the good news. In the thought of Jesus or Paul we do not get the sense of evil as the present *dominating* reality in the world to which theology must respond. Rather, we hear of the overcoming of evil by historical deeds such as exorcism (in the case of Jesus) or the cross of Christ (in the teaching of Paul).

What we find in both Jesus and Paul is a world-transforming, not a world-negating, approach to things. For example, neither provides a radical critique of human government; indeed, both seem to allow for its current validity (Mk 12:13-17 and parallels; Rom 13). Their use of *abba* suggests the very opposite of what one might expect from someone with an apocalyptic world view who senses God is distant and feels alienated from the world. Both have modified the Jewish schema in which God's definite action against sin and evil is seen as happening in "the age to come." As L. Keck says, "There is in Paul an irreducible tension between 'already' and 'not yet' which is generally absent from apocalyptic theology. . . . Jewish apocalyptic theology knows nothing of the sudden appearing of a messianic figure who has already effected salvation through a prior appearance."[13] Likewise in the case of Jesus' thought, this focus on historical actions coupled with both an already/not yet tension and the proclamation of good news is definitive.[14]

Jesus either speaks directly in the first person, tells parables or indicates he has received direct revelation from God (Mt 11:25-27 and parallels), while Paul either speaks on his own authority or claims to have direct revelation from God (Gal 1:12-16, especially v. 16) or possibly from the exalted Christ (see 1 Thess 4:15, though even here it is not clear whether he is referring to a word of the earthly Jesus or the exalted Lord). This is not to say that Jesus and Paul did not share a world view in which "supernatural revelation, the heavenly world, and eschatological judgment played essential parts."[15] If that is all that one means by calling Paul's or Jesus' thought or world view apocalyptic, then undoubtedly the term is appropriate. My point has been to stress that neither Jesus nor Paul by and large use the characteristic language or *forms* of apocalyptic literature to convey their world view.

Usually, however, people who call Jesus' or Paul's world view apocalyptic mean something more than what Collins identifies as characteristic of such a world view. I suspect that often when a person calls Paul's or Jesus' world view apocalyptic, what is usually meant is that it is driven by a conviction that the world as we know it is already or will necessarily be coming to an end soon. In short, the language of the necessary imminence of the end is thought to characterize Jesus' and Paul's world views, and therefore they are labeled apocalyptic in outlook.

This view, associated in the twentieth century especially with scholars like

A. Schweitzer, has increasingly come under attack on several fronts and for several reasons: (1) the language of imminence does not seem to be a *sine qua non* of apocalyptic literature, or for that matter of an apocalyptic world view, if we accept the authors of the heavenly ascent apocalypses as examples of those who manifest such a world view; (2) the Jesus Seminar, by a 3-to-1 margin, now doubts that Jesus expected the end of the world in his lifetime or within a generation; (3) a detailed analysis of the relevant data in both the Gospels and the Pauline literature leads at most to a conclusion that Jesus and Paul considered the imminence of the end possible in their era but not a certainty.

In fact, both Paul and Jesus, like some of their Jewish and Christian contemporaries who wrote on eschatological matters,[16] are capable of combining the language of possible imminence with a discussion of events that must transpire before the end may come. Thus, Paul talks about the full number of the Gentiles who must first be saved before all Israel is saved (Rom 11) and speaks of his own future plans (which seem rather extensive in scope; Rom 15:24-29); yet in the same letter he says, "For salvation is nearer to us now than when we first believed; the night is far gone, the day is at hand" (13:11-12). Jesus on the one hand seems to suggest that time is running out on his disciples (Mt 10:23), but on the other says that the timing of "that day" is unknown even to himself (Mk 13:32).

Since so many scholars still assume that both Jesus and Paul saw the end as necessarily at hand in or shortly after their lifetimes, we need to make a detailed investigation of the language of imminence in their teaching. Therefore, I will devote the balance of part one to this investigation. In the meantime, I have said enough on this point to justify my choice of the word *eschatological* rather than *apocalyptic* when we speak of Jesus' or Paul's world view.

This seems particularly appropriate, not least because the teachings of both Jesus and Paul are historically rather than heavenly directed and future-oriented. By and large neither Jesus nor Paul seems to have couched his message in the form of heavenly visions using bizzare symbols, though both are obviously conversant with and draw on an apocalyptic thought-world. Furthermore, both proclaimed God's mercy on sinners, or even more strikingly the justification/pardon of the ungodly, which contrasts with the usual message of apocalyptic literature about the vindication of the righteous/godly at the expense of the ungodly. Thus, on the whole it would be better to say that they manifest Jewish eschatological world views that include some apocalyptic elements rather than that they manifest apocalyptic world views with some eschatological elements.[17]

Both Jesus and Paul oscillate between the eschatological already and the not yet, being convinced that some crucial matters have already or are now happening and some are yet to come in the future.[18]

The Language of Imminence

Without question, A. Schweitzer has been one the seminal figures in New Testament studies in the twentieth century. Because of works like *The Quest of the Historical Jesus, The Mystery of the Kingdom of God* and *The Mysticism of Paul the Apostle,* his impact upon scholarly thinking about the eschatology of Jesus and Paul has been great. This continues to be true in several important regards, despite the fact that numerous scholars, such as V. P. Furnish, N. Dahl and J. C. Beker, have shown various limitations of Schweitzer's approach (not the least of which is the fact that we cannot completely separate eschatological and apocalyptic material since the former is often contained in the latter and vice versa).

Schweitzer seems to have had an abiding impact on most critical studies of the eschatology of Jesus or Paul in two particular areas. First is the insistence that both Jesus and Paul expected the end of the world within a few years or generations. This, in turn, is believed to have forced early Christians to wrestle with the problem of the delay of the return of the Son of Man and the delay of the end of human history. Second is the argument that both Jesus and Paul, as a result of their imminentism, promulgated a sort of interim ethic, that is, imperatives that would be directly applicable for believers during the short time span left before the conclusion of human history. The attempts to follow Schweitzer in this regard have led to the widespread belief that late-twentieth-century Christians cannot directly follow and apply much of the ethical teaching of Jesus and Paul. At best, it is argued, one must hermeneutically sift the eschatologically conditioned ethical teaching of Jesus and Paul for a few abiding ideas or principles that might still be applicable today. Needless to say, such assumptions would and do drastically affect whether or not the teachings of Jesus and Paul have anything relevant to say to us about our future.

In the first section of what follows, I have chosen to focus on perhaps the most detailed of Schweitzer's works, *The Mysticism of Paul the Apostle,* in order to show some of the significant flaws in his approach to the imminence language in Paul's eschatology. Similar things could be demonstrated in regard to Schweitzer's analysis of Jesus' teachings in *The Mystery of the Kingdom of God* or *The Quest of the Historical Jesus,* and I will deal with this latter work to some degree later. However, Schweitzer's treatment of both Jesus' and Paul's eschatological teachings is *basically* of a piece, and since today Paul is more often seen as one who spoke of an imminent end than did Jesus, we will spend more time analyzing the relevant Pauline data. Afterward, I will show how even Jesus' material need not be read as teaching the necessary imminence of the end.

In a paper first delivered at the one-hundredth meeting of the Society of Biblical Literature and later incorporated into the Harper edition of *Paul and Rabbinic Judaism*, W. D. Davies argued that in Schweitzer's classic work *The Mysticism of Paul the Apostle*

> he enlarged our perspectives and delivered us from provincialisms, but did he also introduce into his interpretation of eschatology mechanical and even magical categories which deprive it of full moral seriousness? For example, does not baptism, the act whereby the believer already has participated in the cosmic redemption, become a magical rite for Schweitzer? . . . Schweitzer's description of Paulinism is often reminiscent of the thought of those whom the Paul of the NT opposed, that is, those who felt that they had already been enriched and had already attained. The fact is that Schweitzer's Paul is so exclusively eschatological that he cannot participate in the full richness of Judaism. Schweitzer so isolated apocalyptic from other currents in Judaism that he deprived Paul of much of his Jewish heritage, even while insisting on his Jewishness.[19]

Davies then called on Pauline scholars to recognize their debt to Schweitzer, but also to realize that "if Schweitzer rightly revolted against the 'liberal' psychological concentration of the nineteenth-century scholars, the time is now ripe for a revolt against the 'dogmatic' eschatological concentration of their twentieth-century successors."[20] That revolt in large measure has not been forthcoming, although major studies such as M. Hengel's *Judaism and Hellenism* and E. P. Sanders's *Paul and Palestinian Judaism* have made it quite impossible to continue the neat dichotomies Schweitzer made between Jewish and Hellenistic categories, and even between the various branches of Jewish thought, as though apocalyptic was an isolated phenomenon.

On issues of Pauline theology, however, there has been no systematic attempt to reassess and critique Schweitzer's perspective, and certainly no revolt against eschatological concentration. The latter is due partly to the fact that eschatological categories have provided abiding insights into Paul and his general world view. It is a measure of the impact of Schweitzer's views in some quarters that even recent studies of Paul (such as Sanders, *Paul and Palestinian Judaism,* or S. Kim's specialized study, *The Origin of Paul's Gospel*)[21] have felt it necessary to interact in some detail with various of Schweitzer's arguments. In some quarters, though, Schweitzer has been largely ignored or dismissed;[22] nonetheless, his eschatological views have by no means been laid to rest. Thus, perhaps now is an appropriate time to raise the spectre of Schweitzer once more and see whether that spectre needs to be consulted further, or exorcised from the discussion once and for all.

—2—

Between
Daybreak and Day:
The Pauline
Evidence

In discussing the development of Paul's thought, Schweitzer states rather boldly: "From his first letter to his last Paul's thought is always uniformly dominated by the expectation of the immediate return of Jesus, of the judgment, and the Messianic glory."[1] Schweitzer, with no argumentation apart from the citing of certain proof texts, takes it as a given that Paul believed from first to last that the Lord would return immediately, that is, within Paul's own lifetime or soon thereafter, and that this conditioned all his thinking and ethical advice. To be sure, this idea has been passed down in scholarly circles as a "well-assured" result of Pauline scholarship, at least insofar as the early Pauline letters are concerned. But was it the *certainty* that Christ would return, or the *timing* of that return, or *both* that shaped Paul's expressions? If it was primarily the timing of Jesus' return that molded Paul's thought, was it the fact that Christ *could* return imminently, or *would* return imminently that explains all the evidence most adequately? What is Paul's conception of the relationship of time and eternity? In order to deal with Paul's thought, scholars must at least assume an answer to these questions.

Following Schweitzer's lead, I agree that 1 Thessalonians may be the earliest
of Paul's existing letters and is surely at least one of the earliest written. Undoubtedly it has a heavy eschatological cast to it, and a certain primitiveness. Nor can
we doubt that Paul was certain about the return of Christ and its importance for
the present. The problem lies in part in the fact that some of the texts Schweitzer
cites do not prove the "expectation of the immediate return" but rather prove the
expectation and anticipation of the return and its consequences. Such texts as
1 Thessalonians 2:19; 3:13 and 5:23 come immediately to mind. Others, such as
1 Thessalonians 1:10 do have a nonspecific time element where Paul speaks of
deliverance "from the coming wrath." E. Best is right to point out: "How quickly
this anger approaches is not said but if it were regarded as infinitely remote, it
would hardly be described as approaching (emphatic by position in the Greek)."[2]
But at most this proves that Paul believed the end *could* come soon, breaking
in suddenly, and thus Christians must be prepared. It is strange that Schweitzer
spends so little time commenting on 1 Thessalonians 4:13—5:11.[3] Conventional
exegesis of this material has assumed that Paul was saying he would definitely
and personally survive until the parousia, yet as D. E. H. Whiteley points out,
"it is not *certain* either that St. Paul expected to live until the parousia in 1 Thess.
or that he expected to die before it in 2 Cor."[4]

Consider for a moment the following possibility. Suppose Paul did not know
and did not pretend to know the timing of the Second Coming, but thought it
possible that it could be soon. Suppose also that he did not know that he would
die before the parousia. Now if he did not know the timing of the parousia or of
his own death, he could not assume that he would die prior to the parousia. This
means that the only category into which he could possibly put himself when
commenting on the parousia is the living (given his ignorance of the timing of both
these events). Paul could not have said, "We who will die prior to the parousia,"
because that would presuppose that he knew that the parousia was some distance
off. The point is, he simply did not know the timing of these events, and thus he
had to prepare and warn his converts because the parousia *might be soon.*

Thus we cannot infer from 1 Thessalonians 4:15 or 4:17 ("we who are living")
that Paul was certain that he would survive until the parousia. If there were only
two categories of Christians in this argument ("those who have fallen asleep" and
"we who are living"), then clearly Paul could only place himself in the latter
group.[5] Moore says, "Paul does not write as one who will certainly be dead at
the Parousia but as one who awaits the Parousia as an event which might occur

at any moment and therefore he reckons with the possibility of his being alive at that time; but this does not mean that he included himself amongst those who would necessarily be alive at its coming."[6]

H. Giesen has pointed out that the term we has a variety of meanings in verses 14-17. In verse 17 it clearly means all Christians, while in verse 15a it means the authors of this letter. It is thus far from certain that the "we" in verse 15b should be taken to imply that Paul felt sure he would be alive at the parousia. Giesen is also right to point out that the issue Paul is addressing here is not the "delay" of the parousia, but the status at the parousia of those Christians who have already died. Giesen conjectures that Paul had previously spoken of the rapture of Christians to meet the returning Christ, but to the Thessalonians this seemed to imply that only the living would be involved. This created a problem when some among their number died.[7]

Confirmation of the validity of this argument comes in what immediately follows (1 Thess 5:2-11). The Day of the Lord is described as something that comes "like a thief in the night." From verse 3 it is clear that Paul implies that this coming will happen unexpectedly or suddenly.[8] The arrival of this event will catch many, who think all is well, by surprise (v. 3a), but its coming should not surprise believers. Why? Not because they know the exact timing or even the general period of time when the parousia will come, but because they are prepared for that day, having been told that it definitely will come, whether sooner or later. Possibly Paul here is countering some in Thessalonica who may have been acting as if they knew the day was definitely at hand and had ceased working or carrying on their daily activities. Against such presumption Paul says emphatically, "For you yourselves know well" (v. 2), thus indicating that they had already been taught not to engage in theological forecasting since the day was coming "like a thief in the night."[9]

Certainly some believers in the early church believed in the immediate return of the Lord. This caused problems when some died prior to the parousia. If there was a problem about the delay in the parousia, then it was already in evidence in Paul's earliest Epistle. But unlike some Thessalonians, Paul himself shows no anxiety about the death of these believers prior to the parousia because apparently he already had taken into account such a possibility. The "thief in the night" concept's implications (whether or not he derived it from the sayings tradition in the early church)[10] likely led Paul to prepare for either eventuality (compare 2 Cor 5:6-10; Phil 1:21-26).

Schweitzer dismisses 2 Thessalonians as a source for knowledge about Paul, partly because of its strange language but mainly because "it opposes the idea that the return of Jesus is immediately at hand."[11] But should we dismiss an Epistle without argument simply because it does not agree with our preconceived understanding of Paul's eschatology? Doing so also ignores the idea that Paul's views may have developed or even changed significantly over a period of time. Various recent studies of Paul's linguistic usages have pointed out how easily and how well he adopts and adapts "the technical language of traditional apocalyptic" to suit his Christocentric theology and vision of the eschaton.[12] Further, W. G. Kümmel makes clear that, except for the use of *epiphaneia* of the parousia, the language and style of 2 Thessalonians is quite Pauline and consistent with his use of apocalyptic language. He adds:

Arguments against the authenticity based on the difference of the expectation of the End in I and II Thess. cannot be regarded as valid. The concepts employed in II Thess. are traditional apocalyptic material: The Man of Lawlessness (II Thess. 2:3) and the Restrainer . . . in 2:7 are apocalyptic figures; the events which 2:3ff presupposes are as compatible and as incompatible with I Cor. 15:23ff. There is nothing surprising about the alleged tension between I Thess. 5:2, where the parousia is expected to come like a thief in the night, and II Thess. 2:3ff, where anticipatory signs must first occur . . . it must be recalled that both conceptions—the End is coming suddenly, and it has historical antecedents—occur together in the apocalyptic of Judaism and early Christianity, and lie within the same perspective. Nor is it true that Paul nowhere else offers such apocalyptic detail (cf. I Thess. 4:15-17; I Cor. 15:23-28, 51f). The "over-realized eschatology" of the false teachers who proclaim "The day of the Lord has already come" (II Thess. 2:2) must by no means be viewed as related to Gnosticism.[13]

R. Jewett also argues that on balance 2 Thessalonians should be seen as authentic Pauline material, and he shows why the arguments of W. Trilling and others against it being genuinely Pauline will not stand close scrutiny.[14] Now if we allow that 2 Thessalonians (especially chap. 2) is authentic, then it becomes very difficult to argue that Paul held, early or late, to the view that Christ certainly *would* return immediately. A period of time before the End is built into the text of 2 Thessalonians 2, as Schweitzer realized. Even supposing that 2 Thessalonians is not authentic,[15] it becomes increasingly difficult to demonstrate from letters written after 1 Thessalonians that Paul held to such an immediate return. If it is not demonstrable in 1 Thessalonians, then it is even less so elsewhere, with the possible exception of 1 Corinthians.

Schweitzer warns in advance that Corinthians, Romans and Galatians are so preoccupied with arguments about the law, righteousness by faith, being in Christ, predestination and the particular affairs of the churches, "that it is possible to forget the expectation which dominates the soul of the writer."[16] Some of the texts that Schweitzer cites in 1 Corinthians tell us nothing about the timing of the parousia, only about its character and attendant circumstances. For instance, in 1 Corinthians 1:7-8 Paul speaks of the eagerly awaited event and what God will do to keep the believer from facing judgment on that occasion. In 11:26 he mentions the fact of the Second Coming, and in 16:22 prays for that day, but he does not discuss the timing in these contexts. In 6:3 he mentions the believer's role at the judgment, but again not the timing.

Notoriously difficult is 10:11, which says, "Upon whom the ends [goals] of the ages have arrived." This could be a reference to the end of human history, except that "ends" is plural and "have arrived" is in the perfect in the Greek text, signifying completed action. Thus, Paul is not talking about something that is *about* to happen, but something that has been finished or completed. Perhaps he is discussing the fact that the Corinthians are living at the time when the goals or ends of these past ages of history "have arrived"—eschatological time has arrived, bringing previous ages of history, such as the age of Moses just referred to, to a close or to a climax.[17] In any case, this verse does not warrant Schweitzer's translation: You are the generation "that will outlive the end of time."[18]

With 1 Corinthians 7:25-40, however, we get right to the heart of the matter.[18a] Paul's advice to the virgins is the same as his advice to the circumcised and the slaves in verses 17-24: "It is good for a person to remain as they are." The reason he offers is *dia tēn enestōsan anankēn*. Could this be a reference to a present or an imminent distress (or necessity)? What kind of distress is Paul discussing? Because of the qualifying word, present/imminent, it cannot be a reference to the anxieties inherent to the married life (compare vv. 32-35). Nor does it appear to be the kind of distress discussed in verse 37.

Perhaps the phrase which best illuminates the meaning of "present distress" is found in verse 29: *ho kairos synestalmenos estin.* Here too we are uncertain about the translation of the key word *synestalmenos.* Are we to translate it "short" or "shortened"? Are these references to some impending and crucial event in the eschatological timetable, or are they a reference perhaps to some sort of persecution that the Corinthians were facing or undergoing because of their faith?

Paul does speak of troubles in verse 28, and elsewhere he uses this word in an eschatological sense of the trials that will befall Christians now that the end times have broken in (see 1 Thess 1:6; 3:3). In verse 28, however, Paul is referring to the tribulations that affect married people in particular and thus it is more likely the sort of distresses that Paul refers to in verses 32-35, not the Messianic woes that he refers to here (compare *ananke* in Rom 13:5; 2 Cor 6:4; 9:7; 12:10; 1 Thess 3:7).[19]

The word *synestalmenos* is a participle, not an adjective, and should be translated "shortened."[20] It then becomes a reference not to a future event but to some past happening that has dramatically changed the state of affairs. Something or someone has shortened the time. Therefore, "for the rest of time" Christians are to live in a different way than others do. Their entire approach toward all things that are part of this world (one's social position, race, marital status) must be different, "for the form/schema of the world is passing away."[21] Note the present tense of "is passing away." Paul is not speaking of some future apocalyptic event but of an eschatological process already begun. As in Romans 13:11-14, Paul in verse 26 is talking about the present time and the things that are already transpiring, not some time that is about to break in or some impending difficulty. The distress is already upon these Christians: "You know already the hour, how it is time for you to wake from sleep. For salvation is nearer to us now than when we first believed" (Rom 13:11). To be sure, this verse refers to something getting nearer, namely salvation, but it is a salvation in which they already now participate in part. Paul's imperatives in 1 Corinthians 7 are not fundamentally grounded in what God had yet to do, but mainly in the indicative of what God had already done and is doing in Christ.[22]

Apparently, the possible imminence of Christ's return only affects Paul's advice in this regard—it gives it greater urgency and causes Christians to strive with more intensity to reach the goal, for the time has been shortened. Christ could return soon. The decisive event in the eschatological timetable already had taken place. No one could say that there was necessarily a long time before God would bring his plan for history to a climax, since Jesus could return at any moment, like a thief in the night (see 1 Thess 5:1-11). Thus, the Christian must live realizing that all worldly things have been made relative by and in the face of the world-changing nature of the Christ-event and its implications for humanity. Worldly things pale in significance in comparison to the Christ-event, but they are not made meaningless. The point is that a person could no longer place ultimate value or faith in the things of this world, for this world's form was already passing away. One can appreciate the things of this world, however, and use them as long as they are seen for what they are.

These ideas lie behind Paul's advice in 1 Corinthians 7:25-40.[23] If my understanding is correct, then what we have is an ethic that is grounded in the already of Christ's eschatological work, but gains urgency and is given a definite contingency because of what God is yet to do in Christ. It is an ethic *affected* by the possible shortness of the time left, but it is primarily *determined* by the eschatological events that have already transpired, culminating in the death and resurrection of Jesus. These events have shortened the time, leaving little of eschatological significance left to happen prior to the parousia. Coming events, such as the parousia and the resurrection of believers (see 1 Cor 15), do have an effect on the present and on the believers' present behavior. Yet the most critical factors are those which have already happened, for without them there would be no Christ (Rom 1:4) and no *Christians* who must die to sin and live to God (Rom 6:11). This is a consummate description of the essence of Christian ethical behavior and how it is patterned on the events, especially the climactic events, of Christ's life (compare 2 Cor 4:10).

In 1 Corinthians 7:29-31 Paul makes a fundamental statement about the Christian's basic orientation to the joys and sorrows, the things and institutions of this world. His major point is that the Christian's existence is no longer to be dictated by the "form of this world." Paul is not advocating withdrawal from, or renunciation of, the world. Rather, the world is the sphere where the believer is called to obey God's will. The "as if" here does not reflect a tension between present and future but a dialectical relationship between a human being and his world. This explains the present tense in these verses. Bodily and worldly relationships have not become meaningless. Rather they are the very spheres where Christ's lordship and demands are asserted (see 6:12—7:28). "What God demands is not withdrawal from the world, but rather a new understanding of the world as the sphere of Christian responsibility (vv 7-24)."[24] "We have to do here neither with Stoic 'indifference' nor with apocalyptic 'renuncation' but rather with Paul's own understanding of Christian existence as a new creation."[25]

Paul does not say that those who are married are to abstain from marital relationships or the obligations of such relationships (v. 29); indeed, he says quite the contrary (vv. 2-5). Nor does he say that Christians should not make use of the world; in fact, his advice in verses 30b and 31 is directed to those who are and will go on doing so, an action he does not forbid. Their attitude, however, is to change. Those buying things must not act as though they are owning these things. Those making use of this world must not act as if they are taking full advantage of the world.[26] Both the having and the not having are to be taken with equal seriousness and are to be thought of from a Christian point of view.

The point is that for Christians the world is not to be the means whereby they attempt to create their own lives or indulge their own selfish desires. "Striving after the goods of this world," however, no longer determines the existence of the Christian. Nor should he forget that it is Christ who is Lord of this earth and its fullness. Humanity is not then its owner, nor do humans determine its destiny. Neither the world, nor humanity, nor Christ is to be regarded from a worldly, or purely anthropocentric, point of view any longer (2 Cor 5:16). Paul agrees with some of the Corinthians that things are not to be viewed according to the flesh but according to the Spirit. He differs radically, however, with the "spiritualists" in Corinth over what this involves.

Paul's desire is that Christians be free from any sort of worldly anxiety that might distract them from the things of the Lord. The unmarried man has no such divided interests, but the married man strives to please both his wife and the Lord. His interests are clearly divided. Likewise, the formerly married woman and the virgin are concerned with the things of the Lord. But the married woman, like the married man, has divided loyalties, or at least divided concerns that can distract her from giving proper devotion to the Lord. Significantly, Paul severely qualifies these statements in verse 35. They are not binding commandments but rather good advice from Paul acting as a pastor concerned that the Corinthians give proper and undistracted allegiance and devotion to their Lord.

Galatians proves to be an even less fertile field for exploring Paul's views of the eschatological timetable. Galatians 1:4 refers to Christ's death, the purpose of which was to rescue us from this present evil age (we are not told how or when). Galatians 6:10 probably does not refer to the time left until the parousia, although we should perhaps translate it, "so then as we have opportunity/time let us do good to all." This leaves us, according to Schweitzer's estimate of the authentic Pauline letters, with a few comments and asides in Romans and Philippians.

Romans 8:18-25 speaks of the liberation of believers and indeed all of creation that is longed for and looked for.[27] Paul does not say when that redemption will come but significantly counsels patience while waiting for that time (v. 25). Romans 16:20 presents the conundrum of how to translate *en tachei*. It may refer to *how* God will deal with Satan (crush him quickly, speedily, with dispatch) or *when* (soon, meaning shortly). A similar problem arises with this same phrase in Luke 18:8. There the text favors the idea that it means suddenly, quickly, especially since an interval before coming is implied by verse 7. As Robertson and Abbott-Smith indicate, the phrase is an adverbial one and so it should indicate manner.[28] Thus Paul likely is explaining to his audience that God's crushing of Satan will not take long and will be done quickly, suddenly, with the comforting implication that God's power is clearly much greater than is Satan's. The point of the key phrase is *how*—not when—this will happen. Romans 13:11-12 deserves closer scrutiny.

It is impossible not to note the eschatological framework of all the advice Paul offers in Romans 12 and 13 (see 12:2).[29] It is also crucial to realize that Paul often inculcates moral earnestness by reminding his audience that the eschatological clock is running and has already passed various crucial hours. Romans 13:11-14 falls into this pattern. His audience are those who know "the time," namely, that it is time to wake up. Salvation is nearer now than when the Romans first believed, and thus they must be alert because the day is at hand. One is struck by the similarities between this text and 1 Thessalonians 5:2-11. The metaphorical language about sleeping and waking, night and day, are characteristic of eschatological discussion.[30] Barrett is right that this is not simply a contrast between "the day of judgment" or "the day of the Lord" and "night"; rather, Paul is characterizing the night as a period of time, not a moment or a single event in time (this present evil age which is "far spent").[31]

What then are we to make of the term *the day*, which is dramatically contrasted to *the night?* This also seems to be a reference to an age, not to the parousia or Day of the Lord. This age is *ēngiken*. The perfect tense of *engizō* requires careful rendering. It is often used in the Gospels to refer to the kingdom (see Mk 1:15; Mt 3:2; 4:17; 10:7). The question that arises is, Should we translate *ēngiken* in such contexts as "has come" or as "is at hand/ near"? As W. R. Hutton has shown, in various texts the more natural translation would be "has come/arrived."[32] C. H. Dodd points out that in the Septuagint *engizō* is sometimes used to translate the Hebrew verb *nāḡaš* and the Aramaic verb *mᶜṭā'*, both of which mean "to reach" or "to arrive." In Luke 10:9 the probable meaning of *ēngiken* is "has come": "the Kingdom has come upon you" (compare Mt 12:28; Lk

11:20).[33] The kingdom is not merely near, but *is here*—it has arrived at least in its initial phases. To be sure, only the context can determine whether or not this is Paul's meaning in Romans 13, and so we must examine the context again.

Paul has said that it is already time for the Romans to wake up (v. 11). In verse 12 he exhorts them to put on "the armour of light," which seems to imply that the time of light and the equipment of the "enlightened" is already here. Confirmation of this idea is found in the similar passage in 1 Thessalonians 5:4-5, where Paul emphatically says, "you are not in darkness," and a little later, "for you sons of light are also sons of the day." The Semitic idiom "sons of" is not unlike the idiom we use when we call someone "a product of his upbringing" or "a child of her time." Thus, Paul's words imply that in some sense the day has dawned, the light has come. A person cannot be a product of or a son of something that does not yet exist! In sum, Romans 13 seems to say that the eschatological age has dawned even during the twilight of this present evil age. Christians then have no excuse for not remaining alert and vigilant. The day of salvation could come soon to consummate the age to come. Since Christians do not know dates or times, they must always be prepared. Cranfield is right to say that

> the primitive Church was convinced that the ministry of Jesus had ushered in the last days, the End-time. History's supreme events had taken place in the ministry, death, resurrection and ascension of the Messiah. There was no question of another chapter's being added which could in any way effectively go back upon what had been written in that final chapter. All that subsequent history could add, whether it should last for few years or for many, must be of the nature of an epilogue.[34]

Not only do the points made above show the vulnerability of the argument that Romans 13:11-14 proves that Paul was convinced that the end of the world *must* come very soon, but so does the context in which these verses are found. As G. B. Caird rightly emphasizes, the "statement that the night is almost over and the day is breaking follows hard on a vast missionary programme which involves the conversion of the whole Gentile world and of all Israel."[35] Such a program, which also included Paul's ambition to evangelize the western part of the empire in the future, strongly suggests that Paul must mean something else by these words than that the end of the world must come soon.

Finally, we must examine certain texts in Philippians to which Schweitzer appeals. Sayings such as Philippians 1:6, 10 or 3:20-22 do reflect the eager anticipation of Paul and other Christians as they look forward to the "day of Christ

Jesus," but they tell us nothing about the timing of that event. Philippians 4:5, however, may indicate such a time. In the midst of various exhortations to rejoice and to be gentle, to be at peace, Paul adds, "the Lord is near." This could mean that the Lord is near either in space or in time. If the latter, it would appear to be a reference to the nearness of the Second Coming, an event about which Paul has already intimated he did not know the date (1 Thess 5).

Both Old Testament and extrabiblical New Testament parallels, however, suggest a different interpretation of this text. In 1 Clement 21:3, for instance, "we see how he is near" is used where the reference is clearly to the nearness of the Lord *spatially* and thus means that nothing escapes his notice.[36] Further, it appears that Paul is thinking here of Psalm 145:18-19. In Philippians, this saying about the nearness of the Lord leads to an exhortation to pray and not be anxious, while in the Psalm we find the following: "For the Lord is near to all who call upon him" (compare Ps. 118;151 in the Septuagint).[37] If this is the correct background for the Philippians text, then this remark is not about the nearness (in time) of the Day of the Lord. Notice also that Paul says the *Lord* is near, not the *Day* of the Lord, which makes perfect sense spatially in light of Paul's in-Christ mysticism, to which Schweitzer draws our attention.

This brings to a close the examination of the material Schweitzer relies upon to prove that Paul's eschatological framework entailed the view that the return of the Lord was necessarily immediate and/or imminent. We have seen that the material will bear another interpretation without forcing the texts in question, or engaging in exegetical gymnastics to avoid the obvious meaning of the text. I agree with Schweitzer that Paul's thought from his earliest letters onward was shaped by a definite eschatological framework, but I disagree about the shape of that framework.

Thus, it appears that throughout his letters Paul attempted to walk a narrow tightrope between overrealized and unrealized eschatological viewpoints. There was an *already* to his eschatology that definitely shaped his world view, but that view was also affected by the *not yet,* the anticipated return of the Lord. Since that return was at an unknown time and since the eschatological age had already dawned, Paul could use an appeal to "that Day" as a means of producing moral seriousness in his audience. Christians must always be prepared since they know not the hour. The *certainty* of that coming, combined with its *possible* nearness, made the exhortations especially effective. On the one hand, Paul did not want to fall into the trap of an overrealized eschatology that suggested that there was nothing significant left to happen in the eschatological timetable (see 1 Cor 4:8-13; 15:12-19), or perhaps nothing significant left to do prior to that Day of the Lord (see 1 Thess 5:12-23; 4:11-12). On the other hand, Paul did not want to suggest that God's work of salvation was all promise and no fulfillment yet (see Rom 8:1-4; 9ff.; 2 Cor 5:16ff.). His ethical exhortations are grounded in what Christ has *already done* for the believer in dying and rising, and they gain added significance from the fact that God is not finished with his work. Christians will be accountable for how they live in the time preceding the parousia (see 1 Cor 3:13-15; Gal 6:7-9).

The amount of discussion Paul devotes to matters involving the parousia seems determined in part by the questions and problems raised by congregations he addressed and in part by his own eager anticipation that God's plan be consummated. Paul reckoned with the *possibility* of a near Second Advent, but we see no signs of any disappointment on his part when various Christians die prior to that event or even when he contemplates his own death prior to that day (see Phil 1:19-26). Had his expectation been that Christ's return was necessarily imminent, we could expect to see an adjustment or significant change in his eschatological framework as he wrestles with the increasingly long interim in his later letters.[38] Such a significant change is nowhere in evidence, which is not to say that Paul's thought did not develop some over the course of his correspondence. The development, however, was along the trajectory of what he had already thought and written as early as 1 Thessalonians if not before. According to J. C. Beker,

> Paul's Christian hope is a matter of prophecy, not a matter of prediction. The incalculability of this hope is for Paul one of its essential marks. . . . After all, Paul is a writer of letters and not of apocalypses; he uses apocalyptic motifs but not the literary genre of apocalyse. Whereas the apocalyptic composition often concentrates on a timetable of events or on a program for the sake of calculating apocalyptic events, Paul stresses to the contrary the incalculability of the end. Instead of narrating apocalyptic events in a temporal sequence of "first," "unless," "then," Paul emphasizes the unexpected, the suddenness and surprising character of the final theophany (1 Thess. 5:2-10). Moreover, the incalculable character of the end motivates Paul to restrain severely his use of apocalyptic language and imagery. . . .Thus the delay of the parousia is not a theological concern for Paul. It is not an embarassment for him; it does not compel him to shift the center of his attention from apocalyptic imminence to a form of "realized eschatology," that is to a conviction of the full presence of the kingdom of God in our present history. It

is of the essence of his faith in Christ that adjustments in his expectations can occur without a surrender of these expectations (1 Thess. 4:13-18; 1 Cor. 15:15-51; 2 Cor. 5:1-10; Phil. 2:21-24). Indeed, the hope in God's imminent rule through Christ remains the constant in his letters from beginning to end, that is, from 1 Thessalonians to Philippians and Romans.[39]

I can only conclude that the Schweitzerian eschatological framework, so far as its time orientation is concerned, leads the student of Paul astray, for while on the one hand he sensitizes us to the pervasiveness of the eschatological element in Paul's thought and to the importance of knowing "the time" (while not knowing the "timing"), on the other hand he misleads us as to what that thought meant and to what it amounted. Nor is Schweitzer's error less severe in regard to the question of the use of apocalyptic material in an eschatological framework. As L. E. Keck rightly says,

> One must not repeat Albert Schweitzer's error, who in the name of reclaiming Paul as a coherent thinker constructed an eschatological scenario from various apocalypses and then claimed that Paul modified it by introducing a special resurrection for believers who had died before the parousia. Even if such a scenario had existed, Paul would scarcely have made a simple adjustment in it. One who had once been "a Pharisee of the Pharisees" but now wrote, "I know and am persuaded in the Lord Jesus that nothing is unclean in itself but it is unclean for anyone who thinks it is" (Rom. 14:14) or that "if you break the law your circumcision becomes uncircumcision" (Rom. 2:25) does not simply make adjustments in inherited thought. Instead, he rethought everything in light of Christ's death and resurrection. In short, if we find apocalyptic theology in Paul, it will have been transformed.[40]

In the end, in his discussion of the law and of Romans 9—11, even Schweitzer is forced to reckon with an interval before the parousia in Paul's thought because Paul believed that the gospel had to be preached to the nations so that the full number of Gentiles could come in before the end.[41] I must conclude therefore that the evidence Schweitzer and others have used to prove that Paul thought the end of the world, or at least the parousia of Christ, would necessarily happen within his lifetime or within a generation thereafter will certainly bear another interpretation. Indeed, the interpretation I have suggested makes better sense of a lot of factors we encounter in the Pauline Epistles, such as Paul's advice about a Christian's relationship to governing officials in Romans 13, which sounds anything but apocalyptic or imminentist in character.

—3—

Dawn's First Light:
The Evidence
from Jesus'
Teaching

In some ways dealing with the Jesus material that might suggest a near end of the world or a return of the Son of Man within a generation is an easier task than dealing with the Pauline evidence, especially if we are allowed to begin our discussion with Mark 13:32 and parallels.

Since I have argued at considerable length elsewhere for the authenticity of Mark 13:32,[1] I will not rehearse those arguments here. This saying amounts to a disclaimer by Jesus that he knows the timing of "that day," which likely refers to the *Yom Yahweh,* the Day of the Lord, which in the Jesus tradition is identified with the day of the return of the Son of Man (for instance, Mk 14:62). Since it is not likely that the early church would invent a saying predicating Jesus' ignorance of such a vital matter, we must give this saying its full weight. Thus, it is improbable that Jesus ever taught or suggested that the world's end, or even the coming of the Son of Man, would definitely and necessarily happen soon. Rather Jesus, like Paul, may have considered those events as *possibly* imminent, but the timing was uncertain since it was unknown.

Such a view meant that one must always be prepared for the coming of that day, since it could be sooner *or* later. This is precisely the message of the parable of the wise and foolish virgins, which is predicated on the assumption of ignorance about the time when the Bridegroom will arrive.[2]

Several other key texts must now be given more detailed scrutiny, beginning with Mark 9:1. Various scholars, such as E. Schweizer, have argued that texts such as Mark 9:1; 13:30 or Matthew 10:23 likely do not go back to a situation in the life of Jesus but rather only reflect the eager expectation of the End that existed among some early Christians.[3] This would make our task much easier, but I will follow the more difficult course of assuming that these sayings likely reflect something about Jesus' own eschatological world view.

Mark 9:1, which has partial parallels in Matthew 16:28 and Luke 9:27, appears to be an isolated logion. Mark, who likely has the most primitive form of this saying, uses it as a bridge between 8:38 and the narrative about the transfiguration, which begins at 9:2. A whole series of questions are raised by Mark 9:1. Does Jesus equate the coming of the Dominion of God with the coming of the Son of Man in glory (8:38)? Does he equate either one of these things with the end of human history or of the world as we know it?

In the narrative outline of all three of the Synoptic Gospels it would appear that the Evangelists have placed this verse so as to introduce the story of the transfiguration, where only three of Jesus' disciples see Jesus in radiant attire.[4] If the first three Evangelists wrote their Gospels well after the time of Jesus' life and death (Mark perhaps as early as the late 60s, Matthew and Luke perhaps sometime in the late 70s or 80s), then it is hardly surprising that they do not see this verse as Jesus' prediction that the world would end within the lifetime of at least some of his audience. However, is seeing this verse as an allusion to the transfiguration, or for that matter to any other event in the latter part of Jesus' earthly life, a misrepresentation of the original meaning Jesus intended to convey by these words?[5]

Some scholars, such as W. G. Kümmel, have stressed that this text must mean that Jesus expected the coming of the kingdom of God *in power* in the relatively near future (while some of his listeners are still alive), but not *immediately*.[6] They then conclude that Jesus was simply wrong on this matter.

By contrast, C. H. Dodd, consistent with his stress on realized eschatology, interpreted this saying in Mark 9:1 to mean "until they have seen that the Kingdom of God *has* come with power."[7] This requires understanding the word *see* to mean *understand,* and it requires taking the perfect participle *elēlythyian* and the words that go with it as the equivalent to a *hoti* clause. To be sure, the action mentioned in the participle must precede the "seeing," but the tense of the participle is determined by the flow of action in the sentence that requires the participial action to be antecedent to the action indicated by *idōsin.* It does not have to mean that the Dominion has already come in power during the ministry of Jesus. The key point, noted by J. Y. Campbell and others, is that the context and grammar of this sentence suggest a future event, not a later awareness of an already present reality.[8] Certainly, both Luke (by removing the clause with the participle) and the First Evangelist (by substituting "The Son of Man coming in his Dominion" for Mark's "the Dominion of God come in power") understood this clause to refer to a future event.

Several keys will help us to understand this text. First, the Semitic idiom "some will not taste death" (Heb 2:9; 4 Ezra 6:26) could refer to spiritual death (Jn 8:52), but this is not its normal meaning. Mark's use of the idiom probably should not be interpreted on the basis of John's, especially since the Fourth Gospel has a tendency to use various terms in a spiritual or metaphorical sense that would normally have a physical or literal sense (compare the use of "water" and "food" in Jn 4:2). As Cranfield points out, the phrase "some will not taste death" focuses on the fact that at least some of those who first heard these words *would* see the coming of the Dominion with power. The phrase is not focusing on the death of those who would not see the coming, and thus it is likely wrong to rule out the possibility that Jesus was refering to something that could happen very soon indeed, not merely within a generation. The phrase means no more than "some of you will live to see" and the emphasis is probably on the word *some,* not on calculations about the timing of this event.[9] Accordingly, an allusion by Jesus to some sort of event during his earthly ministry cannot be ruled out.

Second, in the Markan outline the transfiguration is probably presented as a foreshadowing of the parousia, not the resurrection (compare 8:38; 9:2-3).[10] This might explain why the First Evangelist makes the substitution of the phrase about the coming of the Son of Man for Mark's words about the coming of the Dominion with power.

Third, the use of prepositive *Amēn* with an "I" saying,[11] as well as the general Semitic flavor of Mark's text, supports the suggestion that this saying goes back to Jesus, as does the possible offensiveness of the saying, since it could be interpreted even in Mark's day to be a prediction that failed to come true.

How then are we to understand Mark 9:1? In its original form this saying likely refers to an event that manifests the power of the Dominion of God, probably an event that Jesus thought would happen during his earthly ministry, or very shortly thereafter. If so, then in its original context this saying could refer to any of a number of miracles or perhaps an exorcism (see Lk 11:20; Mt 12:28). If the transfiguration was a historical occurrence, an oblique reference to it is not impossible. Some will think it more likely that this saying refers to Jesus' coming vindication by God's power (see below on Lk 22:18).[12] The text itself does not make clear whether we are to see this event as something Jesus will bring about, or something that will happen to Jesus.

In any event, the crucial point is this: Mark 9:1 cannot be unambiguous evidence that Jesus thought the world's end or the glorious coming of the Son of Man was imminent, much less immediate. Indeed, this verse may well refer to an occurrence during the ministry of Jesus brought about by the earthly Jesus himself.

We can hardly underestimate the importance of Matthew 10:23 to Schweitzer's estimation of the character of Jesus' proclamation. Largely on the basis of this text alone Schweitzer argued that Jesus expected the parousia of the Son of Man (someone other than himself) before his disciples had completed their preaching tour of Galilee. When this did not transpire, Jesus decided to go to Jerusalem and bring the messianic woes on himself and so precipitate the end. In essence Schweitzer argues that Jesus was the first to have to deal with the problem of the delay of the parousia.

> The whole history of "Christianity" down to the present day, that is to say, the real inner history of it, is based on the delay of the Parousia, the non-occurrence of the Parousia, the abandonment of eschatology, the progress and completion of the "de-eschatologising" of religion which has been connected therewith. It should be noted that the nonfulfilment of Matt. x.23 is the first postponement of the Parousia. We have therefore here the first significant date in the "history of Christianity"; it gives to the work of Jesus a new direction, otherwise inexplicable.[13]

Few scholars today would take Schweitzer's precise view on this matter, not least because it artificially combines the circumstances of Mark 6 with Matthew 10 and takes the latter as uttered all on one occasion.[14] Yet what is probably a majority still think that Matthew 10:23 speaks of a parousia expected in the not-too-distant future. Accordingly we must examine this saying closely.

Unique to the First Gospel, this saying is set in the midst of a collection of sayings that has usually been thought to focus on giving instructions to disciples about to embark on missionary activity. This conclusion has been drawn despite that fact that the material in verses 17-22 is drawn from Mark 13:9-13, to which the First Evangelist has appended verse 23. Despite the efforts of several scholars to see in Matthew 10:23 an "apocalyptic persecution saying," most scholars still conclude that it refers to persecution experienced for witnessing about Jesus.[15]

Though some scholars have tried to attribute this saying to the early church, during the period when it is assumed there was great enthusiasm and belief in an imminent return of the Son of Man, there are significant problems with this view. For one thing, by the time the First Gospel was written it was widely known that Christian missions were basically *not* directed toward Jews, and certainly not focused on the land of Israel. Indeed the First Gospel includes the charge to go unto the nations (Mt 28:19). It was also surely known that the parousia of the Son of Man had *not* transpired during or shortly after the time when the first disciples had witnessed about Jesus in the various cities of Israel. On the surface of things, this is hardly the sort of saying the early church was likely to make up and place on the lips of Jesus if they wanted to present him in a positive light. The only thing that might not favor a *Sitz im Leben Jesu* for this saying is the reference to persecution of Jesus' disciples. Even this is not decisive since the Synoptic Gospels contain plenty of evidence of a hostile response to, or at least a context of controversy surrounding, Jesus and his traveling disciples.[16] What then could this saying have meant on the lips of Jesus?

If Matthew 10:23 was originally Jesus' word of encouragement to his disciples to continue witnessing in Israel despite a negative response in various places,[17] then it might mean several things. First, there were plenty of towns in Israel for the disciples to witness in, despite a negative response. They are to carry on with their work for there were enough towns to last them until and beyond the time of the coming of the Son of Man. In this view this saying is a comment on the abundance of places the disciples could and should go and witness in Israel, not on the precise timing of the parousia of the Son of Man. The focus would be on the largeness of their task and the abundance of places to go, not on the shortness of time until the parousia. Second, the phrase "before the Son of Man comes" might *not* refer to the parousia at all. The saying says nothing about the Son of Man coming on the clouds, or coming in glory, or coming with angels.[18]

Various *ēlthon* sayings refer not to the parousia of the Son of Man but to the present earthly activity of Jesus, and at least some of them are likely authentic.[19] Most of these have to do with the purpose or task for which Jesus came and do not seem to be relevant to our discussion. However, a likely authentic Q saying like "the Son of Man has come eating and drinking" (Mt 11:19; Lk 7:34)[20] shows that Jesus is capable of speaking of his present activities using the phrase "Son of Man" and the verb "to come" in its more common sense.

Though we cannot be certain, since Matthew 10:23 is not likely in its original context, it is possible that this verse simply means that the disciples shall not have completed the missionary work in Israel that the earthly Jesus sent them out to do before he rejoins them. If so, it is understandable why in the 80s the First Evangelist did not hesitate to include this saying. He did not take it to suggest anything one way or another about the timing of the parousia of the Son of Man.

In the event that either of the two suggestions mentioned above is wrong, Matthew 10:23 could still refer to the parousia of the Son of Man, but in that case we must ask how the language of imminence functions and what its purpose is. If the function of this saying is to inculcate in the disciples courage and perseverance in the task despite violent opposition, then at most it seems to assume the possible imminence of the parousia, not its necessary imminence. The language functions to reassure that the disciples will not be left to face such opposition alone forever. In short, the purpose of the saying, even if it includes the language of imminence, is not to speculate or teach anything about the timing of the parousia. It is doubtful that this saying can be used as the linchpin for an argument that Jesus predicted the end, or that the parousia would definitely happen in or shortly after his lifetime.

Finally S. McKnight undertook an extensive source- and redaction-critical study of Matthew 10:23 and concluded that the original setting of this saying was eschatological, not missionary, and that it belonged with the sort of material we find in Mark 13:9-13 (note the similarity between Mk 13:13b and Mt 10:23a). Thus the First Evangelist has rightly juxtaposed it with Matthew 10:17-22. This being the case, McKnight concludes that the saying means, "When they persecute you in one place (as part of the final intense persecution associated with the parousia), flee to the next (and so on). I tell you the truth you will not have finished fleeing through the cities of Israel (as cities of refuge) before the Son of Man comes."[21] Even if the saying does have to do with witnessing, in view of McKnight's study it may well have to do with witnessing in the context of the imminent parousia, not witnessing in the context of the earthly ministry of Jesus.

The First Evangelist, to be sure, has placed it near the mission charge, thus in part de-eschatologizing it by giving it a new context, but our concern is with the original intent and focus of the saying in the *Sitz im Leben Jesu.* Thus we must conclude that this saying does not necessarily support the view that Jesus thought the coming of the Son of Man would happen during his ministry or even shortly thereafter.

Several other sayings present fewer problems for the case we are making. For instance, Mark 13:30, if it does go back to Jesus, is set in the collection of eschatological sayings found in Mark 13. As the so-called Markan apocalypse is presently structured, there is a contrast between "these *things*" which are expected to happen soon and "those *days* after that tribulation" which are supposed to begin at some unspecified time later than the distress caused by "these things."[22] Those post-tribulation days are described in verses 24-27 and include the coming of the Son of Man on the clouds.[23] Verses 5-23 describe "these things," which are called the beginning of the birth pains and then are referred to once more in verses 28-31. Clearly, as Lane avers, verses 24-27 cannot be mere birth pains or preliminary signs of something else, for verses 24-27 with their celestial upheaval and Second Coming and the gathering of the elect describe what is properly called the end events.[24] These verses are clearly distinguished from the rest of the chapter, which is involved in discussing the events that lead up to the destruction of Jerusalem and the temple in A.D. 70. These preliminary events are characterized repeatedly as "these things" or "all these things" (vv. 4, 23, 29) in order to set them off from the matters discussed in verses 24-27. Indeed the preliminary events are characterized as occurring during a time when people make false claims about the coming of the Christ (vv. 6, 21-22), for he will not be coming during these events, but only "following that distress." Thus the contrast between verses 24-27, 5-23 and 28-31 is explicitly made in the text in regard to the matter of the timing of the parousia.

In a sort of appendix to this discourse, in verses 32-37 Mark stresses the point that no one knows the timing of the parousia, and therefore one must always watch and be prepared for it. The timing of "that day" (the *Yom Yahweh)* is unknown, not least because the Evangelist never states the relationship between the timing of the preliminary events and what will happen in "those post-tribulation days."[25] Indeed, Mark seems to think it is not only impossible to state the timing of the parousia, but in fact any such preliminary speculation is not to be believed (vv. 6, 21-23).

Here then we have a composite discourse that has as one of its prominent themes what may be called eschatological reservation. It may be that Mark collected this material precisely in order to dampen speculation in the early church about an imminent parousia.[26] It is also true that this discourse serves a definite paranetic function. As W. S. Vorster points out, life is seen in relationship to the future, and therefore great emphasis is placed on correct conduct in preparation for the future.

It is remarkable that almost everything which is said to, and thus about, the four to whom the speech is directed is done by way of imperatives (cf. *blepete* in 13.5, 9, 23, 33; *mē throeisthe* in 13.7, *mē promerimnate* in 13.11; *proseuchesthe* in 13.18; *mē pisteuete* in 13.21; *mathete* in 13.28; *ginōskete* in 13.28, 29; *blepete agrupneite* in 13.33; *grēgoreite* in 13.35, 37 and the singular subjunctives in 14-16).[27]

The question then becomes, How much of this discourse actually goes back to Jesus, and does Mark 13:30 go back to Jesus? A good deal depends on whether one thinks Jesus could have spoken of the destruction of Jerusalem and/or the temple. Much of the language in Mark 13:5-23 is rather stock material drawing on Old Testament descriptions of coming judgments on Israel (see especially Dan 9), as well as typical descriptions of the mayhem caused by war or when a city is sacked.[28] Sometimes in early Jewish literature such descriptions are used to describe the great tribulation that will precede the messianic age or the age to come (compare the mention of famine, familial strife, war and signs in the heavens in such texts as 4 Ezra 5:4—9:3; Assump. Mos. 10:4-6; Apoc. Bar. 27:6-7; 70:3-7). Sometimes such stock descriptions of a world in chaos are used to describe a *past* intervention of God in human history, such as the theophany at Sinai (compare Bib. Ant. 11:3; 4 Ezra 3:18-19). Such descriptions can be used to explain various sorts of historical events in which God is believed to have intervened or is believed to be going to do so. The language is not used solely to describe the final events of human history that lead to the age to come.[29] Thus, either Mark or even Jesus could have used this stock language to describe the impending catastrophe in Jerusalem, without necessarily assuming that that judgment initiated the end of the world.[30]

A reasonable case can be made that Jesus at some point during his ministry had spoken about the destruction of the temple, as is suggested by a variety of likely independent traditions (see Mk 14:58; Acts 6:13; Jn 2:18-22).[31] If this is so, there is nothing improbable about understanding Mark 13:30 to allude to that teaching of Jesus, adding to it the information that Jesus expected this temple destruction, perhaps also coupled with the fall of Jerusalem within a generation.[32] Mark, perhaps writing about A.D. 68 with knowledge of the events already set in motion in Israel, apparently has structured his discourse so the "reader will understand" that what Jesus was talking about when he referred to "all these things" was the destruction of the Holy Place and its attendant circumstances, not the parousia of the Son of Man. Further, Mark indicates that even Jesus professed not to know about the timing of that event. I see no reason to compel us to dispute Mark's interpretation of various Jesus traditions that he has collected in Mark 13.[33] Of course, many have attempted to interpret "this generation" to mean something other than Jesus' contemporaries, or at least his contemporaries that are blind to Jesus' significance (Mk 8:12; Lk 17:25), but such attempts usually assume that "all these things" includes the coming of the Son of Man, which is unlikely.[34]

One final verse, Mark 14:25 and parallels, deserves brief comment here. This saying, whether we take the Markan, Matthean or possibly independent Lukan form of it, says nothing specific about the timing of the end of the world or the coming of the Son of Man. In its original form it seems to reflect Jesus' confidence that the Dominion of God will come and that he will be vindicated one day and share in that dominion. As such this tradition seems to be related to the various traditions that indicate that Jesus spoke about the messianic banquet and those who would participate in it (compare Mt 8:11-12 and the Q parable Mt 22:1-14; Lk 14:15-24).[35] Certainly, nothing here requires us to believe that Jesus affirmed the necessary imminence of the end of the world or of the parousia of the Son of Man. At most what it may suggest is that Jesus believed that the dominion of God would definitely come on earth (something he likely taught his disciples to pray for), and the text may hint that he considered it possible that this event *might* happen soon.

—4—

The
Origin
of an
Orientation

What is the origin of Paul's belief in the possible imminence of the parousia? Is it possible to trace a trajectory from Jesus to Paul on this matter? It is one thing to point out similarities between the thought of Jesus and of Paul on a given matter, but it is quite another to establish a definite case of dependency of Paul on Jesus. Yet there is something to be said for the view that Paul was dependent on the Jesus tradition at least in part for some of his teachings on eschatological matters. Nowhere is that more the case than with regard to the "thief in the night" motif, which perhaps connotes both possible imminence and also uncertainty about the timing of the coming of the key figure in question. There is also an undertone suggesting the suddenness of the breaking in of the time in question.

The "thief in the night" motif seems to have been an important one for early Christians as it is found in various forms in various sorts of material, at least some of which is surely independent of the other examples of this motif. I would suggest that the origin of this motif goes back to the Q saying found in Luke 12:39/Matthew 24:43. This metaphorical utterance, at an early date in the transmission of the tradition, seems to have been clearly understood to refer to the coming of the Son of Man at an unexpected hour.[1] The metaphorical utterance was then picked up and used in various ways in a wide variety of Christian communities—Pauline, Johannine and Petrine (compare 1 Thess 5:2; Rev 3:3; 16:15; 2 Pet 3:10)—in the middle and latter parts of the first century A.D.[2] Always the metaphor is taken to allude to the coming of the Day of the Lord at an unexpected time.[3] This tradition is redirected in the *Gospel of Thomas* to refer to being wary of the world and being on guard against it breaking into the believer's life (*Gospel of Thomas* 21:3). Since this redirection is at odds with all the other examples of the motif it is surely secondary (*Gospel of Thomas* 103).

How then are we to evaluate the original parabolic utterance found in Luke 12:39/Matthew 24:43? Various scholars have urged that the explication of the saying in Luke 12:40 and parallels is a Christian expansion that does not go back to Jesus. This conclusion of course depends on whether one thinks a saying like Mark 13:32 could be authentic, and also on whether Luke 12:40 and parallels is a saying meant to allay fears about the delay of the parousia. Thus, for instance, Jeremias takes the explication in Luke 12:40 to be secondary and assumes that the parabolic saying, while authentic, originally was Jesus' word about the impending crisis about to come upon his fellow Jews.[4] He argues that Christians viewed the parousia as something to look forward to joyfully, not something to watch out for as if it would involve judgment for the believer. There are several problems with these views.

First, even allowing that the explication in Luke 12:40 and parallels is secondary, the parabolic utterance itself suggests the coming of a personal intrusion, not merely the coming of an event (the *Yom Yahweh*).[5] Second, it is incongruous with the view that this saying originally was only about the *Day* of the Lord that we are told in the saying that the coming will happen at an hour or moment. This is much more fittingly predicated of a sudden personal arrival, not the coming of an impersonal crisis or judgment.[6] Third, as J. Fitzmyer says, while the time element is crucial in the saying (the thief will come at an unexpected hour or watch of the night), neither the saying nor the explication says or suggests that the thief has been delayed in coming. "It is simply that the time of the burglary is not known. . . ."[7] Fourth, Jesus' parabolic utterances are replete with warnings *for God's people* about the dangers of not being on guard and not looking out for God's climactic actions. There is always the danger that when the householder returns, his own servants, not some strangers, will be found wanting (compare

Lk 12:36-37 and parallels). In his letters Paul is constantly warning Christians that they too will face judgment when the Lord returns, at least in regard to their deeds (1 Cor 3:13-15; 4:5). Thus, there is nothing incongruous with Jesus warning disciples about the dangers of being caught napping when the thief breaks in.

Thus, Luke 12:39 and parallels, even if the explication in verse 40 is secondary, is speaking about watchfulness because someone is coming at an unknown time, at an hour when he is least expected. This comports with the likely authentic utterance in Mark 13:32. The explication in Luke 12:40 and parallels then is likely correct, even if secondary, and properly draws out Jesus' meaning for a later Christian audience.

We should note three crucial things in Paul's use of the motif in 1 Thessalonians 5:2. First, it may well be, as 1 Thessalonians 4:15 suggests, that Paul is making clear the source of his teaching on these eschatological matters—a word of the Lord. This is probably an allusion to the Jesus tradition, though it could refer to a word of the exalted Lord revealed to Paul. In any case, Paul assumes that his audience in Thessalonica has already received teachings about times and seasons (5:2-3); they already know about the Day of the Lord coming like a thief in the night. This suggests that the teaching was a regular part of early Christian instruction about eschatological matters, at least in the Pauline communities. Nonetheless, the use of the "thief in the night" motif in very diverse parts of the New Testament may well suggest this teaching was disseminated in non-Pauline communities as well.[8]

Second, in 1 Thessalonians 5:1ff. Paul uses the "thief in the night" motif to warn Christians to "stay awake and be sober." In short, it functions as a warning to believers much as the original saying was intended to do.

Third, Paul takes this motif to be a comment on "times and seasons," that though the Day of the Lord will surely and suddenly come, since its timing is unknown one must always be awake and prepared for it. In short, the "thief in the night" motif perfectly encapsulates how both Jesus and Paul convey an eschatological message involving *possible but not necessary* imminence of the end to inculcate moral earnestness and diligence in the believer.

Conclusions

This survey of the relevant data in the Pauline letters as well as in the Gospels has led us to the conclusion that neither Jesus nor Paul seem to have taught that the end of the world or the parousia of the Son of Man (which Paul calls the return of the Lord) would *definitely* come within their lifetimes or within a generation. They do seem to entertain the *possibility* that the end might come soon, hence they warn their respective audiences to be prepared, stay awake, keep watch. However, nothing in this data justifies the conclusion that the teaching of either Jesus or Paul amounted to little more than an interim ethic, or radical contingency plans since the end of the world would *necessarily* come soon. This being the case it is important to examine carefully, as I have tried to do, how the language of imminence functions and what purpose it seems to serve in the teachings of Jesus and Paul.

It seems that its primary function is not to establish any sort of eschatological timetable, but rather to inculcate a sort of moral earnestness in believers so that their eyes will remain fixed upon the goal, eagerly longing for the fullfillment of God's plan for human history. It is in part these decidedly historically oriented approaches of Jesus and Paul that have led us to prefer to talk about the eschatological rather than the apocalyptic world views of these two figures who above all have affected Christians' views about the nature of the future.

One final remark is in order at this point. If at most Jesus or Paul spoke of the *possible* imminence of the final intervention of God or his agent in human history, then it is not appropriate to speak of Paul or for that matter of Jesus as attempting to cope with a problem of eschatological delay. As R. P. Carroll has so aptly put it: "In order to have a delay there must be a specific time or schedule whereby an event, arrival or expectation can be known to be late. Without such information it is not possible to use the term 'delay.'. . . This factor suggests that 'delay of the parousia' treatments of the New Testament may not be built on firm foundations."[9]

PART TWO

The
Dominion
of God

—5—

The Reign
of the Regent:
Paul and the
Basileia tou Theou

At first blush it might seem an unpromising venture to compare Jesus' and Paul's views of the future. Jesus seems to have spoken about the future involving the Son of Man, but Paul never uses the term "Son of Man." While Jesus speaks in parables about both the present and the future, Paul seldom if ever uses *meshalim* to get his message across. Jesus seems also to have spoken about the demise of the Herodian temple and the meek among the Israelites inheriting *eretz Israel*,[1] but Paul shows little or no interest in either the future of cultic religion in Jerusalem or Jewish territorial theology. The contrasts between Jesus and Paul on such matters seem relatively clear and easy to demonstrate. However, some areas of their thought about the future have some striking similarities, and it is our task in this section and the next to examine two of these areas. We will first discuss what Paul and Jesus have to say about the *basileia tou theou* (the Dominion of God) and then about the community of believers as an ongoing entity.

Following the same procedure as in part one, I will start with Paul and work back to the Jesus material, but I will begin with an important observation: it appears that for both Paul and Jesus the *basileia* was an already *and* not-yet matter. They spoke of this *basileia* as something involving both the present and the future, as we shall see. Though it would be wrong to suggest that Paul uses the phrase *basileia tou theou* nearly as often as does Jesus, it would also be wrong to say that "Paul hardly ever makes use of the phrase when he is writing to Greeks. . . ."[2] In at least eight instances Paul uses this phrase to convey something about the new thing God has done or will do in human history. These references are found primarily in the Corinthian and Thessalonian letters, though there is a scattering of references elsewhere. The complete list is as follows: 1 Thessalonians 2:11-12; 2 Thessalonians 1:5-12; Galatians 5:21; 1 Corinthians 4:20-21; 6:9-10; 15:50; Romans 14:17 and Colossians 4:10-11.[3]

G. Johnston and G. Haufe have analyzed these texts in some detail, and I will draw on some of their insights.[4] The first text (1 Thess 2:11-12) comes in a letter that has a strong emphasis on the not yet. For instance, we find not only a lengthy discussion about the matter of those who have fallen asleep in Christ and the coming thief in the night (4:13—5:11), but also in the thanksgiving section of the letter the phrase "wait for his Son from heaven, whom he raised from the dead—Jesus, who rescues us from the coming wrath" (1:10). Further, in the benediction that closes chapter 3 Paul writes: "May he strengthen your hearts so that you will be blameless and holy . . . when our Lord Jesus comes with all his holy ones" (v. 13). In such a context when Paul speaks of "urging you to live lives worthy of God, who calls you into his *basileia* and glory" (his glorious *basileia*), in 2:12 it seems reasonably clear that while the *call* goes out now, the *entering* of the *basileia* comes later. We will see that it is a repeated motif in Paul's use of the language of the *basileia* that he speaks of entering or inheriting this *basileia* in the future. Also, Paul seems to see the *basileia* as a realm in such future-oriented sayings.

The second passage, 2 Thessalonians 1:5-12, only confirms the observations just made. In verse 5, Paul speaks of being counted worthy of the *basileia tou theou*. He then goes on to indicate that this *basileia* will come to God's people when the Lord Jesus returns from heaven in blazing fire with his angels. He further describes this event as "the day he comes to be glorified in his holy people and be marveled at among all those who have believed" (v. 10). The connection between the *basileia* and future glory is found in both this text and in 1 Thessalonians 2:12.

Here I must also mention 1 Corinthians 15:24. Though here the word *basileia* stands alone, it seems reasonably clear that it refers to a realm Christ will deliver up to the Father *after* he returns to earth, and after the resurrection of believers. This action of delivering up is clearly associated with the end *(to telos)*. Some scholars have seen the term "end" as almost a *terminus technicus* in eschatological material, especially because it is used without any qualification.[5] In such contexts it seems to have the meaning of the "decisive eschatological turning point,"[6] not simply the termination of all earthly events (compare 4 Ezra 7:113; 12:34; 6:25; 11:39-46). Thus, Paul is maintaining that the parousia of Christ brings about the final decisive events of human history including the delivering up of the *basileia* to God. The connection of the *basileia* with the active reigning of Christ (compare v. 25, *basileuein)* is clear. I will discuss Paul's view of the parousia in a later chapter, but here I wish to note the definite connection of the *basileia* coming to God's people and being delivered back to the Father when the Lord returns.[7]

Further, 1 Corinthians 15:24 raises the question of whether Paul, in addition to believing in the *basileia tou theou,* believed in a temporary messianic kingdom on earth at the end of human history. Several considerations may favor the view that he did. First, the qualifier *tou theou* is omitted in verse 24. Second, there may have been a precedent for such a belief in early Judaism among those who believed in resurrection and some form of an afterlife on this earth.[8] L. J. Kreitzer has shown that such a temporary kingdom is clearly in evidence in 4 Ezra and 2 Baruch, and the idea seems also to have existed before Paul's time in the Apocalypse of Weeks (1 Enoch 93:1-10; 91:12-17).[9] In any case, such a belief seems to be in evidence in early Christianity (see Rev 20:4-6). Furthermore, Colossians 1:12-14, if it is either Pauline or a legitimate development of Paul's thought, would seem to favor such a view.

Against the view that Paul speaks of a distinct messianic kingdom in 1 Corinthians 15:24 is the fact that 1 Corinthians 15:50-52 alludes to the sequence of parousia, resurrection of believers, followed by the end including the delivering up of the *basileia* to God. Here that *basileia* is called the *basileia* of God, which is inherited *after* the resurrection of believers. Thus, it seems unlikely that 1 Corinthians 15:24 is an isolated reference to a messianic kingdom in Paul's letters. Rather, Gordon Fee is right in saying that Paul's point here is "to demonstrate on the basis of Christ's resurrection the necessity of the resurrection of the dead by tying that event to the final events of the End, particularly the defeat of death (vv. 54-55)."[10] In short, Paul is not arguing for a temporary messianic kingdom prior to the end.

Just as God's *basileia* was something Jesus proclaimed and in some sense manifested during his earthly ministry, so Paul envisions the parousia entailing a role for Christ in relation to the *basileia* of God in the future. Yet there is no question for Paul but that this *basileia* ultimately is God the Father's and must be returned to him. The scenario seems to be as follows: (1) Christ will return; (2) the dead in Christ will rise, the living will be transformed; (3) *to telos* ("the end") will occur, which entails Christ and God the Father on the behalf of Christ causing the subjection of all powers and principalities to God's will, apparently involving their destruction (see 15:24). We are not told that this destroying will be a process taking a *lengthy* amount of time, much less a millennium (though *dei basileuein* in v. 25 may suggest an ongoing process). Indeed, the fact that the last enemy to be subjugated is death suggests that all this subjection happens when Christ returns and the dead are raised. Less probably, *to telos* might simply entail the delivering of the *basileia* over to the Father, the subjugating being something that is happening now during the time between the exaltation and parousia of Christ. This subjugating/destroying is then consummated at his return when the final enemy (death) is overcome by Christ's raising of the dead Christians.

Much depends on how one interprets the crucial sequence of phrases introduced by *hotan* in verses 24-28, how one interprets the use of *tagma, eita* and *epeita* in verses 23-24, and finally what one makes of the *achri* in verse 25. If Paul did believe in a period when the Messiah ruled, in distinction from the Father, Colossians 1:12-14 suggests that age is now, not sometime in the future. Christ then presumably would be ruling God's *basileia* for him, until the parousia.[11] If Colossians is Pauline we can also note that this present *basileia* is called the *basileia tou theou* in 4:11 (however, see below on Col 4:11). More clearly, the present saving activity of God is spoken of in texts like Romans 14:17. I must conclude then that Paul probably did not speak of a messianic kingdom distinct from God's *basileia*.[12]

Three sayings in the Pauline corpus speak of inheriting or failing to inherit the *basileia tou theou:* Galatians 5:21; 1 Corinthians 6:9-10 and 15:50. This language must be related to the idea of being found worthy of the *basileia*, since it is apparent that for Paul there are ethical prerequisites to entering or inheriting this *basileia*. Indeed, Paul is directly or indirectly reminding his audience of these preconditions in all of the first five of the *basileia* sayings we have been examining.[13] In 1 Thessalonians 2:10-11 he speaks of being holy, righteous, blameless and worthy. In 2 Thessalonians 1:8 he says that Christ's parousia will bring punishment to those disobedient to the gospel. The same ethical preconditions for entering or inheriting the *basileia* are clear in Galatians 5:21. Those who engage in orgies, drunkenness, idolatry or the other items condemned in the vice catalog will not inherit the *basileia*.

The exact same sort of thing is said in 1 Corinthians 6:9-10. Here too we have an abbreviated vice catalog, or catalog of the excluded coupled with the very specific remark, "Do you not know that the wicked will not inherit the *basileia tou theou?*" (6:9). G. Haufe has pointed out that the connection of *basileia theou* with the verb *klēronomein* ("inherit") in the future (or present with future meaning) and a negation *(ou)*, characterizes these three sayings, and distinguishes them from all the discussion of the *basileia* in early Judaism outside the Jesus tradition.[14] It is not the case then that Paul is simply using traditional Jewish language about the *basileia* here.[15]

Before we consider 1 Corinthians 15:50, which is slightly different in character from the sayings thus far examined, it will be well to note that even though Paul clearly believes that salvation or justification (at least insofar as it is a present condition or event) is by grace through faith, nonetheless he is quite clear that certain forms of behavior by believers (or unbelievers) can either exclude one from or make one worthy of the future *basileia*. In all the instances studied thus far Paul is clearly addressing Christians and warning them about *their* conduct and its possible effect on whether or not they may enter or inherit the *basileia*. We may wish to call this working out one's salvation with fear and trembling but clearly Paul does not think moral behavior is optional for those who wish to enter or inherit the *basileia*.

Even more pointedly, Paul thinks that ongoing moral failure can *exclude* one from that coming *basileia* even if one is presently a Christian believer. Were this not Paul's viewpoint it would be nearly impossible to explain his choice of language in these five sayings, and we would have to conclude that Paul engaged in idle threats while secretly knowing that there was no possibility of those who were presently Christians being excluded from the *basileia* on the basis of their conduct after conversion. Perhaps we should relate these texts to the material in the Gospels where Jesus either speaks of *rewards* in heaven depending on one's conduct on earth, or warns even believers of possible exclusion from the coming *basileia* because of bad conduct. For instance, Matthew 5:20 reads: "Unless your righteousness surpasses that of the Pharisees and the teachers of the law, you will certainly not enter the kingdom of heaven." Or we may compare Matthew 7:21; 18:3 and parallels or Luke 6:35 and parallels. While some may argue that some of this material goes back only to the First Evangelist or to the editors of the Q material, in a later chapter we will see that by the criterion of multiple attestation various of these *ideas* seem ultimately to go back to Jesus himself, regardless of who was responsible for the final formulation of the material.[16]

Though similar in form to Galatians 5:21 and 1 Corinthians 6:9-10, 1 Corinthians 15:50 has a slightly different content. Here the focus is not on moral qualifications or disqualifications for entering or inheriting the *basileia,* but on *physical* disqualification. In short, Paul is asserting that human beings *in* their present mortal physical bodies cannot inherit the *basileia.* This makes abundantly clear the future character of this *basileia* for Paul, for he insists that one must first have a resurrection body (whether due to resurrection from the dead or transformation of the living) to *inherit.* This means that the *basileia* cannot arrive *until* Christ returns, the dead are raised and the living transformed. In this saying Paul is using traditional Jewish language, if not also traditional Jewish thought about the resurrection, to describe conditions in the *basileia.*[17]

My conclusions about the future *basileia* sayings in Paul may be summed up briefly. Paul seems to see the future *basileia* as a *realm* that one enters or inherits only upon the return of Christ and *after* the resurrection of the dead in Christ and the transformation of the living believers. Paul believes there are various moral and physical prerequisites to inheriting or entering the *basileia.* Put the other way around, immoral conduct can keep even those who are presently Christians out of this future *basileia.*[18]

Of a rather different character are the sayings in 1 Corinthians 4:20-21 and Romans 14:17. In the former Paul uses an *ou . . . alla* formula to make clear what is and is not an essential attribute of the *basileia.* It is not a matter of mere words but of power. The sentence is without a verb, so we must insert "is" or "consists." Both the content of this sentence and its context suggest that Paul is saying something about the present situation that exists among believers. In view of the fact that Paul speaks of the power of the cross and its effect when preached (1 Cor 1:17), and in view of the demonstration of the Spirit's power when Paul preached in 2:4[19] or of God's power in 2:5, it is very likely that the reference to power in 1 Corinthians 4:20-21 should be taken as describing something presently active in the world. Here perhaps Paul uses the term *basileia* to mean something like the dynamic saving activity of God or perhaps the reign of God.[20]

This sort of interpretation of *basileia tou theou* also helps us to understand Romans 14:17. Here we learn that the *basileia* is not food and drink but righteousness, peace and joy in the Holy Spirit. This appears to be a definition of what characterizes the *effects* of the *basileia* in the present. Since the focus is on the effects of the dynamic saving activity of God in the present and not on the activity itself,[21] this text differs somewhat from 1 Corinthians 4:20-21. Nevertheless, like 1 Corinthians 4:20-21, Romans 14:17 is talking about a condition or activity in the present.

Colossians 4:11 speaks of coworkers for *(eis)* the *basileia tou theou.* The text is somewhat oblique, but it too seems to refer to something that exists in the present on earth for which Paul and his coworkers can work. There is also a reference to these coworkers being Jews, which raises the question of whether *basileia tou theou* might be the language Paul especially used in a Jewish context to talk to them about the saving activity of God in Christ. If this is so, it might explain the paucity of references to the *basileia* in some of Paul's letters.

It is interesting that the first two of these present Dominion sayings seem to reflect a polemical context. Paul seems to be correcting misconceptions about what the Dominion of God is in the present era. This also seems to be the case with some of the future Dominion sayings. It does not follow from this, however, that Paul uses this idea only under pressure or duress. Various of Paul's ideas, including justification by faith, he uses primarily in a polemical way or context, but the exceptions to such examples show that Paul has a positive view of such ideas quite apart from their usefulness in polemics.

What may we conclude about the references in Paul to the *basileia tou theou* being a present reality? First, Paul does not suggest that anyone enters or inherits the *basileia* in the present. This language he reserves for the future *basileia.* Second, Paul speaks of the power of the *basileia* being present, and the effects of that power on people being evident in the present. He does not say that the *basileia* is already present per se. Colossians 4:11 may well imply that the *basileia* is present, but it could also mean "coworkers *unto* (the coming) of the *basileia.*" That is, Colossians 4:11 could mean that Paul and his coworkers are involved in mission work with a view to the coming of the *basileia* (or for *basileia* purposes). Paul, it would appear, views the *basileia* at least in the present as something that is primarily spiritual in character and effect, not material or physical. He sees it having to do with the spiritual transformation of human beings in the present, not the physical transformation of the cosmos. He also makes it clear that a *purely* material view of the coming *basileia* will not do. Paul, however, does associate material transformation of both persons and world with what will happen in the future—the return of Christ, the resurrection of believers, the renewal of the world (compare Rom 8:22-25). At the very least then it would seem that the future *basileia* will involve a transformed or transfigured material state and thus will not involve "flesh and blood" in its present perishable or mortal condition.

—6—

The Realm
of Possibilities:
Jesus and the
Basileia tou Theou

When we turn to the Jesus traditions that involve the *basileia* we find some of the same features of usage as we have noted in the Pauline material. For instance, some language suggests that entering the *basileia* is something that will happen in the future and involves a future realm or state of affairs. However, other sayings suggest that Jesus thought that the *basileia* as God's dynamic saving activity was present and working through his ministry, transforming individuals' lives. Before I demonstrate these conclusions and further compare and contrast Paul's and Jesus' views on such matters, we need to look at two recent and influential interpretations of the *basileia* language in the Gospels that are at variance with the approach taken in this book.

Since I have elsewhere dealt at considerable length with the question of the definition of *basileia* or *maȓkûṯ* in the Gospels,[1] I will not rehearse those arguments here. In brief, I argued there that *basileia* has more than one nuance, depending on the context—sometimes refering to God's present saving activity breaking into human history, sometimes referring to a future realm that one may enter as a result of that activity of God. Thus we must reject J. Marcus's recent attempt to suggest that the *basileia* language in the Gospels is not multivalent, but rather always refers to an event or activity to be experienced rather than to a realm.[2] Rather, the word means different things in different contexts, and the time element in a saying is the key to discerning the proper meaning.

Marcus helpfully classifies the *basileia* material into various subtypes: (1) those which imply the kingdom's movement; (2) those about entering the kingdom; (3) those which speak of the kingdom as a possession—something inherited, received, given, possessed; (4) those about being in the kingdom; and (5) parables that use the Jewish formula "the kingdom is like."[3] Marcus is also helpful in pointing out that God's *basileia* when used in a dynamic sense does not merely refer to God's ongoing kingly rule or sovereignty but rather to "the force of his personal self-assertion that manifests his kingship by overpowering the resistance to it in the earthly sphere."[4] I would prefer to speak of God's divine saving activity breaking into human history.

I must raise the following objections to his one-sided interpretation, especially of the entrance sayings. First, examples such as those cited from Psalm 143:2, "do not enter into judgment," or Matthew 25:21, 23, "enter into the joy of your master," are by no means directly parallel to the *basileia* entrance sayings. In the former case the text has nothing whatsoever to do with God's saving intervention in human history or the *basileia*. Rather it speaks of interpersonal human relations. In the second example, the context is a parable and the specific focus of the phrase has to do with a servant sharing (entering into) his master's happiness. Thus, while it is indeed a Semitic idiom to speak about entering into something and mean by it sharing in something, this parable does not use this language to draw an analogy with what it means to enter into the *basileia*. The same applies to Marcus's use of John 4:38b: entering into evangelizing labors is not equivalent to entering into the *basileia*.

Second, Marcus's interpretation of Luke 23:42, far from proving his case, proves just the opposite. It in fact provides evidence of the local use of *basileia* in the Gospels. Here Jesus speaks of himself and the criminal on the cross both being in Paradise before the day is out. The implication is surely that this will happen *after they die*. Note that the thief here asks to be remembered (asks for a place) by Jesus when he comes into his *basileia*. The clear parallel in this text is between *basileia* in the criminal's request and Paradise in Jesus' response, the latter of which is conceived of in a local sense here as well as elsewhere in early

Jewish literature. For example, Paradise is seen as a place of bliss (Ezek 31:8), and even more tellingly as the abode of the righteous *after death* (*T. Lev* 18:10-11; *Ps Sol* 14:3; 1 Enoch 17—19; 60:8; 61:12). This is surely close to the meaning in Luke 23 as well.[5] In addition, the future Paradise was identified not only with the Garden of Eden, but also in some cases with the intermediate resting place for the souls of the righteous dead.[6] Notably, Paul uses it as a synonym for heaven (2 Cor 12:4; compare Rev 2:7). In all these examples Paradise is understood to be a place, in particular a place one will reach after death. The analogy between Paradise and *basileia* in Luke 23 does not suggest that "Jesus' reply . . . is a correction of the thief's futuristic eschatology"[7] if by that one means that Jesus then replaces it with some form of realized eschatology such as Marcus suggests: "already, *from the cross,* Jesus is exercising kingly power."[8]

Third, though Aalen clearly overstated his case for the local sense of *basileia,* he is certainly right about that sense in some cases. I would suggest that Aalen's reference to texts like 2 Chronicles 13:8; Psalm 103:19 and Obadiah 21, which refer to the *malᶜkûṭ Yahweh* in a local sense,[9] or the material about kingdoms in Daniel 7—11 provide much closer analogies to some of the Gospel usage of *basileia* with entrance language than do such Psalms as 15 or 24, which provide us with ritual entrance liturgies. In none of these texts from the Psalms is the *malᶜkûṭ Yahweh* even referred to. Also, in neither the *mᶜšālîm* about the *basileia* nor in the isolated sayings about entrance into the *basileia* does Jesus appear to be drawing on entrance liturgy material from the Psalms. Indeed, Jesus' teaching is in general remarkably free of such cultic language. This may well be because he was at odds with how Jewish religion was being practiced in such settings.[10]

Fourth, when Marcus deals with a text like Mark 10:15 he says that one can receive kingly power but cannot receive a realm.[11] We may properly ask, Why not? The very use of the language of inheritance or possession of the *basileia* in the New Testament suggests just the opposite. If one can possess/inherit the *basileia* one can surely receive it. Surely, in a first-century context, where people like the Herods were indeed receiving kingdoms from Caesar, speaking of receiving God's Dominion would make perfectly good sense.

Other kinds of texts, such as "You are not far from the *basileia tou theou*"(Mk 12:34) or the Q saying in Matthew 8:11/Luke 13:28b-29 about having places at the messianic banquet in the *basileia tou theou* do not make good sense if the *basileia* is not understood in a local sense at least some of the time. In particular, in the Gospels *basileia* seems normally to have a local sense when it is equated with a future entity that one may yet enter, take a place in, or come into. This usage also comports with what we have already discovered about future *basileia* sayings in the Pauline corpus. Thus we must conclude that Marcus has failed to make his case.

It may well be that Aalen has touched on a crucial point when he says that Jesus (and for that matter Paul) did not use the language of epiphany (revealed, appears) to refer to the *basileia tou theou* in the present precisely because he rejected the theocratic interpretation of the *basileia.*[12] For neither Jesus nor Paul does the coming of the *basileia* in the *present* amount to the visible theophanic manifestation of God himself that displaces all human governments, re-establishes Israel in its Davidic glory (see *Ps Sol* 17—18), establishes the sort of Edenic state on earth depicted in texts like Isaiah 60 and has other dramatic supernatural effects on the cosmos and material world as well as on human beings (see Lk 17:20-21). This leads us to consider T. F. Glasson's view of the *basileia tou theou* that Jesus proclaimed.

Glasson advocates what he calls the traditional view of the kingdom of God, that it was the era of redemption inaugurated in part during Jesus' ministry and in full by his death and resurrection.[13] He attempts to de-eschatologize the *basileia* chiefly by negating or minimizing the passages that deal with a future realm at the end of human history called the *basileia,* and by affirming that Jesus had in mind setting up a new covenant and a new covenant community in a new era of salvation.

On the one hand, Glasson seems to be correct that for Jesus as well as for Paul there was a spiritual character to the *basileia* in the present, if by that one means it was chiefly a matter of God's saving activity causing personal transformation, and causing renewal of human relationships between God and human beings and between various parts of humanity, resulting in some sort of community. Riches has rightly pointed out how Jesus denationalized the concept of the *basileia.* Nor does Jesus use it to speak of the final vengeance on Israel's enemies.[14] In a later chapter I will consider whether Jesus, like Paul, *intended* to set up a community. At least for Jesus the *basileia* also meant good news for those who needed physical healing or material help. It involved physical and social transformation as well as spiritual renewal. Indeed, the physical and spiritual aspects of the coming of the *basileia* are too closely intertwined to be radically distinguished in such key texts as Luke 11:20 and parallels, or in the material that suggests that for Jesus table fellowship with sinners in the present was a manifestation of the coming of the *basileia* (see the Evangelists' editorial comments in Mk 2:15; Lk 15:1; Mt 9:10).

Furthermore, it is simply not possible to dismiss all the future sayings, or the note of consummation or finality in such sayings. While we may well speak of "fulfillment without consummation"[15] in regard to the present *basileia* sayings, this will not work with the future sayings that are associated in Jesus' teaching with things like the messianic banquet or the final reconciliation of humanity coming from the east and west, and with the resurrection of dead believers in Paul's teaching. Caution is called for in any investigation of Jesus' use of the *basileia* language, and we are not well served either by severe attempts to reduce all the *basileia*=realm texts to *basileia*=dynamic activity, or by attempts to de-eschatologize Jesus' *basileia* teaching that had a definite future and final element to it.

With all this in mind, we are now prepared to examine some of the texts that may be fruitfully compared to the Pauline texts we have already examined. We must begin with the future-oriented texts that seem somewhat comparable to the first five Pauline texts we examined. There is nothing unique about the fact that either Jesus or Paul spoke of a future *basileia*. On the one hand, the early Jewish Kaddish prayer, like the Lord's Prayer, involves a petition requesting the coming of God's *malkûtā'*. On the other hand, texts like the *Assumption of Moses* 10:1 refer to the future appearance of God's Dominion throughout creation. This is comparable to what is also found in Targum Zechariah 14:9 and Targum Obadiah 21 (see also 1 QSb IV, 25-26; 1QM VI, 6). What this means, as Allison has rightly pointed out, is that there is a rather clear connection in various contexts in early Judaism between eschatological hopes and the *malkûtā'/basileia* of God.[16] It is not surprising then to find such a connection also in the Jesus material. What is surprising is that Jesus also spoke of the manifestation of the presence and power of God's *basileia* in the *present* as well.[17]

It is well to note in passing that various parables widely considered dominical suggest a future *basileia*. These include the parable of the leaven (Mt 13:33/Lk 13:20-21/*Gospel of Thomas* 96),[18] the parable of the mustard seed (Mk 4:30-32/Mt 13:31-32 and parallels; *Gospel of Thomas* 20) and the parable of the seed growing secretly (Mk 4:26-29). These same parables suggest a connection between what is happening in the present in Jesus' ministry and what will happen in the future when the whole lump is leavened, or when the mustard seed produces its large bush, or when the seed growing secretly produces a harvest. Allison probably is correct when he observes that "the seeming contradiction between the presence of the kingdom of God and its futurity is dissolved when one realizes that Jewish thinking could envision the final events—the judgment of evil and the arrival of the kingdom of God—as extending over time, and as a process or series of events that could involve the present" (compare Jubilee 23; 1 Enoch 91:12-17; 93).[19]

Several texts in Mark 10 immediately command our attention. Mark 10:15 (Mt 18:3/Lk 18:17), which also seems to be independently attested in a slightly different form in John 3:3, 5, refers to both receiving and entering the *basileia*. It is not completely clear what sort of sequence of events is envisioned here, but probably the most likely explanation of the earliest form of this text[20] is that one must receive the *basileia* (God's present activity in Jesus' ministry) like a child does here and now, if one expects in due course to enter that *basileia*. As Beasley-Murray notes, the entrance spoken of here is in the future tense, and "there would not appear to be any reason for suspecting that the saying is referring to anything other than participation in the future kingdom."[21] If this interpretation is correct then we actually have here a word about both the presence of the *basileia* and its future. More clearly, Jesus in Mark 10:23-25 (Mt 19:23/Lk 18:24) refers to the difficulty of the rich at some point in the future entering the *basileia*.[22] This text is important to us not only because it makes clear that Jesus saw entrance into the *basileia* as something that happens in the future, but just as crucially for our purposes this likely authentic text suggests that there were certain ethical prerequisites for entering the *basileia*, a motif we have already noted in Paul's future *basileia* sayings.

The material in Mark 9:42-50 and parallels is also instructive. This is a collection of sayings that Jesus likely spoke on various occasions, although originally verses 43-47 may have been a unit. The shocking character of this material favors its authenticity, as does the fact that we can find no *Sitz im Leben* in the early church where such sayings might have arisen and have been applied. Even the severest forms of disciplinary action we know of in the early church do not approach what is suggested here (compare 1 Cor 5:1-5, where expulsion from the community, not execution or corporal punishment, is in view). In verses 43-47 the phrase "entering into life" parallels "entering into the *basileia*." Once again we should note that the context is a discussion about sin that might exclude one from entering into life/the *basileia*. For our purposes the crucial verses are 43 and 47. It is clear that when Jesus speaks of entering life, he is not talking about being born into this life deformed. This is so because he has just dramatically advocated maiming oneself rather than allowing oneself to sin and go to hell. Therefore, here he is discussing drastic remedies for sin, so that one will not be excluded from participation in eternal life, the future *basileia tou theou*.

Since Derrett has shown that Jesus could be speaking here about well-known punishments for various sorts of sin (particularly sexual ones), his words may not be a matter of mere hyperbole.[23] His point would be that even painful dismemberment or corporal punishment is preferable to continuing a life of sin and so missing out on entering the *basileia*. Thus "entering life" is short for entering the life to come, and makes a statement about the quality of the future *basileia*—it will involve entering a form of life hitherto not experienced.[24] This is noteworthy because Paul intimates something similar when he says that "flesh and blood cannot inherit the Dominion" (1 Cor 15:50). The future *basileia* will not entail normal mortal life as we know it. This view seems to have been shared by Jesus and Paul.

Equally important is Matthew 7:21 (compare Lk 6:46). While it is certainly possible that the First Evangelist has formed an original non-Dominion saying into an entrance saying (compare his interest in this subject in Mt 5:21 and 23:13, both in the context of a polemical reference to the Pharisees),[25] this is not certain. In the first place, this saying could have arisen during the ministry of Jesus and reflect his critique of those of his followers who gave him lip service but failed to live out his teaching about God's will. In its original setting "Lord" would likely mean "master" or "respect sir" and not have any particular christological overtones.[26]

Second, I have already noted the connection of ethical prerequisites with a saying about entrance into the *basileia* both in the teaching of Jesus and of Paul, and this saying certainly suits this pattern.

Third, Luke's tendency to edit out Jesus material refering to future eschatological matters is well known. Furthermore, we can believe that Luke would have changed an original reference to God's will to refer to Jesus' will, and so make the saying more useful in a Christian context where violation of the Lord's will meant a violation of the exalted Jesus' will. It is also possible that this saying in its context in Q and/or in the First and Third Gospels could have been directed against false prophets among the Christians. In its original setting, however, it would refer to Jesus' frustration with the shallowness of the commitment of some of his followers to God's will. Thus with the exception of the possible change of an original rhetorical question into a statement in 7:21a, the First Evangelist may well preserve the more primitive form of this saying.[27] If it goes back to Jesus it provides another example of a pattern we have already noted—ethical prerequisites alluded to as necessary requirements for entrance into the future *basileia*.

In chapter three we examined the well-known saying of Jesus about eating and drinking in the *basileia* (presumably beyond death; compare Mk 14:25 and parallels). Here we should examine in detail a likely authentic Q saying that is similar in perspective to Mark 14:25 and parallels and reveals further information about Jesus' views on the future *basileia:* Matthew 8:11-12/Luke 13:28-29. The original Q form of this saying seems to have read, "Many will come from the east and west and sit at table [with] Abraham, Issac, and Jacob . . . in the *basileia tou theou* . . . but [you] will be thrown [into the] outer [darkness]. There people will weep and gnash their teeth."[28] Marshall is probably right that Luke better preserves the sense, though not the order, of the original saying. In Aramaic the force of the saying is that one group (Gentiles) will enter into the banquet with the patriarchs *while* some of Jesus' Jewish contemporaries will be excluded from the banquet.[29] This saying draws on Jewish ideas about a messianic banquet in the age to come. In particular, it draws on a text from the Isaianic apocalypse that is thought to be the origin of the concept of the messianic banquet:[30]

> On this mountain the Lord Almighty will prepare a feast of rich food for all peoples, a banquet of aged wine—the best of meats and the finest of wines. On this mountain he will destroy the shroud that enfolds all peoples, the sheet that covers all nations; he will swallow up death forever. The Sovereign Lord will wipe away the tears from all faces; he will remove the disgrace of his people from all the earth. (Is 25:6-8)

We should note at the outset that this banquet is associated with ideas of Zion as the mountain of God to which in the end all nations will stream to participate in the salvific benefits of Israel's God. The point is that this material presupposes that Israel/Jerusalem/Zion is the center of God's dealing with humans and that if they wish to benefit from these actions they must come to the place where they have that umbilical link with God.

Though Jeremias's reconstruction of the background of Matthew 8:11 and parallels has been criticized,[31] the reference to people coming from the east and west to sit down with the Jewish patriarchs at banquet surely draws on Isaiah 25:6-8 (compare 21:1-5; 1 Enoch 90:30-36; Tobit 13:11), which *includes* the idea of the pilgrimage of the nations to Zion for participation in the benefits God will provide for his people in the end.[32] Jesus then in this saying affirms that "salvation is of the Jews," but also that it is for the "nations." In view of the Old Testament background this surely refers to Gentiles rather than Diaspora Jews. What is striking here is that juxtaposed with the messianic banquet idea in this Jesus logion is the idea of judgment on some Jews, presumably for rejecting the message of Jesus about the *basileia*. There is thus a contrast between some Jews who are cast out, and Gentiles who are given the great privilege of sharing in the eschatological blessings of the *basileia* with the patriarchs.[33]

For our purposes there are several crucial aspects to this saying. First, it is purely eschatologically oriented, as is made clear by the reference to the patriarchs who apparently are going to return or rise from the dead to dine with the nations. Jesus does not envision here some rapprochement between Jew and Gentile in the present or through the normal events of human history. Second, he does, however, allow that Gentiles will participate in this final blessedness— the banquet being the ultimate symbol of reconciliation, joy and receiving God's gracious gifts. Third, the *basileia* here is once again locally conceived as a place or realm where a banquet can transpire. Indeed, though this saying is perhaps to some degree metaphorical, it does appear that Jesus envisons the *basileia* as finally coming on earth to *eretz Israel* and having a material dimension. Fourth, a warning is given that some Jews may be excluded from this final reconciliation of all peoples, apparently on the basis of their rejection of Jesus and his message. Fifth, once again we see the connection between present behavior and future participation in the *basileia* and its benefits.

When we compare the data from this examination of crucial future-oriented sayings in the Jesus tradition to the Pauline material examined earlier, several important matters come to light. Paul generally talks about *inheriting* the *basileia,* Jesus about *entering* it. Thus Paul places more stress on the idea of *basileia* as a possession, Jesus on *basileia* as a realm to be entered. Both place considerable stress on the ethical prerequisites to entering/inheriting the *basileia.* Inclusion/exclusion is based on both the initial and the ongoing human response to some present message that Jesus or Paul has been proclaiming and to various deeds they have been doing. Both seem to envision the future *basileia* as a realm upon the earth, but nonetheless a realm with certain heavenly as well as earthly qualities. For Paul, this amounts to speaking of the *basileia* as something that humans in their present mortal condition cannot participate in, for resurrection bodies are required. Jesus may intimate as much (though this may be debated) when he refers to the presence of the patriarchs sitting at table. The future *basileia* is envisioned as having both elements of continuity and discontinuity with life as we know it. It is not merely seen as a utopian earthly situation, but one that also partakes in some of the eternal qualities of heaven. For both Paul and Jesus it would appear that the future *basileia* involves the final reconciliation of Jew and Gentile (compare Rom 11 to Mt 8:11-12 and parallels).[34]

It is widely agreed among scholars that Jesus likely spoke of a future *basileia* and of the *basileia* being at work in the present. Some see this last aspect as what was unique about Jesus' proclamation in early Judaism.[35] Yet if indeed Jesus spoke about both the presence and the future of the *basileia*, then the tension between this sort of an "already and not-yet" eschatology must also to some extent be unique.[36]

Jesus did speak of a future *basileia* that would bring goodness beyond expectation to this world, but he also made clear that those who do not dream the dream of hope and see it as in part already realized now in his ministry cannot hope to be part of the dream when it fully becomes reality. There are, in other words, human choices and prerequisites required for participation in that future *basileia*, and the chief of these is a positive reaction to the presence and power of the *basileia* as it is manifested in Jesus and his ministry.

Fortunately for us there is considerable evidence, not only in the parables but elsewhere, that supports the view that Jesus spoke of the *basileia* in the present tense. This material is found in Mark, Q, L and M, as Beasley-Murray has clearly demonstrated.[37] By the criterion of multiple attestation alone this idea of the present *basileia* must surely go back to Jesus. The more important question for our comparison with the Pauline material is, *How* did Jesus conceive of this present *basileia*? What is its character?

Since I discussed at length three of the key present *basileia* sayings and argued for their basic authenticity in a previous book, I will simply summarize my findings here.[38] The Q saying Luke 11:20/Matthew 12:28 is perhaps most critical for our purposes. Jesus interprets the exorcisms he performs as clear evidence that the *basileia* has come upon his audience. Here surely the *basileia* is seen as God's dynamic saving power breaking into the life of someone who is spiritually bound, setting him or her free. This freeing, however, is wholistic in character and also brings physical health. Schnackenburg rightly says, "Accordingly, the reign of God is seen as an effective power (not as a kingdom, as an institution, nor as a purely interior reality)."[39] In short, the *basileia* in the present means the in-breaking of God's dynamic saving power or reign, which can affect the whole person. This comports nicely with what Paul says in 1 Corinthians 4:20-21. The *basileia* in the present amounts to God's saving power, not mere talk. This interpretation of 1 Corinthians 4:20-21 is confirmed by examining such texts as 1 Corinthians 1:17-18. Human transformation takes place by the *dynamis theou* (power of God) that comes upon a person when he or she hears and receives the proclamation of the "word of the cross." Hearing the word preached and being changed is different from exorcism, but the character of the *basileia* is the same in both cases—God's dynamic saving activity at work in the present.

Marshall rightly stresses the connection between the activity of the Spirit and the coming of the *basileia* in Jesus' teaching.[40] This in itself strongly suggests that Jesus believed he was bringing in the decisive and final saving activity of God through his own ministry. Note how birth by the Spirit and entering the *basileia* are linked in John 3:3, 5.

Though it does not involve the phrase *basileia tou theou,* Q material like Matthew 11:2-19/Luke 7:18-35 further supports the conclusion that Jesus understood the in-breaking of the *basileia* in and through his ministry to mean God's saving and healing activity in the present.[41] Thus G. Theissen is likely right when he says, "Jesus is unique in religious history. He combines two conceptual worlds which had never been combined in this way before, the apocalyptic expectation of universal salvation in the future and the episodic realisation of salvation in the present through miracles."[42] This conclusion is illuminated when we compare a saying like Luke 11:20 and parallels to Matthew 8:11-12 and parallels.

Now one could argue that a saying like Matthew 8:11-12, especially when coupled with Jesus' apparent table fellowship with sinners and others during his ministry, suggests that he believed that the *basileia* did entail physical eating and drinking. This is also suggested by a saying like Mark 14:25. If this is so, then one might contrast this with what Paul says in Romans 14:17: "the *basileia tou theou* is *not* a matter of eating and drinking" but rather of more intangible qualities—peace, joy, righteousness. Paul then might be seen as the one who began the trend of "spiritualizing" what the *basileia* means in the present. However, close attention to the context of Romans 14:17 suggests that Paul's point is in regard to the stumbling block principle. That is, we should not insist on our freedom to eat whatever we want, since after all what the *basileia* is really about is not the mere right to eat whatever one wants whenever one wants it but about manifesting those qualities of peace, joy and righteousness that lead to peace and mutual edification (v. 19). There is no place for being purely self-serving since the *basileia* has come.[43]

Another key that gives us some information on the character of the present *basileia* in Jesus' teaching is the much-debated, uniquely Lukan saying found at 17:20-21. Most scholars, including even R. Bultmann, have recognized this saying as a genuine utterance of Jesus.[44] It may be that we have independent attestation to this saying in the Greek form of the *Gospel of Thomas* logion 113 where his disciple said to him,

> On what day will the kingdom come? [Jesus said] "It comes not with expectation (of it). They will not say 'Look, here (it is)!' or 'Look there (it is)!' Rather, the kingdom is spread out over the earth, and human beings see it not!"

We may also cite the Coptic version of the *Gospel of Thomas* logion 3:

> Jesus said, "If those who draw you on say to you, 'Look, the kingdom of heaven,' then the birds of heaven will be (there) before you. If they say to you, 'It is in the sea,' then the fish will be (there) before you. But the kingdom is within you and outside you."[45]

The data from the *Gospel of Thomas* must be used with care, bearing in mind that the Gnostic agenda has affected how these sayings have been rendered in this source.

Though some scholars have argued for seeing Luke 17:20-37 as a unit,[46] it is more probable that it is an isolated logion.[47] It may be that Luke is responsible for the Pharisees being said to be the inquisitors here, but on the other hand the question is believable on their lips. Various scholars have noted the parallels in language between Luke 17:21a and Mark 13:21, but the subject matter is rather different. The former text refers to the coming of the *basileia*, the latter to the falsely claimed presence of the Christ. Nonetheless, they are similar in that in both sayings Jesus is setting eschatological reservation over *against* apocalyptic expectation.[48] This, it seems to me, is characteristic of how Jesus addressed such questions, as I suggested in chapter one. In form, Luke 17:20-21 is a pronouncement story, and in view of its lack of clear evidence of Lukan editing and modifications, with the possible exception of the specification of the questioner being a Pharisee,[49] it seems to go back to Jesus.

Jesus' response to the interlocutor answers not only the *when* question about the *basileia*, but also something of the *how* question. The noun *paratērēsis* is a hapax legomenon in the New Testament and, based on the use of its related verb *paratērein* (see Lk 6:7; 14:1; 20:20; Acts 9:24), likely means "observation." The term probably is used here in its secular sense where it can refer to watching for preliminary signs in the heavens presaging some great event.[50] It is also possible that *paratērēsis* alludes to the watching for "times and seasons," that is, engaging in eschatological forecasting based on timetables and premonitory signs in the heavens (see Wisdom 8:8; 1 Thess 5:1; Mk 13:32). This latter may better suit Jesus' early Jewish context. Jesus then would be saying that all such calculation and indeed all scanning of the skies or of earthly phenomena is pointless because the *basileia* does not come in the present with *cosmic signs* and transformation of the cosmos. The *basileia* in the present does not come as Old Testament theophanies are depicted as coming, with earth-shattering consequences.[51] Such watching for visible signs either in the heavens or on earth will thus prove fruitless.

This does not mean that Jesus is claiming that the *effects* of the present coming of the *basileia* on human beings are invisible. Far from it, as Luke 11:20 and parallels make clear! We need to distinguish this from the *basileia's* possible effects on the material universe apart from human lives. Jesus does not claim that the *present basileia* has wrought change in that realm. It may also be that Luke 17:20-21 is denying that *in the present* the *basileia* is a *realm* or entity that can be seen and inspected. Jesus speaks only of the future *basileia* as a realm that one enters.

We now come to the vexed question of how to interpret *entos*. There are three possible meanings and all have their advocates. Coupled with the plural personal object "you," *entos* may mean: (1) within you; (2) among you, in your midst; or (3) within your grasp, possession. This matter could perhaps be settled more easily if we knew for sure that Jesus' audience was the Pharisees, for it is unlikely that he would have said the *basileia* was within them.[52] We cannot be certain about this, however; thus, the various options must be weighed carefully.

The rare Greek word *entos* is an adverb of place that came to be used as a preposition, usually meaning "inside, within the limits of" (see Josephus *Wars* 3.7.10, "within the city"). In its only other New Testament use it means "inside" the cup (Mt 23:26). In favor of the translation "within you," which was the favorite patristic understanding of the phrase,[53] is the use of *entos* in Psalm 39:3; 103:1; 109:22 and Isaiah 16:11 in the Greek Old Testament and Josephus *Antiquities* 5.1.26. The real problem is that Jesus nowhere else speaks of the *basileia* as a purely inward reality or condition. As Fitzmyer puts it, "The presence of the kingdom is never equated with the presence of the Spirit."[54] Or as Marshall puts it, "Jesus speaks of [people] entering the kingdom, not of the kingdom entering [people]."[55]

R. J. Sneed has argued that Romans 14:17 is an expanded paraphrase of Luke 17:20-21 and that in the oral period the point of the Jesus logion was that the reign of God is not realized by Mosaic law observance but by receiving the Holy Spirit.[56] This is based on a doubtful interpretation of *paratērēsis*, and also on the false assumption that Paul equates Spirit and *basileia*. To the contrary, for Paul the Spirit is something the believer already possesses as a sort of deposit or first installment of future blessedness (compare 2 Cor 5:5), whereas Paul speaks of inheriting the *basileia* in the future. Even in Romans 14:17 a distinction between Spirit and *basileia* is possible. The Spirit brings God's dynamic saving and sanctifying activity into the life of the believer. However, the Spirit's presence is not strictly equivalent to that activity. This same sort of distinction is implicit in a statement such as Luke 11:20 (compare Mt 12:28). The Spirit is the agency by which Jesus performs exorcisms, that is, the Spirit brings God's dynamic saving activity in the present (the *basileia)* to bear on a human life. Therefore Sneed's interpretation is unlikely.

The view that *entos* means "among you" or "in your midst" has the support of such texts as Xenephon *Anabasis* 1.10.3; *Hellenica* 2.3, 19; and Herodotus *History* 7.100.3, the last of which gives an example of *entos* with a plural object with this meaning.[57] This then is clearly a possible meaning here, and it does not conflict with what Jesus says about the character of the *basileia* elsewhere in the Gospels.

The third view, that *entos* means "within your grasp," also has had various supporters,[58] but it appears that its meaning in the papyri, on which this interpretation is based, is closer to "in the house of" or "in your domain" rather than "within your grasp."[59] In any case "in your midst" or "in your domain" would seem to be much the same in meaning, both indicating that the *basileia* is present and active within the human community. The thrust of this logion would then be that there is no need to be anxiously calculating or looking for the future coming of the *basileia* (as a realm) when its presence and activity is already in the midst of Jesus' audience through his ministry. This does not mean that Jesus is claiming to be or personally to embody the *basileia,* but sayings like Luke 11:20 and parallels and Luke 17:20-21 certainly indicate that he claims to bring the *basileia,* God's dynamic saving activity to God's people.

—7—

Conclusions

We are now prepared to sum up what we have discovered by comparing the *basileia* material in the Jesus and Pauline traditions. In the future sayings Jesus speaks about entering while Paul speaks about inheriting the *basileia*. Both Jesus and Paul envision a realm on earth where there will be transformed human conditions. Jesus characteristically spoke of a place where the perfect symbol of human reconciliation, a banquet involving both Jew and Gentile, could transpire. Paul, on the other hand, associates the future *basileia* with believers receiving a resurrection body.

When either Jesus or Paul spoke of the *basileia* in the present they were apparently referring to the dynamic saving activity of God intervening in human lives. In fact, one could say Jesus' and Paul's belief in and views about the nature of salvation in the *present* have affected their views of the nature of the *basileia* in the present, if the two concepts are not simply equated.[1] In the case of Jesus, the *basileia* comes or God's salvific action happens primarily through the miracles he performs. In the case of Paul it is primarily but not exclusively through the proclamation of the gospel of Christ's cross and resurrection (see 2 Cor 12:12). The present *basileia* then is primarily associated with God's saving power.

In both the Jesus and Pauline traditions, when the future *basileia* was spoken of it was joined with statements about certain ethical prerequisites for entering/inheriting. This correspondence seems especially significant. For both Jesus and Paul there is an already and a not-yet aspect to the *basileia*. We noted an *ou . . . alla* form to Paul's present *basileia* sayings, which is similar to the form of contrast in Luke 17:20-21. In both cases this suggests that present *basileia* sayings are used to correct common misconceptions in regard to the character or nature of the *basileia* in the present. The term *basileia* can refer to either the present dynamic saving activity of God—his saving power bursting into our midst—or to the results of that activity. When Jesus speaks of the results in the present of the power of God, he characteristically speaks of miracles or exorcisms, while Paul characteristically focuses more on the transformation of human character and relationships (joy, peace). In neither case, however, is the present *basileia* seen as something that has purely spiritual effects, or for that matter purely material effects. Exorcism is most certainly a matter involving the human spirit at least as much as it involves the human body. Both Jesus and Paul also seem to be working with a nontheophanic or nonapocalyptic view of the coming of the *basileia* in the present, insofar as neither of them seems to have associated God's present dynamic saving activity with cosmic catastrophe or cosmic transformation. In both cases the focus is solely on human transformation and the transformation of interpersonal human relationships. Taking all things into account, the correspondence in outlook about both the present and future *basileia* in the Jesus and Pauline tradition is quite remarkable, and by and large seems much more profound than the differences that are also quite apparent.

It is inevitable that since both Jesus and Paul did speak of God's *basileia* coming to God's people, and being entered/inherited (as a realm) by them in the future, we should raise the question, What is the relationship of *basileia* to the community of God's people in the present? To do this we must compare and contrast Jesus' and Paul's views of the community of God's people, and here we will find more notable differences than we have found thus far in our discussion.

PART THREE

The
Community
of Christ

— 8 —

Introduction

It is not my intention to engage in a detailed discussion of all aspects of Jesus' or Paul's views of the community of God's people. My concern here is to focus on the relationship of the *basileia* to that community. On the basis of what we have concluded thus far, certain preliminary observations seem in order.

First, it is easily demonstrated that neither Jesus nor Paul ever equated the present community of God with the *basileia,* even in its present manifestation. If the *basileia* in the present is God's dynamic saving activity, while it could be argued that that activity results in the formation of a community, the two could never be strictly identical. At most one could perhaps speak of a cause-and-effect relationship.

Second, both Jesus and Paul spoke of entering/inheriting the *basileia* in the future at the end of human history when God is concluding his dealings with humanity. Such purely future-oriented language is never used by Paul to speak of entering the community of believers or by Jesus to discuss what it means to become one of his disciples. Paul, for instance, never speaks of inheriting the *ekklēsia!* Indeed both Paul and Jesus seem to have believed that it is the faithful people of God who do his will who will enter the *basileia* in the future. This means that whatever the relationship of *basileia* to the community of faith or the *ekklēsia* Paul speaks of, they could never be simply equated even when the discussion focuses on the ultimate future. It is one thing for believers to inherit/possess/enter the *basileia; it is another thing to be* the *basileia,* and this latter language is not used anywhere in the New Testament. The *basileia* is apparently something God or his agent brings to earth. The community of believers may now benefit from its presence or ultimately participate in its final manifestation, but not be identified with it without remainder.

Third, it has often been suggested that Jesus had no intention of setting up an ongoing community of his followers.[1] This is argued because it is assumed that Jesus believed in and proclaimed the *necessary* imminence of the end of the world. To what purpose would one set up a community if the world was necessarily about to end? This sort of logic should be considered suspect on two grounds. First, we have already made plausible the contention that it is unlikely that Jesus ever proclaimed the necessary imminence of the end of the world. Second, *even if we were wrong in our arguments* and it turns out that Jesus did believe in the necessary imminence of the end, what we know of the Qumran community should lead us to be more circumspect about insisting that Jesus could not have intended to set up a community. At Qumran, eager eschatological expectation, even in some cases a belief in the necessary imminence of the end, could be and was found side by side with the attempt to set up a community of true believers. Detailed documents about the regulation of the community exist side by side with documents manifesting various sorts of eschatological expectation.[2] The question of whether or not Jesus intended to set up a community, and if so what its relationship to the *basileia* is, should be reassessed.

For Paul there is no doubt that he was in the business of preaching with a view to setting up Christian communities in various parts of the Roman Empire, and he sees no contradiction between this and his eschatological world view. Indeed his evangelism is a natural manifestation of that world view.

—9—

Paul
and the
Body
of Christ

Simply on the basis of volume of usage, it appears rather clear that for Paul the term *ekklēsia* is best and most often used to describe the community of Christians. The term in and of itself denotes a group called out, but its connotations seem to have developed along the same lines that the term *synagōgos* developed. The latter term seems to have first referred to the gathering of God's people, then by extension to the people that gathered, and finally to the building where the gathering happened. Behind both of these terms likely stands the Hebrew word *qāhāl*, and in the Aramaic *qahala* or possibly *kenista*. In any event these terms in early Judaism were used to refer to the people of God, or as at Qumran the community of the covenant. In the Septuagint the term *ekklēsia* is used as a translation for *qāhāl* and means either the people of God or the assembly/congregation of God's people. For Paul the semantic field of *ekklēsia* ranges from the assembly/congregation of God's people (hence the use of the phrase *en ekklēsia* in 1 Cor 11:18) to God's people *simpliciter*. Paul *never* uses *ekklēsia* to refer to a building that houses the assembled Christians. It is very likely that his use of the term *ekklēsia* derives from his reading of the Septuagint, from its use in early Judaism in the Diaspora to refer to the assembly/assembling of God's people, and perhaps from the fact that other early Greek-speaking Christians were using the term for the gathering of Christians. As R. Banks has pointed out at considerable length, Paul almost always means a particular local gathering of Christians when he uses the term *ekklēsia*.[1] When he refers to more than one such gathering he uses one of the plural forms of *ekklēsia* (compare 1 Cor 16:19; 2 Cor 8:1; Gal 1:2, 22). Banks rightly concludes that the idea of a unified provincial or national church is foreign to Paul's thought. Banks seems to be wrong, however, in also claiming that Paul never uses the term *ekklēsia* to speak of the church everywhere.[2] I suspect that 1 Corinthians 11:22, "Do you despise the church of God," or even more clearly Galatians 1:13, "I persecuted the church of God," are instances where Paul means more than one local Christian assembly by *ekklēsia*. What we can say with some assurance is that the local assembly of Christians is the focal point for Paul.

Even more crucial for Paul is the fact that each local *ekklēsia* is a full representation of *the ekklēsia*. This becomes especially clear when Paul uses the body analogy in 1 Corinthians 12—14 to describe one local group of Christians—those in Corinth. They locally manifest all the members of the body of Christ. For Paul, they are *the ekklēsia tou theou* in Corinth. Yet it is also clear that for Paul the term *ekklēsia* encompasses more than one household gathering of Christians if there are several such gatherings in one locale. Thus Paul can speak of "when the *whole ekklēsia* comes together" (1 Cor 14:23; compare Rom 16:23). This means that *ekklēsia* cannot simply be equated with *oikos* (house). Rather, Paul speaks of the *ekklēsia* that meets in particular houses (1 Cor 16:19). Banks is right to stress the dynamic rather than static character of this *ekklēsia*. It can be built up and grow, or be harmed and atrophy (see 1 Cor 14:4).

In these early letters of Paul the term *ekklēsia* consistently refers to actual gatherings of Christians as such, or to Christians in a local area conceived or defined as a regularly-assembling community. This means that the Church has a distinctly dynamic rather than static character. It is a regular occurrence rather than an ongoing reality. The word does not describe all the Christians who live in a particular locality if they do not in fact gather or when they are not in fact gathering.[3]

Again, this may be slightly overstating the matter, since Paul can use the term to refer simply to the Christian people of God (Gal 1:13), but it is true that for

Paul God's people become the *ekklēsia* properly speaking when they meet together for worship and koinonia. The *ekklēsia* for Paul is a living entity or organism that grows or atrophies, as people are joined to the body of Christ by the supernatural work of the Spirit. It is fundamentally not an organization, club or society, though it may well have appeared to be such to outsiders who compared it to other such groups in Corinth and elsewhere.[4] *Ekklēsiae* may *have* structures, buildings or organization, but they are not synonymous with them, for in the end *ekklēsia* refers to the people of God gathered, or to the congregation of believers, or to the people *simpliciter*. That there is order to and an organization in the meetings and of the leadership of the *ekklēsia* does not vitiate these conclusions.

Paul also speaks of Christians on earth as already being part of a heavenly commonwealth or community (see Phil 3:19-20; Gal 4:25-27; Col 1:18-24). What we do not find in Paul is the idea of the "invisible church" in the midst of a mass of unredeemed people. The church is the visible body of believers in a given locale—indeed they are at times embarrassingly too visible when they sin and fail (see 1 Cor 5). Banks puts it well when he says the *ekklēsia* is the visible earthly manifestation of a heavenly commonwealth and its qualities. The *ekklēsia* takes on a supranational and supratemporal character not due to some international or provincial organizational structures or some council of churches, but because of its connection with the heavenly commonwealth. Only in Paul's vision of community do we find the idea of a voluntary association with regular meetings of like-minded people coupled with the notion of a shared identity and citizenship with those in heaven, combined with the character of a household unit.

The household character of the *ekklēsia* is shown first by the family terms and expectations applied to believers. They are to treat each other as their actual brothers and sisters, showing fellow Christians the same love, respect and generosity one would show family. Second, the meetings are intentionally in households, which likely explains why in the later Paulines we find, third, the adaptation and adoption of household rules or tables for the family of faith (Col 3:18—4:1; Eph 5:21—6:10).[5] What is a rather unique development here is the concept of the family that is family because of shared faith, not any sort of social, sexual, economic, educational or ethnic ties (see Gal 3:28). Nowhere in the Old Testament is Israel ever called God's family, and even at Qumran there is very little use of family language.[6] There is something distinctive and perhaps almost unique in the household setting, family language and family responsibilities of the early Pauline Christians. However, as we shall see, it would appear that this idea of the family of faith ultimately goes back to Jesus himself.[7]

Finally, we should note that when Paul uses the term *sōma* in the metaphorical sense to describe the *ekklēsia* it is not simply identical with the *ekklēsia*. Paul uses *sōma* when the unity of Christians in a locale is at issue, and the term focuses more on inter-Christian relationships, giftedness and responsibility toward one another, while *ekklēsia* is more of a wholistic term that focuses on a group (whether all or some) of Christians assembling together for worship. Paul calls the latter the church of *God*, while he never speaks of the body of God, only the body of Christ. This is probably partly because there was a congregation of God's people assembling on various occasions before Christ came, but it was Christ's coming, death, resurrection and Spirit-giving that in Paul's view knit believers together into a body. The *sōma tou Christou* is an entity that could exist only after the Spirit was poured out on all Christians (1 Cor 12:12-13). Paul apparently was the first to apply *sōma* to a community within and smaller than the body politic (compare Seneca, *De Clemen* 1.4.3-5) or than the universe (which was sometimes thought to be God's body).

Paul nowhere clearly discusses the relationship of the *basileia* to the *ekklēsia*, but it seems reasonable that he never treats the two terms as synonymous. In fact, one would be hard-pressed to find even one example where Paul uses the two terms in close conjunction with one another.[8] While both *basileia* and *ekklēsia* are understood as dynamic rather than static in character, there is little or no overlap in meaning of these two terms. For Paul *basileia* in the present is God's dynamic saving activity, or his reign in human lives brought about through the Holy Spirit, or the results of that activity. In the future, the *basileia* is a realm that believers may enter, but it too comes as a result of the dynamic action of God's agent at his parousia. It is not something Christians can build up or harm, nor would it have made sense to Paul to talk about God's saving activity in the present growing or being edified.

By contrast, the *ekklēsia* is the assemblying/assembly of the Christian people of God, or simply the Christian people of God. The dynamic saving activity of God changes human lives and makes possible the *ekklēsia*, but the focus of the former is apparently on individual transformation (especially), while the focus of the latter is on the group that results from such individual transformations. In due course Christians who are now the *ekklēsia* may enter the final manifestation of the *basileia* provided their behavior is consistent with or meets the entrance requirements, or at least does not cause their exclusion. The *ekklēsia* has heavenly connections and associations—its head/leader is in heaven (see Phil 1:20). But for Paul the *ekklēsia* is basically an earthly entity or at least the earthly manifestation of a heavenly one, and fundamentally something that exists in the present and during the remainder of human history until Christ returns.

For Paul, however, it appears that entering/inheriting the *basileia* is the same as entering eternal life in the resurrection body when Christ returns. It is thus not temporally bound. Paul might well have been comfortable with the phrase *basileia tou ouranou,* but not with the *ekklēsia tou ouranou.* The commonwealth in heaven is connected to the *ekklēsia* through Christ but not identical with the earthly *ekklēsia,* which has historical purpose, function and manifestation. We must bear these things in mind as we turn to examine Jesus' view of community and its relationship to the *basileia.*

—10—

Jesus
and the
Foundation
Stones

There are various indications or hints in the Jesus tradition that Jesus did indeed intend to set up a community, or call all Israel into such a community. For instance, Jesus' use of family language was distinguishable from its normal usage in early Judaism. He seems to have spoken of his circle of disciples/ adherents as his brothers, sisters and mothers *in distinction from* his physical family (see Mk 3:31-35 and parallels). Elsewhere I have called this the language of the family of faith.[1] This occurs not only in the primitive tradition in Mark 3:31-35 and parallels[2] but also in various other strands of the Gospel material (compare Mt 25:40ff.; 28:10; Jn 20:17).[3] It would seem that early Christians simply carried on using family language based on the precedent in the Jesus tradition after the Easter events (for example, 1 Cor 15:6), for it is difficult to explain its ubiquity not only in Paul's letters but elsewhere in the New Testament if Jesus never used family language in this specifically religious way.

A second fact about the ministry of Jesus that most all scholars would agree on is that there was an inner circle of disciples that came at a very early date to be called the Twelve (see 1 Cor 15:5, citing earlier tradition).[4] If indeed Jesus directed his ministry to Israel it seems clear that "twelve" must have some sort of communal significance. I have argued elsewhere that Jesus chose twelve not to *be* but to *free* Israel, to be his *s^elûḥîm* to Israel, calling them back to God in view of the in-breaking of the *basileia*. It would seem as well that he intended for them to have some sort of juridical function over Israel when the *basileia* as realm finally came to *eretz Israel*.[5] Mt 19:28/Lk 22:30 suggests that Jesus envisioned this happening not during the current course of his ministry but at the culmination of human history. Surely the reference to judging and thrones indicates that this activity will not transpire until the *Yom Yahweh,* the day of judgment.

Third, Jesus' use of the term "Son of Man" also suggests that he may have intended to set up some sort of community. If, as many scholars still think, Jesus did use such terminology of himself with allusion to *that Son of Man* in Daniel 7, this in itself may suggest he intended to form a community. The Son of Man in Daniel 7 represents God's suffering people in the very presence of the Ancient of Days. But even beyond this point, if Jesus had *any* sort of messianic self-understanding,[6] it is hardly likely that he would not have thought it was his task to form or reform some sort of community. What is a messianic figure without a people?[7] G. Lohfink has put it this way:

> After a history of more than a millennium, the people of God could neither be founded nor established, but only *gathered* and *restored.* It was precisely this that Jesus sought. . . . It is not just any movement of gathering and awakening, but the *eschatological* gathering of God's people. The central content of Jesus' preaching after all, was that with his appearance the time was fulfilled. The ancient promises for the last days had become reality. The reign of God had begun to arrive. In this eschatological situation, Israel had to grasp the salvation it was offered; it had to repent and let itself be gathered for the reign of God.[8]

I would agree with most of this, except that it seems to me that Jesus' message amounted to more than just a matter of reforming early Judaism in a way that would leave all its essential features intact. He envisioned a more radical reform that included the annulment of the laws of clean and unclean.[9]

In any event, if I am right about any of the three factors mentioned above, and bearing in mind what was said earlier about the Qumran community and eschatological matters, it should not be dismissed out of hand that Jesus had in mind the setting up of a community. One text that might give us some real clues as to what Jesus had in mind is Matthew 16:17-19. This text has often been dismissed as a later church formulation.

Typical of this view is the argument of F. W. Beare. He points out that nowhere else does Jesus speak of *ekklēsia* much less *my ekklēsia*. This suggests to Beare the formation of a sect within Judaism, and the historical evidence does not suggest that Peter ever held the role predicated of him in Matthew 16:17-19.[10] This last point, however, far from arguing against the authenticity of this saying, counts in favor of it. We must ask, What Evangelist writing in the 80s, if not later, and certainly *after* Peter's death would have invented such a saying when it was well known that Peter never assumed such a role in the early church?

Frankly, this is more difficult to believe than the alternative—that Jesus did say something along these lines but that historically we have no evidence that they were fulfilled during the lifetime of the historical Peter. I have already noted that the term *ekklēsia* is regularly used in the Septuagint for the assembly/assembling of God's people and thus is hardly a specifically Christian term. In any event, it is doubtful that Jesus spoke such a saying *in Greek,* and so the proper question would be whether Jesus could have ever spoken of a *qahala* or a *kenista,* Aramaic terms that could be translated with *ekklēsia.* I will pursue this matter further in a moment. Here I will simply pause to note that several important recent critical and detailed studies of Matthew 16:17-19 have concluded that there are likely at least some authentic elements in this saying.[11] Thus various factors may favor that this saying at least in part goes back to Jesus,[12] and we should at least investigate them.

First, as G. Bornkamm pointed out, while the use of *ekklēsia* in Matthew 18:18 seems more like a Christian use of the term, the usage in 16:17ff. is different. Thus he concludes that "one must certainly affirm that Matt. 16:17ff is of an earlier date than 18:18."[13] Also favoring the view that this saying is primitive and not invented by the First Evangelist is the significantly higher number of Semitisms/Aramaisms, more than in other sayings of comparable length in the Gospel that do reflect extensive redactional work, if not whole-scale creation, by the Evangelist.

Out of some eighty words in Matthew 16:17-19 are the following Semitisms/Aramaisms: (1) Bar-Jonah, which is probably an Aramaic patronymic; (2) the use of Hades in the sense of Sheol to refer to death, with gates of Hades referring to the doorway into the grave; (3) the reference to binding and loosing probably in the early Jewish sense of what one is bound to do and what one is permitted to do; (4) the phrase "flesh and blood," a typical Jewish periphrasis for a mortal human being (see 1 Cor 15:50); (5) the reference to the keys with likely allusion to Isaiah 22:15-25; (6) the use of *petros/petra,* which probably goes back to the Aramaic nickname Jesus gave Peter (Kepha[s]), a name independently attested in the early 50s at 1 Corinthians 1:12, which also suggests that there are some authentic elements in this saying;[14] and (7) though *ekklēsia* does not occur elsewhere in the arguably authentic sayings of Jesus, its use here in a sense akin to what we find in the Septuagint, coupled with the fact that Jesus does use eschatological images for the community of God's people in his parables and elsewhere (flock, plant, city of God) makes it plausible he might have spoken of a *qahala* or *kenista.*[15]

Possible evidence for the very early date of Matthew 16:17-19 has sometimes been found in Galatians 1:11ff.[16] Paul speaks of the fact that God *revealed his Son* to him, and that he had no need to confer with *flesh and blood* for this information. This may well suggest that Paul knew some such tradition as in Matthew 16:17, and that Paul is making a claim for himself comparable to that of Peter's. Peter (who is called Cephas at Gal 1:18, another possible point of contact with our text) is the one Paul says he went to visit in Jerusalem (1:18), and clearly in 2:7-8 Paul makes a point of comparing his ministry with Peter's. Also, in 2:9 Paul mentions the *styloi,* columns or pillars normally made of rock or stone. Is this an allusion to what we find in Matthew 16:18, "this *petra*"?

As J. R. Mantey has ably demonstrated, there is no known example in contemporary Greek literature where *petra* means the same thing as *petros.* A *petros* is a small stone or piece of a rock, but a *petra* is by contrast a ledge or shelf of rocks, and usually is used to refer to a cluster of rocks, such as a cliff. It can on occasion mean a huge boulder of bedrock as in Matthew 7:24, or as in Josephus a massive boulder that only a catapult could throw.[17] This raises the possibility that this saying is not a play on words at all but indicates that Peter, as the representative disciple, is the sort of confessing person, along with other such "rocks," on which Jesus will build his community. Jesus would be saying that he will build his community not on one small stone, but on a bedrock or ledge of such stones.

If this is the meaning of Matthew 16:18 then not only could Paul allude to it in Galatians 2:9, but also a reference to it might be found in such texts as 1 Peter 2:4-5 or perhaps more likely in Ephesians 2:20. In any event, if Matthew 16:17-18 *is* alluded to in Galatians 1—2, it is quite believable that this is information

Paul obtained from Peter himself whom he says he visited and conferred with sometime in the late 30s. Paul then would be describing his own revelation about the Son in comparable terms because his authority was being questioned. If, as some have argued, what we have in Matthew 16:16-18 is a postresurrection logion that was perhaps originally part of the content of Peter's experience of the risen Lord, the parallels to the Pauline material in Galatians 1—2 may be even sharper.[18] The setting of this saying is uncertain, however, especially in view of the fact that the fragments of this tradition found in John 14:1-2 and 20:23 are found in widely differing contexts than the placement of the material in Matthew.[19]

It is frankly difficult to separate out tradition from redaction in Matthew 16:17-19, not least because, as B. Meyer and others have pointed out, not only are there Semitic ideas throughout the three verses, but in form the three verses are a unity. The text is a triad, with each of the three parts having three lines made up of a thematic statement that is then made clear by an antithetically structured distich.[20]

Blessed are you Simon bar-Jona
for flesh and blood has not
revealed [this] to you
but my heavenly Father.

And I say to you:

You are Peter
and on this bedrock
I will build my *ekklēsia,*
and the gates of Sheol
will not prevail against it.

I will give you the keys of
the *basileia* of heaven.
And whatever you bind on earth
will have been bound in heaven.
And whatever you loose on earth
will have been loosed in heaven.

Due attention will have to be given to the verb tenses in this pericope, for even if it does go back ultimately to Jesus we will note that *oikodomeō* and several succeeding verbs are not in the present tense but rather in the future. The First Evangelist certainly does not take this to indicate that Jesus then and there at Caesarea Philippi was establishing a community during his ministry. Indeed, in light of the larger Matthean context (see 16:21), it appears clear that he assumed that Jesus meant that this event would happen sometime after his death. This means that the First Evangelist does not use this traditional material to claim that Jesus founded the Christian *ekklēsia* during his ministry.

The image of building something on a rock has plenty of Jewish precedent, and E. Schweizer especially has brought the important parallels together in his commentary.[21] The following points are worth reiterating. First, the rock on which the temple in Jerusalem was built was sometimes thought of as sealing the gateway to Sheol, and that same temple was seen as the gateway to heaven. In fact, Mishnah Yoma 5.2 calls this rock "Shetiyah," which means "foundation." If Jesus was alluding to that rock, he would be suggesting that he was setting up an alternate center of religious life founded upon the basis of a confessing Peter.[22] If this is alluded to here then it may relate to those sayings where apparently Jesus claimed, or at least was understood to have claimed, that the temple would be destroyed and he would build another shortly thereafter (see Mk 14:58; 15:29 and parallels; Jn 2:19; Acts 6:14).[23] This again suggests that if this saying goes back to Jesus it reflects a claim that a community would be established after Jesus' death.

Second, the Qumran material includes two traditions of relevance—1 QH 6.23-28 and 4 QpPs. 37.3(2).16. The former speaks of the hymnist being brought to the very gates of Sheol, using the imagery of the primordial flood, but God rescued him and brought him into a secure city built upon a rock amid "sheltering gates that vouchsafe no entrance, and secure bolts that do not shatter." The pesher on the psalms speaks of the Teacher of Righteousness building a community. Of less direct relevance is the later rabbinic tradition about Abraham being a rock on which God builds the world. Not only does this tradition postdate our logion by a considerable amount of time, but it may in fact be a counterpolemic against Christian claims based on Matthew 16:17-19.[24] Of more relevance than any of this data is the material in Isaiah 22, which we will examine shortly. We should note, however, that the gates of Sheol is equivalent to the gates of death, not hell, as is evident from such texts as Isaiah 38:10, Job 17:16, 38:17 and Psalm 9:13. This makes it unlikely that this text was originally about the struggle between Satan and the church during the post-Easter period.[25]

J. Marcus has urged that Matthew 16:18 presents us with a military metaphor suggesting the rulers of the underworld bursting forth from the gates of hell to attack God's people on earth.[26] Against this is the following: (1) the already-noted usual meaning in the Bible of the phrase "gates of Sheol"; (2) the fact that elsewhere in the Bible death is personified as an aggressive and hostile being that attacks human beings (such as 1 Cor 15:55); it is death that will not prevail over Jesus' *ekklēsia*; (3) the only other possible example in the New Testament where *Hades* equals hell is in the uniquely *Lukan* parable of the rich man and Lazarus (Lk 16:19-31); and (4) the keys to the *basileia* of heaven are not the same as the keys to heaven's gate, pace Marcus, and so there is no contrast here between the keys and the gates of Sheol, representing heaven and hell respectively. In fact, in the Matthean redaction the *basileia* that is the Son's and that the Son can bestow authority over is *on earth* (see Mt 13:38, 41, where world and *basileia* are paralleled). This part of the text makes good sense as it stands, based on the Jewish idiom Jesus would have known and could have used in which the gates of Sheol represent death and its powers. I must stress again that we must take the future tenses seriously. The text does not say Jesus there and then gave Peter the keys, but that he would do so in the future. This text is more on the order of a promise than a dispensation.

Here we must carefully consider the material in Isaiah 22:15-25. The parallels with our text are numerous and notable: (1) the address in Isaiah 22 is to a steward who has hewn a habitation or tomb for himself in the rock, that is, he has bought a one-way ticket to the gates of Sheol (v. 18); (2) the steward Shebna will then be deposed and disposed of, being replaced by Eliakim, who then will have authority committed to his hand; (3) Eliakim is said to be the father to the *house* of Judah and to Jerusalem; (4) to him is given the key of the house of David, which he shall open and none shall shut and vice versa. In short, he has the final authority and power over this gate to David's house. The power here is clearly an earthly one, involving an earthly realm.

These parallels suggest that Jesus is bestowing some kind of earthly authority on Peter in relationship to the entering of the *basileia*, presumably at the end of human history and on earth. Also bestowed on Peter is the power of binding and loosing, which in view of the Jewish parallels likely refers to making decisions about what is required (what one is bound to do) and what is allowed (what one is permitted or free to do) in Jesus' community.[27] It is possible that binding and loosing refers to allowing people in or excluding them from the community, which would more closely link this material with the Isaiah 22 background.[28] On this view Peter is given authority in relationship both to behavior in the community and to entrance into the eternal *basileia* at the end of history. This text does not suggest, any more than does any other Matthean text, that the *ekklēsia* and the *basileia* are one and the same.[29] Nor is it clear that Peter alone is being labeled here as the foundation of the later community known as the Christian *ekklēsia*.

R. H. Hiers's suggestion that the reference in Matthew 16:19 is to the binding of demons and the setting free of their captives must also be given serious consideration, especially in view of the use of binding language elsewhere in the New Testament to refer to exorcism or binding of Satan, as well as the use of keys to refer to binding of Satan in a pit (see Mk 3:27; Lk 13:16; Rev 1:18; 20:1-3; T. Levi 18:10-12; CD 6.13). The reference to the gates of hell could also point us in this direction,[30] and Jesus' bestowal of powers of exorcism on some of his first followers is well attested in several strands of the tradition. On this showing, Peter is given the power over the forces of darkness and assured that they will not prevail over him or the community Jesus is founding. The two problems with this view are that it probably requires that binding and loosing refer to persons, rather than to two different groups of beings, and here the keys have to do with the *basileia* and admission into it.

In the end two elements in Matthew 16:17-19 are perhaps to be attributed to the Evangelist's hand. First is the modifier "my" that has been attached to *ekklēsia*. "Jesus certainly never intended the founding of a mere sectarian community, for such an intention would not have been compatible with his appeal to all Israel, and we can specify no point in time after which Jesus' appeal to all Israel is abandoned."[31] The second element in this saying that may be considered suspect is the reference to binding and loosing, if it is referring to something like *halakôt* and in effect makes Peter into a sort of Christian rabbi. This would comport well with the theological interests of the First Evangelist in the law and its fulfillment.

Otherwise, however, there is little or nothing about this saying that could not plausibly go back to a *Sitz im leben Jesu*. The drift of the saying would be that Jesus ascribed some special role to Peter, and presumably to the other "rocks" that were his disciples *in the future* when there would be a new (or true) community founded. Their role would have to do with proclaiming and aiding people to enter the future *basileia* of God. Alternatively, the saying may simply reflect the sort of ideas we also find in Matthew 19:28 and parallels and refer to some juridical function at the end of human history in relationship to Israel. Whichever is the case, while this saying certainly does suggest that Jesus promised to build an *ekklēsia,* it does not suggest that he was already doing so by or during his ministry. As such, the saying seems to fall into the same field of ideas as the promise to raise up the eschatological temple after a short time.

That Jesus might have spoken about building an eschatological temple should not be lightly dismissed, not only because there is evidence from two different sources in the New Testament that suggests Jesus may have spoken about his doing such a thing (see Mk 14:58; Jn 2:19), but also because, as D. Juel has pointed out, at least two texts (2 Sam 7:13/1 Chron 17:12; Zech 6:12) were considered messianic texts before the time of Jesus, and both of them refer to a Messiah-king building the temple when he comes.[32] Furthermore, we know that *prior* to the destruction of the temple in A.D. 70, the equation of temple with community of believers was made not only in the Christian community but elsewhere (compare 2 Cor 6:16 to 1 QS 8.4-10; 9.3-6; CD 3.18—4.10; 1QpH 12.3).[33] Taken together with the evidence we discussed earlier, Mark 14:58 and John 2:19 may provide corroboration that Jesus spoke of building a community of believers.

—11—

Conclusions

What may we conclude from this part of our discussion? First, while it appears likely that Jesus did in fact speak of building a community of God's people, he nowhere equates that community with the *basileia tou theou,* which he sees as a present saving power and a future realm that the faithful members of God's people may enter at the end of human history. On this score, there is little to differentiate the essential understanding of the relationship of community to *basileia* in the Jesus tradition from what we also found in the Pauline material. In the Pauline material, however, we have a much more developed understanding of community, a community that is essentially grounded in Christ and in particular in his death and resurrection. There is no evidence of this sort of developed christological and soteriological understanding of the basis of community in the Synoptics. Paul speaks of a community existing in the present, based on the past salvific events, and looking forward to the parousia. Jesus by contrast simply speaks of a future community, as well as a future entering of the *basileia.* No clear time frame is specified in the Synoptics in regard to these future realities. Thus there are more notable differences in regard to the matter of community between the Jesus and Pauline traditions, than on the matter of the *basileia*.

This discussion raises in an acute way the question of how Jesus and Paul viewed the future of Israel either as a people or as a nation, and to this matter we must turn in the next chapter.

PART FOUR

Paul, Jesus
and the
Israel of God

—12—

Introduction

There are many ways one could ferret out how Jesus or Paul viewed Israel and its future. One way to approach the matter would be to evaluate how Paul or Jesus viewed Torah, temple and territory, three of the major elements that shaped an early Jew's view of his people. The difficulty with this sort of indirect approach is that neither Paul nor Jesus seem to have had much to say about the Jewish territorial doctrine per se.[1] Furthermore, Paul has almost nothing to say about the temple and its cultic activities, and what little we know of Jesus' attitude toward the temple suggests a highly critical approach much like that which is evidenced in some of the Qumran literature. Interestingly, Jesus' attitude about the temple seems to contrast to a significant degree with his attitude toward his own people, especially the least, the last and the lost within Israel.[2] In short, his attitude about the former does not necessarily indicate his attitude about the latter. Finally, both Paul's and Jesus' attitudes toward Torah are complex, and though they certainly do affect each man's views about Israel in general, it is quite difficult to sort out the implications.

Because of these considerations, and also because our concern is not simply to examine Paul's and Jesus' view of Israel, but their views on *the future of* Israel in God's plans and in human history, I have chosen to focus on the direct evidence that bears on this matter. Again, I will begin first by considering Paul's views on these matters.

—13—

Paul
and the Plight
of His
People

Any study of Paul's views of Israel must necessarily focus on Romans 9-11, but it would be a mistake to neglect other relevant material such as 1 Thessalonians 2:14-16; Galatians 4:21-31; 2 Corinthians 3 and Ephesians 2:11-22.[1] In fact, scholars such as W. D. Davies have sought to trace a development in Paul's thought on Israel by examining these texts in chronological order.[2] Davies urges that in Romans 9-11 we find a mellower, more mature Paul less ready to urge that God has permanently rejected non-Christian Jews and replaced them with the church than was earlier the case. Accordingly, we will need to consider these other texts carefully as well.

Since most scholars believe that 1 Thessalonians is Paul's earliest letter, we will begin by examining the much-controverted material in 1 Thessalonians 2:14-16.[3] It has been urged with some cogency that at least verses 15-16 are a later anti-Semitic interpolation into this letter. If so, then this material will tell us nothing about Paul's view of Israel. The theory of interpolation has been urged not simply because of the apparent anti-Semitism of the material that seems to speak of a period when Christianity had made a clean break with Judaism, but also because the judgment spoken of there is most naturally correlated with the demise of Jerusalem in A.D. 70.[4]

The problems with the interpolation theory are formidable, however. First, there is no textual evidence for the omission or even displacement of these verses, unlike the case with a text like 1 Corinthians 14:34-35.[5] Second, as D. Wenham has shown, a strong case can be made that Paul is drawing on material from the Jesus tradition here—in particular the Q material found in Matthew 23:29-36/ Luke 11:47-51 and Matthew 23:37-38/Luke 13:34-35.[6] Third, the critique of early Judaism found in these verses is not very different in tone or content from various of the Old Testament woe or judgment oracles (see, for example, Is 29—30, especially 30:12-14; Jer 5; Amos 2:6-3:8).

First Thessalonians 2:14-16 reflects a trenchant critique of acts of violence commited against Christ and early Christians by *some* Jews, and thus is not even a form of anti-Judaism, much less anti-Semitism.[7] In fact Paul, following the precedent in the Jesus material, places this critique within a salvation-historical perspective,[8] making clear that this reflects a pattern of behavior engaged in by some Jews throughout Jewish history at the expense of their own earlier prophetic figures.[9] O. H. Steck has made a good case for Paul drawing on traditional material here, not merely on the earlier prophetic critique of Israel but on the Jesus tradition. In particular, he compares Mark 12:1b-5 to 1 Thessalonians 2:15, Mark 12:7 to 1 Thessalonians 2:16, Mark 12:8 to 1 Thessalonians 2:15 and Mark 12:9 to 1 Thessalonians 2:16.[10] Paul may be drawing on Jesus' own prophetic critique of Israel here, but in any case it would be better to see 1 Thessalonians 2:14-16 as part and parcel of a passionate intramural debate that does not reflect some sort of racial prejudice against the Jews or a rejection of Judaism *in toto*. The theology and life of early Judaism was exceedingly diverse, and it was perfectly possible to critique one form or various aspects of Judaism strongly without rejecting it as a whole, as the Qumran literature makes apparent.[11] This is likely what Paul is doing here, especially in view of evidence elsewhere that suggests not only that Paul sought to be the Jew to the Jew (1 Cor 9:20, and thus had not rejected Judaism *in toto*), but also that he had hopes of converting some Jews through his ministry (see 2 Cor 11:24; Phil 3:2).[12] As W. Marxsen has stressed, the theme of persecution unites the whole subsection of 1 Thessalonians 2:1-16. Thus for thematic and also literary reasons verses 14-16 should not be expunged as an interpolation.[13] K. P. Donfried has pointed out the parallels between 2:13-16 and 1:6-9a particularly in regard to the themes of imitation and affliction.[14]

Several aspects of 1 Thessalonians 2:14-16 are crucial for our purposes. First, note how Paul, though a Jew, distinguishes himself from "the Jews" (v. 14) whom he is critiquing here. This is similar to what he says in Romans 9:24 as well as elsewhere (compare 1 Cor 9:20; 2 Cor 11:24). This suggests that what Paul usually means by "the Jews" is not merely something ethnic but rather something religious, that is, non-Christian Jews.[15] This hints at a rather clear distinction in Paul's mind between himself and other Christians on the one hand, and "non-Christian" Jews on the other.

This fundamental distinction seems to be *most* characteristic of the way Paul thinks about non-Christian Jews. His judgment about them is chiefly informed by the fact that he and other Christians believe that a crucified Jew named Jesus is Messiah, whereas they do not. This is not to deny various elements of continuity that Paul believes exists between himself and his fellow kinfolk according to the flesh (see below on Rom 9:1-5, and such texts as Phil 3:4-6; 2 Cor 11:22). Nor is it to deny that Paul has a positive evaluation to offer of various aspects and advantages of early Judaism. It is, however, to suggest that the perceived discontinuity rather than continuity is what most shapes Paul's evaluation of non-Christian Jews. He views them in the light of what he now has in Christ, and so ultimately he is willing to say that whatever of this Jewish heritage he considers of profit to him, he is willing to forego in view of the surpassing greatness of knowing Jesus Christ (Phil 3:7-8). It is inconceivable that Paul might ever have asserted the converse of this statement!

This feeling of discontinuity, or cognitive dissonance, is expressed vehemently in 1 Thessalonians 2:15 not least because Paul holds at least some of his fellow non-Christian Jews in some sense responsible for the death of Jesus as well as for the persecution of the church in Judea, and for the hindering of Paul's own ministry to Gentiles. Here he is most angry with these persecuting non-Christian Jews.[16] The dissonance is not simply created by the persecution—that merely exacerbates the problem. The chief cause of the dissonance is because of the rejection of Jesus as Messiah by most Jews. This is why Paul will go on to argue in Romans 11:17-21 that non-Christian Jews have been broken off from the true people of God (albeit temporarily, he hopes) *due to their unbelief.* I see no evidence either early or late in the Pauline corpus to suggest that Paul ever ceased to feel this way about his fellow (non-Christian) Jewish kinfolk. Indeed, it is clear even in Romans 9—11 that Paul is still in great agony over the majority of his non-Christian Jewish contemporaries' lack of Christian faith, and he even hopes that Gentile Christians and their faith will provoke some Jews to jealousy, and thus to conversion through his ministry.[17]

The second aspect of 1 Thessalonians 2:14-16 that calls for comment is the reference to heaping up their sins to the limit. This likely draws on texts such as Genesis 15:16; Daniel 8:23 and 2 Maccabees 6:14, but more proximately on the Jesus tradition found in Matthew 23:32. The fact that Paul so strongly relies on the Jesus tradition here likely implies that he thought he was simply continuing the sort of critique that Jesus had earlier made of their fellow Jews. The concept of filling up sins to a preset limit suggests that God has given people a certain period of time to act as they will before he brings his judgment upon their iniquity. In other words, probably we should closely connect 1 Thessalonians 2:16b and 16c. The evidence that some early Jews did indeed persecute Christians and/or hindered the Gentile mission of Christians, though there may have been no systematic effort to do so, is found not merely in 1 Thessalonians 2:14, but also in several other texts (Gal 1:22-23; 2 Cor 11:24; Acts 17:4-5 on Thessalonica, also Acts 13:45-50; 14:2, 19). It is not quite clear, however, whether Paul has Jewish or pagan persecution in mind in our text. The fellow countrymen could be Jews who lived in or around Thessalonica, but perhaps it would be best not to press this suggestion. Paul is in any event extremely angry with those who do such things and says that Jews who were involved in such behavior in Judea displease God and fill up their sins.

The third aspect that we need to consider is a notable *crux interpretum*. How are we to understand *eis telos* in 2:16c? There is no denying that the verb *ephthasen* (or *ephthaken*, as read by B, D*, 104 and a few other manuscripts) is in the past tense. This has led to any number of conjectures about which particular act of judgment on "the Jews" Paul has in mind. The very variety of suggestions attests to the general uncertainty about what Paul had in mind.[18] The whole debate may be beside the point if either the past tense verb here represents a prophetic perfect or if *eis telos* has a different meaning than is often assumed. The following are the possible meanings of *eis telos:* (1) at last, finally (RSV, NIV); (2) completely, to the uttermost;[19] (3) forever, to the end, lasting forever (NEB); (4) until/unto the end (see Mt 10:22);[20] and (5) on the basis of the Semitic background to the phrase a combined meaning has been suggested—fully and finally. This last suggestion takes the phrase to be following the superlative meaning of NTSH.[21]

The basic question is whether *eis telos* is some sort of adverbial phrase that modifies the verb "has come" or some sort of phrase modifying "wrath" and thus indicating some kind of time factor. A remarkably clear parallel to our text is *Testament of Levi* 6:11: "*ephthasen de hē orgē kyriou ep autous eis telos.*" While this testament, in view of the fragments of it found at Qumran, predates Paul's letter by a considerable amount of time, there are probable Christian interpolations in the document as we now have it (see *T. Levi* 4:1; 14:2).[22] Furthermore, as E. Best points out, some manuscripts of the testament do not have 6:11.[23] It is thus wise not to press the parallel, as the text in the testament may even be based on 1 Thessalonians 2:16c.

There are difficulties with taking *eis telos* to mean "at long last" or "finally," as this meaning lacks clear attestation in biblical Greek.[24] There are also difficulties with taking the phrase to mean "forever" or "to the end," as it requires that the verb's meaning be stretched to "has come (so as to last) forever." It is also hard to believe that Paul would understand the phrase to mean "completely" or "to the uttermost" in view of the fact that he and other Jews had in fact been converted to Christ since Jesus' death.

If, however, we take the meaning of *eis telos* to be "until/unto the end," as J. Munck has suggested[25] (a meaning of the phrase found not only in Mt 10:22 but also in Mk 13:13/Mt 24:13; see also Rev 2:26; Hermas *Sim* 9.27.3), then there is no need to argue for a prophetic aorist here and the other difficulties mentioned above are eliminated. The prophetic use of the aorist is not found elsewhere in the New Testament in any case. It is more natural to take *ephthasen* to refer to something that has already transpired. Taking the phrase as temporal and modifying "wrath," which is perfectly possible, also comports with Paul's approach to non-Christian Jews in Romans 9—11. There Paul urges that these Jews have been hardened or broken off, until the full number of the Gentiles is saved, after which they too will be saved.

Paul then would be stressing in 1 Thessalonians 2:14-16 that due to their unbelief in the Messiah Jesus, God's wrath has come upon these non-Christian Jews "until the end"—until the final events in human history. On this view, Paul is not talking about a final, total or complete judgment or rejection of non-Christian Jews by God but rather a temporal and temporary one. If this is correct, it removes the basic reason for arguing that Paul later significantly changed his mind about his kinfolk. Nevertheless, we must not overread 1 Thessalonians 2:14-16. Paul does not inform us here of what will happen to the Jews at or after the *telos*. Perhaps it had not yet been revealed to him. All that one can say from this text is that Paul sees non-Christian Jews, perhaps especially those who persecute the church, as under God's wrath.

We must now turn to that most polemical of all Pauline letters—Galatians. Its tone is set right from the beginning and is evident not only from what Paul says, but from what he deliberately omits. Only in Galatians among the capital Pauline letters is the thanksgiving section missing.

Paul is writing to a situation where Judaizers (Jewish Christians) are trying to impose various Old Testament laws (such as circumcision) on both Jewish *and* Gentile Christians whom Paul had converted in Galatia. Paul sees this as a serious threat to his gospel, to his offer of freedom and salvation in Christ to all with no conditions or prerequisites except faith. Paul's anger in this letter then is not directed against "the Jews" per se as was the case in 1 Thessalonians 2:14-16, but in all likelihood against certain Judaizing Jewish Christians. This fact must be kept steadily in view, especially when we examine the so-called allegory in Galatians 4:21-31.

C. K. Barrett has argued plausibly that Paul, not only in Galatians 4:21-31 but also in chapter 3, is taking up texts that his opponents the Judaizers have made much of in their attempt to persuade the Galatians to be circumcised and to keep the law. In particular he says that

> Paul's opponents in Galatia followed up their quotation of the passages (see 3.16) on the seed of Abraham by an argument based upon the two women, Sarah and Hagar, by whom Abraham had children. The seed of Abraham, understood physically, issued in legitimate and illegitimate children. The Galatians were urged to legitimize themselves.[26]

Paul, in response to arguments by his opponents that seem to have been convincing to his Galatians, urges in a tour de force that (1) the legitimate "seed" of Abraham is not law-abiding Jews or Jewish Christians and those who follow their lead, but rather Christ; (2) the true children of Hagar the slave woman are those who insist on following the dictates that came down from Sinai, and the true children of Sarah are those who have accepted the blessings of Abraham on the basis of faith in Christ, looking to the Jerusalem that is from above rather than the earthly Jerusalem. This stands on its head what was likely the argument of Paul's opponents. The more obvious way of handling the material in Genesis 15 was to argue that the descendants of Hagar and Ishmael were Gentiles who had no natural claim on the benefits of the covenant with Abraham, whereas the descendants of Sarah and Isaac, who were Jews, did.

Paul ends his argument with a flourish, hinting that the Galatians should cast out the slave woman and her son (4:30). In view of 2:4 ("false brothers had infiltrated . . . to make us slaves") and perhaps also 2:12, it seems evident that Paul is here referring to the Judaizers as the descendants of Hagar who had infiltrated the Galatian Christian community. If so, then his argument in 4:21-31 is not directly with Judaism, but a Judaizing form of Christianity that Paul thinks betrays the very essence of the gospel.

Nevertheless, what Paul says in both Galatians 3 and 4 has some definite implications for his views of non-Christian Jews. In the first place Paul makes clear that he views the Mosaic covenant as a parenthesis that served as a *paidagōgos* of God's people between the Abrahamic covenant and the new (3:24).[27] It was added after the Abrahamic covenant "until the Seed to whom the promise referred had come" (3:19). In short, though the Mosaic law had an important function in its time, it was superceded by what Christ made available to all when he came, and so now God's people have reached their spiritual majority and have become heirs in Christ (so 4:1-7). To go back to keeping the law was tantamount to submitting again to bondage and thus renouncing the law-free gospel Paul preached.

In light of this sort of argument, which leads up to the typology in 4:21-31,[28] it is not incidental or accidental that Paul tells us that Sarah and Hagar represent two different covenants (4:24). He is deliberately contrasting the two to make his point, and he does not hesitate to say that the earthly Jerusalem is no longer his own or other Christians' true mother; rather, "the Jerusalem that is above is free, and she is our mother" (4:26).

The reference to *ediōken* in 4:29 should not divert us from seeing that Paul is still contrasting his approach to matters with that of the Judaizers, for surely, as Fung points out, his use of the term here has the more general sense of "harass" or "trouble," which is what Paul has accused the Judaizers of doing to the Galatians (see 1:7; 2:4; 3:1).[29] Paul certainly is not intimating in what immediately follows in 4:30 that the Galatian Christians should cast non-Christian Jews out of Galatia! This means that we cannot agree with H. D. Betz when he sets up the simplistic contrast as follows: Hagar vs. Sarah=old covenant vs. new covenant=present Jerusalem vs. heavenly Jerusalem=*Judaism vs. Christianity.*[30] In the first place, Galatians is part of an intramural debate between the Jewish-Christian Paul and other Jewish Christians over the character of the "gospel" or the new life in Christ, and what its implications are for Christian behavior vis-à-vis the ongoing viability of one specific Old Testament covenant, the Mosaic covenant. The contrast here is between the Abrahamic and new covenants on the one hand and the Mosaic covenant on the other. Paul links the former two covenants together by means of interpreting the "Seed" as Christ. For Paul the Abrahamic promises are fulfilled in Christ and for those who are in him. Thus, while it is true that Paul is arguing that the new covenant is replacing the Mosaic covenant as the basis of relating to God, he is not simply arguing that Christianity replaces Judaism. Rather, he sees Christianity as the legitimate development and fulfillment of the Abrahamic form of Judaism and of the promises given to Abraham. This same sort of argument surfaces again in Romans 3:21—4:25. The argument then is about which form of Judaism is the legitimate one—the Christian form with its link to the Abrahamic covenant, or the Mosaic form as here maintained by the Judaizers and elsewhere by non-Christian Jews.

W. D. Davies is right to insist over against Betz and others that

in accepting the Jew, Jesus, as the Messiah, Paul did not think in terms of moving into a new religion but of having found the final expression and intent of the Jewish tradition within which he himself had been born. For him the Gospel was according to the Scriptures: it was not an alien importation into Judaism, but the true development of it, its highest point, although in its judgment on the centrality which some Jews had given to a particular interpretation of the law it showed a radicalism which amounted to a new creation.[31]

In the second place, it is quite precarious to insist that *all* of the readers of this letter would have been Gentile Christians, though doubtless the majority were (see 5:2; 6:12). It is equally precarious to urge that Paul is defending Gentile Christianity at the expense of Jewish Christianity. Rather, his vision is of Jew and Gentile being united in Christ (Gal 3:28), without ethnic distinctions or customs being assigned any soteriological significance or being allowed to sever the bond of fellowship (see 2:11-21). When circumcision, keeping kosher, sabbath-keeping and the like are assigned some sort of salvific or status-granting significance especially for Gentiles, Paul opposes them.

Thus one should not insist on the basis of the material in Galatians 3—4 that Paul is rejecting Judaism per se. What he is rejecting is that Christians—whether Gentile or Jew—are obligated to keep the Sinai covenant and its stipulations. Rather Christians are called to fulfill the "law of Christ" (Gal 6:2). This does not amount to some form of antinomianism per se, but a belief that the Mosaic covenant is no longer binding on true believers. Paul here opposes the Judaizing of some Jewish Christians, not Judaism *in toto.*

Before completing our discussion of Galatians we must turn to one of the more controversial texts: Galatians 6:16. Is Paul here calling the whole church, just Jewish Christians or non-Christian Jews "the Israel of God"? Here again we must pay careful attention to the whole context as well as to the content of this verse. Paul has just stated emphatically that the only thing that matters is a new creation. Neither circumcision nor uncircumcision counts at all. In short, one of the things that mattered most to Jews and to Judaizing Christians alike and most set them apart from Gentiles counts not at all in the new divine economy so far as Paul is concerned. Paul then goes on (v. 16a) to pronounce *shalom* and mercy on all those who "walk in" this rule that he has just enunciated (v. 15).

In this context we must examine the phrase *kai epi ton Israēl tou theou.* Paul nowhere else calls either a group of Christians or for that matter a group of non-Christian Jews "the Israel *of God.*" The qualifier here may be important, and Betz has urged that it suggests a contrast with "Israel after the flesh," a phrase Paul does use elsewhere (1 Cor 10:18).[32] It is also possible that Paul is taking up a favorite phrase of his opponents in Galatia and reapplying it in a different way. Perhaps, however, the most helpful way to look at Galatians 6:16b-c is in light of the Nineteenth Benediction of the Shemoneh Esreh, which reads, "Bestow peace, happiness, and blessing, grace, and loving-kindness, and mercy upon us and upon all Israel, your people." This blessing seems to have been extant before Paul's time, and it appears Paul has adopted and adapted it here.[33]

As Betz notes, the distinction in this *barakat* between the present congregation and the larger group called Israel seems to be paralleled in Galatians 6:16 by *autous* on the one hand and Israel on the other. "Peace and mercy upon us" has become by Paul's modification "peace upon them and mercy." What then are we to make of *kai epi ton Israēl tou theou?*

It is possible to take the *kai* as epexegetical and translate it "even" or "namely" (NIV, RSV). The problem with this view is that Paul does not seem to use *kai* in that way elsewhere in his letters.[34] We must ask, Would Paul offer a blessing on those who do not follow the principle just enunciated in verse 15 and in the same breath turn around and bless those who do? That is what is required of the interpretation that insists that "the Israel of God" refers to non-Christian Israel and that translates the *kai* as "even."

If Paul is adapting the Nineteenth Benediction it is more natural to take the *kai* as a simple copulative here, translating it "and." There is, however, one other possibility, raised by M. Zerwick—*kai* could mean "that is."[35] On this view Israel and *autous* both refer to the same group. It would also be clear that Israel refers to the church, both Jew and Gentile who are following the rule enunciated by Paul (thereby excluding the Judaizers from this blessing and calling all the other obedient Christians Israel). This intepretation is quite possible, but perhaps the edge should go to seeing the *kai* here as a simple copulative, in which case we can determine who "the Israel of God" is only by the larger context.

That "the Israel of God" does *not* refer to either non-Christian Jews or Judaizing Jewish Christians follows from the fact that Paul is here blessing whoever *(hosoi)* does follow the rule he has set forth, and these two groups clearly do not.[36] That "the Israel of God" probably does not refer solely to non-Judaizing Jewish Christians follows from the fact that Paul has been trying in this letter to unify the Christian community in Galatia, not bless or endorse distinctions within it. This is, after all, the letter in which Paul chastises Peter for acting on the basis of such distinctions (2:11ff.) and also comments, "There is neither Jew nor Greek . . . for you are all one in Christ Jesus" (3:28). It follows then that by "the Israel of God" Paul means the larger Christian community, both Jew and Gentile, as he extends the blessing beyond the local congregation of those *(autous)* who are following his rule.[37] The blessing rests upon all those who are a part of the new creation God has brought about in Christ Jesus.[38]

What then may we say about Paul's view of non-Christian Jews, the Israel according to the flesh, and their future in God's plans on the basis of Galatians? Paul really says little or nothing about God's future plans for non-Christian Jews in this letter. He does, however, make clear that those who insist on taking up the yoke of the Mosaic law are perverting the covenant that Jesus inaugurated when he came. By implication, he also sees this as a perverting of the original intent and approach of the Abrahamic covenant as well. Further, it seems that Paul holds that the church, both Jew and Gentile in Christ, are the true Israel of God. However, Paul neither states nor implies in this letter that non-Christian Jews have been simply abandoned by God. While Paul's thoughts about the future of non-Christian Jews certainly may have developed after writing Galatians, nothing here conflicts with what Paul later says in 2 Corinthians 3 or in Romans 9—11, nor as we shall see do those texts anywhere suggest that Paul simply abandoned his earlier views on this matter.[39]

The material in 2 Corinthians 3 involves us once again in a tale of two covenants.[40] Here, perhaps for the first time in early Christianity, is there mention of an "old covenant" (v. 14).[41] This phrase does not appear to have been used again of any portion of Torah before Melito of Sardis toward the end of the second century A.D. The argument in 2 Corinthians 3 is somewhat complex and has often been debated, but what is not in dispute is that once again Paul is combatting problems among his converts and the thrust of the material, as was the case in Galatians, is rather polemical. The use of the adjective *palaias* with the term "covenant" probably should be seen as pejorative in view of the way Paul argues in 2 Corinthians 3.

It will be useful to work our way from what is clearer about this passage to what is more obscure. That Paul is discussing the Mosaic law given at Sinai is indisputable due not only to the explicit reference to Moses at 3:7, but also to the repeated reference to letters engraved on stone (vv. 3, 7). In fact, the reference is to the Ten Commandments in particular, though as representing the essence of the more extensive Sinai covenant.

Second, it is reasonably clear that Paul is contrasting two sorts of ministries involving two covenants that have in his mind two very different effects on people. Paul identifies his own work as the ministry of the new covenant that is "of the Spirit" and gives life (v. 6). This is in contrast to the ministry of the old (Mosaic) covenant that is "of the letter" and leads to death.

Paul does not deny for a moment that the Mosaic law came "trailing clouds of glory," nor that its judgments are right and truly represent the will of God. He says in Romans 7:12, 14 that the law is holy, righteous, good and even spiritual, and nothing here contradicts that evaluation of the essential goodness of the Mosaic law. Rather, Paul is engaging in what may be called a salvation-historical argument. In essence it goes as follows: No one disputes that the Mosaic covenant came attended with splendor. The fact is, however, that its glory or splendor has been eclipsed by the greater splendor of the new covenant, and so not only the glory on Moses' face but the Mosaic covenant itself is being annulled (v. 11). Not only so, but the effect of the glorious Mosaic covenant on fallen human beings is condemnation. It is death-dealing, not life-giving (see vv. 6-7). The Mosaic law cannot empower or enliven its recipients so that they might obey it. Thus the ministry of Moses stands in contrast to the ministry of the new covenant in this crucial regard—only the latter brings life by means of the Holy Spirit.

At this point we need to deal with the much-controverted matter of to what the veil refers. In verse 13 it refers to what Moses literally put over his face, but thereafter the matter is less clear. Is the veil over the law, or in the minds of the Israelites (v. 14)?[42] Verse 15 seems to indicate that the metaphorical veil is *epi tēn kardian autōn*. This comports with what is said in verse 14a—that their minds have been hardened/made dull.[43] The only other place that Paul says something like this of non-Christian Jews, using this verb, is in Romans 11:7 (compare the noun form in Rom 11:25). This suggests that he already held at least some of the views articulated in Romans 9—11 when he wrote 2 Corinthians.

Several aspects of the interpretation just offered for this whole passage need to be defended. In the first place, Paul is not merely talking about a legalistic *approach* or *attitude* to the Mosaic law here, though he would no doubt object to that as well.[44] The contrast is between the actual effect of the Mosaic law itself on fallen human beings (condemnation, spiritual death) as opposed to the effect of the Holy Spirit and Christ on people (life, 3:6; righteousness, 3:9; enlightenment, veil removed in Christ, 3:15). As such the argument differs little from that in Romans 2—3; 5:20-21 and, of course, 7—8. Paul's view of the Mosaic law stands in contrast to the tradition we find in *Exodus Rab.* xli.1 (on Ex 31:18), "While Israel stood below engraving idols to provoke their Creator to anger . . . God sat on high engraving tablets which would give them life." In Paul's view the law has precisely the opposite effect!

Second, the verb *katargeō*, which Paul uses in various forms (3:7, 11, 13, 14), is a crucial one. Twenty-two of its twenty-seven occurrences in the New Testament occur in the undisputed Paulines, and always elsewhere in Paul it refers to something replaced, invalidated or abolished, not merely to something faded.[45] There is no reason to doubt that Paul is using the verb the same way here, especially in view of his contrast in the passage between the ministry that brings death and that which brings life.

Third, only Christ the Lord or the Spirit can take away the veil over the hearts of the Israelites. But when the veil is taken away, what does Paul think the Israelites will see? His arguments suggest that they will see that the Mosaic law has a temporary, not a permanent, glory, unlike the new covenant (v. 11, *to menon en doxē)*, and thus a temporal and temporary part to play in the divine economy of salvation.[46] His argument suggests that they will see that the Mosaic covenant, far from giving life, had just the opposite effect on fallen human beings. When the veil, or hardheartedness, is removed, though the law will be seen as a good and glorious thing in and of itself, it will also be seen to have had bad effects, and thus in the end needed to be superceded by a more effective covenant that gives life and righteousness.

I cannot stress enough that the argument here is *not* about either human attitudes or approaches to the law[47] or about the character of the law itself per se. Rather the argument is about the *effect* of the Mosaic law and covenant on fallen sinful humans as opposed to the effect of the new covenant and the Spirit.

Finally, it is not completely clear in verse 14 whether the veil or the covenant is being annulled. In view of verse 11 where the neuter participle *to katargoumenon* in accordance with the neuter substantive in verse 10 must be interpreted as applying to "the entire ministry of the old covenant symbolized by Moses,"[48] it is more likely that the reference in verse 14 is to the old covenant being annulled. Furthermore, when Paul speaks of the removal of a veil (v. 16) he uses the more appropriate term *periaireitai*.[49]

In various ways 2 Corinthians 3 comports with what we have already discovered about Paul's view of Israel in Galatians and in 1 Thessalonians. In Galatians 4 and 2 Corinthians 3, Paul contrasts two covenants. In the former he associates the keeping of the Mosaic law with slavery, and in the latter he says the law's effect is condemnation and death. It may well be that the wrath he spoke of in 1 Thessalonians 2 as resting on non-Christian Jews is simply another way of saying what he says here—that their minds have been hardened. In both cases Paul is talking about an action of God on non-Christian Jews that has already transpired in history. But if Paul's argument about the covenants and the glory is a salvation-historical one, comparing earlier and later covenants and their attendant glory and effects, we should hardly be surprised that in Romans 9— 11 Paul will try the same kind of approach when dealing directly with the issue of the status and future of "the Israel according to the flesh." To that crucial material we now turn.

In Romans 9—11 a very viable case can be made that Paul is presenting an "apocalyptic Gospel."[50] He is after all claiming to be revealing to his audience a *mystērion* (11:25) about how it is that "Israel" has been temporarily hardened until the full number of the Gentiles have been saved, and then "all Israel will be saved." This *mystērion* about Gentiles being saved first while the majority of Jews are hardened and then Jews being saved at the end of human history is not something one could deduce simply by studying human history, or for that matter by examining the Scriptures. Early Jewish exegetes normally concluded that the

Gentiles would flow into Zion *after* Israel had first been restored to its intended glory (see Ps 22:27; Is 2:2-3; 56:6-8; Micah 4:2; Zech 2:11; 14:16; Tobit 13:11; 14:6-7; *Ps Sol* 17:34; *T. Zeb* 9:8; *T. Ben* 9:2). Paul here reverses the order of things.

There are other telltale signs that Paul is presenting an argument based on an apocalyptic revelation from God. Not only does he seek to peel back the tapestry of history and reveal the sovereign divine hand guiding it to its intended conclusion like other pieces of apocalyptic literature, but his reason for doing so is very much the same as the raison d'être of a great deal of apocalyptic literature—to justify the ways of God to human beings or to answer the query, Has the Word of God failed? Additionally, there are some hints of the periodization of human history in Romans 9—11 (the arguments about fullness, 11:12, 25; about partial or temporary hardening, 11:7, 25, 32; and also about the *telos* of the law, 10:4). As in other apocalyptic literature things seem to have gone all wrong for at least some of God's people, but by revealing this mystery about the future of Israel Paul wishes to make clear, using the language of election, predestination and foreknowledge (see 9:11, 23; 11:2, 5, 7, 32), that in the end all will turn out all right. Finally, it would seem that Paul, not unlike what is found in some apocalyptic documents (see Rev 14:3), is willing in a general sense to talk about a certain limited number of those saved, at least in the case of Gentiles (11:25, *plērōma*).[51]

Yet though the *source* of the information Paul calls a *mystērion* in Romans 11 may well have been an apocalyptic revelation that he received, and though the content of what he received in this revelation may also explain some of the characteristically apocalyptic elements or motifs in Romans 9—11, the present *form* of these chapters reflects a profound meditation upon numerous Old Testament texts and is not simply the record of an apocalyptic vision.[52]

What R. B. Hays says about Romans as a whole especially can be applied to chapters 9—11:

> This text is most fruitfully understood when it is read as an intertextual conversation between Paul and the voice of Scripture. . . . Scripture broods over this letter, calls Paul to account, speaks through him; Paul, groping to give voice to his gospel, finds in Scripture the language to say what must be said, labors to win the blessing of Moses and the prophets. . . . If, however, we attend carefully to Paul's use of the quotations, we will discover them spiraling in around a common focus: the problem of God's saving righteous-

ness in relation to Israel. The insistent echoing voice of Scripture in and behind Paul's letter presses home a single theme relentlessly: the gospel is the fulfillment, not the negation, of God's word to Israel.[53]
In fact more than half of all the Old Testament quotes in Romans occur in 9—11 and about 40 per cent of these are from Isaiah. Almost a third of all the verses in these chapters involve a quote or paraphrasing of the Old Testament.[54]

There is no dispute that Romans 9—11 is a literary unit with its own characteristics. In particular, it consists to a large extent of a rhetorical dialog with an imaginary interlocutor, which explains the inordinate number of questions (see 9:14, 19-22; 10:14-15, 18-19; 11:15), usually followed by declarative answers and scriptural arguments or quotations.[55] The danger of overplaying the factors just mentioned is that Romans 9—11 might be and sometimes has been treated as a sort of appendix or afterthought to the main argument of Romans. In view of Romans 3:1, 3 as well as the announced theme in 1:16-17 ("to the Jew first and also . . ."), this is a serious mistake, as we shall see. Nevertheless, the change in tone from 8:39 to 9:1, and the closing doxology in 11:33-36 do set off chapters 9—11 as a new development or subsection in Paul's argument in this letter.[56]

Though it may be too much to say that theodicy is the main theme of Romans, it is certainly a major one. Paul is not interested in the abstract question of why there is evil in a world created by a good God, but rather how it can be that the majority of Jews have rejected the crucified Messiah Jesus and are thus outside the context where the promises of God are being fulfilled, even though God's word and promises have not failed, not even to those Jews now outside the church. Paul does indeed seek to justify the ways of God to his audience, which seems to have been predominantly Gentile (see 11:13).[57] As N. A. Dahl says, Paul's statement in 1:16, "I am not ashamed of the gospel: it is the power of God for salvation to every one who has faith, to the Jew first and also to the Greek" (RSV), not only prepares us for the discussion in Romans 1—4 about the status and relationship of Jews and Gentiles, but the phrase "to the Jew first" hints in advance at what is only fully explained in Romans 9—11.[58] Paul prepares us even further for chapters 9—11 by raising the question in 3:1-5, "What advantage, then, is there in being a Jew, or what value is there in circumcision?" and giving a partial answer there. The dialogical form of the discussion in 3:1-5 also presages what is to come in 9—11. The preliminary answer is twofold: (1) God has entrusted Jews with his word; and (2) God is faithful to his word even if some Jews have proved faithless.[59] Thus, the theme of Romans 9—11 is prepared for in advance and serves as a sort of undercurrent in the letter that explodes with force into the light of day only after Paul has fully presented the essential character of his gospel in the first eight chapters.[60]

Romans 9—11 traditionally has been divided into three subsections. E. Käsemann's presentation of this division is rather typical: (1) following the introductory material in 9:1-5, 9:6-29 presents the first theme of the validity and goal of election; (2) 9:30—10:21 presents the discussion of Israel's guilt and fall; and finally (3) 11:1-36 includes the mystery of salvation history.[61] A different way to look at this material is by noting that Romans 9—11 has a structure analogous to the structure of a lament psalm: (1) 9:1-5, Lament over Israel; (2) 9:6-29, Has God's word failed? Defense of God's elective purpose; (3) 9:30—10:21, Paradox: Israel failed to grasp the word of faith attested by God in Scripture; (4) 11:1-32, Has God abandoned his people? No, all Israel will be saved; (5) 11:33-36, Doxological conclusion.[62] Too often Romans 9—11 has been seen as a discourse on predestination and free will, but it is better seen as an attempt to show how God's current dealing with both Jews and Gentiles is fully consistent with his revealed will both in Scripture and in the gospel Paul preached.[63] Paul's anxiety expressed in these chapters is not about Gentiles being included in God's people, but rather about Israel's *apparent* exclusion.[64] He is at pains to explain this anomaly. In a sense Romans 9—11 represents Paul's *apologia* for his kinfolk who have not accepted Christ.[65]

It will be well as we examine this material to keep in mind three questions that Paul attempts to answer: (1) Has God rejected his first chosen people once and for all? (2) If not, why then did the Jews reject Jesus, if he was indeed the Jewish Messiah? and (3) What is the relationship and status of Jew and Gentile in Christ? To this one might also add, Is there any continuity between Israel and the church, and God's basis of dealing with and accepting each one? Throughout this passage "Israel" refers to non-Christian Jews.

Romans 9:1-5 lists the advantages Jews have been given by God—the adoption as sons, the glory, the covenants, the giving of the law, the worship, the promises, the patriarchs and finally the Messiah "according to the flesh," in his human ancestry. This listing, however, only exacerbates the problem and makes it all the more problematic that Israel has rejected Jesus.

God had chosen Israel to be the scene upon which his saving purpose should be worked out. This was what made the fact of Israel's present rejection doubly offensive. What was evidently God's purpose seemed to have failed altogether in its effect. It is not Jewish nationalism, but a glaring theological paradox which sets in motion the argument of chs. ix-xi.[66] Even here Paul distinguishes himself from non-Christian Jews, calling them "those of my own race" even though he also calls them his brothers. The point is that the physical tie and the listed advantages are what Paul shares in common with them, not the most crucial factor of faith in Christ. This is true despite all of Paul's apostolic labors.

It appears that as Paul lists the advantages in verses 4-5 he is thinking through a logical historical sequence. Israel was made God's sons (and daughters) in the exodus. They saw his glory in the pillar of fire and the cloud. God then made a series of covenants with them.[67] There may well be a theological reason for saying "covenants." In Paul's view there were two great covenants in the Old Testament, the Mosaic and the Abrahamic, and he did not simply assimilate the one to the other, as we have seen in Galatians 3—4. Once the covenants had been established then the law and divine worship were thereby set up, and the promises became something to which God obligated himself. Mentioning promises leads Paul to think of the persons who received them, the patriarchs, or about whom they spoke—the Messiah.

With the introduction out of the way Paul proceeds to give a sort of history lesson showing that God has always worked on the principle of election, which also involves selection within the elect group. This in turn leads him to the discussion of the fact that there had always been a righteous remnant of God's people.[68] The argument moves in two directions at once—not all of Abraham's physical descendants are truly Israel *and* not all of Israel is made up of Abraham's physical descendants. The striking thing about the way Paul's argument proceeds is that he is not merely arguing that God had the right to choose only some, but that even among the elect God had the right to break some of them off and include others. Election it would seem does not necessarily entail the guarantee of salvation for particular individual Israelites.[69] In any case, Paul here is interested in the current and future historical fate of non-Christian Jews, not their eternal destiny.

Paul begins to make his point by arguing, "It is not the children of Abraham's flesh, born in the course of nature . . . [but those] who come by promise who are counted as Abraham's seed" (9:8). This comports with what Paul has said earlier in Romans 2:28-29: "A man is not a Jew if he is only one outwardly, nor is circumcision merely outward and physical. No, a man is a Jew if he is one inwardly; and circumcision is circumcision of the heart, by the Spirit, not by the written code." In Romans 9 Paul will indicate that the righteous remnant is determined by God's grace, those who have come by God's promise. He will, however, turn around and say in the succeeding chapters that faith in the promises is the basis of inclusion, and disobedience the basis for exclusion. It is important to hold these two ideas in tension and not to try to emphasize one at the expense of the other, since Paul held to both ideas at once. In due course Paul is going to argue that God has in fact consigned *all* to disobedience so that he might have mercy on all (11:32), an argument very similar to what Paul has said earlier in the Epistle (3:9, "Jews and Gentiles alike are all under sin").

Paul is especially concerned to squelch the idea that physical descent determines the elect, and he accomplishes this by carrying the argument through two generations. One could object that Ishmael was not chosen because he was illegitimate. Paul responds by pointing out that Jacob and Esau both came from the same Jewish mother and father, in the same act of conception, and yet Jacob was chosen and Esau was not. This shows that it was God's divine election, mercy or promise, not human circumstances, that determined God's choice. The question then is *not,* Has God reneged on his promises to Israel? but rather, Who counts as Israel? Romans 9:6 is emphatic on this point—not all who are descended from Israel are (true) Israel.

Paul does not speak of a "new Israel," nor does he speak of the *replacement* of one Israel by another here. His argument is about the way the one true people of God have developed through history.[70] He does, however, redefine who the people of God are, countering both popular Jewish notions about the claim Jews had on God because of their physical descent (see Mt 3:9/Lk 3:8; *Mish. Sahn.* 10:1), but at the same time countering attitudes that some Gentile Roman Christians seem to have had that suggested that Gentiles had replaced Jews as God's chosen people (11:19).

For our purposes it is necessary to focus on several key matters in Romans 9—11: (1) the righteous remnant concept Paul offers as a partial explanation of God's dealings with his people; (2) the hardening of Pharaoh and of some Jews; (3) Christ as the *telos* of the law in 10:4; (4) the analogies in 11:16-24, especially the olive tree analogy; and (5) the *mystērion* described in 11:25-27.

The remnant theme is effectively introduced in Romans 9:27 by the quotation of Isaiah 10:22-23 and is further developed in 10:16-11:5, climaxing with the statement, "So too, at the present time there is a remnant chosen by grace."

Immediately prior to this conclusion Paul used the classic example of the Elijah story found in 1 Kings 19 to drive home the point that God has never been without a people, there has always been a righteous remnant. This argument refutes two ideas at once: (1) that God has simply replaced Jews with Gentiles as his people, for it is very clear that in 11:5 Paul has in mind some Jews who are this current remnant; and (2) that God's word has failed. "That only a minority of Jews have believed the word of faith about Messiah Jesus is only to be expected by those who can read the ways of God in the history of his people."[71] For Paul the case of Elijah and the seven thousand true Israelites has typical and typological significance. His argument is, "As was true then, so likewise now."

In short, the remnant idea is not simply God's compensation now for the fact that the majority of Jews have rejected Jesus. Paul says this is the way it has always been with God's people. In view of the fact that the remnant discussion involves the statement "But not all the Israelites accepted the good news. . . . Faith comes from hearing the message, and the message is heard through the word of Christ" (10:16-18) followed by the texts cited in 10:18-21 making clear that the Jews have heard the gospel of Christ, it becomes clear that for Paul the current remnant of grace are Christian Jews, not devout or zealous non-Christian ones.[72] Paul in fact takes his own experience as exhibit A that God has not rejected his people, but this implies that now they are only accepted "in Christ" (compare 11:1-2). The righteous remnant now is the Jewish Christians. This will become even more apparent when we consider the olive-tree analogy.

In the course of the discussion in Romans 9—11 Paul speaks of two hardenings. He implies the hardening of Pharaoh in 9:16-18, stating that *hon de thelei sklērynei* (v. 18). In 11:7 he makes a distinction between Israel and the elect. Nonelect Israel *epōrōthēsan.* Then finally in 11:25 Paul says, *hoti pōrōsis apo merous tō Israēl gegonen.* Verse 25b makes clear that at least in the case of Israel this is a temporal and temporary condition. In each case, God is the one who performs the hardening. Paul uses a different term for the "hardening" of Pharaoh than for that of Israel. Concerning Pharaoh, he uses the verb *sklērynō,* which normally has the nuance of "harden" or "stiffen."[73] *Pōroō* from *pōros* (compare 11:25 *pōrōsis)* has the basic meaning of "petrify," and when it is used in the New Testament in the "divine" passive it has the metaphorical sense of "to become deadened or insensible" (see Mk 6:52; 8:17; Jn 12:40; 2 Cor 3:14). *Pōroō/pōrōsis* is usually used metaphorically to describe the heart attitude or condition of the persons in question. Several texts stand in the background here, notably Deuteronomy 29:4; Isaiah 29:10 (which are cited in 11:8) and probably also Isaiah 6:10. For Paul this amounts to a temporal, not final, judgment on those in question, as becomes especially clear in 11:25. This hardening has happened "until" *(achris)* some specific point in time.

The translation of *pōrōsis apo merous* in 11:25 is in dispute. *Apo merous* could be taken adverbially with *pōrōsis* rather than with Israel, in which case we would translate "a partial hardening." Favoring this view is the fact that Paul always uses the phrase *apo merous* adverbially (Rom 15:15; 2 Cor 1:14; 2:5). However, grammatically it is just as possible that *apo merous* is adjectival and modifies Israel here (compare RSV, NJB),[74] and this is especially likely in view of what Paul says in 11:7—"The rest were hardened/made insensible." Here Paul says nothing about the hardening being partial, but rather that part of Israel was hardened. Elsewhere he will say of the same group that they have been broken off from the people of God, albeit temporarily (11:17, 24). Furthermore, the position of *apo merous* and its apparent contrast with "all Israel" in verse 26a favors the view that Paul means a part of Israel has been hardened.[75] The implications of this must have their full force: Paul is arguing that *temporarily* some Jews are not a part of the people of God because of their unbelief in the Messiahship of the crucified Jew, Jesus. Paul nowhere in Romans 9—11 suggests that there are two peoples of God.

Certainly the most debated verse in all of Romans 9—11 is 10:4. How shall we understand the word *telos* there? Do we take the *gar* as closely linking 10:4 with 10:3? The sentence reads literally, "For Christ [is] the *telos* of the law for/unto righteousness to everyone who believes." As Dunn points out, the term *telos* in Greek is ambiguous or multivalent.[76] The sense of end=completion or termination does not exclude the sense of end=goal, but in Paul *telos* seems always or almost always to include the sense of end=termination/completion whatever other nuances it may have (compare 1 Cor 1:8; 10:11; 15:24; 2 Cor 11:15; Phil 3:19).

Just as important is the context, where in 10:5-6 Paul contrasts the righteousness that is "of the law," which involves human deeds, and the righteousness that is "of faith," which is a matter of receiving, believing and confessing the grace gift of God, Christ Jesus, who bestows right-standing apart from human deeds. Verse 3 is equally important, for there too Paul speaks of Jews whose zeal is commendable, but it is not a zeal according to knowledge, for in seeking to establish their own righteousness they have not known the *dikaiosynē* that comes as a free gift from God.

We must bear in mind that Paul's argument here is salvation-historical not christological.[77] He is trying to explain how it is that many Jews have not received the *dikaiosynē* that comes from God through faith in Christ. He is not trying to demonstrate that Christ is the aim of the law, or that Christ embodies the righteousness the law promised, though he might well have affirmed those ideas as well in another context. The sense here is rather close to that in 2 Corinthians 3:13-14, where the point is the end *(telos)* of the Mosaic covenant, spoken of metaphorically as the end of the glory on Moses' face, which was being annulled. As a means of right-standing, or establishing one's own righteousness before God by works (9:32) rather than by faith, the law is at an end, and Christ is the one who brings it to this end.[78] This interpretation agrees with what we have already seen in Galatians 3—4 and 2 Corinthians 3, and makes sense of the immediate context of Romans 10:4 as well.[79] Barrett puts it this way: "*Telos,* whatever logical nuances it may bear, signifies an historical process. The clue to this process is provided not here but in Gal. 3.16: the historical figure of Jesus is the seed of Abraham, and thus includes in himself the process of election and the law, for he precedes and concludes both."[80]

The analogies or metaphors in 11:16-24 play a crucial part in Paul's overall argument as he builds to a climax at the end of chapter 11. Again we will need to work from what is relatively more clear to that which is less clear to make sense of this material.

In the first place Paul has chosen as his dominant image that of the olive tree (vv. 17, 24), not the vine image. Israel is rarely described in such terms in the Old Testament (Jer 11:16; Hos 14:6). In fact, it is striking that in its use in Jeremiah we read, "The Lord called you a thriving olive tree with fruit beautiful in form. But with the roar of a mighty storm he will set it on fire, and its branches will be broken. The Lord Almighty, who planted you, has decreed disaster for you, because the house of Israel and the house of Judah have done evil and provoked me to anger. . . ." The context of Hosea 14:6 is also one of God's judgment upon his people, though followed by restoration ("His splendor will be like an olive tree," compare v. 4). This suggests that the reason Paul chose this metaphor rather than the more popular vine metaphor is because of the broken condition of Israel, with some being part of the "olive tree" and some at least temporarily being broken off from it. Some of Israel, indeed the majority, currently stands under God's judgment, of which Jeremiah spoke.

The context here makes clear that Paul is speaking of a cultivated olive tree into which, contrary to good horticultural practices, wild olive branches have been grafted. As Davies notes, the wild olive tree never produced useful oil.[81] Since Paul clearly identifies the Gentiles with the wild olive branches that have been grafted in, he is seeking to put overweening Gentile Christians in their place in two ways. He makes it clear that Jewish Christians are the natural branches and the Jewish forebears are the root of the tree, thus giving Jews precedence in this people of God, and that the Gentiles bring nothing into the union. God simply grafts them in by pure grace. They stand only by faith, and may be broken off like the Jews before them who were guilty of unbelief.

This metaphor makes abundantly clear how Paul in all of Romans 9—11 has been providing an *apologia* of sorts not only for God but also for Jews in general, and perhaps Jewish Christians in particular. This may suggest that a problem existed in Rome with Gentile Christians disparaging or even writing off Jews, perhaps even Jewish Christians. By this argument Paul attempts to set things straight as to who is indebted to whom, making clear that the Gentiles are the "unnatural" ones among the people of God.

While it is rather certain that the branches are Jews, broken off due to unbelief, is it as certain who is the root? On the basis of 1 Enoch 93:5, 8; Philo *Rer. Div. Her.* 279 and Jubilees 21:24, it seems likely that the reference is to the patriarchs and perhaps to Abraham in particular. This conclusion probably finds support in Romans 4:1-2, where Paul speaks of Abraham "our forefather *kata sarka.*" This would make sense in view of several other considerations. Paul is about to explain that the basis of being grafted in or being broken off is faith or unbelief respectively. In Romans 4, as was already the case in Galatians 3, Abraham is seen as the point of origin for the people of God, even to the point of Paul arguing in Galatians that Christ is *the seed* of Abraham. Further, when Paul begins his salvation-historical argument in Romans 9:6 he starts with Abraham.

What this argument amounts to is a claim that there is only one continuous people of God throughout human history, beginning with Abraham (or perhaps the patriarchs) and continuing to the present. Individuals may be broken off or grafted in but there has always been only one people of God, and conversely God has never been without a people.

Who then are the *tines* (compare *en autois,* v. 17) who remain grafted into the olive tree and are not broken off, to which the wild branches are added? Clearly it is not the Gentile Christians, who are the wild branches and who have not been grafted into non-Christian Israel, but into the *ekklēsia.* This means that the remaining branches are Jewish Christians like Paul, who are also the righteous remnant we discussed earlier. Here Davies' summary is helpful:

> From what have the unbelieving Jews been cut off? It cannot be that they have been cut off from the Jewish people considered as an ethnic entity: they are still Jews. The branches broken off (the use of the passive verb . . . indicates the action of God), then, are those Jews, and they are the majority, who have refused to be part of true Israel, the remnant that believed in Christ. The olive in 11:17 stands for the community of Christian believers, the Church, at first composed of Jewish Christians of the root of Abraham.[82]

It is more difficult to sort out whether the various metaphors in verse 16 all refer to the same thing. It is logical to conclude that the reference to root and branches in verse 16 has prompted the following extended metaphor and thus that they both refer to the same thing. Dunn has argued that the first fruits, in view of Paul's use of *aparchē* elsewhere (Rom 16:5; 1 Cor 16:15; 2 Thess 2:13), likely refers to the first Christian converts.[83] This then probably refers to Jewish Christians. It is possible that first fruits refers to the patriarchs in analogy with the root in the other metaphor. This latter view makes better sense in view of verse 15, where Paul has been discussing the reconciliation of the presently estranged Jews back into the people of God. Paul's point then is that even the currently estranged Jews are still set apart by God *(hagia)* and will ultimately be reconciled back into the true people of God. As Paul goes on to say in verse 28, "They are loved on account of the patriarchs, for God's gifts and call are irrevocable."[84] This necessarily leads us into a discussion of the crucial material in 11:25-27.

First, verse 26 cannot and should not be isolated from verse 25. This is so not only because verse 26 begins with the linking words *kai houtos,* but also because these two verses represent one continuous sentence and it seems unlikely that Paul would change the meaning of Israel, which he uses in both verses from one half of the sentence to the next. Throughout Romans 9—11 Paul has been careful to use the term only for "the Israel after the flesh," that is, non-Christian Israel, and so the burden of proof must be on those who insist that in verse 26 Israel means something different than it meant in verse 25. *Houtos* normally has the meaning of "so" ("in this manner"), but when combined by *kai* with the previous two clauses, as it is here, it could have a sequential sense "and then" or "and thus" or "and without further ado."

The sentence presents a historical sequence: (1) a part of Israel has been hardened (2) until the full number of Gentiles have been saved; and then (3) all Israel will be saved.[85] This understanding of verses 25-26 is also supported by what 11:15 says—first is the reconciliation of the world (Gentiles) while the non-Christian Jews are rejected and then these Jews will be accepted, which will mean or signal "life from the dead," presumably the last resurrection.[86] This interpretation also makes sense in light of verse 23, which indicates that God can graft non-Christian Jews back in again. It may be, as Wagner suggests, that Paul knew some such tradition as in Mark 13:10 and has in part expanded on it here.[87] Allison has noted that in intertestamental literature a pattern occasionally emerges as follows: (1) contemporary Israel has missed the mark and needs to repent; (2) before the end comes she will do so; (3) when she does so the end will come; (4) salvation will then come to the Gentiles (*T. Dan* 6:4; *T. Jud* 23:5; 4 Ezra 4:38-43). This same sort of pattern (at least in regard to points 1-3) can be discerned in Acts 3:19-20. When Israel turns to her Savior, "times of refreshing"—the final eschatological blessings—will transpire. Paul has had to modify this pattern to include the idea that Gentiles have repented and believed *before* Israel by and large has done so.[88]

But when and how will this regrafting take place? Paul does not say directly but he does provide us with two clues. If the reference to "life from the dead" in verse 15 is meant literally, and surely the qualifier *ek nekrōn* points in that direction, as does the prior reference to the reconciliation of the world mentioned in 15a,[89] Paul probably is thinking of some sort of eschatological miracle, *not* a mission to the Jews after the *plērōma* of Gentiles is converted. This view is also favored by 11:26b, which likely refers to either God or more likely Jesus coming and turning godlessness away from Jacob.

If by Zion in this quote from Isaiah 59:20-21 (compare 27:9) Paul means heaven or the heavenly Jerusalem (see Gal 4:26), then it seems likely that Paul means this eschatological miracle will happen at the parousia. Elsewhere Paul clearly connects parousia and resurrection of the dead (see 1 Cor 15:23-24). F. Mussner has put it this way: "If God himself has hardened the hearts of the Israelites, then 'logically,' only he, and not the church, can lead them out of this hardening. Not the converted Gentiles save 'all Israel'—an absolutely unbiblical thought—but only God alone."[90] Nevertheless, Paul does affirm that an ongoing mission to the Jews is in order *prior* to the end of the Gentile mission, even if it produces little fruit (see Gal 2:7-8).

What then does Paul mean by "all Israel"? If the Old Testament usage is any clue, the phrase does not mean every last Israelite but the corporate whole with some exceptions (1 Sam 7:5; 25:1; 1 Kings 12:1; 2 Chron 12:1; Dan 9:11; Jub 50:9; *T. Levi* 17:5). The much-quoted *Mish. Sanh.* 10.1 deserves one more airing: "All Israel have a share in the world to come . . . [except] he that says that there is no resurrection of the dead . . . and [he that says] that the Law is not from heaven . . . and he that reads the heretical books, or that utters charms over a wound. . . . Also he that pronounces the Name with its proper letters."[91] Paul gives us no list of exceptions to this, not even those who refuse to confess that Jesus is Lord even after he returns. Thus "all Israel" in verse 26 must mean the corporate whole of Israel, or at least the vast majority of Israel, both those who are now Jewish Christians and the rest who will be saved after the full number of Gentiles has been saved.[92]

How is this event to transpire? Will it be a mass conversion of Jews to Christ by the preaching of the gospel at the end of history, or a Jewish response only to and at the parousia of Christ? F. Mussner is probably correct that the proper stress must be placed on the connection Paul makes between verse 26a and the fulfillment of Scripture in 26b. The salvation of Israel will transpire as it is written in Isaiah 59:20-21, and thus will involve an eschatological miracle, a direct response to the coming of the Deliverer Christ.[93]

Paul concludes his argument as he began it, by stating clearly that God's gifts and call are irrevocable, and that salvation for all is on the basis of mercy (and faith), not on the basis of some claim humans and perhaps in particular Jews might presume to make on God (11:28-32). On the basis of the *mystērion* Paul reveals, he can also claim that God's word has not failed, despite only a minority of Jews currently believing in Christ, for God is not finished with "the Jews" yet. We may perhaps sum up Paul's vision of salvation history in schematic fashion:

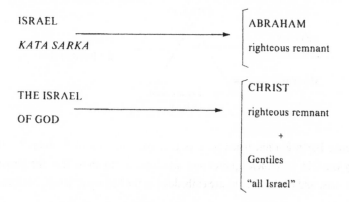

This schematic does not clearly show that for Paul the righteous remnant existed *within* Israel *kata sarka,* while since Jesus came, the righteous remnant consists of Jewish Christians in the *ekklēsia* and they are united with Gentiles. Paul never says "not all Christians (whether Jew or Gentile) are true Christians," though his arguments about "false brothers" in Galatians 2 might lead one to think that he operated with an *ecclesiola in ecclesia* theology. What is reasonably clear is that for Paul at no time in human history is there more than one people of God. This means that what he calls the *ekklēsia* (Jew and Gentile united in Christ) is a development of Israel, not a replacement of Israel. It may rightly be called the "true Israel" in the present age, though he chooses to call it "the Israel of God."

This schematic would have a slightly different look if we attempted to combine the "laology" in Galatians with that in Romans 9—11.[94] Then it would look like two pyramids narrowing to a point in the middle, namely to Christ who is seen as *the seed* of Abraham, or to put it another way, *the* righteous remnant of Israel, before there were any Jewish-Christian followers. The second pyramid would then expand out to include all those who are in Christ now, and at the bottom would be added one more eschatological layer, "all Israel." It would look something like the following:

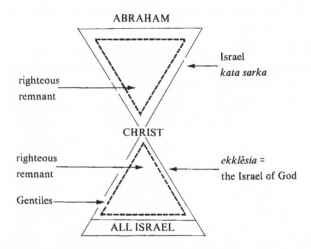

In a sense Barth is right when he says that the intention of Romans 9—11, especially the Old Testament quotes and allusions, is "to show that the history of Jesus Christ and of the nations are embedded in the history of Israel, continues that history, and leads to its fulfilment."[95] Beker is perhaps more explicit and nearer the mark:

Israel's priority is real, but it is not located in Israel's achievement of "covenant-keeping." It lies exclusively in God's salvation-history and therefore in His election and promises to Israel. . . . Israel's continuing function for the Gentile is grounded in both her salvation-historical priority as the people of the promise and her eschatological destiny. The consummation can not come unless Israel is saved. For unless Israel is saved, God's faithfulness to his promises to Israel will remain forever ambiguous.[96]

At the close of his letter to the Romans, Paul reiterates the themes found in Romans 9—11. Here he describes Christ as a servant of the "circumcision" to confirm the truth of God's promises to the patriarchs (15:7). He reminds his audience at the end that "if the Gentiles have shared in the Jews' spiritual blessings, they owe it to the Jews to share with them their material blessings" (v. 27). Though this is a plug for the collection for the poor saints in Jerusalem (v. 26), it shows clearly how much Paul is preoccupied with the theme of the interrelationship of Jews and Gentiles in God's salvation-historical plan (Rom 1—15). Though justification is not a minor theme of this letter, it should be clear that Paul brings up the matter of justification in the course of working out what it is that God is doing with Jews and Gentiles in his salvation-historical plan. All of what Paul says in 1:16-17 must be taken seriously as the announcement of the theme of this letter, not merely "the righteous will live by faith."

Before I conclude this discussion of the Pauline material it is necessary to examine Ephesians 2:11-22. Whether this material was written by Paul or by one of his coworkers or disciples, it seems to be a legitimate development of what we have already heard in Galatians, 2 Corinthians and Romans. We will start by examining Ephesians 3:6 and work our way back to Ephesians 2.

Ephesians 3:4 indicates that the subject of discussion is a *mystērion,* but is it the same one Paul was discussing in Romans 9—11? The answer must be in part yes, for in 3:6 he describes the Gentiles literally as "co-heirs, one body, and co-partakers in all that is promised" with Jews through their acceptance of the gospel of Jesus Christ. "It is the distinctive message of Ephesians that no Gentile can have communion with Christ or God unless he also has communion with Israel."[97] But this is not really unique to Ephesians, for it is at least part of what Paul is arguing for in Romans 9—11.

Ephesians 2 explains how this *mystērion* has been made possible. Through the death of Christ the "dividing wall of hostility" between Jew and Gentile has been broken down, and Gentiles, who were once excluded from citizenship in Israel, are now included in it (vv. 12-14). Here "Israel" refers to Jew and Gentile united in Christ, which comports with Paul's use of the term in Galatians 6:16. However, the author still maintains the precedence of the Jews in salvation. The argument is once again about the inclusion of Gentiles into Israel, the already existing people of God. It is not about replacement of Israel with the church. The church is simply seen as the development of Israel in the direction God always intended (see 1:10-11). Nor is there talk of a new Israel here. Such language apparently arises in Christianity only when there were no longer any Christian Jews or their numbers had dwindled to an insignificant few. Also, what citizenship means to the author of this document is at least in part getting in on the promises of the covenants (v. 12), a theme heard previously especially in Galatians 3—4.

What then is the dividing wall of hostility Christ abolishes? Though this has been much controverted, the straightforward way to translate verse 15 is, "the law of commandments in regulations he has abolished." This possibly means only those commandments or regulations which separate Jews from Gentiles (such as circumcision, keeping kosher or the sabbath, and so forth).[98] Against this Lincoln has stressed that the divisiveness "was produced by the very fact that Israel possessed the Torah; and so in order to remove the divisiveness, Christ had to deal with its cause—the law itself. . . . It is clearly the law itself and all its regulations, not just some of them, which are in view."[99] If the author is developing what has already been said in Romans 10:4, he may indeed mean the abolition of the law as a means of works-righteousness or right standing with God. Here the emphasis is on the law as something that divides Jews from Gentiles, whereas in Romans the focus is on law as a means of obtaining righteousness in the sight of God. In both cases it would seem clear that the Mosaic law is in view, though the sense in which it is abolished is expressed differently. Romans 10:4 and Ephesians 2:14-15 do agree that in whatever sense the law has been abolished it is Christ who has terminated it.

Ephesians 2 concludes with a picture of Jew and Gentile being built into a temple or household of God, and the Gentiles are called "fellow citizens with God's people" (v. 19). The crucial question here is, Who are the *hagioi* (saints) mentioned in verse 19? In view of the trajectory of the argument thus far in Ephesians 2 one would expect this to be a reference to Jews of some sort (see also 3:6). Against the view that *hagioi* means all believers must be the fact that in verse 12 this group of Gentiles (v. 11) that the author is addressing as "you" was said to be excluded from citizenship in Israel. It is much more likely then that *hagioi* refers to Jewish Christians, or less probably the patriarchs, to whom Gentiles have been joined in Christ.[100] Here again the precedence of Jews is given its due. Nothing in Ephesians contradicts anything in Paul's earlier letters, and in the main it seems to be a faithful development, especially of several of the themes in Romans 9—11. Jew and Gentile united in Christ are seen as the true development of Israel and so are considered true Israel by Paul and, if it is not by Paul, the author of Ephesians. There is thus a sense in which this is "one new being" made out of two formerly separated groups (2:15), but also preserved is the idea that there is some continuity with Israel as it existed prior to the death of Christ.

What then shall we say about Paul's view of Israel and its future? First, Paul sees non-Christian Jews, or at least those who have rejected the gospel, as temporarily under the curse or wrath of God (compare 1 Thess 2 and Rom 11), but in what may have been a new insight when he wrote Romans, Paul also affirms that even they have a positive future in the plan of God. Second, Paul's vision of the people of God in the present is Jew and Gentile united in Christ—the Israel of God (compare Gal 6:16 to Eph 2:12-13). Third, Christ is the basis of this unity of Jew and Gentile and the means through which even Gentiles have access to the promises given to Abraham (Gal 3—4; Eph 2—3). This necessarily entailed that Christ replaces the law as the center of religious focus, and in fact "ends" the Mosaic law at least as a means of right-standing with God (through works of the law) and as a means of separation from Gentiles (Rom 10:4; Gal 3—4; 2 Cor 3; Eph 2). For Paul there is only one true people of God, and in Galatians and Romans in particular he traces its trajectory from Abraham through the righteous remnant to Christ and then to the righteous remnant in the present (Jewish Christians) to whom have been joined Gentiles who profess Christ, and with whom "all Israel" will finally be joined, apparently at the eschaton.

Though we may argue that this is a very peculiar view of Judaism, nonetheless what we have read in these passages is part of an intramural debate about Israel and its future, with Paul insisting that the crucifed Jew Jesus holds the key to understanding the past, present and future of God's people. He is the "end" of the law, the seed of Abraham and finally in a striking metaphor the keystone, capstone or head of the corner of the temple/household God is building out of Jewish and Gentile believers,[101] though he could also be viewed as the stone of stumbling for non-Christian Jews in the present (see Rom 9:32-33; 11:11). Christ is then in a paradoxical way both the divider and ultimately the unifier of God's people in Paul's vision of things (see Rom 11:26c-27). This amounts neither to anti-Semitism nor anti-Judaism but a most profound re-envisoning of the people of God seen in the light of the Christ event. It must be judged as such.

—14—

Jesus
and the
Jews'
Just Due

In some ways Jesus' views on Israel and its future are easier to discern than are
those of Paul. When Jesus spoke there was no *ekklēsia* like the one Paul had to
deal with, nor had the community that Jesus spoke of forming taken shape.[1]
Furthermore, Jesus never distinguished himself from "the Jews" as Paul did on
occasion. Thus for Jesus, unlike Paul, there was no question about what the
relationship of *ekklēsia* to Israel was, nor was he ever even partially looking in
on Israel from the outside. Jesus' life and ministry were defined by and apparently
almost entirely confined to Israel.

Since we have dealt with many of the texts that have a bearing on Jesus' view
of Israel, I will now summarize some of the major views by various scholars, as
well my own insights, and then analyze texts that tell us about the *future* of Israel,
and texts that seem to reveal Jesus' view of Gentiles vis-à-vis that future.[2]

E. P. Sanders has denoted four different scholarly interpretations of how Jesus
viewed Israel.[3] First, G. Bornkamm's view, which draws on Bultmann's existen-
tialist approach, is that Jesus addressed people *as individuals*. This view denies
any special status to Israel. Indeed, Bornkamm affirms that "through Jesus'

words and actions the illusion of the inalienable, as it were legal rights of Israel and its fathers is attacked at the root and shaken to pieces."[4] The second view, which is essentially that of Sanders himself, is that Jesus addressed all Israel and intended reform, only condemning abuses or certain individual "elements" in early Judaism. The third view is that Jesus, perhaps like the Qumranites, wanted to establish the true Israel, a remnant of the pious, pure and loyal. The fourth view is Sanders's assessment of what Jeremias was arguing in *Jesus' Promise to the Nations*.[5] He claims that Jeremias argued that Jesus addressed all Israel, but only *pro forma*. Jesus held the common view that Israel would be restored before the end of human history and that *then* Gentiles would enter the kingdom. Jesus also knew in advance that Israel would reject his preaching, but he offered it anyway so their destruction would be justified.

However, Sanders's assessment of Jeremias is questionable. Jeremias never says that Jesus' appeal to his fellow Jews was only *pro forma*. What he says is that "the promise of salvation given to 'the fathers'. . . and to 'the sons . . . of the covenant' must first be fulfilled . . . the children must first be fed, before the incorporation of the Gentiles into the people of God could be effected." Jeremias does go on to draw the dubious conclusion that Jesus saw his ministry to Israel as a fulfilling of a precondition to or as a means of incorporating Gentiles into the Dominion of God. It does not follow from this however that Jeremias thought the ministry to Israel was purely *pro forma*.[6]

The real question that concerns us is whether or not Jesus had anything positive to say about the future of Israel and/or its national hope. Various scholars have thought that Jesus did affirm a nationalistic hope in some form. For instance, consider the words of G. B. Caird:

> He intended to bring into existence the restored nation of Israel, promised in the Old Testament prophecies. It was to this end he accepted baptism at the hands of John, to this end that he appointed the Twelve to be his associates, instructing them that their number was a symbol of their relation to the twelve tribes of Israel. This was why he spoke of his followers as a "little flock" . . . this was why he predicted the raising up of a new temple made without hands, to take the place of the old hand-made temple, and why he interpreted his own forthcoming death as the sacrifice by which God was sealing his covenant with the renewed Israel. . . . Yet the success of his mission in no way depended on the acceptance of his preaching by the nation as a whole, for he had already brought into existence, in nucleus at least, the Israel of the new age.[7]

W. D. Davies takes a somewhat different tack. He affirms that Jesus was concerned to gather a community of people to share in his ministry, and he sent his disciples not to the nation of Israel, but to the "lost sheep of the house of Israel"—to the people as people, not as a national entity. He hoped to reconstitute the chosen people within the matrix of Israel, not to affirm their political hopes.[8] If Davies is right, then one would expect Jesus to have said little about the future of Israel. On the other hand, if Caird is right it is hard to see why Jesus seems never to encourage the political hopes of his people.

My own assessment of Jesus' view of Israel may be summed up as follows: Jesus addressed not just a part of Israel but the whole of Israel, calling her to repentance in view of the in-breaking of the Dominion of God in and through his ministry. It appears that Jesus warned of the possibilty of judgment if the manifestation of the Dominion in his ministry was rejected (see Mk 12:1-9). Jesus gathered disciples, including an inner circle called the Twelve, *not* so that they would be a new Israel, but in order that they might help him to free Israel, calling her to repentance. In short, the Twelve were Jesus' *šᵉlûḥîm*. Jesus by design confined both his own and his disciples' ministry primarily if not exclusively to the people who lived within Galilee and Judea, believing he was sent only to the "lost sheep of Israel," by which he apparently meant Israel as a whole.

During his ministry Jesus did show special concern for the least and the last of Jewish society and apparently derived a good deal of his following from among them. If the parable of the sower is any indication (Mk 4), Jesus expected and got a mixed response to his announcement of the Dominion and his call to repentance, as John had before him. In due course, Jesus seems to have contemplated his own demise as a means of achieving what he had not accomplished during his ministry. Finally, as we have seen in chapter ten, Jesus seems to have envisioned a community being founded in the future, based on Peter and presumably those of like faith and commitment. Jesus did not set out to set apart a righteous remnant but to reform the whole of Israel in view of God's present eschatological action in their midst. Finally, Jesus also envisioned a role for the Twelve, "judging" the twelve tribes of Israel when the Dominion was fully realized on earth at the eschaton. This key saying (Mt 19:28/Lk 22:30) may have been part of the Q material originally. Though I have already dealt with this saying at some length in *The Christology of Jesus,* we must return to it in a moment, looking at it from a different angle. In itself Matthew 19:28/Luke 22:30 is enough to show the error in arguing that Jesus had nothing to say about the future and future hopes of Israel and is also sufficient to demonstrate that Jesus did not identify his inner circle of followers as the new Israel.

How *radical* a reformer of Israel did Jesus intend to be? Was he simply an advocate of restoration theology,[9] or did some of his teaching strike at the heart of early Judaism and in effect attempt to redefine what it meant to be God's true people? I have suggested that the latter is nearer the mark. For instance, I believe it is likely that Jesus defined holiness in purely moral terms, rejecting the laws of clean and unclean, and also defined the people of God on the basis of adherence to God's will, speaking of a family of faith.[10] Both M. Borg and J. Riches have shown that one of the major clashes between Jesus and some of his contemporaries, perhaps especially the Pharisees, was over holiness issues.[11] How striking it is that we nowhere find in the Jesus material any affirmation of things like circumcision, offering animal sacrifices in the temple, or exclusive claims that heredity determined whether or not one was a Jew![12] On such matters Jesus seems to have developed some of John the Baptist's prophetic teaching to its logical conclusion (that God could raise up children of Abraham from stones, heredity being no guarantee of blessing when the Dominion came). This theology in turn led to a calling of all Israel to repentance, even the pious and Torah observant, lest judgment overtake them all. In this context we should evaluate what Jesus has to say about the future of Israel. As with Paul the crucial question seems to be, Who counts as Israel?

Let us now re-examine Matthew 19:28/Luke 22:30. It is difficult to decide who has preserved the most primitive form of this logion. The reference to sitting on twelve thrones in the Matthean version is surely original, since Christians would hardly invent a throne for Judas. On the other hand, in all other respects the Lukan form of the saying seems more primitive except for the reference to "my kingdom." Thus the original saying probably promised participation in the messianic banquet to the disciples in the Dominion, and also a role for the Twelve in relationship to the judging of Israel.

As Fitzmyer has pointed out, Psalm 122:3-5 seems to lie in the background here: "Jerusalem. . . . That is where the tribes go up, the tribes of the Lord. . . . There the thrones for judgment stand, the thrones of the house of David."[13] If this saying lies in the background perhaps *krinō* means "rule" or "judge" in the sense that the Old Testament judges did, but on the other hand both Matthew 25:31-46 and 1 Corinthians 6:3 may suggest that it means having a role in the final judgment of Israel, which has been gathered before the throne.

Another saying may also be in the background here. *Ps. Sol.* 17:28 reads, "And he shall gather together a holy people, whom he shall lead in righteousness, and he shall judge the tribes of the people that has been sanctified by the Lord his God." Here again "judge" has the more positive sense of "to rule." Davies has carefully critiqued the drawing of parallels between our text, 1 Corinthians 6:3 and Revelation 21:14.[14]

There is one further consideration. What of the saying of Jesus about "this wicked generation" being judged even by notable or notorious Gentiles? Two observations can be made about the Q material found in Matthew 12:41-42/Luke 11:31-32. First, even if it does go back to Jesus[15] it speaks of a judicial testimony by Gentiles, not a role for the Twelve. Second, the testimony is against "this wicked generation," not against the gathered tribes of Israel. As Marshall says, "The phrase 'this wicked generation' is used to characterize the contemporaries of Jesus as sharing in the perversity of faithless Israel."[16] Behind the usage stand texts like Deuteronomy 32:5, 20; Judges 2:10; Psalm 78:8 and 95:10. We should also compare the usage in the Gospels (Mk 8:12, 38; 9:19; Lk 11:50-51 and parallels; 17:25; 21:32 and parallels). We will see that this phrase is *not* used to characterize all Israel, but simply a faithless generation or group of Israelites. It probably then is of little or no help in ferreting out the meaning of Matthew 19:28/Luke 22:30.

On the whole Matthew 19:28/Luke 22:30 probably refers to the Twelve, perhaps with the Son of Man ruling the gathered tribes of Israel at the eschaton. Less likely is that they will be part of the judicial separating of wheat and chaff in Israel at the final judgment. Either way, however, Jesus envisions the gathered people of Israel participating in the eschatological events, and for at least some of them that participation will be positive. This means at the very least that Jesus *did* envision a future for Israel, and for at least some of Israel that future will involve a positive role and experience.[17]

The second important saying is the eschatological beatitude found only in Matthew 5:5. This is a direct quote from Psalm 37:11 in its Septuagint form, but this in itself does not rule out that it may go back to Jesus. The Hebrew form of Psalm 37(36):11 reads, "the meek shall possess land," even though the Revised Standard Version renders that verse "But the meek shall possess *the land.*"[18] Since Luke does not have this beatitude and since Matthew 5:5 is sometimes found before and sometimes after 5:4 in the manuscripts, various scholars have thought it redactional or secondary.[19] Davies and Allison have argued that 5:5 was found in the

Matthean version of Q and is not redactional since it does not betray any typical Matthean vocabulary or interests. They do not think it goes back to Jesus, but rather reflects an early Christian commentary on "Blessed are the poor."[20]

The problem with the conclusion of Davies and Allison is that the manuscript support for the order 5:5 then 5:4 is nowhere near as strong as that for 5:4 followed by 5:5. The former order is found in the Western text (D), followed by 33 and various minuscules and by some church fathers (notably Clement and Origen). The latter reading is supported by the important and diverse witnesses Aleph, B, C, K, W, Delta, Theta, as well as various minuscules and also Tertullian and Chrysostom. On purely text-critical grounds the order 5:4 followed by 5:5 has a decided edge (B rating in the UBS), and Metzger rightly points out that the reversal can be explained:

> If verses 3 and 5 had originally stood together, with their rhetorical antithesis of heaven and earth, it is unlikely that any scribe would have thrust ver. 4 between them. On the other hand, as early as the second century copyists reversed the order of the two beatitudes so as to produce such an antithesis and to bring πτωχοί and πραεῖς into closer connection.[21]

We must conclude that the juxtaposition of 5:3 and 5:5 is probably secondary.[22] What then would 5:5 have meant if it did come from Jesus' lips? The inheritance of the land was a part of the historic prerogative of Israel promised by God (cf. Deut 4:1; 16:20). Perhaps because it was part of the Matthean redactional agenda to spiritualize some of these beatitudes (compare Mt 5:3 to Lk 6:20), it is often argued that *tēn gēn* in 5:5 has the more general sense of "earth," or may even be a synonym for the worldwide Dominion of God.[23] This flies in the face of the fact that it is a direct quote of Psalm 37(36):11, where the reference is surely to *eretz Israel.* In any case our concern is what this would have meant to Jesus and his audience, not to the First Evangelist. If indeed Jesus spoke of the gathering of the twelve tribes at the eschaton in one place, that place would surely be in *eretz Israel,* and thus it is more likely than not that *tēn gēn* should not be generalized or spiritualized here. What Jesus seems to have in mind is something like Isaiah 61:7: "Instead of their shame my people will receive a double portion, and instead of disgrace they will rejoice in their inheritance; and so they will inherit a double portion *in their land,* and everlasting joy will be theirs" (italics mine).

Jesus could well have drawn some of his material for the beatitudes from Isaiah 61. Verse 9 speaks of the people whom the Lord has blessed, and verse 2 speaks of comforting those who mourn. Verse 1 refers to good news for the poor (compare Lk 6:20). Verse 6 speaks of feeding on the wealth of the nations (compare Lk 6:21). Twice the people are said to be the *locus* where God has bestowed his righteousness (compare Is 61:3, 10 to Mt 5:6). Verse 1 proclaims the release of captives and those oppressed or persecuted, and verse 4 the restoration of the land devastated by oppression and persecution (compare Mt 5:10 and parallels). There is more than enough evidence here to conclude that Jesus drew on various parts of Isaiah 61 in his eschatological beatitudes, and this suggests that he also may have interpreted Psalm 37(36):11, which implies *eretz Israel,* in light of the more clear reference in Isaiah 61:7 to "their land." Note the temporal difference between the first and third of the beatitudes in Matthew. The first refers to a present possession or at least a present claim on the Dominion. The third beatitude refers to a future eschatological inheritance of the land. These two beatitudes should not be identified as two ways to say the same thing, despite second-century copyists who reversed the order of verses 4 and 5.

In the texts from Deuteronomy referred to above, such promises of possessing the land are made contingent on following the decrees and laws of God. In Psalm 37:27 this is equally clear: "Turn from evil and do good, *then* you will always live securely. For the Lord loves the just and will not forsake his faithful ones." Isaiah 61:3 as well refers to those who will be called "oaks of righteousness." In all these texts there are moral preconditions to inheriting one's portion of the land. In Matthew 5:5 land is promised to "the meek," not to all Israel.[24]

Who then are the meek? If the Hebrew *'nwm* lies in the background here the term means something like "one who knows their need for God," or, as Guelich puts it, *praeis* is "focusing on one's dependent relationship to God."[25] E. Schweizer has suggested the translation "powerless."[26] "The *praeis* are not so much actively seeking to avoid hubris (an attitude) as they are, as a matter of fact, powerless in the eyes of the world (a condition)."[27] This naturally suggests that Jesus is talking about some of the people he was most concerned about within Israel—the least and the last. Some of these people had responded enthusiastically to his preaching and had followed him.[28]

What may we conclude on the basis of Matthew 5:5? It is less clear than Matthew 19:28 and parallels, but if it does go back to Jesus it may well reflect his belief that at least some Israelites would inherit *eretz Israel,* when the Dominion of God finally came in full. It seems likely that Jesus did hold out a future hope for at least some in Israel, even if in the present he was being rejected by the majority "in this wicked generation." When we ask whether Jesus' vision might also have included non-Jews in this eschatological state and perhaps even in Israel, it requires that we examine several texts of a different sort. First, a word about early Jewish attitudes toward Gentiles is in order.

It is not true that all early Jews felt an implacable hatred toward Gentiles.[29] Certainly some early Jews felt this way, as is clear from some of the Qumran data (see the War Scroll), from Jubilees 15:31 and from 4 Ezra 6:55-57. We can also point to a pronouncement by R. Eliezer ben Hyrcanus about Gentiles having no part in the world to come (see *Tos. Sanh.* 13:2, also the saying in *Mekilta Ex.* 21:30). These views must be balanced against the considerable evidence that many early Jews favored and engaged in proselytizing Gentiles.

This evidence has been well laid out by A. Segal and does not need to be repeated here.[30] His conclusion is amply warranted: "Jewish prosyletism was both real and controversial."[31] It was controversial because there were some who did not agree with it, perhaps even many. "[A]ttitudes ranged from a total denial of a mission to the gentiles to an extreme interest in it. . . . Different Jews and different Jewish sects reached different opinions about proselytism and defined conversion differently."[32] Matthew 23:15 and Josephus *Antiquities* 20.2.3-4 both attest to this ongoing phenomenon of proselytism. Since Israel was a house divided on this issue, it cannot be assumed that we know what Jesus' views on such matters must have been. It is thus necessary to examine certain key texts.

The first and most important of these texts is the Q logion found in Matthew 8:11-12/Luke 13:28-29. The belief in a messianic or eschatological banquet of the saved at the end of history seems to have been widespread in early Judaism and existed at least as early as the late prophetic period (see Is 25:6-7; 65:13-14; Ezek 39:17-20; 1 Enoch 62:14; 2 Bar 29:4; 4 Ezra 6:49ff.; 2 Enoch 42:5). It is also found in several layers of the Gospel tradition (see Lk 14:15; Mt 22:2-14; Mk 14:25) besides the text we are now examining. Thus it is likely that Jesus did believe in such an idea.[33] Another view that went back to the late prophetic period was that Gentiles would stream to Zion in the end to participate in or contribute to the blessedness of Israel (see Zech 8:20-23; Mic 7:12; Is 60:11; Ps 47:9; Is 54:15 LXX; Amos 9:12 LXX [compare Acts 15:17]; Tob. 13:13; *T. Ben* 9:2; *Ps Sol* 17:31; 4 Ezra 13:13).

The earliest form of this saying seems to have been: "Many will come from east and west and sit at table with Abraham, Issac, and Jacob in the kingdom of God, but you will be thrown into the outer darkness. There people will weep and gnash their teeth" (compare 2 Esdras 1:38-40).[34] Does it at least in substance go back to Jesus? R. Bultmann intimates that it is not an authentic saying.[35] Against this must stand several considerations.

First, the thought-world and language is very Semitic. The patriarchs are referred to and ultimate blessedness is described in terms of table-fellowship. The early Jewish idea of the damned and saved being able to see each other (compare Lk 16:23) may be present, and the Semitic phrase "sons of the Dominion" is used here of Jews. This last phrase also rules out the idea that Diaspora Jews are those who are streaming in and displacing some who have a claim on the Dominion. It is also probable that the Aramaic circumstantial clause stands behind the participial construction as in Luke 13:28, "When you see Abraham . . . and you yourselves cast out."[36] Second, this saying comports with other likely authentic words of Jesus in which he does speak of displacement of some Jews by others at the banquet (compare Lk 14:15-24).[37] Third, if this saying does not go back to Jesus then one would have to posit that it was created quite early on by Jewish Christians *while* the mission to the Jews was still ongoing (see Gal 2:8-9). But is it really likely that Jewish Christians intent on bringing more Jews into the Christian community would invent a saying suggesting that some or many Jews would be excluded from the Dominion at the eschaton and their place be taken by Gentiles? This hardly seems plausible. We thus conclude that this saying is likely authentic and in its simplified form goes back to Jesus.

What do we learn from this saying? First, that Jesus believed in the participation of the Jewish patriarchs in the messianic banquet. This is hardly surprising and shows that Jesus was not interested in replacing Judaism with some other non-Jewish form of religion. It was Jews that had been promised a place in God's final Dominion, and Jesus foresaw at least some Jews receiving the benefits of such a promise. Second, Jesus, like some of his Jewish forebears and contemporaries, believed in the eschatological inclusion of Gentiles in the blessings of Israel's salvation at the end of history. The shocking aspect of this saying is the displacement motif. Jesus is not merely arguing for Gentile inclusion in final blessedness but for the displacement of some Jews by Gentiles.[38]

In its original setting (which possibly the First Evangelist preserves, although this is uncertain), this saying was probably directed against "this present wicked generation," certainly not against all Jews, and certainly not against those who had responded positively to Jesus' message. What is striking about this saying is that Jesus envisions Gentiles sitting down and sharing table-fellowship with the patriarchs. Normally this would be understood to entail ritual defilement for the Jews involved.[39] Yet Jesus did not believe in such ritual defilement, and so it is hardly surprising that his vision of the messianic banquet did not include the idea of observing such distinctions or laws.[40] Jesus' vision of the Dominion then seems to include both Gentiles and Jews in final blessedness. This vision also seems to be in evidence at least in part elsewhere in the Jesus tradition. For example, the parable of the mustard seed in Mark 4:31-32 and parallels (compare Gosp. Thom. 20:2) comes to mind.[41] The reference to birds nesting in the mustard bush *when the bush has fully grown up* may well refer to Gentiles being allowed to benefit from the eschatological blessedness of Israel (compare Ezra 17:23; Dan 4:12, 21).[42]

The foregoing discussion, however, really tells us nothing about Jesus' estimation of Gentiles in his own day. As Jeremias has shown, Jesus confined his ministry as much as possible to "the lost sheep of Israel," and his only positive contact with Gentiles involves two stories of healing *at a distance* (Mk 7:24-30 and parallels and the story that immediately precedes Mt 8:11-12).[43] Furthermore, Jesus is apparently both harsh and coarse with the Syro-Phoenician woman,[44] even though in the end he grants her request. This story also supports the view that Jesus saw Jews as having precedence over non-Jews in terms of God's blessings (Mk 7:27 and parallels). What is important about Mark 7:24-30 and parallels is that Jesus would *allow* that a non-Jew might receive even miraculous help from and during his ministry. Thus while non-Jews are not excluded from God's mercy even in the present, Jesus does not direct his ministry toward them.

Three further sayings in Mark also concern us: 13:10 and parallels, 14:9 and parallels and 11:17. Mark 13:10 is widely regarded as a Markan creation, not only because the vocabulary is distinctively Markan, but also because, had Jesus so clearly indicated a mission to Gentiles prior to the end of the world, it is difficult to understand why the early church prior to Paul felt no compulsion to engage in such a mission, and in fact severely critiqued Paul's efforts to carry out such a mission.[45] Yet it does appear that Paul may have known some form of Mark 13:10 (see Rom 11:25b), and so in some form it may go back to Jesus.

It is possible that a saying such as this, or related sayings such as Mark 14:9 (and even a saying like Mt 28:19a), originally may have been less specific than they are now. That is, perhaps near the end of his ministry Jesus may have alluded to the proclamation of the good news *eis holon ton kosmon,* and this was taken by the first Jewish Christians to mean that the news should be spread throughout the Diaspora and directed to Diaspora Jews, though Gentiles would not be excluded. This would explain not only what we find in Acts, where the regular pattern of Christian mission is to go to the synagogues first and only afterward to others, but also why it is that Paul insists that the gospel is for the Jew first (Rom 1:16). In due course a Gentile mission was deliberately undertaken, and Mark and the First Evangelist wrote their Gospels in the light of such a mission, hence the form of such sayings as Mark 13:10, where *panta ta ethnē* probably does allude to going to the Gentiles, as does *ta ethnē* in Matthew 28:19a.

What this means is that even if such sayings as Mark 13:10; 14:9 and Matthew 28:19a did ultimately go back to some original utterance of Jesus, and many scholars would deny the likelihood of this suggestion, we cannot be sure whether Jesus was suggesting a mission to Gentiles or perhaps to Diaspora Jews. Finally, only Mark, who was likely writing primarily to Gentiles, includes the words *pasin tois ethnesin* in the quote of Isaiah 56:7 at 11:17 in the temple cleansing story. It is an exact quote of the Septuagint, not the Masoretic Text version of Isaiah 56:7. For these reasons it is usually urged that Mark has added this quote here.[46] Even so, the question must be raised whether Jesus' action in the temple, which took place in the Court of the Gentiles, has any significance for his view of Gentiles. One could argue that Jesus was making the point that Gentiles had a right to use the temple as a house of prayer and be included in the Jewish cultus. If so, then we have one more piece of evidence that Jesus believed that Gentiles could be included in the benefits of what God had provided to the Jews.

What then can we say with some assurance about Jesus' view of Gentiles? First, he believed that some Gentiles would be included in the messianic banquet as replacements for some unworthy Jews. He seems to have adopted and adapted the expectation that at the end Gentiles would flow to Zion and worship the true God. Second, Jesus was willing to help Gentiles during his ministry, but his ministry was not directed toward them. Third, it is disputed whether Jesus ever spoke of a mission to Gentiles. Barrett stresses that "if Jesus had in fact given orders that such a mission should take place in the interim between his resurrection and his return, his followers could hardly have disputed whether it was right to undertake it."[47] Fourth, while Jeremias has conjectured that such sayings as Mark 13:10 refer to the eschatological proclamation to the Gentiles by an angel, this conclusion can be doubted, and even if true, it adds little to what we have learned on the basis of Matthew 28:9 and parallels.[48] Finally, Jesus seems to have focused his ministry and that of the Twelve on Israel during his lifetime, though he was willing to help others who came to him.

—15—

Conclusions

We are now in a position to compare and contrast Paul's and Jesus' views of Israel and its future. First, both Paul and Jesus do seem to have envisioned an eschatological future for Jews. Second, they both believed that Gentiles would be included with Jews in the final salvation of God. Neither of them proclaimed a complete replacement of Judaism by some totally non-Jewish form of religion. Gentiles were to be grafted into the ongoing Jewish people of God. Jesus seems to have envisioned this process happening at the eschaton; Paul, on the basis of a special *mystērion*, believed that God had planned for it to happen before the end. Paul partially reversed the traditional order of things, envisioning a salvation of some Jews while the full number of Gentiles were being saved, and only after that would the majority of Jews be saved. The apostle to the Gentiles also affirmed that "Christ became a servant of the circumcised . . . to confirm the promises given to the patriarchs" (Rom 15:8 RSV) and this assessment is only confirmed in the Synoptic Gospels. Jesus directed his ministry specifically to Israel, which he saw as basically lost unless they repented and heeded the message the Baptist and he were proclaiming.

Paul explained the rejection of Jesus by most of his Jewish contemporaries as a temporary condition that God would use to bring many Gentiles to faith in Christ. Neither Paul nor Jesus tried to deny that the response of the Jews to their respective messages was largely negative. Jesus' critique of "this wicked genera-tion" not only makes clear the largely negative response to his ministry, but also indicates that Jesus did not believe that the promises would apply to every Is-raelite regardless of their faith response to God's message and messenger. Jesus, perhaps more radically than Paul, was even willing to talk about final replace-ment of some Jews by Gentiles at the messianic banquet, while Paul only spoke of a temporary hardening until the end. Jesus also seems to have envisioned a territorial promise being fulfilled at least for some Jews at the eschaton, but Paul mentions nothing of this sort. What Paul does say does not exclude the possibility that God might fulfill some territorial promise to some Jews.

In some ways assessing Jesus' view of Israel and its future is easier than as-sessing Paul's. Both of them apparently agonized over the lack of positive re-sponse by Jews to the good news (compare the Q material in Lk 13:34-35 and parallels to Rom 9:1-5).[1] Both of them affirmed in one way or another Israel's first claim on the blessedness God had promised his people (compare Rom 1:16-17 to Mk 7:27 and parallels). Jesus is in a rather different historical position than is Paul. Jesus never distinguished himself from "the Jews" as Paul at times did, and he certainly never had to wrestle with the relationship of the *ekklēsia* to Israel as did Paul. Both Paul and Jesus did have some vision about salvation finally including both Jews and Gentiles in one people of God.

One of the most salient differences between Paul and Jesus is that they spent their lives and directed their ministries by and large to two different groups of people—Paul to Diaspora Gentiles and Jesus to Palestinian Jews. This may well explain various of the notable differences between Jesus and Paul on these mat-ters, but their respective places in the historical timetable and how they viewed salvation history as a result of that difference probably have more to do with their differences in perspective than anything else.

In the end both Paul and Jesus agreed on the most fundamental things. First, God had not abandoned his first chosen people, nor would they all be excluded from the final blessedness in the Dominion of God. Second, Gentiles could and would be included, though only with Jews in this final blessedness. Third, God never had more than one people at any point in human history.

Fourth, though both Paul and Jesus redefined "the Israel of God" on the basis of their definition of who was true Israel, and on the basis of their critique of such crucial matters as Torah and temple, neither of them simply envisioned the replacement of old Israel with a new one. Rather, new Israel grew out of old Israel, though with some significant differences that led to later distinctions.

Fifth, both Paul and Jesus rejected the belief that being a true Jew was defined or determined necessarily by one's heredity, and they rejected the belief that heredity allowed any Jewish individual to claim that God was obligated to fulfill his promises for him or her in particular, with or without a faith response to God's word.[2] This is confirmed by re-examining the material in part two above, which showed that both Paul and Jesus affirmed that certain moral requirements were prerequisites to entering or inheriting the final Dominion of God. God could raise up true children of Abraham from stones if he wished, and thus all Jews must be called to repent and believe the good news. This was the gospel both Paul and Jesus preached, and yet paradoxically it was also a gospel that gave Jews the first opportunity to respond and that prophesied that Jews would ultimately take part in the messianic banquet or final state of bliss.

Sixth, neither Paul nor Jesus seem to have affirmed the laws of clean and unclean, or for that matter the strict observance of the sabbath, at least in its Pharisaic form. It is also notable that Jesus said nothing about circumcision, and what Paul had to say about it is largely negative—since it was something that divided people in the *ekklēsia*.

Both Paul and Jesus seem to have had a vision of God's people united in one group on the basis of faith and doing God's moral will. As A. Segal has remarked, "From a legal perspective Paul may not have startled the Jewish Christian community so much by saying circumcision was unnecessary for Gentile salvation *per se*, as claiming that the saved Jews and Gentiles could form a single new community and freely interact."[3] Jesus does not speak of such a community existing before the eschaton. Nonetheless, his adaptation of John's call of everyone to repentance and faith, coupled with his acceptance of even notable sinners without observance of the ritual law, so long as they would repent and believe the good news, provided a new basis for receiving forgiveness from God, apart from the cult and ritual observance of the law.[4] He did also speak of a community he would found in the future that was to be based on individuals who affirmed some sort of messianic faith. This in turn prepared the way for the gospel as Paul preached it, a gospel that focused on neither Torah nor temple.

Lastly, both Paul and Jesus were part of an intramural debate about Israel and its future and also about who could be counted as a true Jew. Neither Paul nor Jesus could be said to be anti-Semitic, though both were strongly critical of early Judaism, especially in its Pharisaic form. In effect they both advocated a rather radical renovation or reinterpretation of early Judaism. Early Judaism was exceedingly diverse and complex, and in the end we may doubt whether even their radicalism should have placed them entirely beyond the boundaries of early Judaism. W. D. Davies in fact affirms that "the separation of Christians from Jews was a 'forced withdrawal' in which both sides were responsible."[5] Certainly, neither Paul nor Jesus ever ceased to see himself as a Jew striving to be faithful to his own vision of what the one true God required of him both as a Jew and as an individual called to be a *šālîaḥ* of God.[6]

PART FIVE

The
Day of the
Lord

—16—

Introduction

Part one discussed the chronological aspects of Paul's and Jesus' views on the event commonly called the parousia, but it is now time to investigate their views on the character of that event. It was not a part of early Jewish expectations about a Messiah that he would *return* to earth after his death. The idea of a *second* coming does not appear in the literature prior to the time of Jesus and Paul. We might well expect to find something unique about the teaching of Paul and perhaps even Jesus that stands out from its Jewish matrix. Paradoxically, these traditions about a return have a great deal of indebtedness to Old Testament ideas about theophanies and in particular the theophanic event known as the *Yom Yahweh*. Thus we will spend some time investigating Old Testament ideas about the "Day of the Lord."

The *Yom Yahweh*

Most scholars agree that the concept of the *Yom Yahweh* first emerges in the Old Testament with Amos in the middle of the eighth century B.C., though it draws on previous accounts of theophanies in the Old Testament.[1] There has been no end of debate about the origin of the concept. Does it ultimately derive from Old Testament Holy War traditions in which Yahweh intervenes in history and fights for his people, as G. Von Rad thought (see Zech 14:3)? Or should we see its origins as lying in the Old Testament cultus perhaps connected to some sort of New Year Festival, at which time Yahweh's enthronement was celebrated and dramatized, as S. Mowinckel suggested, or perhaps connected to some autumn cultic festival, as J. Gray alleged? Although we cannot debate this matter at length, a few comments are in order. On the one hand, Von Rad's arguments seem flawed because there are too many texts where the judgment connected with the *Yom Yahweh* is *on Israel,* not merely and in some cases not at all on their enemies (Amos 3:12-13; 5:15; Zeph 1; 3:11; Is 1:8-9; 7:17). On the other hand, as F. C. Fensham points out, there is no direct proof that Israel ever celebrated a New Year Festival following the Babylonian model.[2] It seems likely that at least in part the Sinai theophany and other Old Testament theophanies, perhaps with some influence from the Holy War traditions, have been drawn on to portray the *Yom Yahweh.*

What is more certain is that possibly as early as Amos, but more certainly in Zephaniah and the later prophetic literature the *Yom Yahweh* had taken on eschatological overtones and was used to describe a definitive and possibly final manifestation of God's redemptive-judgment. I use the term "redemptive-judgment" intentionally because almost always the concept that the phrase *Yom Yahweh* represents is an act of God's judgment on some which is at the same time a redemption of others. This is especially the case when the *Yom Yahweh* is said to be judgment on Israel's enemies and thereby redemption of Israel. Yet even when the *Yom Yahweh* is said to be directed against Israel, there is also almost always talk of a remnant that survives or is saved "though as through fire" (compare Zech 14:2). When a prophet uses the idea of the *Yom Yahweh,* most often the stress lies on judgment, on a *Dies Irae,* though this is not always the whole picture. Amos is, however, conveying the most characteristic idea when he says, "Woe to you who long for the *Yom Yahweh!* Why do you long for the *Yom Yahweh?* That day will be darkness, not light" (5:18). This accent on wrath speaks against the connection of the concept with any enthronement ceremony or positive celebration. Amos is suggesting that, contrary to popular belief, when Yahweh does indeed come it will be for judgment, even on his own people.[3]

The following motifs, found in the Sinai theophany recorded in Exodus 19 (see also 1 Kings 19), recur in various of the *Yom Yahweh* passages: descriptions of lightning, smoke, fire, earthquake and even cosmic upheaval. To these accompanying manifestations the *Yom Yahweh* traditions add the concept of judgment, sometimes even on Israel. This may also entail judgment on the land, sometimes taking the form of a locust plague (Joel 2) or some other form of destruction. For instance, Zephaniah 1:2-3 reads, "I will sweep away everything from the face of the earth. . . . I will sweep away both men and animals; I will sweep away the birds of the air and the fish of the sea. The wicked will have only heaps of rubble." It is not surprising that this day is then sometimes called "the Day of Yahweh's vengeance/wrath" (Is 22:5; 34:8; Zeph 1:18; 2:2-3; Ezra 7:19).

It is also crucial to bear in mind that the specific phrase *Yom Yahweh* is never used to describe days and events in the past. It is always applied to a coming or imminent judgment from God, and certainly as early as Zephaniah the concept has eschatological overtones. Interestingly, the *Yom Yahweh* traditions are several times connected with the idea of the flow of the nations to Israel at the end of history, only in this case the nations are not said to be converted to Judaism but are either instruments of God's wrath against Jerusalem (Zech 14) or are said to be more faithful to the one true God and his justice than are "the people of the house of Jacob" (Is 2). That the *Yom Yahweh* is not something confined to a literal twenty-four-hour day but rather is an event that goes on for some time is made clear in Isaiah 34:8 where *yom* parallels *sana* (year). The Day of Judgment is also called a year of retribution. One further development of the *Yom Yahweh* tradition bears mention at this point. By the time Malachi was written we find the idea of a prophet sent before "the great and terrible Day of the Lord" not merely to warn of the day's coming, but possibly by effecting change among Israel to avert the coming that will "smite the land with a curse" (Mal 4:5-6).

It is not possible here to show how the idea of a day of judgment associated with the final theophany of God developed in the extracanonical early Jewish literature. What is important to us is that in this so-called intertestamental literature the stress on judgment is developed even further than in the Old Testament, though the idea of redemption is also not absent from this material. For instance, we read in 1 Enoch 100:4-5:

> In those days, the angels shall descend into the secret places. They shall gather together into one place all those who gave aid to sin. And the most high will arise on that day of judgment in order to execute a great judgment upon all the sinners. He will set a guard of holy angels over all the righteous and holy

ones, and they shall keep them as the apple of the eye until all evil and sin are brought to an end.[4]

Note that the primary character of "that day" is judgment from which the righteous get protection. In 2 Enoch 66:6-11 likewise the righteous simply escape "the Lord's great judgment." It is not surprising in literature that arises out of a persecuted or oppressed group of Jews to find a stress on God's judgment on the nations, but it is telling that we also find, for example in the Testament of the Twelve Patriarchs, a stress on redemption as well as on judgment. For instance, in Testament of Judah 22:2 we read, "My rule shall be terminated by people of an alien race until the salvation of Israel comes, until the coming of the God of righteousness, so that Jacob may enjoy tranquility and peace, *as well as all the nations*" (my italics). Testament of Levi 4:4 is equally telling: "Blessing shall be given to you [Levis' sons] and to all your posterity until through his son's compassion [the king's] the Lord shall visit all the nations forever" (compare 18:1ff.). This is especially striking since the author of the document apparently saw the Day of Judgment as near at hand (see 1:1).[5] Yet there are also clear passages like Testament of Judah 23:3 where God's judgment against faithless Israel is spelled out in graphic detail. The *Yom Yahweh* is usually called the great Day of the Lord or the Day of Judgment, and it retains and in some cases enhances the Old Testament's stress on judgment, even on God's people, but there is also a message of redemption of the righteous connected with it.

A further source of background material that has bearing on our study is found when one explores the meaning and use of the term *parousia* before and during the New Testament period. The word means "presence" or "arrival." From the Ptolemaic period to the second century A.D. there is clear evidence that the term was used for the arrival of a ruler, king or emperor. The Latin equivalent was *adventus*. For instance, a third-century B.C. papyrus refers to a crown of gold to be presented to a king at his parousia.[6] Or again a parousia of King Ptolemy the Second (circa 113 B.C.), who called himself *sōtēr*, is expected and it is said "the provision of 80 artabae . . . was imposed for the *tou Basileōs parousian*. . . ."[7] Such examples from both the Hellenistic and Roman periods could be multiplied. For example, in memory of the visit of Nero to Corinth, special *adventus/parousia* coins were cast that read *Adventus aug[usti] Cor[inthi]*.[8] These coins were cast during the general period when Paul was writing to Corinth (1 Cor 15:23).

Equally interesting is the evidence G. D. Kilpatrick has collected showing that "parousia" often was the Hellenistic term for a theophany.[9] For instance, in the

Greek form of the Testament of the Twelve Patriarchs, at Testament of Judah 22:3(2) and Testament of Levi 8:15(11), we find it used to refer to the final coming of God. Josephus uses the term *parousia* for the divine appearances in the Old Testament theophanies *(Ant.* 3.80, 202-3; 9.55; compare 18.284). Of perhaps equal importance is another sort of "sacral" use of the term, found in an inscription from the Asclepion at Epidaurus, which reads *tan te p[a]rousian tan auto[u] [p]arenephanize ho Asklapio[s]*—"and Asclepius manifested his parousia"[10] (compare 2 Thess 2:8). It is important to realize that one should not make too sharp a distinction between the sacred and the profane use of *parousia*, not least because by Paul's time the emperor was already being given divine status of a sort. E. Best puts it this way:

> These two usages are not so far apart as might seem for court and sacral language are closely linked. It is difficult to believe that those who used the term in the Hellenistic world were unaware of this significance. . . . The word then was chosen to express the concept in Greek because it carried the nuance of movement and probably, . . . because it carried from Hellenistic culture the idea of a ceremonial visit of a ruler to his people which would be for them a joyful occasion.[11]

With this background we are prepared to examine the Pauline and Jesus traditions that draw on this sort of material and apply it either to the return of Christ or the coming of the Son of Man.

—17—

Perusing
the Parousia:
The Pauline
Evidence

Paul may have been the first person to use the term *parousia* to refer to the return of Christ.[1] The term itself does not mean "return" or a "second" coming; it simply means "arrival" or "presence." Applying it to Christ's coming from heaven in a sense changes what the word connotes. The word occurs twenty-four times in the New Testament, fourteen of which are in the Pauline letters. Paul and others used the term to refer to the arrival or presence of Paul or one of his coworkers (see 1 Cor 16:17; 2 Cor 7:6-7; 10:10; Phil 1:26; 2.12). Scholars have called Paul's use of a letter as a substitute for his physical presence "the apostolic parousia."[2] Neither of these uses concerns us here, except to say that they show that the term does not have to connote the arrival/presence of a deity or king.

It may seem puzzling that Paul only uses the term *parousia* of the coming of Christ from heaven in three letters, all of them early—1 Thessalonians where it is most prevalent (2:19; 3:13; 4:15; 5:23), 2 Thessalonians 2:1, 8-9 and 1 Corinthians 15:23. This is perhaps explained because the situations Paul was addressing in the Thessalonian correspondence and in 1 Corinthians required him to

speak at some length on matters pertaining to the eschatological future.[3] In 1 and
2 Thessalonians Paul must correct certain misunderstandings about future eschatology, while in 1 Corinthians Paul must correct an overrealized or overspiritual-
ized eschatology by setting over against it the eschatological future.

The phrase Paul more frequently uses to speak of Christ's return is the "Day
of the Lord" or the "Day of Christ." As W. Baird has so clearly demonstrated,
linguistic variety in talking about things eschatological is characteristic of the way
Paul approaches these matters even within one letter.[4] It is impossible to demonstrate a clear developmental schema in regard to Paul's thinking about Christ's
return. This becomes especially clear not merely because in the latest generally
undisputed Pauline letter Paul is still talking about "the Day of Christ Jesus"
(Phil 1:6) and "eagerly awaiting" his return from heaven (Phil 3:20), but also
because it is impossible to know how much weight to give to the contingency/
coherency factor. The stress on future eschatology early on and less emphasis in
later Pauline letters may as easily reflect the change in audience and problems
Paul is addressing as a change or shift in the apostle's thinking.

At this point I digress to consider ideas about the development of Paul's
thought since they affect how one views Paul's parousia teaching. The idea of a
decisive and enduring shift in Paul's eschatological thinking from a predominantly horizontal to a predominantly vertical (otherworldly) eschatology somewhere
between the time of 1 and 2 Corinthians is confounded by the fact that in the
crucial 2 Corinthians 5 text Paul speaks not only about being "at home with the
Lord" in heaven (v. 8) but also of "all appearing before the judgment seat of
Christ" at some time subsequent to being at home with the Lord (vv. 9b-10). This
conclusion is further confirmed by Baird's comparison of the "early" material in
1 Thessalonians 5 to the "late" material in Romans 13:

> Nevertheless, the notion that Paul has made a change in eschatological lan-
> guage which he consistently maintains is confounded by a comparison of
> Rom. xiii, one of Paul's latest letters with 1 Thess. v. The distinctive feature
> of these two texts is the description of the imminent eschaton (note the use
> of *kairos* in Rom. xiii.11; 1 Thess. v.2) in terms of contrast between night and
> day. In 1 Thess v.4, the Christians are told that they are not *en skotei* while
> in Rom. xiii.12 they are admonished to throw off the works *tou skotous*. In
> 1 Thess. v.6 the readers are instructed not to sleep, and in Rom. xiii.11 they
> are told it is time to wake up. In 1 Thess v.7 the faithful are warned against
> being *methuskomenoi* while in Rom. xiii.13 they are advised not to walk

methais. The Thessalonians are encouraged to put on *(enduō)* the breastplate of faith and love and the helmet of the hope of salvation (v.8); the Romans are instructed to put on *(enduō)* the armour of light (xiii.12).[5]
Even less convincing than the decisive shift between 1 and 2 Corinthians theory is the view of C. L. Mearns that the earliest eschatology of the church and of Paul was realized eschatology; future eschatology was developed because of the death of Christians and the need to correct enthusiasm.[6] At most one can say that Paul's eschatological language manifests a rich variety and complexity and as time went on he put less stress on future eschatology than he did in some of his earlier letters, for reasons that are not completely clear. This did not, however, amount to abandoning one form of eschatology for another, as Romans 13 and Philippians 1 and 3 make clear.

As time went on and it became clearer to Paul that his death was likely to come before the parousia, he quite naturally reflected more on life in heaven with the Lord. This increased focus on vertical eschatology is evident in those letters where his death may have seemed rather near (such as 2 Corinthians and Philippians). In short, the contingent circumstances of Paul's audience or of Paul's own life may best explain the differences of eschatological emphasis and focus in Paul's various letters.[7] Paul never really de-eschatologizes his thought. In fact, he does not even expunge the purely future elements of this eschatology even in his latest letter. His thought has an eschatological framework from start to finish, but unless we bear in mind the interplay of Paul's soteriology, Christology and *theo*logy with that eschatological framework we will not fully understand his thinking. The eschatological framework is shaped especially by Paul's belief that Jesus is the crucified and risen Messiah who has *already* made salvation available to all but has *not yet* completed the full work of salvation. This is why Paul can speak of salvation as both present and yet future.

Also, because of his Christology, Paul (1) speaks without precedent from his Jewish background of a *return* of Messiah from heaven; (2) bifurcates the resurrection into that of Christ and that of those who belong to him;[8] (3) speaks of the final judgment sometimes as an act of God and sometimes as an act of Christ; and (4) speaks of the *Yom Yahweh* sometimes focusing on Christ's role and sometimes focusing on God's. The already/not-yet tension in Paul's eschatology is caused by what he believes is already true about Jesus Christ and has been accomplished by him, *and* by what he will yet do at the parousia. Paul never totally resolves this tension either by stressing the already at the expense of the not yet or vice versa, precisely because he always believes that he stands between the resurrection of Christ and his return. Philippians 3:20 must be given its full weight—Paul was still eagerly awaiting the Lord from heaven even as his life approached its end.

Behind all of Paul's theologizing stands the christological narrative of faith about one Jesus who came, died, rose and would return. For Paul the performance of this narrative on the stage of history is still in *medius res*. Paul cannot conclude the drama prematurely, for the main actor must first return to the stage for a final act. I would thus suggest that partially fulfilled messianism is the essence of Paul's thought and largely explains why the eschatological framework takes the shape it does in his thought.[9] With these things in mind, we must now return to the discussion of Paul's use of parousia language.

It is reasonable to expect Paul to use the royal imagery and accompanying appropriate metaphors and terms when he speaks of Christ's parousia, and we might expect the description of "the Day of the Lord" to draw more on Old Testament theophanic and *Yom Yahweh* traditions. To a certain extent this expectation is justified, but since it is also the case that "parousia" could refer to the arrival of a deity, it is not surprising that in some Pauline texts where the term is used we also find theophanic terms and imagery. As we shall see, 1 Thessalonians 4:13—5:11 bears evidence of this sort of cross-fertilization of ideas. Also, for Paul the parousia, the final judgment and the resurrection of the dead are closely intertwined, the latter two being dependent on the former event. Thus, there is some overlap of ideas from traditions about resurrection as well as from those about the *Yom Yahweh*. I am reserving my discussion of resurrection until part six in order to focus better here on the initial event that precipitates the other eschatological events—the "arrival" of Christ from heaven.

Paul's first reference to the parousia is at 1 Thessalonians 2:19. It is clear that the meaning of the term here is "arrival" since Paul conveys the idea of presence by another phrase *(emprosthen tou kyriou)* and since he says *en tē autou parousia*—"in/at his arrival/coming." A distinct note of joy permeates this whole passage, and there is no hint that the converts will undergo judgment. Paul speaks of his converts being his crown in which he will boast when the Lord comes. It seems probable that Paul is drawing on the idea of a joyful celebration when a parousia of a king happens. It may also be that the reference to the crown is drawn from such a complex of ideas (see above on the Flinders Petrie Papyrus, which reads in part *allou stephanou parousias iB)*. What Paul will present to the

King when he returns is his converts who are his crown. F. F. Bruce is right when he says, "When Christians spoke of the parousia of their Lord, they probably thought of the pomp and circumstance attending those imperial visits as parodies of the true glory to be revealed on the day of Christ."[10]

At 1 Thessalonians 3:13 is a similarly worded phrase, only God the Father has been added to what was said in 2:19. Now converts will be in the presence of the Father *en tē parousia tou kyriou hēmōn Iēsou meta pantōn tōn hagiōn autou.* Here Paul has drawn not only on secular parousia traditions but also on the *Yom Yahweh* material found in Zechariah 14:5 (LXX), which speaks of the coming of the Lord God with *pantes hoi hagioi.* It is not surprising then that overtones of judgment are found in 1 Thessalonians 3:13. The converts are being presented to God and Christ for his final review. The hope is that they will be seen to be blameless and holy on that day. Here it is appropriate to remark that the eschatological material in 3:13 serves a parenetic function (cf. 1 Cor 15:32-34, 58). In fact, 1 Thessalonians 4—5 and Romans 13 are set in *paranetic* sections of their respective Epistles.[11] Paul is indeed writing as a pastor attempting to exhort and encourage his converts about various matters; the eschatological material is not purely didactic in function.[12] In view of the Zechariah 14 background here, it seems likely that *hagioi* in 1 Thessalonians 3:13 refers to angels, not believers.[13] Thus Jesus will not come alone at the parousia.

The next reference to the parousia is in the midst of a complex paranetic section in which Paul is trying to reassure the Thessalonians about Thessalonian Christians who have already died.[14] The function of 1 Thessalonians 4:13-18 is to encourage (v. 18) the Thessalonians by assuring them that the Christian dead are at no disadvantage because they have died prior to the parousia.[15] Indeed, Paul makes clear that the dead will take precedence over the living in the resurrection and in the going to meet Christ in the air.

For our purposes several points are of considerable importance. Paul clearly connects the parousia here with both the resurrection and the meeting with Christ in the air. The latter two are precipitated by and thus depend on the parousia. Paul sees all three of these eschatological events as made possible only by Jesus' own death and resurrection. This comports with 1 Corinthians 15 where, for Paul, Jesus' resurrection is presented as the first portion of the general resurrection. The apostle believes that Christ's resurrection makes certain that believers will likewise be resurrected. This is clearly implied in 1 Thessalonians 4:14-16 and stated explicitly in 1 Corinthians 15.

Second, there are no connotations of judgment here. Thus, while the material
presented by Klijn from 4 Ezra 4:1-5 is interesting, it has to do with the simul-
taneous appearance of the living and the dead at the final judgment, not the
meeting of the Lord in the air by both the living and the dead.[16] Paul here is
sailing in waters that are basically uncharted in early Jewish apocalyptic and
eschatological literature.

Third, verse 14 says that God will bring with Jesus *(achei syn autō)* the dead.
This might suggest that the Christian saints are returning with Christ from heav-
en. If verse 16 is an explanation of what Paul means by "bring with him" in verse
14, then what he means is that when Christ comes the dead in Christ will be
raised. Paul does not pause to explain how the dead in Christ are reunited with
their bodies, or whether at this stage in his thinking he believes that the Christian
dead are "asleep" with their bodies rather than being in heaven until Christ
returns.[17] In view of what Paul says elsewhere in 2 Corinthians 4—5 and in view
of precedents in early Jewish literature for a belief in life in heaven, it is probable
that Paul already believed when he wrote 1 Thessalonians that to be away from
the body means to be present with the Lord.[18] Paul's purpose here, however, is
not to offer speculation on the relationship of the resurrection to life in heaven.
It is perhaps significant that here as in 1 Corinthians 15 Paul says nothing about
the resurrection of the non-Christian dead. What verses 14-15 do suggest is that
Paul sees the dead Christians as persons who still can be addressed and com-
manded at the parousia.[19]

Fourth, from Paul's description of what accompanies the parousia, namely the
loud command, the voice of the archangel and the trumpet call of God, it seems
clear that Paul sees the parousia as a public event. Here only audible, rather than
visible, factors make this apparent. The reference to clouds in verse 17 perhaps
also reflects the use of the Old Testament theophanic imagery, but this is uncertain since Paul is talking about a meeting in the air that naturally suggests the
reference to clouds. It is possible that the three audible components that announce the parousia are three different ways to describe one phenomenon.[20]
More important, Paul is likely drawing on *Yom Yahweh* traditions for the tradition about the trumpet blast (see Is 27:13; Joel 2:1; Zech 9:14; 2 Esdras 6:23;
Sib. Oracl. 4:174; 1 Cor 15:52), though the other two audible phenomena are
apparently unprecedented in the literature. In any case, the reference to the archangel confirms our earlier interpretation of the *hagioi* in 1 Thessalonians 3:13.

It is probable that Paul is drawing on the secular parousia imagery, for when a king went to visit a city his herald would go before him to the city walls to announce with trumpet blast and audible words the coming of the king. It might even include the "cry of command" to open up the city gates so as to let the visiting monarch in (compare the use of this tradition in the entrance liturgy in Ps 24:7-10).

This suggestion becomes more than a conjecture when we point out that in 1 Thessalonians 4:17 Paul refers to the *apantēsin.* Cicero, in the course of his description of Julius Caesar's tour through Italy in 49 B.C., says, "Just imagine what *apantēseis* he is receiving from the towns, what honors are paid to him" *(Ad. Att.* 8.16.2; compare 16.11.6 of Octavian). This word refers to the action of the greeting committee that goes out to meet the king or dignitary at his parousia who is paying an official visit to the town, and escort him back into the town on the final part of his journey. "These analogies (especially in association with the term *parousia)* suggest the possibility that the Lord is pictured here as escorted the remainder of his journey to earth by his people—both those newly raised from the dead and those who have remained alive."[21] Thessalonica, a Hellenistic town founded by the Macedonian king Cassander, was a free city within the Roman Empire from 42 B.C. The recipients of 1 Thessalonians would surely have been familiar with what Paul was implying by the use of the secular Hellenistic language of a parousia.

It is more than likely that while Paul does not tell us where the Lord and the Christians go after meeting in the air, the inference that he intended and that his audience would have taken was that they all would return to earth together. This means that while Paul does speak of a "rapture" into the clouds to meet the Lord, he is not to be taken as an early advocate of the Dispensationalist view of a pretribulation rapture of the saints so that they will avoid the messianic woes that precede the end of history.[22]

Indeed, Paul seems to affirm that he and other Christians have already been experiencing such woes since Christ's death and resurrection. Thus he speaks of "the sufferings of this present time" (Rom 8:18) or "the present distress" (1 Cor 7:26). First Thessalonians 3:4 would seem to point in the same direction—"we told you beforehand that we were to suffer affliction" (RSV). Romans 1:18 says, "The wrath of God is *presently* being revealed from heaven." Finally, if Colossians is Pauline, it points in the same direction: "I complete what is lacking in Christ's afflictions" (1:24 RSV). Of this last text E. Lohse has written:

The concept of a definite measure for the last days determines the phrase "what is lacking in Christ's afflictions." Just as God has set a definite measure in time (cf. 4 Ez. 4.36f.; Gal. 4.4) and has determined the limitation of the tribulations at the end (Mk. 13.5-27; par.), so he has also decreed a definite measure for the sufferings which the righteous and the martyrs must endure (1 En. 47.1-4; 2 Bar. 30.2). When this has been completed, the end is at hand.[23] J. J. Collins adds, an "accurate generalization of apocalyptic patterns might say that the final judgment is preceded by a time of great distress, which may on occasion contain a historical description of the time of the author, but most often is future prediction, either entirely or in part."[24]

That Paul might have affirmed that Christians would suffer in the great tribulation before the end is not surprising since in early Judaism a belief in the saints going through the tribulation was not uncommon. Thus we find the idea in Daniel 7:21-22, *Jubilees* 23:23, *Assumption of Moses* 9:1-7, *Apocalypse of Elijah* 4:21 and 1 QH III,13—IV,26.[25] Evidence also exists that some early Jews, such as some of those at Qumran, believed that the great tribulation had already begun or was beginning (see 4 Ezra 5—6; 9:3; *M. Sota* 9:15; *Assump. Mos.* 8—9; 1 QH III—IV). If this was indeed Paul's belief, as seems to be the case, it may in part explain why he could so readily speak of the possible imminence of the parousia. Yet when we consider 2 Thessalonians 2, even if Paul does believe he and other Christians are already suffering the messianic woes, it does not follow that Paul could not also conceive of certain important events still being yet to come prior to the parousia.

Since we have discussed 1 Thessalonians 5:1-11 in chapter two and will examine it again when we look at Paul's use of the phrase "Day of the Lord/Christ," and since this material does not use the word *parousia,* I will not examine this material here.[26] It is appropriate however to ask whether Paul is drawing on oral or written sources in 1 Thessalonians 4:13—5:11.

Paul tells us in 1 Thessalonians 4:15 that he is drawing on sources, but this reference has been understood in various ways: (1) that 4:15 refers to a revelation of the exalted Lord either to Paul himself or to a Christian prophet; (2) that 4:15 cites an *agraphon,* an otherwise lost saying of Jesus; and (3) that Paul is drawing on some version of a saying from the Jesus tradition—possibly something like Matthew 24:31: "And he will send his angels with a loud trumpet call, and they will gather his elect from the four winds, from one end of the heavens to the other." If this saying does lie in the background here Paul has certainly offered an interpretive paraphrase of it. Most scholars have of late tended to favor the view that Paul is quoting an utterance of a Christian prophet or sharing his own personal revelation.[27] Yet we should not lightly dismiss Paul's drawing on the Jesus tradition not only in 1 Thessalonians 4:15 but throughout 4:13—5:11.[28]

For one thing, there are many echoes in this material and in 2 Thessalonians 1—2 of the eschatological discourse recorded in Mark 13/Matthew 24/Luke 21. Beasley-Murray points out the following:

1) 1 Thess 4:15ff. = Mk 13:26-27/Mt 24:31;

2) 1 Thess 5:1-5 = Mk 13:32-33/Lk 21:24-35;

3) 1 Thess 5:6ff. = Mk 13:35-36; cf. vv. 33, 37;

4) 1 Thess 5:4-10 = Mk 13:22;

5) 2 Thess 1:11-12 = Lk 21:36;

6) 2 Thess 2:1-2 = Mk 13:26-27;

7) 2 Thess 2:3 = Mk 13:5/Mt 24:12;

8) 2 Thess 2:4ff. = Mk 13:14;

9) 2 Thess 2:7 = Mt 24:12;

10) 2 Thess 2:8-12 = Mk 13:22; cf. Lk 24:11; Mk 1:36;

11) 2 Thess 2:13 = Mk 13:27; cf. Lk 21:8;

12) 2 Thess 2:15 = Mk 13:23; cf. v. 31.[29]

D. Wenham tries to demonstrate that a presynoptic eschatological discourse of Jesus circulated in the early church that Paul and others may have used.[30] I would not rule out either the existence of such a discourse or Paul's use of it.

The two most solid parallels in 1 Thessalonians 4:13—5:11 to the synoptic eschatological discourse are the thief-in-the-night motif and the coming of the Lord from heaven.[31] Most of the parallels listed above come from 2 Thessalonians, not 1 Thessalonians. In Beasley-Murray's later assessments of Mark 13 and parallels he has argued that Mark drew together various traditions from various sources and wrote them up in his own style.[32] For my part it seems probable that Mark 13 and parallels is a composite of various different early Jesus traditions. If there was a Q apocalypse the situation may have been different, but we cannot be sure of this.[33] I would add that the cumulative effect of the above list of biblical references is that it appears that Paul has drawn on and added to one or two Jesus logia in his eschatological discussions in 1 Thessalonians 4—5, and that he seems to be more heavily dependent on such traditional material in 2 Thessalonians 1—2. Since 1 and 2 Thessalonians were written at such an early date (circa A.D. 50), we may have evidence here that Paul was familiar with important parts of the Jesus tradition even before he began his missionary work. If so it should not surprise us that Paul's essential views on eschatological matters are consonant with what we can reconstruct of Jesus' views on these matters.

Our next text for scrutiny is 1 Thessalonians 5:23, which is in essence the reformulation of what we have seen at 3:11-13. In both cases we are dealing with a wish prayer. Here again Paul stresses the prerequisite of a certain sort of moral character as necessary if one is to be prepared to meet the Lord at his parousia. This is reminiscent of our discussion of the Dominion sayings in Paul. Here the emphasis is on God's sanctifying work in the believer, whereas those texts place more stress on human conduct. Paul expects this process of sanctification to be complete at the parousia, or at least to be completed at the parousia, more likely the former.[34] Verse 24 reassures the audience that God will finish the good work he has begun in them. The paranetic thrust and function of this material is once again evident.

When we turn to 2 Thessalonians 2:1, 8-9, we find a tale of two parousias, one of Christ (vv. 1, 8) and one of the "man of lawlessness" (v. 9). The former is a royal and divine one, while the latter is a pseudo-divine one. The "man of lawlessness," as in the story of a pagan god's parousia into his temple (see above on Asclepius), will come into God's temple, proclaiming himself to be God (or a god). In 2 Thessalonians 2:8 Jesus, by contrast, is said to take on the role of the Prince of the House of David mentioned in Isaiah 11:4 (LXX) who comes to "smite the earth with the word of his mouth and destroy the wicked one with breath through his lips."

In this same verse we have the only New Testament occurrence outside of the Pastoral Epistles of the term *epiphaneia*. Like *parousia,* this term is another cultic word meaning "appearing" that was also used of divinized emperors or the visible appearing of a god.[35] The point of the seemingly redundant phrase *tē epiphaneia tēs parousias autou,* "with the appearing of his coming," is to make Christ's parousia seem more grand and significant than that of "the man of lawlessness." Christ's coming involves the appearing of one who is truly royal *and* divine, whereas the coming of the "man of lawlessness" is simply the coming of a false god. The use of *epiphaneia* may also be because Paul apparently sees this man of lawlessness as a political figure in the mold of an Antiochus Epiphanes who desecrated the temple. Perhaps more fresh in Paul's mind would be Gaius Caligula, who attempted to have his statue set up in the Jerusalem temple in order to assert his claims of divinity in A.D. 40 (Philo *Leg. Gai.* 203-346; Josephus *Ant.* 18:261-301). Jesus then is presented as a counter political force of greater power who will come as the Prince of David and destroy the man of lawlessness.

Much in 2 Thessalonians 2:1-12 is obscure; thus it is not surprising that there are almost as many conjectures as commentaries about the man of lawlessness and *to katechon* (v. 6). Unfortunately, Paul is covering ground that he already covered in part with his audience (v. 5) and so he simply assumes they will understand this presentation of eschatological truth that uses apocalyptic language to a certain extent to convey its message. For us, who do not have this prior information, the material is necessarily cryptic and no good purpose is served here by engaging in further speculation.[36]

What can be said with reasonable certainty can be summed up as follows. First, Paul is trying to correct the impression of some Thessalonians that the parousia, also called the Day of the Lord (v. 2), is already present.[37] Second, Paul corrects this impression by referring to certain events that must precede the parousia, namely the *apostasia,* which can mean political rebellion or religious apostasy and here may convey some of both ideas, and the coming of the man of lawlessness. These events, or at least the latter of them, have not yet occurred (compare vv. 7-8) and so Paul's point is that even the necessary preliminary events that immediately precede the parousia of Christ have yet to transpire. Third, 2:1 once again refers to the same idea we have seen in 1 Thessalonians 4:17, namely the gathering of Christians to Christ when he comes. Fourth, in addition to this positive notion, parousia as applied to Christ in this passage clearly is associated with an act of judgment by Christ on the "son of perdition." The purpose of this material is to inject a note of eschatological reserve into a group of Christians with some form of overrealized eschatology, which in turn may have affected the willingness of some of them to work (see 3:6-11).

Finally, in early Jewish and Christian eschatology the theology of imminence or of a sudden end could be and was often juxtaposed with an accounting of some events usually involving a time of tribulation and distress that must transpire before the end. Sometimes the language of imminence is even accompanied by periodization or calculations. The New Testament writers are notably reticent about offering specific calculations but they do juxtapose the language of imminence with the recounting of preliminary events that must come first. This is seen not only in the Thessalonian correspondence, the synoptic apocalypse and the book of Revelation, but also in the Qumran literature and in some of the pseudepigraphical material (see 1 QM passim on preparations for the work of the community members in the imminent messianic woes; see 2 Bar 36-40 and

2 Esdras 10:60-12:35 on calculation).

One should not argue that 2 Thessalonians 2 is non-Pauline since it entails the chronicling of events prior to the parousia. Paul would have seen no contradiction between what is said in 1 Thessalonians 4—5 and what is said here. For Paul the mystery of lawlessness is already at work, but the "man of lawlessness" has not yet made his appearance nor has Christ come back. There is an already and a not-yet even to the preliminary eschatological events. The mystery of lawlessness that may perhaps be associated with the suffering of the messianic woes is already happening. The *apostasia* and the man of lawlessness are yet to come.

The final parousia text is in the middle of Paul's lengthy discussion about the resurrection in 1 Corinthians 15. At verse 23 Paul is in the midst of chronicling the climactic events of human history in some sort of order *(tagma)*. Here the resurrection of believers is integrally connected with and dependent on the parousia of Christ. As such this material varies little from 1 Thessalonians 4. Once again Paul says nothing about a resurrection of the non-Christians at the parousia. It is not completely clear whether Paul thinks parousia and resurrection of the Christians precipitates what he calls the end *(telos)*, which could entail some further eschatological events, or whether parousia and resurrection constitutes "the end" after which we have the eternal Dominion of God upon earth.[38] The use of *eita* in 24a would seem to favor the former view, while the content of verse 24 favors the latter. What is not in doubt is that for Paul the resurrection of Christians amounts to the overcoming of the last enemy, death, and so the parousia is what triggers the final triumph of Christ over the forces of darkness.

Here we must consider those passages where Paul uses the phrase "the Day," or "the Day of the Lord/Christ." That Paul means the same event by these phrases as the parousia is evident from the fact that the terms are used interchangeably in some of the passages we have already discussed (see 1 Thess 5:2, 4 which has both "the Day" and "the Day of the Lord"). It is interesting that in Paul's earlier letters we find either the phrase "the Day" (1 Thess 5:4; 1 Cor 3:13; Rom 2:5; compare 13:12) or "the Day of the Lord" (1 Thess 5:2; 2 Thess 2:2; 1 Cor 5:5) or even "the Day of our Lord Jesus Christ" (1 Cor 1:8) or "the Day of the Lord Jesus" (2 Cor 1:14). Philippians, however, has "the Day of Christ Jesus" (1:6) or "the day of Christ" (1:10; 2:16) without the qualifier "Lord."[39]

It has often been conjectured, probably rightly, that Paul has taken over the "Day of the Lord" phrase from the Septuagint and instead of using it to refer to Yahweh he now predicates it of Christ. That such a transfer has been made is clear from comparing 1 Thessalonians 4:14-17 to 5:2. Whether Paul is the first to make this transfer of the *Yom Yahweh* language is uncertain. However, this usage is perfectly logical in view of the early Christian confession "Jesus is Lord," which Paul takes up and uses. It is simply a matter of pursuing the logic of the confession to its end. The christological importance of this transfer of the titles of Yahweh to Christ should not be minimized as it means that, for Paul, Christ is to be confessed and worshiped as in some sense God. In the use of the *Yom Yahweh* language, however, the focus is on Christ taking over the *functions* of Yahweh, bringing in the final judgment and redemption that is predicated of Yahweh in the Old Testament.[40]

It should not surprise us that when Paul uses the *Yom Yahweh* language the theme of judgment is usually found in the immediate context. Thus, for instance, in 1 Thessalonians 5:3, which follows our first reference to "the Day of the Lord," we read, "destruction will come on them suddenly." This comports with the use of the thief-in-the-night metaphor that stresses the sudden unexpected intrusion aspect of the parousia. In both 1 Thessalonians 5 and Romans 13 there is a play on the contrast between day and night in conjunction with talking about preparedness for the coming of "the Day." Though Christ will come like a thief in the night, when he does so "the Day" will dawn. In 1 Thessalonians 5:5 "the Day" is associated with light and Christians are by the use of a Semitic phrase labeled "sons of the Day."

In 1 Corinthians 3:13 we read again of judgment on "the Day," involving a fire that will test the quality of a Christian's or perhaps in particular a Christian church planter's works. The individual Christian escapes, but only like one passing through the flames, even if his work is burned up (v. 15). It is important to recognize that 3:15 is an analogy (compare Amos 4:11) that is meant to indicate a narrow escape, not literally to describe the condition of the believer on that day. Nonetheless, the theme of final judgment somehow affecting the believer strikes a note we have not come across in our discussion. The theme of exposure of the true character of something at the final judgment is conventional. Once again, the material has a paranetic function meant to inculcate care in one's actions, especially in regard to how one builds the *ekklēsia.*

In Romans 2:5 Paul speaks of "the Day of God's wrath," a day when God's righteous judgment will be revealed. The subject of this activity is God, not Christ (compare 2:2-3). Yet 2:16 shows that for Paul both God and Christ are involved in this final judgment, for he says that God will judge people's secrets *dia Chris-*

tou Iēsou. He has already mentioned the idea of God and Christ working together on "the Day" in 1 Thessalonians 4:14—it is God who brings Jesus at the parousia. Here, as in Romans 13:11-14 the reference to "the Day" of judgment serves a paranetic purpose—to encourage moral earnestness, good deeds, repentant hearts, preparedness and the like. The use of the term *apokalypsis* makes evident that only on "that Day" will the condition of a human being become fully evident. God is not unjust for he renders "to each according to his works," quoting the Old Testament principle from Psalm 62:12 and Proverbs 24:12.[41] It may also be that Paul is drawing on Zephaniah 1:15, 18, 2:2-3 and 3:8 for the idea of the *Yom Yahweh* as a day of wrath. In the Romans passage Paul seems to be drawing on the Jewish idea of a treasury of works that provides a sort of "heavenly bank account."[42] This idea is found in the Jesus tradition (Mt 6:19-20; Lk 12:33) and is well known in early Judaism (see Tob 4:9-10; 4 Ezra 6:5; 7:77; 8:33, 36; Apoc. Bar. 14:12). Paul, however, has turned the treasury of merits into a treasury of wrath. What some are storing up is more and more judgment for themselves![43]

Since we have dealt with 2 Thessalonians 2:2 we pass on to 1 Corinthians 5:5. Here Paul speaks of a redemptive-judgment that happens on "the Day of the Lord." On the one hand, this verse could mean that the body will be destroyed but the human spirit saved on the Day of the Lord.[44] On the other hand, the contrast could be between *sarx* as sinful inclination/nature, the "flesh" in a moral sense, and the human spirit. In view of 1 Corinthians 15 where Paul indicates that the body will have a part in final salvation it seems unlikely that Paul might be suggesting some sort of spiritual salvation apart from the body. While some Corinthians might have believed that the body was doomed to destruction but the spirit was immortal or savable, Paul did not. In addition, if in fact the phrase "destruction of the flesh" means physical death, here it is difficult to see how that could be remedial. Yet clearly from the purpose clause Paul intends this action to be remedial *(hina to pneuma sothē).* It is thus likely, as most early church commentators suggested (Origen, Chrysostom, Theodore of Mopsuestia), that Paul means that the man should be put outside the Christian community for the destruction of what was carnal in him, his sinful inclinations, so that he might ultimately experience eschatological salvation.[45] If this is the correct interpretation, then Paul is talking about temporal judgment now, but salvation at the "Day of the Lord."

Like some of the earlier texts we examined, 1 Corinthians 1:8 stresses moral preparedness for the Day of the Lord, though it makes clear, since this is a promise, that God is the one who keeps them strong to the end. In content 1 Corinthians 1:8 is almost exactly the same as 1 Thessalonians 5:23, though the language has been modified a bit. First Corinthians 1:8 involves a promise; 1 Thessalonians 5:23 a wish prayer. First Corinthians 1:8 speaks of "the Day of the Lord Jesus Christ," the most expansive of Paul's phrases for the return of Christ; 1 Thessalonians 5:23 speaks of the parousia. First Corinthians 1:8 speaks of being "irreproachable" *(anenklētous)*; 1 Thessalonians 5:23 of "being kept blameless" *(amemptōs)*. Both verses use *en* to introduce the phrase about the parousia/Day. The nearly identical phrasing in these two verses must be taken as strong evidence that for Paul the parousia equals the Day of the Lord Jesus.

In 2 Corinthians 1:14 Paul boasts of his converts (presumably to the Lord) "in the Day of the Lord Jesus." This seems to suggest that Paul expects to be a witness at the final review of Christians. One of the distinctive features of the Pauline letters is the way Paul uses *kauchēma* "boasting." Of the fifty times this word and its cognates appear in the New Testament, forty-six of them occur in Paul's letters. Ordinarily this term refers to an arrogance or vanity that deserves condemnation. Paul, however, uses it most often in a positive sense to refer to justified pride in something or someone.[46] G. B. Caird suggests that the use of this language is a carryover from Paul's Pharisaic days when he believed that a person's destiny depends on his/her record. For a Pharisee like Paul it was not enough just to pass God's scrutiny, one must excel in life and so pass with something of which one could be justly proud.[47]

We must always keep in mind that when Paul speaks of the events that ensue at the parousia and he associates them with the End *(telos;* see 1 Cor 1:8; 15:24), he is referring to the end of the present world order, but he also believes that at "the end" another world order will begin.[48] He calls this eschatological world order "the Dominion of God." In short, when Paul speaks of "the end" he is not referring to the "end of the world" in the sense of the complete destruction and termination of the earth and universe or the end of all human life or relationships. In 2 Corinthians 1:14 Paul suggests a time of celebration when he may converse with his Lord and brag about the faith and perhaps also the lives and deeds of his converts. On the whole, Paul is noticeably reticent to describe or discuss the life to come on earth when Christ returns. He simply uses phrases like "we shall be with the Lord forever" or "we shall inherit the Dominion." There can be little doubt, especially in view of 1 Corinthians 15, that he does envision such a future life happening on earth. Resurrection of the body and renewal of the earth (see

Rom 8) is integral to Paul's view of the completion of the process of redemption. Philippians 1:6 is very much of a piece with 1 Thessalonians 5:23 and 1 Corinthians 1:8. Once again we have a word of encouragement. Paul assures his converts that God will carry to completion his work in them "until the Day of Christ Jesus."[49] The advice and encouragement Paul gives on such matters he gives with a real sense of urgency. This is because "the advent was imminent . . . in the sense that it might happen at any time, not because it must happen within a given period of time."[50] Philippians 3:20 makes clear that Paul loses neither his belief in imminence nor the urgency that comes from that belief in his later letters. More often in Paul's letters he expresses this urgency as a sense of anticipation of the good that is to come as a result of God's work in believers, as in Philippians 1:6, but sometimes this sense of urgency involves real anxiety for Paul when some of his converts seem in danger of apostasy and of missing out on the Dominion of God (see 1 Cor 9:27; Rom 11:21-22; Gal 5:21).

Philippians stands out from the earlier Epistles in its use of the phrase "the Day of Christ" or "Day of Christ Jesus," but the content differs little from what we have heard before. Philippians 1:10 in fact is an even closer parallel to 1 Thessalonians 5:23 and especially 1 Corinthians 1:8 than is Philippians 1:6. Once again Paul offers a wish prayer that his converts may be morally discerning in their choices and conduct and so be blameless/faultless *(aproskopos) eis hēmeran Christou.*[51] Philippians 2:15 echoes this same theme, and verse 16 reiterates Paul's desire to boast of his converts when Christ returns. The ideas Paul associates with the parousia/Day of the Lord vary little from the earliest to the latest of Paul's undisputed letters.

Paul is not limited to using either the word *parousia* or the phrase "Day of" when he wishes to talk about the return of Christ. For instance, at 2 Thessalonians 1:7 he speaks of the revelation *(apokalypsis)* of our Lord Jesus Christ from heaven (compare Phil 3:20), and we read virtually the same words in 1 Corinthians 1:7.[52] In both cases Paul uses apocalyptic language to describe the parousia.

Finally, note how Paul can speak of Christians appearing before the *bēma* of Christ for judgment of their deeds and receiving their just due accordingly (2 Cor 5:10). "The life of faith does not free the Christian from the life of obedience."[53] Rather one may insist that grace or justification by faith equips the believer for such a life.[54] There is little doubt that the middle aorist subjunctive *komisētai,* "receive," has a retributive force here (see Eph 6:8; Col 3:25).[55] Paul also makes clear that this judgment is distributive—each *(hekastos)* will receive according to what she or he has done. We are not judged as a group, but the whole life of each believer is seen as a unity that can be looked back on *(prassein* is in the aorist).[56] While it is possible that the "we all" refers to all persons, in light of whom Paul is addressing in verses 9-10, the object of this judgment is probably the sum total of all Christians.[57] *Phaulos* here should probably be translated worthless, poor or paltry rather than simply evil *(kakos).*[58] Notice that Paul can equally well in Romans 14:10-12 speak of Christians appearing before the *bēma* of God and giving an account to him. Paul's basic view of what will happen at the parousia does not seem to change much throughout his letters, but he uses a variety of ways to express the same set of ideas.

These ideas may be summarized as follows: (1) Christ will return with his angels; (2) the elect will be gathered to him in the air and whether they are dead or alive they will also receive resurrection bodies; (3) the deeds/words/intentions of Christians will be reviewed and judged, and they will be rewarded or punished accordingly. Thus, Paul repeatedly urges and prays for his believers' moral preparedness for "the Day," which is associated with both judgment and redemption by God or Christ or both. It is not clear where Paul draws the line between conduct that keeps one out of the final Dominion of God and conduct that is merely punished while the believer ends up being saved. (4) Paul is also notably silent on the future resurrection or judgment of non-believers, though clearly he believes that various morally unprepared people will be excluded from the Dominion (see Gal 5:21). This is probably because in his letters he is too busy exhorting and preparing those who are Christians to comment on the fate of others (but compare Rom 2:7-10). (5) Paul envisions being able to boast about his converts to Christ on "the Day." (6) In view of the various events Paul associates with "the Day" it is rather clear that he does not envision "the Day" as a twenty-four-hour day but as a period of time that begins with the event of Christ's return from heaven to earth.

By way of conclusion I may also point out that we have seen that Paul uses the term *parousia* or the phrase "Day of the Lord" interchangeably for the same event. It is also striking that Paul's use of these terms is confined to some of his earlier letters—1 and 2 Thessalonians and 1 and 2 Corinthians. Yet this is primarily a matter of terminology, for the idea of the "Day" is also in evidence in Romans 2:5-16 and 13:11-14, and is especially clear in Philippians 1:6, 10, 2:16 and 3:.20, though now Paul calls it the Day of Jesus Christ. We should not argue that Paul abandoned his theology of the return of the Lord at any point during his ministry. Nor does he exchange a purely future eschatology for a realized one. There is, however, understandably more emphasis given to vertical eschatology as time goes on and Paul sees himself as more likely than not to die before the parousia.

Paul uses the parousia language to convey the idea of a royal and divine coming of Christ while he predominantly draws on the *Yom Yahweh* material when he speaks of the "Day of the Lord." Yet the imagery does overlap. Judgment can be discussed even when the term *parousia* is used, and redemption can be in focus when either the parousia or the *Yom Yahweh* language is used. The parousia language is used to express the idea of a rapture of living and dead believers when Christ returns, but the use of this terminology leads one to think that he believes that the sequel entails a return to earth with Christ. Paul is also capable of holding in tension a belief in events that must precede "the Day" but also a belief in the possible imminence of "the Day." In most of these matters Paul does draw on Jewish eschatological and apocalyptic ideas. However, since Paul now views such matters in the light of Christ he reinterprets the tradition he has inherited so that he may convey the unique idea of a *return* of Messiah from heaven, and of Messiah sitting on the *bēma* to judge the lives of Christian believers. To what degree he may have been drawing on the Jesus tradition for these unique ideas and the formulation of some of the precedented ideas may be debated. The parallels especially between 1 Thessalonians 4:13—5:11 and 2 Thessalonians 2:1-12 and Mark 13/Matthew 24/Luke 21 suggest considerable use by Paul of some form of the material in the synoptic apocalypse. It is our task at this point to see what Jesus may have had to say about such matters.

—18—

Future Shock:
Jesus on
the Coming
Son of Man

That Jesus used the phrase *bar enasha* to refer to himself is a conclusion widely accepted by scholars.[1] Due weight must be given to the fact that nowhere do Paul or other New Testament authors, apart from the Evangelists, call Jesus the Son of Man.[2] This suggests that the phrase as applied to Jesus did not originate in the early church but goes back to a *Sitz im Leben Jesu.*

It is also widely accepted that the one category of Son of Man sayings from which some authentic utterances of Jesus are most likely to derive are the future Son of Man sayings. If, however, we also allow that there is even *one* authentic present Son of Man saying in which Jesus identifies himself as the *bar enasha* (for example, the Q saying Lk 9:58/Mt 8:20),[3] then we are confronted with the likelihood that Jesus spoke in some sense of his own future return or at least vindication beyond death. This conclusion is based on the reasonable argument that it is unlikely that Jesus could have referred to *two* Sons of Man![4] We must then ask what some of these future Son of Man sayings tell us about Jesus' future expectations.

At the very outset a negative conclusion is in order—it is unlikely that Jesus ever used the term *parousia* to refer to some future eschatological event. This conclusion is based not only on the fact that it is unlikely that Jesus gave his Son of Man sayings in Greek but also on the fact that the only use of parousia language in the Gospels is confined to Matthew 24, and in each of the verses in question the use of "parousia" is surely redactional.[5] For example, though the Q sayings in Matthew 24:27, 37 use the term *parousia,* the Luk⸍n parallels in 17:24, 26 have no reference to a parousia but rather refer to "the Son of Man in his day" (17:24) and "the days of the Son of Man" (17:26). Furthermore, we have clear evidence in Matthew 24:3 that it is part of the redactional agenda of the First Evangelist to change what is found in his source to the term *parousia.* In the Markan source the term is not found at 13:4. Again, in the Q saying about Noah at Matthew 24:37-39/Luke 17:26-27, only the Matthean form has the term *parousia,* and most scholars would urge that the Lukan form of the saying is likely closer to the original at this point. Accordingly, the redactional character of the term in Matthew 24 must be considered virtually certain. This means that Jesus did not speak of an "arrival" in the future Son of Man sayings, but used some other form of language to refer to that event.[6]

The preceding remarks should not be taken as an affirmation of T. F. Glasson's theory that Jesus never spoke of the coming of the Son of Man to earth in the future. Glasson's view is that the origin of the idea of the parousia, or Second Coming, lies with Paul or the early church, which adopted and adapted the theophanic language of the Old Testament, in particular the *Yom Yahweh,* and thereby created a new concept.

The problems with Glasson's views in this regard are as follows: (1) Glasson must interpret all allusions to a future coming of a Son/Messiah/King in the parables as redactional, as a revision of parables that were originally only crisis parables; (2) he must insist that the original version of the saying found in Mark 8:38 is now found in Luke 12:8-9 and parallels despite the fact that Luke tends to de-eschatologize his sources; (3) he must argue that Mark 13:32 does not refer to the Second Coming, but he does not explain what the reference to "that day" means; (4) he must interpret Luke 17:22-37 to refer to judgment on Jerusalem, not an actual coming of the Son of Man; and (5) he must deny that Mark 14:62 refers to a coming to earth of the Son of Man, despite the fact that the saying draws on theophanic traditions of God's coming down to earth.[7] Glasson places himself in the position of trying to explain away too many texts, using a variety of expedients to accomplish his ends, and his theory dies the death of too many qualifications. We thus turn to the future Son of Man sayings with hope that we may discern something about Jesus' vision of the ultimate human future.

N. Perrin has argued that the future Son of Man sayings should be divided into three categories: (1) sayings reflecting Daniel 7:13 (such as Mk 14:62 and parallels; Mk 13:26-27); (2) judgment sayings (such as Lk 12:8-9; Mk 8:38); and (3) comparison sayings (such as Lk 17:24 and parallels; 17:26-27 and parallels; 11:30 and parallels).[8] Here we will investigate those sayings which most frequently have been thought to go back to a *Sitz im Leben Jesu.*

In *The Christology of Jesus* I argued for the authenticity of Mark 14:62.[9] This saying is not about the exaltation of the Son of Man, for he is already seated in this saying. Rather, it is about his coming with the clouds for judgment. The reference to coming with the clouds alludes to a coming from heaven and immediately comes from Daniel 7:11, but ultimately it is probably drawn from the *Yom Yahweh* traditions such as those in Zephaniah 1:15 and Joel 2:2. A. L. Moore points out that the whole scene in Daniel 7 is enacted on earth, and so the Son of Man's coming even in Daniel 7 probably should not be seen as an ascent to the Ancient of Days in heaven.[10] It is worth noting that when the author(s) of the Similitudes of Enoch uses the material in Daniel 7 he depicts judgment as happening once the Son of Man sits on the throne (see 1 Enoch 45:3; 55:4; 62:5). Thus the overtones of coming for judgment are very likely in Mark 14:62.

In chapter three we examined at some length Matthew 10:23.[11] It seems probable that this saying goes back in some form to Jesus. What is not so certain is that it is about the eschatological coming of the Son of Man. Let us suppose, however, that the saying is about what the church later called the parousia. What do we learn about Jesus' view of this event? Unlike Mark 14:62, which suggests that the Son of Man will come from heaven for judgment, Matthew 10:23 does not state clearly from where the Son of Man is coming. The most one can say is that it suggests that the Son of Man will come back to, and possibly for, his followers, which suggests a coming to earth in general and to Israel in particular. Little more can be said about Jesus' view of the coming of the Son of Man on the basis of this saying.

At this point let us consider several likely authentic sayings from the Q material to advance our discussion a bit further. Three sayings come to mind from the Q apocalypse that may prove revealing: Luke 17:24/Matthew 24:27; Luke 17:26/

Matthew 24:37; and Luke 17:30/ Matthew 24:39b.

Luke has placed this material in his travel narrative, separating it from its likely original context, unlike the case with the material in Luke 21. The original form of Luke 17:24 and parallels seems to have read, "For as lightning comes from the east and shines as far as the west, so will the Son of Man be [in his day]."[12] The phrase *en tē hēmera autou* may in fact be secondary since it does not appear in p[75], B, D and various other manuscripts.[13] On the other hand, a case can be made that the phrase was omitted in some manuscripts because of homoeoteleuton.[14] The decision on this matter is of no small importance since it affects whether the analogy is with the Day of the Son of Man or with the person the Son of Man. In view of verse 30, however, the phrase was probably in the original Q text. Few have objected to the authenticity of this saying, though Bultmann, among others, has urged that Jesus was speaking of someone other than himself in this authentic word.[15] Against this view must stand not only the considerations previously mentioned but also a saying like we find in Matthew 11:5-6/ Luke 7:22-23.[16] As Jeremias says, such a saying would be senseless: "to the question whether he was the one to come Jesus would, rather, have had to reply 'No I am not he. I am only his forerunner and his prophet.' In other words, the fact that Jesus made claim to be the fulfiller excludes the possibility of one coming after him."[17] In short, Jesus expected no successors.

What then is the point of Luke 17:24 and parallels? It is saying that the Day of the Son of Man will be unmistakably evident when it happens, just as lightning that crosses the entire sky illuminates the whole area. A possible secondary point is that the Day will come as suddenly and be as startling as a bolt of lightning.[18] Lightning is associated with theophanies in the Old Testament (see Ps 18:14; 144:5-6) and also is found in apocalyptic sources as a means of revelation (see 2 Bar 53:9). Luke 17:24 and parallels seem closer to the material in 2 Baruch 53:9 than to the Old Testament texts. Thus Luke 17:24 and parallels indicate that the Day of the Son of Man will be visible to all and theophanic in nature.

In Luke 17:26/ Matthew 24:37 we find another analogy, this time with the days of Noah. In early Jewish literature the days of Noah and those of Lot were often associated with each other as examples of notable wickedness that received their due punishment from God (see T. Naph. 3:4-5; 3 Macc 2:4-5; Wisdom 10:4, 6; Phil Vit. Mos II,52-65).[19] In view of Luke 17:27 and parallels, that is certainly how our saying should be interpreted as well—it is about judgment on the wicked.

But is the plural "days of the Son of Man" the original form of this saying? If so, then one might think on the basis of the analogy that the reference is to the wicked and dark days that finally lead up to the coming of the Son of Man.[20] On the other hand, one could argue that while the plural "days" is original, it is due to the analogy with Noah's time and that in fact the reference really is to the coming of the Son of Man for sudden judgment on the wicked, as also happened to Noah's contemporaries. In a probably authentic word Jesus elsewhere refers to Sodom and "that day" (Lk 10:12/Mt 10:15), which may suggest an analogy here as well with the Day of judgment. As Kümmel insists, for Luke, in view of the juxaposition of the two likely independent sayings 17:24 and 26 in closely proximity it would seem that "the day of the Son of Man" has the same meaning as "the days of the Son of Man." These are just varying ways to speak of the time of the coming of the Son of Man.[21] Kümmel adds: "Both texts completely correspond in their emphasis on the threatening and incalculable nature of the eschatological day with Jesus' attitude. . . . There is no need to doubt their belonging to the oldest tradition."[22]

The reference to Lot in Luke 17:28-29 may be secondary since it is not found in the Matthean form of Q, but this does not affect our judgment on Luke 17:30, which has a parallel in Matthew 24:39b. In fact, Luke 17:30 may be the original conclusion of the material in Luke 17:27/Matthew 24:38. Luke 17:30 and parallels is striking because in its likely original form ("and so it will be on the day when the Son of Man is revealed") we have the only case where the Son of Man is the subject of the verb *apokalyptai.* Higgins has pointed to an interesting parallel in 1 Corinthians 3:13, which says, "For the day will disclose it, because it is revealed *(apokalyptetai)* in fire."[23] In both texts the language suggests a sudden act of judgment. This should not surprise us since "the motif of the sudden and unexpected end is a feature of Jesus' preaching. This is the theme of the parable of the watchful servants . . . (Lk. 12.35-8) [and] the immediately following short parable of the burglar (Lk. 12.39 and par. Matt. 24.43)."[24] Jesus associates this judgment with the coming of the Son of Man.

In these three sayings (Lk 17:24, 26, 30) and their parallels it seems likely that Jesus does draw on the Old Testament theophanic material to some extent to express his teaching about the coming Son of Man. In particular he draws on the *Yom Yahweh* material seen as a day of wrath. Even in his use of the phrase "the Day of the Son of Man" he may be drawing on the *Yom Yahweh* phrase or perhaps on a set of ideas that stand behind 1 Enoch 61:5, which speaks of "the day of the Elect One." I have argued that it seems likely that Jesus was cognizant of some of the material now found in the Similitudes of Enoch, perhaps in an oral form.[25] In the Similitudes "the Elect One" is the same as the Son of Man and is depicted as the eschatological judge sitting on a throne (see 1 Enoch 45:3; 55:4; 62:1-3, 5; 69:27, 29).[26] Surprisingly, S. Mowinckel concluded that the idea of a Day of the Son of Man does not derive from *Yom Yahweh* material but is a natural outworking of the Son of Man material in Daniel 7.[27] This is probably correct in the main though some of the theophanic imagery also seems to have been used in these Q sayings. It is even possible that the idea of a *coming* of a Son of Man with the clouds to earth was derived by Jesus from Daniel 7:13.[28] In any event the evidence thus far all attests to a close connection of the ideas of judgment with the future coming of the Son of Man.

Once it is accepted that a saying like Luke 17:24 and/or Mark 14:62 is likely authentic, this immediately raises questions about the provenance of a saying like Mark 13:6-7 and parallels. This is all the more the case since Paul seems to have known this material in some form (compare 1 Thess 4:16-17 to Mk 13:26-27 and parallels). Mark 13:26-27 and parallels is part of a larger unit, Mark 13:24-27 and parallels, which originally may have been handed down together from the period of oral transmission. That this material, like the rest of the material in Mark 13, can be called a form of "paranetic eschatology, or eschatological paranesis" should be kept steadily in view.[29] This is no doubt partly due to the way and the purposes for which Mark has shaped his material, but it would seem likely that this material functioned the same way in Mark's source. In any event, verses 24-27 form "the climax of the eschatological drama" presented in Mark 13.[30] How much of this material can be ascribed to Mark's source and how much to redaction? R. Pesch thinks that all of verses 24-27 came from Mark's apocalyptic source, while J. Lambrecht argues that every clause of Mark 13 was formulated by Mark.[31] These are not mutually exclusive options since it is likely that Mark has made all the sources he used in his Gospel his own, writing his Gospel in his own style and vocabulary. We must consider more substantive arguments against the authenticity of Mark 13:26-27.

The basic argument against the authenticity of Mark 13:26-27 is that it is part of "a pastiche of OT quotations which is part of a detailed apocalyptic programme" and that "the saying is secondary in form to [Mk] 8.38 and 14.62 and represents a development of Christian exegetical traditions based on Dn. 7.13."[32] These objections seem at first glance quite substantial. Let us consider the last one first.

It is claimed that Mark 13:26 has been developed out of 8:38 and/or 14:62. As Beasley-Murray points out, "Arguments that this saying is the result of a conflation of Mark 14:62 with Daniel 7:13 are not convincing, since the verse obviously fails to include the motif of the exaltation of Jesus, so important to Mark 14:62."[33] It is also worth stressing that the term *opsontai* ("they shall see") probably should not be seen as derived from Mark 14:62 since the latter text is addressed exclusively to people condemning the Son of Man who, it is implied, will face his judgment when he comes, while here "seeing" refers to a universal seeing that involves both the elect and the condemned and perhaps both heavenly powers and earthly humans.[34] Also, Mark 14:62 says that the Son of Man will come *meta tōn nephelōn tou ouranou,* while in Mark 13:26 we read of a coming *en nephelais meta dynameōs pollēs kai doxēs.* It is unlikely that this latter description is simply a development of the former one. Furthermore, the reference in Mark 13:26 is to the Son of Man's own glory, whereas in 8:38 it is the glory of his Father that is in view. My point in both cases is that there are significant differences between Mark 8:38, 13:26 and 14:62 that are not purely stylistic. In short, it is unlikely that Mark 13:26 is simply a development of one or both of these other sayings.

The obvious allusion to Daniel 7:13 in Mark 13:26 is evaluated variously, depending on whether one thinks Jesus actually referred to himself or even to a future coming one using the language of the *bar enasha.* If Mark 14:62 is once accepted as authentic, then an allusion to Daniel 7:13 is not an obstacle to Mark 13:26 being an authentic word of Jesus.

More important, the argument that the early church developed a Son of Man theology on the basis of Daniel 7 that does not go back to Jesus is weak. Besides the fact that Paul and other New Testament writers, including Luke (in Acts), show no tendency to develop or even really use such a theology, it cannot be lightly dismissed that "Son of Man" is found on the lips of Jesus in the Gospels and almost nowhere else. Very few examples can be argued plausibly to be the result of purely redactional activity (Mk 2:10 and Lk 18:8b may be exceptions to this rule). One would also have to posit that this theology arose very early after Easter but that by the time of Paul, Mark and Luke it already was disappearing. The so-called sayings with rivals (sayings with both a Son of Man and a non-Son of Man form) suggest that in fact the earlier Jewish phrase "Son of Man" was already being replaced in the tradition even before the Gospels were written, possibly even prior to Q. I thus conclude that Perrin's arguments about Mark

13:26 are weak at best.[35] The arguments against the authenticity of Mark 13:26 then should not prevail, especially in view of the evidence that Paul knew some form of Mark 13:26-27.

What then of Mark 13:27? This saying draws on a long tradition involving the concept of the eschatological gathering of the elect, and especially echoes Deuteronomy 30:3 (compare Is 11:12; 27:12-13; 60:1-2; Tobit 14:7). There is nothing particularly Christian about this saying at all. It could easily be uttered by any early Jew with a future hope for God's people, especially since "the elect" are not identified in this saying and probably originally referred to the gathering of dispersed Israel. There is certainly nothing here that could not have gone back to a *Sitz im Leben Jesu.*

If then it is more probable than not that Mark 13:26-27 does go back in some form ultimately to Jesus, what does it teach us about his future hope? First, as was already implied in Luke 17:24 and parallels and to some degree in Mark 14:62, the Son of Man's coming is envisioned as a theophanic event of universal scope and impact. Second, in Mark 13:26-27 "all of the actions are attributed to the Son of Man: he not only comes, but he gathers the elect through the ministry of angels, and the elect are 'his.' "[36] Here the emphasis is on redemption of the elect, whereas in Luke 17:24 and parallels and in Mark 14:62 the emphasis was on judgment, as is also true of Luke 17:26 and parallels. Third, if Mark 13:27 does in fact go back to Jesus we may have another form of the idea of the gathering of God's elect together in one place, which comports with the messianic banquet tradition in Matthew 8:11 and parallels. Mark 13:27 would likely have originally been understood to refer to a gathering of the dispersed Jews.

It is now in order to ask how Paul's handling of the tradition in Mark 13:26-27 and parallels, which is in 1 Thessalonians 4:16-17, is similar to or different from the original thrust of the tradition. The following concepts are found in both texts: (1) descent of a figure from heaven; (2) angel(s) involved in gathering the elect; and (3) the gathering of the elect, which is universal in scope. The differences are also notable: (1) Paul speaks of the Lord's coming, Jesus of the Son of Man; and (2) Paul is referring to living and dead Christians being gathered together to meet the Lord, while Jesus may have been referring to elect Jews in the Dispersion. If this latter point is right then Mark 13:27 is in some ways nearer to Romans 11:26-27.

—19—

Conclusions

Our study of Jesus' and Paul's views on the coming *Yom Yahweh* has led to some intriguing discoveries. In some ways Paul's and Jesus' views on this matter are remarkably similar. Both have adopted and adapted theophanic texts from the Old Testament, in particular some of the later prophetic *Yom Yahweh* material, and have used it to describe the *return* of a figure already known to have had a career on earth. The idea of the *return* of an already known figure is in fact the one major component in both Jesus' and Paul's views of the ultimate future that stands out from its context in early Judaism. All the rest—judgment, redemption, gathering of the elect, resurrection, all precipitated by a final theophanic event—is not without precedent in early Judaism.

The fact that this figure is invested with the attendant beings and circumstances predicated of God in the Old Testament is not without import and would seem to amount to a significant modification of early Jewish monotheistic traditions. Early Jews were expecting the coming of *Yahweh* on the *Yom Yahweh,* not some other agent or figure, however well invested with divine authority, power, garb and entourage he might be. The only *real* exception to this rule is some of the material found in the Similitudes of Enoch, and it may be that Jesus in fact drew on some of this material in his future Son of Man sayings. Paul goes one step further than the Jesus tradition, to the point of even calling this figure by Yahweh's name—*Adonai*/Lord. It may well be, as L. W. Hurtado has suggested, that some of the agency material, the treatment of exalted angels and the treatment of some patriarchs in early Jewish literature paved the way for these developments in both the Pauline and Jesus material.[1]

Both Paul and Jesus, it would seem, focus on the ultimate fate of the elect in these events. In the material we have examined Paul says little if anything about the ultimate fate of the nonelect. Jesus in Luke 17:26 and parallels implies a bit more about the judgment of the nonelect. Paul speaks of a coming parousia or Day of the Lord in his early letters, and these two traditions have cross-fertilized in Paul's presentation of the return of Christ. The apostle focuses only on the Day of the Lord material in his later letters, calling it the Day of Christ. Jesus draws on no parousia traditions, which is not surprising since he probably did not speak these sayings in Greek, and he spoke to an exclusively Jewish audience.

Paul, it appears, was capable of holding together the idea of the possible imminence of the parousia with the idea of some preliminary events. In the likely authentic sayings we have examined from the Jesus tradition, Jesus mentioned no preliminary events. This is not to say that he did not affirm some. If even one of the collected sayings found in Mark 13:14ff. and parallels goes back to Jesus, it may be that he too affirmed one or more preliminary events.[2] In particular, Jesus may have predicted the coming destruction of the temple. However, as Mark 13 is presently structured, the only events *immediately* associated with the coming of the Son of Man are cosmic, not historical in nature (13:24-25).[3] Even these verses, however, may simply reflect the use of theophanic language to indicate the coming of the divine one, and may not have been intended to describe actual cosmic phenomena.[4]

Both Paul and Jesus affirm a moral resolution of all matters of good and evil at the close of human history as we know it. This resolution is brought about by divine intervention, not the completion of some human agenda. It is quite clear in both the Pauline and Jesus material that human beings, including the elect, are acted upon and are portrayed as passive recipients of what this heavenly figure causes to happen to them. There is also the implication that this final resolution of matters is universal in scope and thus inescapable, though both Paul and Jesus stress that moral preparation now will mean that the Coming will bring redemption rather than judgment for those ready for it. Thus, for both Jesus and Paul this eschatological material with some apocalyptic elements is used to serve a paranetic purpose—whether for comfort or warning. In short, it is used to aid or confirm certain forms of moral decision making in the present that amount to preparation for the eschatological future. History for both Jesus and Paul has a sudden closure involving a final review of human lives. Though that closure is in divine hands, the implications are that preparation for it to a large extent rests in human hands.

PART SIX

The Resurrection of the Dead

—20—

Introduction

As should be evident in our discussion of various eschatological topics, a great deal more can be said about Paul's views on these matters than about Jesus' views. This is due in part to the problem of isolating authentic sayings of the historical Jesus, but even if all the Gospel material were to be taken at face value we still have a much smaller data base for discussing Jesus' views. The chapters on the Pauline evidence thus far have necessarily been disproportionately longer, and the chapter to follow will be no different.

Paul spoke of resurrection early, middle and late in his letters (see 1 Thess 4:13ff.; 1 Cor 15; Phil 3:10-11). For Paul the subject of resurrection—not only of Jesus, but also of Christians including himself—is one of the constants that he affirms throughout his correspondence. In one sense this should hardly surprise us because Paul was by background a Pharisee, and apparently from the time he became a Christian the heart of his preaching focused on the death and resurrection of Jesus the Messiah. By turning at this point to the examination of the relevant texts in the Pauline corpus we will be able to better clarify the shape of Paul's resurrection faith.

—21—

Body
Language:
Paul and the
Resurrection

The great merit of J. C. Beker's treatments of Paul's theology is that he clearly shows that Paul's understanding of resurrection, including the resurrection of Jesus, must not be studied apart from the eschatological framework of which it is an integral part.

> Resurrection language is end-time language and unintelligible apart from the apocalyptic thought world to which resurrection language belongs. . . . Thus the resurrection of Christ, the coming reign of God, and the future resurrection of the dead belong together. . . . When the resurrection of Christ is isolated from its linguistic apocalyptic environment and from the reality of future apocalyptic renewal, it may well retain its traditional nomenclature in expositions of Paul's thought, but it becomes something radically different. It becomes actually a docetic miracle in the midst of history without affecting the historical process itself, that is, an event in the midst of history rather than at the end of history for the sake of history's transformation. Attention now

shifts to resurrection as the end of the incarnation, as a closure event rather than an inaugural event.[1]

Beker's judgment is on target, though for reasons already indicated in part one I think the term *eschatological* rather than *apocalyptic* should be used to describe what Beker is discussing. He is also right that the attempts to remove the ontological and historical referents from Paul's views on resurrection do less than justice to Paul's perspective.[2] Whether or not we are comfortable with the idea, Paul believed not only in the spiritual resurrection of the human spirit in this life, and the new perspective on life which that brings, but also in the literal resurrection of people at the end of history as we know it. Furthermore, this resurrection is linked to actual environmental renewal of the earth itself (see Rom 8:18-25). The destiny of believers and the destiny of the earth are inexorably linked together.

Where Beker has skewed Paul's perspective, in my judgment, is that while rightly highlighting Paul's eschatological framework, he has done so at the expense of Paul's Christology. As I noted in the last chapter, what causes Paul to alter his eschatological framework, which he inherited from early Pharisaic Judaism, is precisely the past and future work of Christ. Not only does Christ's return trigger the resurrection of believers, but in Paul's view there will be no resurrection of believers if Christ has not been raised. In short, it is the narrative of Christ's career that causes Paul to bifurcate his doctrine of resurrection and to make the resurrection of believers dependent on both Christ's resurrection and his return. The parousia component especially distinguishes Paul's views from those of other Jews about when and how the resurrection of believers will transpire. W. D. Davies said, "It is erroneous thus to make Paul conform too closely to current apocalyptic speculation. That in his eschatology, the Apostle drew upon the latter for his terms will be obvious, but the character of that eschatology was determined not by any traditional scheme but by that significance which Paul had been led to give to Jesus."[3] With these general caveats in mind, we are now prepared to trace the trajectory of Paul's thought on resurrection (both Christ's and believers') as it is evidenced in the capital Pauline letters.

It is hardly surprising, in view of his Pharisaic background, that Paul places so much stress on resurrection, both Christ's and the believer's. There was also, quite apart from Pharisaic teaching (see *Gen Rab.* 14:5; Acts 23:6-8), considerable precedent for such a belief not only in the Old Testament (see Is 26:19; Dan 12:1-3) but in the intertestamental period (see 2 Macc 12:43-44; 7:10-11; 4:9; 14:46).

This belief became a sort of test of true Jewishness after A.D. 70 (see *Mish. Sanh.* 10:1; *B.T. Sanh.* 90b; *2 Bar* 50:1-4).[4] The majority of the references to resurrection in early Judaism suggest a very materialistic view of the resurrection (but see Josephus, *Wars* 2.10.11; Wis 3:1-4). In other words, to many if not most early Jews and especially to Pharisaic ones the idea of a nonmaterial resurrection would have amounted to a contradiction in terms.[5] G. W. E. Nickelsburg has, however, rightly cautioned us "that in the intertestamental period there was no single Jewish orthodoxy on the time, mode, and place of resurrection, immortality, and eternal life."[6]

There was apparently considerable debate in regard to the degree of continuity and discontinuity between the body one has in this life and the body one gained after being raised from the dead. Thus 1 Corinthians 15 in particular shows that Paul was part of that ongoing debate. Nickelsburg has also shown that the idea of a general resurrection and judgment of all the dead (not just the believing dead) in early Jewish literature is rarely found prior to the end of the first century A.D. (see *2 Enoch* 65:6-7; *Apoc. Mos.* 13:3; 41:3; *T. Ben* 10:9; *Sib. Or.* 4:176-90; 4 Ezra 7; *Wis.* 1-6 is a possible exception, as is Dan 12:2). When a universal resurrection is spoken of its function is almost always to make possible the final rendering of justice for all. By contrast in the earlier Jewish texts that speak of a resurrection of the righteous the function of resurrection is vindication, rescue or reward (see 2 Macc 7).[7] When Paul speaks of resurrection, whether of Christ or of Christians, this latter, more positive, thrust and connection with vindication or reward comes to the fore (see Rom 1:4; 1 Cor 15).

Very little in 1 Thessalonians will help us to obtain a clear fix on Paul's view of resurrection. First Thessalonians 1:9-10 is probably a pre-Pauline fragment of the early church's preaching to Gentiles.[8] In point of fact the material in these verses is quite close to the examples of Paul's missionary preaching in Acts 14:15-17, and especially in Acts 17:31.[9] Whether or not this is a citation of a traditional formula, Paul clearly endorses its content as a good and useful summary of what the Thessalonians had initially accepted when they converted. Verse 10 speaks of God having raised Jesus from/out of *the* dead (persons).[10] Though this implies resurrection from death, what the text actually says is that Jesus was brought back from the midst of the realm of the dead persons (Sheol).[11] Paul normally uses the verb *egeirein,* either in the active or passive, to speak of resurrection. He does not use *anistanai* in the transitive.[12] That is, Paul never speaks of Jesus raising himself, rather he is always passively acted upon by God (see, for example,

Rom 4:24-25; 6:4, 9; 7:4; 1 Cor 6:14; 15:12-17, 20; 2 Cor 4:14; 5:15 and so forth).[13]

In 1 Thessalonians 1:10 Christ's resurrection is connected with the believer's future deliverance from God's wrath. In fact, almost always when Paul speaks of Christ's resurrection he does so in connection with the events that will transpire when Christ returns. He clearly does not see Christ's resurrection as an isolated historical anomaly but as an eschatological event that is the harbinger and in some sense the trigger or at least the prerequisite of future eschatological events. Paul is surely dealing with Christians in Thessalonica who had speculated about such eschatological matters, and it may even be that the Thessalonian Christians were reflecting the characteristics of a millenarian movement.[14] If so, then it would appear that Paul is trying to offer a certain amount of "eschatological reserve" while still affirming much of the substance of the Thessalonians' beliefs about the future. Here Paul grounds the believer's future status in the belief in the past Christ-event.

I have already dealt with 1 Thessalonians 4:14 in the previous chapter but note here that the future resurrection of deceased believers is linked with the past death and resurrection of Jesus. The link here, however, is unlike that in 1 Corinthians 15. Here belief in Christ's resurrection is seen as the proper grounds for believing that deceased Christians will likewise be raised. Verse 16 also makes clear that Paul is only referring to the future of "the dead in Christ," that is, dead Christians. Christ's resurrection is not a guarantee or proof of the future general resurrection of all the dead.[15] Finally, since in verse 17b Paul says "and so [or 'in this way'—*kai houtōs*] we shall be with the Lord *forever* [*pantote*]," this must count strongly against the idea that this text is talking about some *interim* stay with Christ in heaven during a period of earthly tribulation.

This brings up a very crucial point that I shall develop at length when we turn to 1 Corinthians 15, but it bears mentioning here. For Paul resurrection means final conformity to the likeness or image of God's Son, even in regard to one's body. In other words, resurrection seems to have a very specific positive content that has to do with the consummation of Paul's ideas about the *imitatio Christi*. In such a context it is hardly surprising that Paul never speaks of the resurrection of nonbelievers. If one has not participated in the process of being conformed to the image of the Son in this life (Rom 8:29), it is hardly to be expected that one would get the final installment or completion of this ongoing process later. Resurrection ushers the believer into the new world and the kingdom promised to them by God. Vos has it right when he says:

If we may judge of the resurrection of believers *mutatis mutandis* after the analogy of that of Christ, we shall have to believe that the event will mark the entrance upon a new world constructed upon a new superabundantly dynamic plane. . . . The resurrection constitutes, as it were, the womb of the new aeon, out of which believers issue as, in a new, altogether unprecedented sense, sons of God. . . . The analogy and its bearing upon our problem become most clear when the passage Rom. 1:3-4 is somewhat closely analyzed. . . . The Resurrection (both of Jesus and of believers) is therefore according to Paul the entering upon a new phase of sonship characterized by the possession and exercise of unique supernatural power.[16]

The truth of this observation will become readily apparent when we examine Romans 1 and 1 Corinthians 15 more fully below. However, I submit that this theological truth already stands behind what Paul says in texts like 1 Thessalonians 3:13 and 5:23 where the ongoing process of sanctification is seen as preparation for the coming of Christ. The work of the Spirit in the present in the believer is preparing that believer not only for the final judgment of Christ, but for the final work of the Spirit for the believer, that is, resurrection in the likeness of Christ's glorified body. For Paul, Christology, pneumatology, soteriology, eschatology and ethics are so closely interwoven that any attempt to treat one or another of these aspects of Paul's thought in isolation from the others does less than justice to them all. This is especially true when we come to what is for Paul a *sine qua non* of Christian faith—the belief in both Christ's and the believer's resurrection.

One last aspect of Paul's discussion in 1 Thessalonians 4:14-17 bears scrutiny. Resurrection here, as in 1 Thessalonians 1:10, has to do with something that happens to a dead person, not a living one. First Thessalonians 4:17 may imply that some similar transformation will happen to living believers but it is not called resurrection here. Since 2 Thessalonians adds nothing to our discussion, we will pass on to 1 and 2 Corinthians.[17]

The first passage under consideration, 1 Corinthians 6:14, comes in the middle of Paul's discussion about the proper use of the human body. Resurrection is introduced here to explain why it is important to act morally in and with the body—body is meant for the Lord and in fact will participate in the eschatological state of salvation. Verse 14 makes the analogy between Christ's resurrection and that of believers quite explicit. Both are raised up by God's power. The context makes clear that by resurrection Paul means something involving a body. In view of the future verb *katargēsei* in verse 13, the future *exegerei* is surely to be preferred in verse 14 (compare 2 Cor 4:14).[18] Again we see a clear connection made between the believer's present condition and conduct and his future condition. Ethics circumscribes bodily conduct because the body has a place in the eschatological future of the believer. Paul is countering the "spiritualizing" tendencies of Corinthian eschatology and soteriology. "This affirmation stands in bold contrast to the Corinthian view of spirituality which looked for a 'spiritual' salvation that would finally be divested of the body."[19]

There has been much debate over what Paul is combating in 1 Corinthians 15. On the surface of things verse 12 seems to give a straightforward answer—some in Corinth were saying, "there is no resurrection of the dead." Paul attributes this view to only "some" *(tines)*, but these some were evidently sufficient in number and/or in importance in the Corinthian church for Paul to correct the problem in this letter to the church as a whole. Indeed, the space Paul devotes to this problem suggests that it is part of the larger general problem in Corinth of what may be called spiritualized eschatology, which Paul has been correcting all along in this letter.

Could these "some" be the same ones who were also baptizing for the dead? It is often pointed out that the practice of baptizing for the dead surely implies some hope about the future of the deceased ones for whom proxy baptism is being undertaken. Paul, by implication, certainly seems to think there is some connection, at least in the minds of those receiving this peculiar baptism, between this practice and one's hope for the future of these deceased persons. What is not clear from verse 29 is whether that future hope entailed a hope for some sort of resurrection or rather some sort of less material participation in eternal life. Paul does not specifically identify the some who are denying the resurrection with "those" who are receiving proxy baptism.

It also seems reasonable to maintain that if Paul in 1 Corinthians 15:12 had wanted to say that some were asserting there is no *more* resurrection, that is, no future resurrection, he would have said *anastasin ēdē gegonenai* not *anastasis ouk estin*.[20]

Perhaps the problem lies with the fact that we have overlooked the qualifier in verse 12—what is being denied is not just "resurrection" *simpliciter* but resurrection of the dead *(nekrōn)*. A. J. M. Wedderburn asserts "that 'resurrection' would mean, especially to Hellenistic readers, something physical, earthy, which only gradually came to be spiritualized as groups of Christians . . . sought to

reconcile their Hellenistic or gnostic aversion to the body with the ineluctable
presence of the idea of resurrection in . . . Christian tradition."[21]

However, there is evidence in 1 Corinthians that at least some of the Corinthians themselves already had been involved in such a spiritualizing of matters.
Besides the fact that a case can be made for some proto-Gnostic tendencies in
Corinth, if 1 Corinthians 6:13b is a quote of the Corinthian's view that God will
destroy the body, thus implying that salvation has nothing to do with it, or if
in fact 1 Corinthians 4:8 ascribes to various Corinthians an overrealized, as well
as an overly *pneumatic,* view of salvation in which the new life called by Christians "resurrection" is seen as a matter of life in the Spirit here and now, it is
not hard to believe that some Corinthian Christians were denying "resurrection
of the dead." Wedderburn says, "For the Corinthians what they treasure as life-
giving and divine is the *pneuma* specially granted to them and not the *psychē*
which is in every [one]."[22] Resurrection of dead persons might well have connoted
to such Corinthians "the standing up of corpses" (see Acts 17:31-32). This would
have seemed repugnant to those who saw salvation/new life in a purely spiritual
vein, whether in this life or the next.

Thus we should not try to envision a group of Christians in Corinth who flatly
denied "resurrection," whether Christ's or believers' per se.[23] Paul would hardly
have addressed such persons as *adelphoi* (15:1), in view of how strongly he feels
about resurrection being a sine qua non of Christian faith (see 15:12-19). Nor
would he have reminded them that they had already believed in the resurrection
if it were not so (15:11).[24] Rather, he is trying here to correct an overly spiritual
and an overrealized view of resurrection. He corrects the former by stressing that
resurrection involves a body. He corrects the latter by setting forth a sketch of
the order of future eschatological events, including resurrection of the dead. The
Corinthians apparently thought the body was at best something inferior, temporary, of no eternal significance, and at worst some of them may have seen matter
as tainted or even evil. In either case they did not envision eternal life/resurrec-
tion as involving a body. This is not surprising in an environment where the
dominant idea of immortality was still the immortality of the soul.[25] K. A. Plank
sums up the matter well:

> The problem in Corinth is not the denial of the kerygma but its enthusiastic
> interpretation: the scandal of the crucified Messiah has been overcome by an
> uncontrolled exaltation christology; obedience to his lordship has been lost
> through sacramental realism that understands redemption to have already

been effected. The difficulty is not the failure of the Corinthians to believe in the resurrection, Christ's or their own, but the fact that they believed "too much"! . . . To oppose the Corinthian position and be true to his own Paul must be both "for and against a theology of the resurrection."[26]

Paul's discussion of resurrection in 1 Corinthians 15 draws on a variety of sources. First, there are traditions from the early church about the death, burial, resurrection and appearances of Jesus (15:1-7). These traditions would seem to go back to the early Jewish Christians, perhaps even to the earliest ones in Palestine.[27] Second, Paul draws on traditional eschatological and apocalyptic elements from his Jewish heritage, modifying them in light of his Christology and soteriology.[28] This would include his adopting and adapting Pharisaic beliefs about the resurrection of believers. Third, it seems that Paul draws on a common Jewish metaphor to describe death and resurrection by analogy with the planting and sprouting of a seed (see *B.T. Sanh.* 90b).[29] Fourth, Paul may be drawing on some conventional Hellenistic rhetoric and rhetorical devices.[30] Paul has taken all these sources and modified them, however, making them his own in order to present in a compelling way his vision of what resurrection means and entails. Particularly notable is the way Paul brings into the discussion a comparison of groups of two related yet distinguishable things: (1) two kingdoms (or two administrators of the one kingdom, first Christ then God); (2) two Adams; and (3) two bodies.[31]

This detailed examination of 1 Corinthians 15 must focus on the matter of Paul's view of the future resurrection of believers since this is a book about Paul's and Jesus' views on the future. This will require a discussion of the first and last Adam typology, the first-fruits/latter-fruits analogy, the seed analogy and the whole question of continuity and discontinuity between the present body and the resurrection body, the place of resurrection in the eschatological schema of things (its relationship to "the end," the parousia and final victory over death) and finally the comparison between the resurrection of dead believers and the transformation of living believers at the parousia.

The Adam/Christ typology is found both in 1 Corinthians 15 and in a somewhat different and more developed form in Romans 5. In 1 Corinthians 15 the typology is used to speak of the two progenitors of the human race who have passed on different sorts of life to those who come from them. There are both similarities and differences between Adam the type, and Christ the antitype. Both are truly human beings, and both are representative heads of a race of human creatures whose character and actions have a dramatic effect on those who come forth from them. In various ways the differences outweigh the similarities. The powerful effect of Adam's nature and action on all humanity was death (v. 21), but the powerful effect of Christ's nature and action was life—both life in the Spirit now and future resurrection of the dead. Is then the parallelism of verse 22 a perfect one? "In Adam all die"—that much is clear. Does the "all" in verse 22b mean that all human beings will one day be made alive in Christ? Verse 23 likely provides the answer, saying that those who gain a resurrection like Christ's are "those who belong to him." Thus the parallelism is not perfect, which warns us here and elsewhere in this chapter that when Paul is using an analogy it must not be pressed to comment on things that go beyond the point of the analogy and of the immediate focus of Paul's thought.

In regard to verses 44-49, where we find the analogy developed further, Jeremias has provided us with the following chart:

v. 45	*ho prōtos Adam*	*ho eschatos Adam*
	psychē zōsa	*pneuma zōopoioun*
vv. 47-48	*ho prōtos anthrōpos*	*ho deuteros anthrōpos*
	ek gēs, choikos	*ek ouranou epouranios*[32]

Though we should beware of using the concept of corporate personality here, Paul does seem to be operating with some sort of federal or representative headship theology. Adam, as representative head of the human race, sinned for us and hence we died through his act. Paul focuses on this idea more in Romans 5 than here, but there are overtones of this theology even in 1 Corinthians 15. This becomes especially apparent when Paul links sin and death in verses 54-56. As K. W. Trim says, "For Paul, sin, death, and corruption form a dynamic unity."[33] Nevertheless, Paul in verse 45 is quoting from Genesis 2:7, which says that Adam became a *nepeš hayah*, "a living being." This is what *psychē zōsa* must mean here. Thus the focus is on the fact that we inherit our natural physical life from the "first Adam." By contrast we receive life in the Spirit, and eventually resurrection of the body from the one who became a "life-giving spirit" by means of the resurrection. In short, the focus of the contrast here comports with what Paul says elsewhere in this chapter about two sorts of life and bodies.

Christ "the eschatological Adam" started the human race over again, and he was obedient even unto death. As a result, after his death and resurrection he became a "life-giving spirit." The first Adam merely had natural life, the second Adam was a dispenser of the sort of life only the *pneuma* can give. He gained this capability by himself being the "first-fruits" of the resurrection. In a sense the "eschatological Adam" is starting a new creation, being the first-fruits of the dead. But in another sense he is the end and goal of the human race. There will be no more human founders after him. He brings in the eschatological age, the new creation, the end of God's plan.

Adam was strictly an earth creature—he came from earth, he returned to earth and his body and life were natural and physical. Insofar as we are his descendants we are earthly, physical, contingent and have a natural life principle. The last Adam, on the other hand, was both from heaven and heavenly in nature in some sense. What was it that was unearthly about him? The only clue that Paul gives us here is that he became a life-giving Spirit. This likely refers to what was true of him after the resurrection (Rom 1:4), not what was true of him either in pre-existence or during his earthly ministry.[34] We must always bear in mind that this analogy functions as a part of the larger argument for and about the resurrection, both Christ's and ours. Just as there is no forgiveness of sins for believers if Christ is not raised (v. 17), so also Christ is not a life-giving spirit if he has not been raised. For Paul both Christology and soteriology hang on the historical reality of Christ's resurrection.

Paul also wants to clarify that what is available through Christ is not merely an equal and opposite reaction to what comes through Adam. To be sure, what is available through Christ is the antidote for the negative things one has received through Adam, but it is also qualitatively different and better. Salvation, and ultimately the resurrection, entails more than just paradise regained. This is clear in Romans 5:15, where Paul says openly that the gift is not like the trespass, but it is also clearly implied in 1 Corinthians 15. The resurrection ushers the believer into a kind of life that is far superior to the natural life that Adam experienced even before the fall, and certainly it is a kind of life that totally eclipses what we have received through Adam. Paul wishes the Corinthians to view resurrection and new life in the light of this salvation-historical perspective.[35]

The Corinthians appear to have viewed spiritual matters and even the resurrection from a purely experiential and ecstatic perspective. It was something that God's Spirit provided them here and now. Their perspective was essentially vertical rather than horizontal. In their view, what they had came down to them from heaven in the present. To counter this Paul offers both historical and developmental analogies as well as an eschatological schema. He stresses the bodily character of resurrection to counter the overspiritual interpretation of salvation.

The crucial nature of the analogy, first-fruits/latter-fruits, is made clear by M. J. Harris. "This essential unity between the firstfruits and the harvest is basic to the whole argument of 1 Corinthians 15. To affirm Christ's resurrection is to affirm that of his people (1 Cor. 15.12, 20, 23). To deny their resurrection is to deny his (1 Cor. 15.13, 15-16). Each implies or is involved in the other."[36]

In the Old Testament the first-fruits was the first part of the annual harvest of grain or wine or other products that was to be offered up to God (see Ex 23:16, 19; Lev 23:10; Num 18:8, 12). As Harris points out, the relationship of first-fruits to the harvest is that of the part to the whole.[37] There is more to the analogy than this, however. The first-fruits both presage and also promise or prove that there will be latter-fruits.[38] In short, Christ's resurrection makes possible, believable and in Paul's mind certain that believers will one day rise. It is also likely that Paul's language of imminence in regard to the end, insofar as it involves both parousia and resurrection, has been strongly affected by his Christology. A. L. Moore puts it this way:

> The nearness of the end is bound up with the person of Jesus Christ, in whom the events of the end, including their open, unambiguous manifestation, coinhere. In him, death, resurrection, ascension, and Parousia belong together. They do not belong together as a general principle but as a matter of theological, or more exactly of Christological fact.[39]

There is a sense in which Pauline theology has a twofold proleptic realization of the end. Christ's resurrection and believers having the Spirit are both pledges and pointers that the resurrection of believers will yet happen. Thus Paul can speak not only of the first-fruits of the resurrection (1 Cor 15:20, 22) but also of the first-fruits of the Spirit (Rom 8:23). In both cases Paul uses the term *aparchē*. It is perhaps not surprising that Paul does not speak of the Spirit as first-fruits in 1 Corinthians 15 since that would play right into the hands of the spiritualists in Corinth.

First Corinthians 15:23b makes clear that this connection between first-fruits and latter-fruits is not a connection between Christ and all humanity, but rather between Christ and "those who belong to him." Christ's resurrection then does not simply trigger or guarantee the resurrection of all the dead in some sort of cause-and-effect relationship. The middle term between Christ's resurrection and that of others is belonging to Christ, being in him—in short, having Christian faith. The Christian's future is dependent upon and connected to Christ's past. As many have said, Paul believes that Christ's history is the believer's destiny. This destiny is not something that is inevitable apart from ongoing Christian faith. Thus we must see that in the *aparchē* analogy Paul is giving the Corinthians another chance to broaden their horizons and gain a salvation-historical perspective, and is also placing the discussion in the context of the larger idea of the *imitatio Christi.*

One further point is necessary about the first-fruits analogy. In 1 Corinthians 15:20 Paul says that Christ is the first-fruits of those who have "fallen asleep." Paul's use of the verb *koimaomai* probably does not suggest that he is affirming some sort of doctrine of soul sleep, as if death were a matter of lying down to pleasant dreams. This is unlikely since Paul sees death as the last enemy (15:26). While it is possible that he is simply adopting a Jewish euphemism for death, Paul may be using sleep here (and in 1 Thess 4:15) to mean that death is no more permanent nor potent than a sleep in the hands of a God who raises people from the dead. It is something a believer will rise up from very much alive and renewed. It is possible that Paul draws on a usage of "sleep" found in the Jesus tradition in various places (see Mk 5:39 and parallels; Jn 11:1-13).

In any event, it is clear that Paul sees resurrection in this passage as something that happens to those who are already dead. Neither in 1 Corinthians 15 nor in 1 Thessalonians 4 does Paul explicitly call what happens to those believers who are alive at the parousia "resurrection." This is because the resurrection Paul is talking about is different from the one some of the Corinthians apparently affirmed. Paul believes that resurrection is *ek nekrōn.* Finally, the first-fruits/latter-fruits analogy suggests that Paul saw the resurrection body of believers as of the same sort as Christ's resurrection body. This suggestion is confirmed by various other things Paul says elsewhere (see Phil 3:21).

We now turn to the seed analogy. We will examine it in the whole context of the discussion of the nature of the resurrection body in 1 Corinthians 15:35-50. The key to understanding the analogy, without pressing it too far, is to analyze the elements of both continuity and discontinuity between the present body and the resurrection body. For the sake of clarity, I will present these elements here at the beginning of the discussion.

Elements of Continuity	*Elements of Discontinuity*	
	Sown	*Raised*
(1) same person	perishable	imperishable
(2) a body	in dishonor	in glory
(3) life in a body	in weakness	in power
	natural body	spiritual body

It would seem that part of the problem for the Corinthians in regard to resurrection of the dead was its inconceivability. Paul argues by way of common analogy, using the idea that a seed put into the ground dies and then is brought to life again miraculously. This is untrue, but it was widely believed and Paul is simply drawing on this commonplace to make a point about resurrection, not about horticulture. In verse 36 the Corinthians who are denying the resurrection from the dead are likened to the fool in the psalms who fails to take into account God's actions in the process.

The first subsection (vv. 35-41) has two major points. First, resurrection is a miraculous event brought about as God wills it, just as he causes the crops to grow. Paul is not talking about some sort of bizarre natural process whereby one plants bodies in the ground that eventually rise up. Second, what is put in the earth is a naked seed that has to be clothed with a new and different body, just as dead believers must.

It is difficult to keep the balance between continuity and discontinuity, between the present body and the resurrection body. If there is a stronger emphasis here it seems to be on the discontinuity between the present physical body animated by a natural life principle and the resurrection body, which is animated by the Spirit.

Verse 38 argues not only that God gives each seed a plant body but also that each one has its own body.[40] It becomes clear that Paul conceives of resurrection as something that happens to each deceased believer who gets his or her own distinct resurrection body. There is no corporate body of Christ being raised. To punctuate that there are different kinds of bodies, he stresses that even in this physical existence there are different sorts of flesh—human flesh is not the same as bird or fish flesh, for instance. So also there are different sorts of bodies, both earthly and heavenly. Furthermore, verse 40 makes clear that these different bodies also have different sorts or degrees of splendor, just as stars differ in splendor.

While Paul does speak of a resurrection body and resurrection of dead people from out of the realm of dead persons, he does not seem to speak of resurrection of or in the *same* body.[41] We may properly ask what "somatically identical" might mean if it does not entail "materially identical."[42] For Paul what makes a body a body is not just its form but its substance. In particular, the analogy he has been developing has focused on the matter of the difference of *material substance* between the natural body and the resurrection body, and between one kind of creature's body and another's. We may perhaps urge that Paul saw a continuity in the form or shape of the two bodies, but we cannot argue that he held that the resurrection body is the *same* body, since it has different material substance. Doubtless, Paul was aware that bodies decayed rather rapidly, and so resurrection could not merely be a matter of revivifying a corpse (see vv. 46-50, "dust"). The body in its present condition, whether alive or dead, is not equivalent to the resurrection body, nor does the latter simply develop out of the former. In fact, what Paul says is that God will give the naked seed a body after it dies (vv. 37-38). The image is not the horticulturally correct one of a "body" or plant form developing out of the seed, but of a body being given to the seed.[43]

Here I must say something about the popular theory of R. Bultmann and M. E. Dahl that for Paul the term *sōma* refers to the person as a whole. On this view, a human being does not *have* a *sōma*, he *is* a *sōma*.[44] Remember that Bultmann was so insistent about this view that when it became evident in various places in 1 Corinthians 15 that this is not what Paul means by *sōma* he then accused Paul of inconsistency, caused by a failure to think abstractly.[45] Part of the reason that many have been persuaded that Bultmann was right is because it is often assumed that early Jews did not think dualistically about human nature. This sort of generalization should be rejected, as has been shown by Nickelsburg, J. W. Cooper and others.[46] Furthermore, the conclusions of the careful linguistic study of R. H. Gundry should be given their due:

We conclude that in neither the Pauline epistles, nor the literature of the NT outside those epistles, nor the LXX, nor extra-biblical ancient Greek literature does the definition "whole person" find convincing support. . . . Rather, apart from its use for a corpse, *sōma* refers to the physical body in its proper and intended union with the soul/spirit. The body and its counterpart are portrayed as united but distinct—and separable, though unnaturally and unwantedly separated. The *sōma* may *represent* the whole person simply because the *sōma* lives in union with the soul/spirit. But *sōma* does not mean "the whole person," because its use is designed to call attention to the physical object which is the body of the person rather than to the whole personality. Where used of whole people, *sōma* directs attention to their bodies, not to the wholeness of their being. . . . For the whole [person] in the unity of his parts, *anthrōpos* is ready to hand. . . . *Sōma*, however, remains faithful to its solely physical meaning.[47]

The *sōma* is the material part of human personality, and what constitutes it as physical substance Paul calls "flesh and blood," though doubtless this is just shorthand for all the material part of human personality. Put another way, while human bodies differ in form and so are distinguishable, they are alike in that all are constituted of *sarx*, in the neutral sense of the term.[48] It is also striking how different Paul's view on such matters is from Plato's. For Plato a human being is essentially *psychē* not *sōma* (see Phaedo 63B-C), while Paul argues that a Christian's destiny is to cease to be *psychikos* and become *pneumatikos*.[49]

In verses 39-41 it is clear that the issue is the substance and not merely the form of bodies. But what sort of body is the resurrection body? Here we must consider the contrast between the *sōma psychikon* and the *sōma pneumatikon*. As M. J. Harris and others have pointed out, adjectives and qualifiers ending in *ikon* almost always carry an ethical or functional meaning.[50] It is unlikely that Paul means a body made out of spiritual substance. Rather, he is urging that the resurrection body will be animated and fully empowered by the Spirit, rather than by a natural life principle as it is now. The *sōma psychikon* is a body empowered and animated by a natural life principle, in contrast to a body totally empowered by the Spirit. I take it that when Paul speaks of bearing the image of the man from heaven he is referring to having a body that partakes of the qualities of heaven—that which is immortal, imperishable and glorious. It is possible that Paul agrees that the believer's resurrection body in some sense comes from heaven. If so, then Paul does not develop this point in 1 Corinthians 15. All he says is, *kai hoios ho epouranios toioutoi kai ho epouranioi* (v. 48).

By *psychē* (v. 45), Paul means a human being, not the immaterial or immortal soul. By *psychikon* (v. 44) Paul is not referring to a "soulish" or spiritual body; to the contrary, he means a body that has physical or natural life in it. This body is *contrasted* with that which Paul wishes to call spiritual. J. W. Cooper points out that even in 1 Corinthians 15 Paul is capable of thinking in terms of limited dualism between the body and the person who inhabits the body. This limited dualism becomes more pronounced or evident in 2 Corinthians 5:1-10.[51] Paul is willing to argue that the present body is perishable, but he does not argue that the human being is perishable. Rather, once the believer dies, she or he "sleeps" in Christ. It is dead *persons* who receive new resurrection bodies, that is, a new form of life. Moule reminds us that talking about a "spiritual" body is not unprecedented in early Judaism. Other early Pharisees seem to have thought along these lines.[52] Yet Paul does not mean an "immaterial body" or a body made out of spirit by the phrase *pneumatikon sōma*. He means a body totally energized or empowered by the Spirit.

Undoubtedly, it would have been a jolt to the Corinthians to hear that being *pneumatikon* had something to do with bodies and bodily existence, not merely spiritual life as believers already experienced it. The truly spiritual person for Paul is ultimately the one who has the resurrection body.[53]

What then do we make of the statement in verse 50 that "flesh and blood cannot inherit the kingdom of God"? Earlier in this study I suggested that this means that a human being in a merely natural or physical condition cannot inherit the kingdom. Jeremias argues that by "flesh and blood" Paul means the living, while by "the perishable" Paul means corpses in decomposition. On this view Paul would be saying that neither the dead nor the living can inherit the kingdom in their present condition.[54]

The problems with this argument are severalfold. First, the abstract noun *hē phthora* is not a technical term for the dead or even for decomposing bodies. Second, the sentence makes much better sense if we have a case of synonymous, not synthetic, parallelism. *Both* the term "perishable" and the phrase "flesh and blood" refer to the fact that the present physical human form is subject to decay and is wasting away (see 2 Cor 4:16). That is why Paul says (v. 53) that it is *this* corruptible body *(phtharton touto)* that must put on an incorruptible body. This surely must include the body of the living as well as the dead (see v. 52b). Third, J. Gillman's extensive arguments about the structure of 1 Corinthians 15:50-53 support the view that "the perishable" is not a reference to decaying corpses or the dead. As Gillman says, since Jeremias wants to contrast flesh and blood with corruptible, it seems necessary then to also maintain that one must contrast the kingdom of God with incorruptible, but this makes no sense.[55] Fourth, elsewhere when Paul contrasts corruptible living human beings with the incorruptible God using the term *phthartos,* this term refers to a living human being and is used in a series describing various other living creatures (see Rom 1:23). When Paul uses the phrase "flesh and blood" the focus is not on simply being alive as opposed to being dead, but rather on the contingent character of physical life—it is frail and subject to decay and death.

Here we should compare 1 Corinthians 15:39, where the phrase "all flesh" refers to persons and all other creatures in their finite and transitory physical nature.[56] Paul believes that there must be a drastic change in the condition of both the living and the dead if they are to inherit the kingdom. They must take on an imperishable, immortal and powerful body in order to inherit the kingdom.

We now examine briefly how Paul views the place of the believer's resurrection in the eschatological schema. We saw in 1 Thessalonians 4 that there was an integral connection between the parousia and the resurrection. The imagery suggested that the one event precipitated the other. Indeed, the parousia seems in Paul's theology to be the one crucial event that not merely presages but actually precipitates the resurrection of believers. In 1 Corinthians 15 it becomes clear that the resurrection of believers is dependent on two episodes in the Christ event: Jesus' resurrection and the parousia. Verse 23 makes this quite clear: "Christ, the firstfruits; then, *when he comes,* those who belong to him." What is much less clear is whether what follows in verse 24 follows the resurrection of believers in chronological sequence. The *eita* in verse 24a would seem to indicate a further development after the resurrection of believers.

The problem with this conclusion is severalfold. First, we have seen in 2 Thessalonians 2:8 that Paul affirms that the forces of darkness, or at least the paramount human (?) embodiment of them, will be destroyed *by the appearing of his coming.* Second, there is the further logical problem that if the last enemy to be destroyed is death (1 Cor 15:26), is Paul really arguing that believers will be raised in a deathless body and yet death has not yet been totally destroyed? It would seem more appropriate to maintain that death, the last enemy, is finally destroyed *by God's raising of believers.* I thus incline to the view of G. D. Fee:

> With the resurrection of the dead, the end, or goal has been reached; an "end" that has two sides to it. On the one hand, the resurrection of the dead will mean that Christ has subjugated and thereby destroyed, the final enemy death, expressed in this case in the terminology "every dominion" and "every authority and power." That this destruction of the "powers" refers to the defeat of death is made certain by the supporting argument from Scripture that follows. On the other hand, with the final defeat of the last enemy the subjugation of all things has taken place, so that Christ might turn over the "rule" to God the Father. The rest of the argument spells out how this is so.[57]

In other words, once the resurrection of believers happens the last enemy is conquered and the turning over of the kingdom to the Father immediately ensues. Here we may finally find another clue as to why Paul speaks of inheriting the kingdom *of God.* The act of inheriting only takes place once the dead believers are raised and the kingdom has been turned back over to the Father. Thus it is a kingdom ruled by the Father, not the Son, that they are inheriting. Here also we see why inheriting cannot transpire before the parousia and the resurrection of believers. On the one hand, believers must be in the right immortal and imperishable condition to inherit the kingdom. On the other hand, Christ must also complete his victory over the forces of darkness and turn the kingdom over to the Father before they may inherit. Thus, for Paul *to telos* refers to a complex of events, including resurrection of believers, which means final victory over death, turning over of the kingdom, and inheriting of that kingdom. These events are made possible by the two Christ events: the resurrection of Christ and his return.

Finally, we must turn to the question of the relationship of what happens to the living at the parousia vis-à-vis what happens to the dead. Paul addresses this concern in verses 51-52. It is hard to escape the conclusion that for Paul, however different the transformation of the living and the dead believers may be, the end result is the same. Both, in the end, partake of life in an immortal, imperishable, glorious body. In short, Paul is not so concerned about the process as the final product of that final eschatological change the believer will undergo.

Verse 52 indicates that the dead will be raised. Unlike 1 Thessalonians 4, Paul does not really specify here that this will happen *prior* to the change of the living, but this text does not rule out such a thought. In any event, Paul calls what happens to *both* the living and the dead a change *(pantes de allagēsometha,* v. 51). Verse 52b seems to suggest that Paul wishes to call what happens to the living only a change, *not* resurrection *(allagēsometha* again). The verb *allassō* is used only in these two verses in the New Testament. The contrast in verse 52 plus the use of the term *all* in verse 51 must strongly suggest that Paul uses the verb of both living and dead in verse 51, but only of the living in verse 52.[58] In these verses it becomes clear that Paul also sees both resurrection and change as happening instantaneously at the parousia.

Some have speculated that comparing 1 Corinthians 15:51 to 1 Thessalonians 4:15 suggests that Paul has modified his view somewhat of how many of his contemporaries will be alive at the parousia. In 1 Thessalonians 4:15, it is argued, he believes the majority would be alive, while in 1 Corinthians 15:51 he may have thought that only a minority would live until the parousia. Paul, in fact, does not engage in such chronological speculation in either text, but both do suggest that Paul considered it possible that Christ could come during his and his contemporaries' lifetimes.

Having considered Paul's discussion in 1 Corinthians 15 at some length now, it becomes clear that for Paul resurrection is something that happens to the dead—both to Christ (as the reference to burial in 15:4 intimates) and to Christians (vv. 51-52). Also, Paul calls the final body believers will have a "spiritual" body, not a resurrection body. This is perhaps because he believed that only some Christians, properly speaking, would be raised. Also, for Paul the final state involves embodied existence, indeed existence in permanent bodies. Both this fact, and the fact that Paul envisions "the End" happening not in heaven but on earth when Christ returns, strongly suggests that for Paul the kingdom will be an earthly one, albeit with heavenly qualities.

This comports with Romans 8:19-25, where Paul envisions the transformation of the earth when believers experience the redemption of their bodies. Thus, while in 1 Corinthians 15 Paul is focusing on final human resurrection or transformation, it is highly probable that he sees this as but a part of a larger process of the renewal of the whole of material creation. The kingdom will be inherited on earth and that requires not only transformed persons but also a transformed earth. Thus Beker is quite right that for Paul the destiny of believers and of creation are inextricably linked together: "the present paradox of victory *amid* death (2 Cor. 4:11) can be sustained by the hope in the transformation of all creation, that is, in the victory *over* death."[59] For Paul the resurrection of Christ only finally can mean victory for Christians and the world if it is linked to and makes possible the resurrection, or "change," of Christians and the transformation of the world. In short, Paul's realized eschatology necessarily entails future eschatology, and if one abandons the latter one seriously distorts the meaning and significance of the former for the believer. Among other things one abandons Paul's teleological perspective about the future.

Neither in Romans nor in 2 Corinthians is resurrection—either of Christ or of believers—a major theme. It is also true, however, that in both documents there is sufficiently clear evidence of Paul's continued belief in these realities that it is not possible to argue that Paul has simply abandoned his future eschatology for a present one, or for one realized at death in heaven. We will turn our attention to 2 Corinthians now.

The first reference of relevance is found in 2 Corinthians 1:9b. Here and elsewhere Paul relies on traditional and sometimes scriptural formulae to express his doctrine of resurrection. It appears likely that Deuteronomy 32:39 and 1 Samuel 2:6 (LXX) stand in the background here, and possibly the second of the Eighteen Benedictions: "You O Lord, are mighty for ever, you make the dead to live. . . ."[60] Romans 4:17 should be compared as a near parallel. In both texts Paul likely draws on traditional Jewish liturgical expressions without really Christianizing them.[61] Though we do have a traditional formula here, Paul's use of it indicates his endorsement of the idea that it expresses.

More specifically Christian is 2 Corinthians 4:14: "Because we know that the one who raised the Lord Jesus from the dead will also raise us with Jesus and present us with you in his presence." Here we see the characteristic paralleling of Christ's and believers' resurrections in words very similar to those in 1 Corinthians 6:14. The future tense of *parastēsei* coupled with the fact that Paul speaks of both his converts and himself being presented to Christ simultaneously makes clear that he must be talking about what will happen not at death but at the final consummation.[62] The scene here envisioned may be the presentation before the judgment seat on which Christ sits (see 2 Cor 5:10), but it is more likely that at least the major focus of this verse is sharing in the triumph over death that Christ has already experienced.

Furnish rightly points out that Paul is also stressing that he will be with his converts on that great eschatological day. "As Paul indicates more explicitly in other places (1:14; Phil 2:16; 1 Thess 2:19) this being together with his converts in the presence of the Lord will be the crowning evidence not only of the authenticity of their faith but also of the authenticity of those by whom they have come to faith."[63] Paul then seems to allude here to the fact that his converts will be his "crown of boasting" on that day and that when he is presented with them they will be evidence provided to the Lord on which his judgment of Paul may be based. Certainly nothing here suggests that by the time he wrote this letter Paul had abandoned his eager expectation of the eschatological future on earth in favor of a purely otherworldly solution to the problem of death. But this leads us to a discussion of the much-debated material in 2 Corinthians 5:1-10.

These verses should be seen as part of the major subsection that begins at 4:7. Paul simply extends his argument contrasting the temporal and temporary with the heavenly and permanent, the inner with the outer and the invisible with the visible, into 5:1-10. As we shall see, the earthly tent or building corresponds to the earthen vessels (4:7), outer person (4:16), body (4:10) and mortal flesh (4:11). We must also keep steadily in view throughout this section that Paul is adopting and adapting the limited dualism found in early Judaism in such places as 1 Enoch 39:4: "And there I saw another vision, the dwelling places of the holy, and the resting places of the righteous. Here mine eyes saw their dwelling places with his righteous angels, and their resting places with the holy."[64] Paul's thought differs, however, in that limited dualism is eventually resolved into a form of monism because of his belief in the future resurrection of believers, as we have already seen in 2 Corinthians 4:14.

There are various clear hints in 5:1-10 that Paul is discussing, among other things, a future resurrection of believers. First, as R. P. Martin has pointed out, the contrasts in 2 Corinthians 5 between the present physical body and the future spiritual one are the same sort as those in 1 Corinthians 15. The language is different, but the ideas are basically the same. Here we hear of *tou skēnous* as opposed to *oikodomēn*, or *epigeios* as opposed to *oikian acheiropoiēton*, or *katalythē* as opposed to *aiōnion en tois ouranois*. This should be compared to the chart listing discontinuities earlier in this chapter. Second, due attention must be paid to the verb *stenazō* in 5:2, 4, which is found elsewhere in Paul only in a letter *later* than 2 Corinthians to describe the groaning we experience in this body as we look forward to the liberation that will come when we obtain the future resurrection body (Rom 8:23). Third, the phrase in verse 4, "what is mortal may be swallowed up by life," closely parallels 1 Corinthians 15:54 where the same verb, *katepothē*, is used to speak of death being swallowed up in victory. In both 2 Corinthians 5:1 and 1 Corinthians 15:48-49 the future life is contrasted with the form of existence that can be characterized by the adjective *epigeios*. We might also point to the concept of nakedness, though it is used somewhat differently in 1 Corinthians 15 than it is in 2 Corinthians 5.

Nevertheless, in view of the obvious similarities between these two texts and bearing in mind the fact that both 1 Corinthians 15 and at least this portion of 2 Corinthians were addressed to the same audience within a reasonably short span of time, it would be hard for the audience *not* to assume that Paul was at least in part discussing the same subject he had already broached in the earlier letter.

V. P. Furnish is right to point out that Paul is not developing a thanatology per se in this material.[65] His focus here is on various forms of life, not death. Yet it would be wrong to ignore the fact that in 5:1 he alludes to death, and death is something that happens to persons individually, not corporately. Furthermore, why would Paul speak of longing for something that he already has, that is, participation in the body of Christ? It is unlikely that Paul is speaking about what has or will happen to Christians corporately. The bodies he has in mind are those of individual Christians like himself, not the corporate body of Christ. The bodies Paul is expostulating about are each individually subject to disease, decay and ultimately death.[66]

In 2 Corinthians 5:1 Paul seems to be drawing on a saying from the Jesus tradition—Mark 14:58 (compare *katalysō-katalythē; oikodomesō-oikodomēn; acheiropoiēton-acheiropoiēton).*[67] To be sure, he is putting it to a different use, for originally the saying was in part about the temple in Jerusalem. Yet in the Christian interpretation of this saying found in John 2:21 at least the second half of the saying was understood to refer to Jesus' resurrection body, not some final eschatological temple in Jerusalem. Paul also calls both the church corporately and the bodies of individual Christians temples of the Holy Spirit (compare 1 Cor 3:16 to 6:19). It is possible that Paul knew the early Christian interpretation of Mark 14:58 in terms of the resurrection of Jesus in a new body, and now having alluded to it, applies the same idea to individual believers as part of his larger stress on the *imitatio Christi.*[68]

If Paul is not speaking of some sort of corporate resurrection of the body, whether in the past (at baptism?) or future, might he be suggesting that the resurrection body now can be received in heaven at the point of death? Moule has been a noted advocate of the view that in 2 Corinthians 5:1-10 we have evidence that Paul had changed his mind in this sort of direction.[69] On the one hand, Paul does speak of this new building as "eternal in the heavens." In verse 2 as well, this building is called a heavenly one, and in verse 8 Paul speaks of preferring to be away from the body and at home with the Lord.

On the other hand, there are some solid reasons to reject this view. First, Paul speaks of the heavenly state in verse 8 as a matter of being away from *the body (ek tou sōmatos),* not merely being away from "this present body."[70] This is made more clear in verse 3 where Paul uses the term *gymnoi.* Being found naked is not described here in moral terms as if it meant being found wanting at the final judgment. The final judgment does not enter the discussion until verse 10. Rather, "being naked" is contrasted with the putting on of the heavenly building. Paul's use of *gymnos* is not unlike that elsewhere in Hellenistic Jewish sources like Philo (see *Leg. All.* 2.57-59), as well as in older Greek sources such as Plato (*Crat.*

403B; *Gorgias* 524D). In both contexts the term *naked* refers to the disembodied state that ensues once one dies. J. N. Sevenster is right to point out that Paul's view of being disembodied differs significantly from both Plato and Philo:

Paul does not consider this "being found naked" as something desirable, but he shrinks from it. He hopes that it will last as shortly as possible, if he has to go through it at all. In the writings of Plato and Philo the logical conse-quence from their anthropological starting-point is that the being *gumnos* is for them a state, for which they long.[71]

Paul's sighing with anxiety is not the "Greek" longing to be freed from the burden of the body so much as it is a longing to be "further clothed."

The textual problem in verse 3 probably can be resolved by accepting the reading that has the best manuscript support—*endysamenoi*.[72] Thus the text should read "we groan, longing to put on our heavenly house, since indeed we shall put it on and we shall not be found naked."[73]

Jewish attitudes about nakedness are well attested (see M. Ber. 3.5). The Co-rinthians likely would have been familiar with the idea of nakedness being equat-ed with being stripped of the body at death, as this idea has appeared in Greek literature (Plato *Cratylus* 403B; *Phaedo* 67DE, cf. 81C.; *Republic* IX.577B; in Latin literature see *Historia Augusta, Hadrian* 25). But in this case what is decisive in deciding what Paul means by nakedness is the context: "Where *gum-nos* is opposed to the concept of being clothed in verse 3 and synonymous with that expressed by *ekdusasthai,* and where this clothing is expressly seen in terms of embodiment, then *gumnos* quite naturally must be seen as referring to a state of disembodiment."[74]

It is also necessary to give due attention to Paul's changing of verbs between *ependysasthai, enduesthai,* and *ekdysamenos.* The first of these verbs means "to put on over" something, like the putting on of an overcoat over another garment, while *enduesthai* (see 1 Cor 15:53-54, another clue that we are dealing with the same subject as in 1 Cor 15) simply means "to put on," and *ekdysamenos* refers to taking off.[75] Paul uses these variations in verb forms to express his longing to live until the parousia and simply be further clothed by the resurrection body, rather than having to be unclothed at death.

It may not be pressing *ependysasthai* too far to point out that Paul does not speak of the transforming of the old garment here, unlike in 1 Corinthians 15. Rather, here he intimates that what happens to the living at the parousia is more like putting something on top of what one already has. This comports nicely with what Paul says in 5:1-2, that we have a heavenly building that is eternal *en tois ouranois*. Though this is obviously a metaphorical way of putting things, and Paul mixes his metaphors, speaking of both buildings and being clothed, all of this suggests the idea of the resurrection body, at least for the living *not* being "somatically" identical with the present body. Paul speaks as one who has a body currently wasting away but knows there is already another to replace it "in the heavens." In fact, in 5:2 Paul says that the building comes from heaven *(ek ouranou)*.

While it might seem strange that Paul sees dying and going to be with the Lord in heaven a matter of nakedness when at the same time he also thinks that "we have a building from God . . . in the heavens," the idea of both nakedness and also garments in heaven is attested elsewhere in early Jewish-Christian literature (see Rev 6:9-11). There are no major difficulties in seeing 2 Corinthians 5:1-10 as simply a development of Paul's previous discussion in 1 Corinthians 15 with no significant change in ideas about what resurrection and the resurrection body might amount to. Barrett has summed up matters well:

> It is important to see the resemblance between what is said in this chapter, and in 1 Cor.xv. on the one hand, and Philippians on the other. There is little sign of development in Paul's thought on this subject beyond the fact that as time advanced he found that he must take with increasing seriousness the possibility of his own death, and in doing so took with increasing seriousness the sense in which even the dead are with the Lord.[76]

By way of closing remarks about the intermediate state, Ellis urges that "the 'intermediate state' is something that the living experience with respect to the dead, not something the dead experience with respect to the living or Christ."[77] Besides the fact that this does not comport either with early Jewish ideas about the spirits of the righteous dwelling with God or with early Jewish-Christian ideas such as that found in Revelation 6:9-11 or a parable like that found in Luke 16:19-31, it simply does not make sense of 2 Corinthians 5:1-10. Why should Paul long to miss death and go straight from life in this body to life in a resurrection body if he believed that there is no real interim period of "nakedness" for the dead anyway? Thus, while Paul is not here focusing on the interim state but only alludes to it in passing, it is reasonably clear that he believes in such a state. It is also clear that he finds such a state a mixed blessing. On the one hand, it involves the bliss of going and being with the Lord, which is far better than the trials and suffering of this life away from the Lord. On the other hand, for Paul life without a body is not life in the full sense of the word but a form of nakedness that is to some degree embarrassing and no happy final state of affairs.

If Paul had to choose between life in heaven and life in a resurrection body on earth there is no question but that he prefers the latter. This preference, expressed in 2 Corinthians 5:3, is reiterated later in his life (see Phil 3:11), as is his preference for going and being with Christ over remaining in this veil of suffering and decay (compare Phil 1:21-23 to 2 Cor 5:8). Thus, going to heaven, while it is a great gain in one's closeness to Christ, is still decidedly a second best to life in a resurrection body. Herein we see how different are Paul's views from those of most modern Christians for whom going to heaven is seen as the ultimate form of eternal bliss. There are no more significant references to resurrection in 2 Corinthians apart from the passing reference to Christ's death and resurrection in 2 Corinthians 5:15.

Romans 1:4, which likely represents Paul's adaptation of a traditional Jewish-Christian confessional formula, has several elements of interest to us.[78] *Oristhentos*, which is a hapax legomenon in Paul, means "appointed," "determined" or "designated to be."[79] Christ was designated to be the Son of God *in power* from the resurrection of the dead. This indicates that Jesus entered into a new stage of his work that was more exalted and powerful than when he was Son of God in weakness during his earthly ministry. This new power seems to be associated with his having the "Spirit of power" or perhaps his being raised by the "Holy Spirit." The key phrase for our purposes is *ek anastaseōs nekrōn*. This does not mean "as from his resurrection from the dead" but "as from the resurrection of the dead." In short, the phrase associates what happened to Jesus with the general resurrection of the dead. This comports with the first-fruits analogy in 1 Corinthians 15, but it also should be compared to the unique tradition in Matthew 27:52-53, where Jesus' resurrection is seen to be accompanied by the resurrection of various saints.[80]

Here the resurrection of Jesus is seen as the prerequisite to his being installed at the right hand of God as Son of God in power. Without resurrection Jesus would not be who he has become to believers—the Son of God in power and thereby a life-giving spirit.

In Romans 4:24-25 we begin to see Paul reflecting on the *present* benefits to believers of Christ's resurrection. We are told not only that God raised Jesus from the dead, but also at least part of the reason why: because of or for *our* justification/ vindication.[81] This makes clear again how crucial Christ's resurrection is for Paul's theology in general. There is a sense in which everything hinges on it. Jesus would not fully be the Christ without the resurrection, nor would he be the Son of God in power, a Son who could be a present help to believers, without the resurrection. It is equally true that Christians would still be in their sins, which is another way of saying they would not be justified/acquitted without Christ's resurrection. There would be no eschatological hope of a resurrection like Christ's for believers if God had not raised him from the dead.

This makes abundantly clear how Paul's beliefs about the future have been shaped and are determined christologically. Paul does not affirm a general resurrection of all the dead. Indeed he does not posit any resurrection even for believers without there first being a resurrection of Jesus. Paul has reshaped his prior Pharisaic eschatological beliefs in light of his newfound christological convictions. The Christ event is both central to and determinative for Paul's eschatology. Here Beker has placed the emphasis in the wrong spot, and it has led him to make Christology something less than the formative part of theology for Paul.[82]

Romans 6:4-9 continues the trend of relating Christ's resurrection to the *present* life and behavior of Christians. Christ was raised from the dead so that *(houtos)* we might now walk in newness of life. Lest we suspect that this stress on the present effects of Christ's resurrection has led Paul to abandon the parallel between Christ's resurrection and the believers at the parousia, in the very next verse (6:5) Paul reiterates this parallel. Note, however, how closely the theme of *imitatio Christi* is tied to the discussion of resurrection. A statement is made claiming that if we have in this present life been united with Christ in his death (experienced death to sin, the burial of the old nature), then we shall also rise in a resurrection like his. The *ei* here could be translated "since" rather than "if," but in either case Paul is talking about the consequences of being united with Christ in his death.[83] Future resurrection in the likeness of Christ depends on present faith in and union with Christ. This is stated another way in verse 8, but the point is the same. Present experience and behavior (v. 4c) determines whether one will experience a resurrection like Christ's in the future. The future tense of *esometha* must be taken seriously in verse 5. Believers have not yet obtained the likeness of Christ's resurrection that Paul is talking about.

In Romans 8 we find two more examples of Paul's linking the believers' present condition with their future resurrection. In verse 11 the future "giving life to your mortal bodies" is made dependent on the Spirit's current presence and work in the believer.[84] The same point is made in a different way in verse 23. This verse raises the question whether, since Paul calls what believers have of the Spirit "firstfruits," he sees the "redemption of our bodies" as an act of the Spirit, or the point at which one receives the fullness of the Spirit. This requires that we take "of the Spirit" as appositive here, or possibly possessive, rather than partitive. The epexegetic sense possibly should be preferred, in which case Paul means that having the Spirit in the present *is* the first-fruits of the eventual harvest that will belong to believers.

In verse 11 we note the clear linking of Christ's and believers' resurrections— or at least their final transformation. A further implication is possible. For the first time it is possible that Paul is suggesting that the resurrection body will be numerically and "somatically" identical with the present body. This is not certain because Paul is addressing the condition of the living. It is in living Christians that the Spirit now dwells, and notice that in verse 11 we are told that it is through the Spirit that *now* dwells in them that life will be given to their mortal bodies. It follows from this that in both verses 11 and 23 Paul likely is referring to the transformation of the living believers at the parousia rather than to the resurrection of the dead. This would explain why he speaks of the "redemption of *our* bodies" (v. 23). Paul seems still to be entertaining the possibility of being alive at the parousia (see 13:11). This may explain why in neither verse does he speak of the believer being raised *ek nekrōn*. He does not do so because he is addressing what will happen to living believers should Christ soon return. Thus, neither of these verses count against the view that Paul still thought of the exchange of one body for another in the case of dead Christians. In short, even in Romans 8 we do not read of the resurrection of the flesh of dead believers.

Other verses in Romans lend some insight into Paul's view of resurrection. In 8:30 it appears that Paul is thinking of the final eschatological state of the believer when he speaks of being glorified. Confirmation of this will be found when we examine Philippians. There is a further reference to Christ's death and resurrection in 8:33, with the implication that Christ has the role he does at God's right hand interceding for us as a result of the resurrection.

In Romans 10:9 belief in Christ's resurrection is seen as a sine qua non for being saved. Here Paul probably is citing an essential part of an early Christian creedal formula, and once again we see how the onset of the eschatological realities are seen as beginning in the climax of Jesus' life.[85] The resurrection of Jesus is as essential for the Christian as it was for Christ. Romans 14:9 adds the thought that the reason or purpose for which Christ died and lived again was so that he might be the Lord of both the dead and the living. It has been pointed out that "the Lordship of Christ is in the theology of St. Paul always connected with His resurrection, not His life, which was a period of humiliation (Rom. viii. 34; 2 Cor. iv. 10, 11)."[86] We may add that assuming lordship is also in Paul dependent on Christ's death. There is for Paul a belief that Christ did not, at least in the full sense, exercise his lordship until after his resurrection. Only then did he assume the position of a *kyrios* at God's right hand (see Rom 8:34; Phil 2:11). Paul always seems to look at Christ in terms of the narrative of the drama of salvation and the successive stages of the Christ event.

In Romans we have seen a new theme emerge in Paul's discussion of the resurrection. In various texts Paul closely connects the believers' present condition or behavior either to Christ's resurrection or to believers' resurrection or to both. It appears that the common denominator is the Holy Spirit, who is involved in both the resurrection of Christ and of Christians, and in the present in the ongoing conforming of the believer to the image of the Son (see Rom 8:23-29). Paul does not isolate belief from behavior or events past and future from their present consequences or importance. Rather, these matters are all closely bound together in Paul's gospel. At the heart of the matter is resurrection *and* walking in newness of life.

To conclude the discussion of Paul's view of resurrection we turn to Philippians 3:10-11 and 21. The first thing that we notice about 3:10 is that Paul, perhaps for the first time, seems to be willing to describe a present experience as knowing Christ and the power of his resurrection.[87] This idea is found more clearly in Colossians 2:12 and 3:1.[88] But is it absolutely certain that Paul is speaking of a present experience of resurrection in 3:10?

Against such a view is the following: (1) in 3:11b it is clear that Paul is referring to the future resurrection; and (2) in verse 12 Paul says that he has *not* already obtained various things he had just spoken of; for instance, "gaining Christ" in verse 8 seems to refer to a future event. The construction *hina* plus the subjunctive of the verb "gaining" does not suggest something already obtained, or at least already completely obtained.[89] The construction in verse 10 is different. Here we have an infinitive with the genitive definite article. Inasmuch as this clause is parallel to the two previous *hina*-plus-subjunctive clauses, it seems that a future referent is intended in verse 10 as well. In fact, we might translate verse 10: "that I might know him in the power of his resurrection."[90] We must conclude that it is not certain that 3:10 speaks of a present experience of resurrection, though it cannot be ruled out.

In any event Paul expects to share in "his sufferings" in this lifetime, becoming like Christ in his death "if somehow I might attain the resurrection from the dead" (at the parousia). The *ei* plus a subjunctive verb suggests an element of doubt; Paul in all humility here is not taking for granted that he will attain that resurrection unless he has been conformed to Christ's image in his sufferings first. Here again is the suggestion that future participation in bliss is contingent on what the Christian does between now and then. It is true that *ei* plus the subjunctive verb may convey the idea that Paul is not presuming on the divine mercy, but we must not overlook the clear connection between 10b and 11. Verse 11 cannot stand alone but is dependent on what has come before it, that is, the conforming of onself (present ongoing activity) to his death.

The theme of *imitatio Christi* is plain here both in regard to suffering and dying with Christ and in knowing the power of *his* resurrection. Verse 11 speaks of resurrection *ek nekrōn*, "from out of the dead," which probably again suggests the idea of a resurrection of the righteous from among the realm of dead persons. The noun Paul uses appears to be one he himself coined, *ekanastasis*, with the added prefix *ek* to strengthen the idea that resurrection is out of, or from, the dead.[91]

Philippians 3:21 adds some further nuances. R. P. Martin points out the detailed parallels between 3:20ff. and the Christ hymn in 2:6-11:

form (2:6, 8)	conform (3:21)
being *(hyparchōn*—2:6)	"is" *(hyparchei*—3:20)
likeness *(schēma*—2:7)	change *(metaschēmatizei*—3:21)
humbled *(etapeinōsen*—2:8)	"lowly body" *(tapeinōseōs*—3:21)
every knee bow (2:10)	subject all things (3:21)
Jesus Christ is Lord (2:11)	the Lord Jesus Christ (3:21)
glory *(doxa*—2:11)	"body of glory" *(doxa*—3:21).[92]

It may be that both sections in Philippians ultimately are of liturgical or creedal origin.[93] Paul, however, uses the language of the hymn to further the presentation of the pattern of the *imitatio Christi.* Is Paul envisioning living until the parousia and being "changed" into the likeness of Christ rather than being raised? If so, then he is not suggesting that resurrection is "of the body" or "in the same body" one had while on earth. Against this conjecture is 3:11 in which Paul seems to expect to die before the parousia (compare 1:19-26).

Note the element of doubt expressed in verse 11. Paul's thought may run as follows: "If I die while sharing in the sufferings of Christ then I hope to attain to the resurrection." In verse 21 Paul may be contemplating the other possibility—that he might live to be changed at the parousia (see 1 Cor 15:51). A temporal interpretation of 4:5b might also support this conjecture. In Philippians, Paul may well be oscillating back and forth between the possibilities of dying before or living until the parousia and resurrection of the righteous.

What is more clear is that Paul expects a dramatic transformation from "the body of our humiliation" to a glorious body like the risen Christ has. Here there is a stress on discontinuity—the body that we will get at the parousia will *not* be humiliating or subject to disease, decay, death. In verse 21 Paul announces the cosmic scope of the renewal he envisions. The transformation of a believer's body will be accomplished by the same power that enables Christ to subject all things to himself. Here the echo of both the Christ hymn in Philippians 2 and 1 Corinthians 15:24-28 is clear. As Hawthorne puts it, "The energy by which he transfigures mortal bodies is the energy by which he subdues the universe and subjects all things to his authority. The resurrection of the dead and the transformation of broken persons is but one part, the most significant part, to be sure, of the great drama of cosmic redemption."[94] For Paul the ultimate goal for Christians is complete conformity to the image of Christ, even in one's body, which will be made into the image of Christ's glorious and powerful resurrection body.

We have seen clear evidence that resurrection for Paul entails bodies from first to last. Paul never totally spiritualizes the idea of resurrection, for even in the same context where he speaks of walking in newness of life he goes on to speak of a future resurrection involving bodies. It is not clear that Paul taught the resurrection of bodies or of the flesh, but it is clear that he spoke of the resurrection of Christians out from the realm of the dead who would receive a resurrection body.

In the end Paul himself would prefer to experience the transformation of living believers rather than the resurrection of dead ones, but the final product of either process is life in an immortal, powerful and glorious body like Christ's. For Paul the theme of *imitatio Christi* in the body refers not only to what God is doing to and for the believer, but also to some degree to how one behaves in the body. *Imitatio Christi* is indeed a matter of both working out one's salvation with fear and trembling and God energizing the person to will and to do. Yet when it comes to the resurrection this is an action that the believer can only passively receive. Paul never speaks of either Christ or Christians raising or transforming themselves. Believers may well qualify or disqualify themselves for such a resurrection by proper or improper conduct that does or does not conform to Christ's character, but they cannot earn, achieve or cause their own resurrection.

The resurrection of Christ is the foundation stone of Paul's gospel, providing the basis for the offer of forgiveness of sins and justification. Resurrection is also the goal for believers; it is that which one strives to attain. There is a sense in which the theme of resurrection circumscribes the Pauline narrative of salvation, providing both its basis and its dramatic climax. In the end, being a Christian means being like Christ not only in character here and now, but also in body and in power then and there.

We cannot help but note the paranetic thrust of the way Paul uses the theme of resurrection in such varied texts as 1 Corinthians 15 and Philippians 3. He uses it to encourage or instill moral striving, and offers himself as an example of one who is still striving precisely because he believes in the resurrection from out of the dead for believers. This is the true and climactic form Paul's hope takes. To deny the resurrection, whether of Christ or of Christians, since this is two parts of the same event, is to jettison the essence and basis of Christian hope. Without this very concrete object of hope, preaching is pointless and Christian living is in vain. In short, for Paul the basis of ethics, Christian living, preaching and even Christology (for there would be no living Lord Jesus Christ without the resurrection) is the resurrection.[95]

There is no clear evidence that Paul ever wavered on this point or seriously modified the character of his belief in resurrection. He certainly did not exchange it for a belief in life in heaven, which at most Paul saw as an interim condition, which while good in comparison to this life, was no satisfactory conclusion to the process of redemption. Life in heaven for Paul was decidedly second-best to experiencing life in a resurrection body forever animated by the eternal Spirit.

Thus, for Paul the drama of redemption must have an earthly conclusion, or else salvation is not complete. Without such a conclusion there can be no renewal of the earth as well as of believers. Without such a conclusion there can be no inheriting of the kingdom of God on earth, or fulfilling of the earthly promises of God to Israel. Without such a conclusion there is no point to a doctrine of a parousia, a return of Christ to raise the dead and to be with his people forever in the Dominion of God.

It is hardly surprising that Paul never speaks of a general resurrection of the dead. For him resurrection was the final step in being conformed to the likeness of Christ so that one might participate in God's eternal Dominion. Only Christians had this hope, in Paul's view. It is Christ in the believer that provides the hope of glory, the hope of sharing in his glorious resurrection.

Thus the drama of salvation has three main acts: (1) the death and resurrection of Christ, which makes possible salvation; (2) the new creation, first-fruits of the Spirit, newness of life, forgiveness and justification the believer experiences now as a result of Christ's resurrection; and (3) the future resurrection/transformation of believers at the parousia. In the end Paul varies little from the early Jewish-Christian picture of what final salvation will and must look like in Revelation 21—it will entail not only new believers but also a new heaven, a new earth and a new Jerusalem on earth that has come down out of heaven (compare Gal 4:26 to Rev 21:9ff.). The realities that already exist in heaven will find their final purpose and resting place on earth. Then and then only will the kingdoms of this world become the kingdoms "of our God and of his Christ."

—22—

Before and Afterlife: Jesus and the Resurrection

There is much less that we can say about Jesus' views on resurrection, but the one thing we can affirm with some certainty is that Jesus believed in a future resurrection, and that he believed that resurrection entailed a significant discontinuity with life as we now experience it in the body. There is surprisingly little evidence of any detailed discussion by Jesus on the subject of resurrection in the arguably authentic material within the Synoptic Gospels. This likely means that in the main Paul got his doctrine of resurrection *not* from the Jesus traditions (apart perhaps from his use of Mk 14:58), but from his Pharisaic background and perhaps to a greater degree from the early Jewish-Christian reflection on resurrection, especially as it is found in early Jewish-Christian creeds and hymns. Paul did not simply take over such traditions but applied his own fertile mind to them, adopting and adapting such traditions and adding to them in his own inimitable way. We point this out in advance because the overlap between Jesus and Paul on the subject of resurrection seems to be meager in comparison to the overlap we have found between their teachings on other eschatological subjects.

Our first text, Mark 12:18-27 and parallels, is one I have given detailed attention to in a previous book.[1] This passage has good claims to go back to a *Sitz
im Leben Jesu* for various reasons. Besides the fact that there is no evidence that
the early church debated the issue of Levirate marriage, a practice already in
general disuse in Jesus' day, there is also no evidence of a tendency in the Jesus
tradition to make Sadducees Jesus' interlocutors. Furthermore, as we have already seen in Paul, when the early church spoke of resurrection they thought of
Christlikeness, not of being like the angels. We may be rather sure then that the
substance of the discussion in Mark 12:18-27 is authentic.

From this pericope we learn that Jesus affirms the reality of the resurrection
in some form, and that he stressed the discontinuity between bodily existence as
we now know it and life after the resurrection. Despite confident assertions by
various scholars, it does not seem likely that Jesus is arguing for a marriageless
and sexless existence in the life to come.[2] Rather, the point is that since there will
be no more death once the resurrection takes place (angels being deathless beings)
then the circumstances that precipitated Levirate marriage and questions about
it will no longer exist. Jesus' questioners seem to have assumed that life in the
world to come would simply be a continuation of the circumstances currently
existing. In short, they overemphasized the element of continuity between this life
and the life to come.

Jesus counters such suppositions with a stress on discontinuity that appears to
involve the fact that no new marital relationships will be initiated. The phrases
"to marry" and "giving in marriage" are the traditional ways of speaking of the
act of *marrying* in a patriarchal culture where men marry and women are given
by their fathers in marriage. Nonetheless, this passage may imply that previous
marital relationships will cease as well.

Jesus places the discussion of resurrection in the context of beliefs about the
Jewish patriarchs (Abraham, Isaac and Jacob); that is, in the context of the
believing people of God. Thus it may be significant that verse 25 speaks of
resurrection *ek nekrōn,* resurrection out of the dead.[3]

Verses 26-27 are somewhat difficult to decipher, but the thrust of the use of
Exodus 3:6 seems to be that since Abraham, Isaac and Jacob are still alive, and
not simply dead or in Sheol as the Sadducees supposed, then a belief in the
afterlife in some form is suggested even by the Pentateuch. Verse 27 does not go
on to say that the three patriarchs have already been raised from the dead, only
that they are alive, and thus presumably Jesus assumes they will be raised. The

sequence of verses 26-27 suggests that Jesus thought that the dead, paradoxically enough, were still alive in some sense, but that according to verse 25a they had yet to experience the resurrection from the dead.

The crux of the matter is what being like the angels in the resurrection amounts to. Luke 20:36 provides us with an interpretation by the Evangelist, and it is probably the correct one. It amounts to having a deathless, but not necessarily a genderless, existence. There is some irony in this argument since Sadducees apparently did not believe in angels either (see Acts 23:8).[4]

Thus this text warrants our believing that Jesus affirmed a future resurrection of at least the believing dead, and that the state of those raised would be deathless and that no new marriage relationships would be initiated. Jesus stresses discontinuity between this life and the life to come. It is interesting to note that Luke 20:34, while it may be redactional, speaks of being worthy of the resurrection, and verse 36 suggests that we truly become sons of God once we have experienced the resurrection. Such words are not at all improbable on the lips of Jesus, not least because both of these verses have a thoroughly Semitic way of speaking about these matters. Nevertheless, most would see verses 34-36 as essentially redactional and so we will base nothing on this conjecture.

We now turn to the more difficult question of whether or not Jesus affirmed his own resurrection. If he believed in a resurrection of the righteous in general it is not at all improbable that he thought he would be among them. Did he speak of his own specific vindication beyond death?

Several texts suggest that Jesus expected to participate in life in the Dominion beyond death. Mark 14:25 springs immediately to mind and has good claims to authenticity. First, there is no evidence of any appearance traditions in which Jesus shared bread *and wine* after his resurrection with his disciples, or *wine alone,* or the Lord's Supper. Nor is there evidence of a post-Easter eucharist tradition that involved *only* the drinking of wine with disciples.[5] It is not likely that this saying was created out of some post-Easter tradition. Second, it probably draws on the tradition of the messianic banquet, and we have already argued that Jesus did envision such a banquet at the eschaton (see also Lk 14:15).[6] We may also point to the evidence from Qumran (1QSa), where it appears there is an eschatological meal of bread and wine in which the Messiah(s) partake.[7]

It is possible but not probable that this saying originally had another setting,[8] but in this case the setting is not crucial to understanding the logion's meaning.[9] Jesus is affirming his participation at the messianic banquet. In view of a saying

like Matthew 8:11 and parallels, this surely implies that Jesus assumed that he
would be blessed and vindicated by God beyond death. What this text does not
mention is resurrection *per se*. Since, however, the messianic banquet tradition
surely implies bodily life of some sort, by implication this text intimates that
Jesus believed that after his death he would be raised and would participate in
the messianic banquet in the Dominion.

It is striking how free from later Christian theologizing Mark 14:25 is. It never
mentions Jesus' death, nor the connection of his death to resurrection, nor resurrection in a short period of time. It may be connected to the interesting Q
material found in Matthew 19:28/Luke 22:30, in particular the Lukan form of
the saying. It seems that Jesus also envisioned the Twelve being raised and
participating in the Dominion banquet or at least in the final judging of Israel.
Are there, however, sayings where Jesus is more specific about his own resurrection?

Here we are confronted with the problems of the saying(s) in Mark 8:31, 9:31,
10:33-34 and parallels. Many scholars have suspected that behind these three
sayings lies one original saying or at most two. The saying most often suspected
of being a *vaticinium ex eventu* is 10:33, and we shall not treat it here. The chart
provided by Taylor makes clear the points of contact between these sayings and
the Passion narrative itself, and this makes it possible that the church and/or
Mark may have embellished one or more of these sayings in light of the early
Christian confession.[10] We are not concerned here about the authenticity of the
idea that the Son of Man *must* be crucified, but about the authenticity of the idea
of Jesus' resurrection or vindication beyond death. Mark 8:31 commends itself
as the most primitive form of the saying.

The original form of the saying seems to have spoken of Jesus being killed
(without specification of the means) and being raised after a short period of time.
It has been noted that the verb *anastēnai* is used only in these three Son of Man
prophecies, while elsewhere Mark uses *egerein* to speak of the event of resurrection (16:6).[11] G. Strecker, in a thorough form-critical study of this text, has
concluded that 8:31 is pre-Markan in character. He points not only to the use
of *anastēnai* but also to *apoktanthēnai* instead of *stauroō*, which Mark and the
early church preferred (15:33ff.; 16:6). Further, the use of "after three days"
(contrast Mk 14:58; 15:29) also points in this direction.[12] These valid points also
distinguish this saying from the language of the Markan passion narrative, which
makes it unlikely that Mark or his source created this saying on the basis of the

early accounts of Jesus' death.

While the placement of Mark 8:31 may be Mark's, for he has schematized his Gospel in such a way that the statements about the Son of Man's sufferings do not occur until after the "who" question is answered at Caesarea Philippi, the investigation of the substance of this saying suggests that 8:31 has not been created by Mark or shaped in light of the later Christian creed, which apparently never spoke of the rising of the Son of Man (compare 1 Cor 15:4). The earliest Greek form of the saying likely had the phrase *meta treis hēmeras anastēnai*, not "on the third day" as in Luke 9:21, which is more like the later Christian creedal formula (see 1 Cor 15:4).[13] The phrase *meta treis hēmeras*, if it goes back to an Aramaic original, probably meant "after a short while" since the word for "three" was used to express several or a few.[14]

What then do we learn from such a saying if it does go back to Jesus? We learn that Jesus expected to be vindicated beyond death, in particular after he was killed. It is not surprising that a prophetic figure like Jesus might, in the wake of what happened to the Baptist and others like him before the Baptist, contemplate a violent end to his life. Nor, if he believed in the rightness of his cause and ministry, would it be surprising if he believed God would vindicate him by means of resurrection. There was precedent for such a belief among the tales about the Maccabean martyrs.[15]

The only element that may prove surprising is that Jesus expected resurrection in a short period after his death. Yet this saying does not say that he expected to be raised alone apart from the resurrection of the righteous. Indeed it tells us nothing about what Jesus believed to be the relationship of his resurrection to that of other believers, nor how he viewed the nature of resurrection. It only indicates that he believed he would be raised. As such it is not difficult to believe that such a saying in its most primitive form goes back to Jesus.

What have we learned about Jesus' views on resurrection? First, Jesus believes in a resurrection of the righteous. Second, he argues for a significant discontinuity between this life and the resurrection state. The latter involves a deathless existence like the angels have, and is devoid of any new acts of marriage. Third, Jesus seems to affirm his own participation in the messianic banquet and thus by implication his resurrection. Fourth, if Mark 8:31 in some form goes back to Jesus, it appears that Jesus not only affirmed his resurrection after a violent death, but that he expected this vindication in a short period of time after his death. Later Christian reflection amplified and clarified this tradition in light of the Easter events.

—23—

Conclusions

Both Jesus and Paul shared a common eschatological framework that included a belief in resurrection. Both seem to have focused on the resurrection of the righteous, though it is possible that Jesus in particular also spoke of the general resurrection (see Jn 5:28-29). More clearly, both seem to have spoken of resurrection from out of the realm of the dead. It would seem that for both Jesus and Paul resurrection involved bodily life here on earth, not merely spiritual life in heaven. This is so for Jesus because he affirmed messianic banquet traditions and also the coming of the Son of Man to earth for judgment. It is true for Paul because he also speaks of the renewal of the earth in the same breath with the resurrection of the believer. Both Jesus and Paul associate being "in the Dominion" with what happens after resurrection. This is quite explicit in Paul, but it also seems to be implied in the authentic words of Jesus.

Jesus may have associated resurrection with the coming of the Son of Man (see Mk 13:26-27), but it is clear that for Paul resurrection of believers only happens after the parousia, or return, of Christ. It does not appear likely that Paul was directly dependent on the Jesus tradition for his teaching on resurrection, with the possible exception of his use of Mark 14:58. It is not completely clear, however, that Jesus himself originally alluded to resurrection in that saying. Both Paul and Jesus saw a significant discontinuity between the life we have in the body and the resurrection state. The continuity lay in the fact that dead believing persons were being raised, and that they would have bodies and life in those bodies. The emphasis, however, in both 1 Corinthians 15 and in Mark 12:18-27 and parallels lies on discontinuity. The resurrection state involves a deathless existence. Paul calls this glorious, Jesus angelic.

While Paul's teaching on resurrection comports with what little we can discern that Jesus said about the matter, Paul goes far beyond what little we know of Jesus' views, developing ideas in light of specifically Christian concerns with Christology, ethics and other matters. It would seem that Jesus' teaching did not place as much stress on resurrection and in particular on Jesus' own resurrection as Paul places on the resurrection of Christ and of Christians.

Nevertheless, both Jesus and Paul stand together in affirming resurrection as the ultimate state of affairs, which stands in contrast both to some Jews such as the Sadducees and to many pagans for whom the only sort of afterlife contemplated was the life of the immortal soul once the body was shed. In this regard both Jesus and Paul stand in continuity with the form of early Judaism that was to survive the disaster of A.D. 70—Pharisaic Judaism. This fact should not be minimized as we contemplate the meaning of all this data for contemporary Jewish-Christian dialog, a subject we will turn to in our concluding chapter.

PART SEVEN

Jesus, Paul
and the
End of the World

—24—

The Eschatological Schema

Our study thus far has been exegetical and historical, but in these final two chapters I hope to make the "hermeneutical leap" and ask about the value and validity of eschatology for the Christian faith at the end of the twentieth century. This chapter summarizes the previous chapters while the next offers tentative exploratory remarks rather than definite conclusions.

Perhaps the most fundamental conclusion I have thus far demonstrated is that to a significant degree Jesus and Paul did indeed share a common eschatological world view. They both believe in such things as a future coming of the Dominion of God on earth, a future resurrection of believers and the future coming of an agent of God (Christ or the Son of Man) who will bring in a day of final redemption and judgment. It also appears that both Jesus and Paul spoke specifically about Jesus' vindication beyond death by means of resurrection. Paul certainly and Jesus probably did speak of a community, an *ekklēsia/qāhāl* of those who were followers of Jesus. They also believed in a future for Israel, that

God had not revoked promises to faithful Jews.

At least two elements of these shared beliefs do not appear to derive from early Judaism: (1) the idea of a dying and rising Messiah; and (2) the idea of an agent of God assuming the role of Yahweh on the *Yom Yahweh*. To this I might add the idea of a *second* coming, which is certainly not present elsewhere in early Judaism but seems to have been affirmed at least implicitly by Jesus because he both identified himself as and with the Son of Man. More certainly, the concept of the return of Christ on the Day of the Lord is clearly found in the Pauline corpus. We have also uncovered considerable evidence that at various points and in various ways Paul seems to have been indebted to the Jesus tradition for some of his eschatological ideas, especially when he differed from his Pharisaic heritage.

It is striking that for both Jesus and Paul the *ekklēsia, basileia* and Israel are distinguishable entities, though not without some overlap. Israel and the *basileia* already existed according to the teaching of Jesus, but the *ekklēsia/qāhāl* is yet in the future. For Paul the *ekklēsia,* which also can be called the Israel of God, is *the* legitimate development of Israel, but at the same time Paul can still speak of an "Israel according to the flesh," a non-Christian Israel for which God yet has plans. This means that Paul does not simply equate the term *church* and the term *Israel* without qualification. While the *basileia* for both Paul and Jesus is something that happens to and in the midst of God's people even in the present, it is not simply identical with them without remainder. In the present, *basileia* refers to the in-breaking of the reign of God and thus could never be equated with the effect of that in-breaking—transformed individuals or the community of transformed individuals.

The distinction between *ekklēsia* and *basileia* is especially clear in the sayings that speak of obtaining, inheriting or entering the *basileia*. When the *basileia* is spoken of as a realm it is never identical with the *ekklēsia/qāhāl* but rather is the goal of those in the *ekklēsia/qāhāl*. Thus for both Jesus and Paul, while the *basileia* (reign of God) is in evidence in the community of Jesus' followers, we cannot make the equation *basileia=ekklēsia/qāhāl*. It is equally true that both Jesus' sending of his disciples out to the lost sheep of Israel and Paul's discussion of ethnic Israel in Romans 9—11 make impossible the simple equation Israel *in toto* (or even new Israel)=the *ekklēsia/qāhāl*.

Neither Paul nor Jesus speak of the displacement or replacement of *all* Jews by some new entity called Israel. Nor is there any evidence that either Jesus or

Paul envisioned two different peoples of God existing simultaneously. For Paul the Israel of God made up of Jew and Gentile united in Christ is the true or legitimate development of Israel in the present, but non-Christian Jews are not broken off from the true people of God forever. The crucial point then is that God is not finished with Israel yet. Likewise, Jesus also speaks of a division within Judaism. True Jews are those who respond positively to the good news of Jesus' preaching and heed the call to be his disciples. Yet Jesus would not likely have warned his Jewish opponents of the dangers of rejecting him had he believed that they were irretrievably lost. Indeed he saw it as his task and the task of his disciples to recover "the lost sheep of Israel."

This means that in some sense the modern dialog between non-Christian Jews and Christians must be seen as an interfaith dialog; in other respects it is a family discussion in which the church must realize its indebtedness to Judaism. Though it is a very delicate matter, both Christians and non-Christian Jews must at some point also discuss the matter of the current and ongoing existence of messianic Jews, those who accept Jesus as Messiah. This is so not least because Paul was a Jew, and he always envisioned some Jewish Christians in the *ekklēsia*. Furthermore, it is difficult to imagine that Jesus ever conceived of the idea of an *ekklēsia/qāhāl* that did not include Jews. Surely what evidence we have suggests that for Jesus, his Jewish followers were those who would constitute or at least be the basis of his future *ekklēsia/qāhāl*. Thus, the question of the nature of continuity of the church with its Jewish heritage, and the relationship of church and synagogue is raised most acutely by the existence today of messianic Jews. The interfaith dialog between Jews and Christians must come to grips with the status of the messianic Jew both in Judaism and in Christianity.

It would be untrue to say that Paul's ideas are simply expansions of what he took from the Jesus tradition. Paul himself was a creative thinker, and especially in regard to his teaching about the future of Israel, the resurrection of believers and the parousia, we see him adopting, adapting and even creating concepts that are not found in the Jesus tradition. He felt free to use not only ideas from his Pharisaic background but also secular concepts to convey what he meant.

Nothing in the eschatological teaching of Paul is clearly incompatible with what we can reconstruct of the teaching of Jesus on such matters. Here Schweitzer was basically right when he said,

> Paul shares with Jesus the eschatological worldview and the eschatological expectation. . . . The only difference is the hour in the world clock in the two

cases. To use another figure, both are looking toward the same mountain range, but whereas Jesus sees it as lying before Him, Paul already stands upon it, and its first slopes are already behind him.[1]

I would modify this statement by adding that Jesus also believed in an already as well as a not-yet aspect to the coming of God's Dominion, and so his eschatology was not purely future-oriented. What is true is that Paul focuses more on those eschatological events which from his perspective have already happened, in particular the death and resurrection of Jesus, than Jesus does. Jesus' teaching is definitely more future-oriented in this respect. One also gets the feeling that for Paul, the *most important* eschatological events have already happened in Christ, though this does not cause him to trivialize or abandon his conviction that the remaining eschatological events are crucial not only for the salvation of believers but also for the renewal of the world.

What is most striking in the teaching of both Jesus and Paul is how they envision the ultimate future as happening in this world, not in heaven. Jesus barely mentions heaven (see the possibly authentic material in Lk 16:19-31; 23:43), and Paul sees it as a state of nakedness, an interim condition that is less desirable than experiencing the resurrection body here on earth. For both founders of Christianity, redemption was only final and fully complete if it entailed the human body and the space-time world in which we live. In short, neither of these early Jews had an essentially otherworldly view of eternal life or salvation, if by that we mean a schema in which things are only finally set right in some realm other than this world. I suspect that "pie in the sky by and by" would hardly have been a complete vision of redemption to either Jesus or Paul. Caird affirms that human salvation

> is not to be conceived as the rescue of favoured individuals out of a doomed world to participate in an otherworldly existence totally unrelated to life on earth. Man's personality is so intimately linked with his environment that he must be saved in the context of all the corporate relationships and loyalties, achievements, and aspirations, which constitute a genuinely human existence.[2]

Where then does that leave a church which by and large has substituted a heavenly conclusion to the eschatological schema for an earthly one? Is the original eschatological framework of Jesus and Paul believable in this day and age? Before we explore these questions it will be well to summarize in a chart the eschatological schema Jesus and Paul seem to have shared.

The Eschatological Schema

The Coming of the Dominion in the Present	(J/P)
The Death and Vindication/Resurrection of Jesus	(J/P)
The Building of the Ekklēsia/Qāhāl	(J?/P)
The Proclaiming of Good News to all Nations	(J?/P)
The Desecration/Destruction of the Temple	(J/P)
The Coming of God's Agent (the Son of Man/Christ)	(J/P)
"All Israel Saved"	(J?/P)
The Gathering and Resurrection of the Elect	(J/P)
The Final Judgment (Including Judgment of God's People)	(J/P)
The Inheriting/Obtaining of God's Dominion	(J/P)
The Messianic Banquet	(J)

Though I have tried to place these events in general chronological order, it should be clear that some rearrangement may be required. For example, when Paul speaks of the presence of the *basileia* he means something that can be true only now that the Spirit has fallen upon the *ekklēsia.* Jesus seems to mean that healing or exorcism is an indicator that the Dominion of God has already broken into the midst of God's people. On the basis of the criteria for authenticity normally applied to the Jesus tradition, it cannot be shown for *certain* that Jesus spoke of a proclamation to the nations or of the building of an *ekklēsia,* though I have argued that at least the latter is likely. It is also uncertain whether when Jesus spoke of many coming from east and west to sit at table with Abraham he envisioned a large number of Jews being gathered and saved, or whether he foresaw Jews being displaced by some Gentiles when the Dominion finally came on earth. The former is more likely, and perhaps the point of the saying originally was that faithful Jews from the Diaspora would replace Jesus' unfaithful listeners ("this generation") at the banquet.

Paul does not seem to have spoken of a messianic banquet, but it is notable that in the context of his discussion of the Lord's Supper he says that whenever Christians eat or drink they proclaim Christ's death until he comes. In other words, Paul makes some connection between eating and drinking and the Lord's return (see 1 Cor 11:25-26). This is not the same thing as speaking about the messianic banquet after the return. It can also be argued that what Jesus meant by the coming of the Son of Man and what Paul meant by the parousia of Christ were two different things. On the whole, I think this is unlikely, for it is striking that they agree that an agent of God will bring in the *Yom Yahweh* with its final judgment, not God himself. It appears that they are talking about basically the same concept. Jesus is not, for instance, speaking of some coming on earth of a messianic figure or Son of Man *prior* to the *Yom Yahweh.*

Furthermore, we have found absolutely no justification in the teaching of either Paul or Jesus for the notion that there will be two Second Comings of Christ—one invisible and one visible. The language about the rapture in 1 Thessalonians 4:17 does indeed speak of a meeting of Christ in the air, but the parousia imagery in the context strongly suggests that thereafter both Christ and believers return to earth. This also leads to the further point that there is no hint in either the teaching of Paul or of Jesus that believers will avoid going through what is variously called the messianic woes or the final tribulation that precedes the Second Coming (see Mk 13:20).[3] Indeed, Paul seems to think that the church in his day was already beginning to experience those woes. In addition, Paul in particular emphasizes that Christians will appear before the judgment seat of Christ and be held accountable for their actions (2 Cor 5:10).

The saying in Mark 13:32, as well as the lack of a clear statement in Mark 13 of what is the chronological relationship between preliminary events and the final return of Christ with attendant cosmic effects, should have long since ruled out prognostications about the end of human history. Then, too, the fact that the Jesus tradition and Paul share the use of the thief-in-the-night motif to talk about the Second Coming should have discouraged such speculation as well. No doubt even before the New Testament canon was closed such speculations were already being made in the Christian community, but it is also true that even in the second century a wise church father was warning against any confidence in attempts to match current historical events and persons with the biblical data. We must keep steadily in view that such attempts thus far in church history have all without exception been wrong! Irenaeus, in *Adversus haereses* ("Against All Heresies") 30:1-3, written in the second half of the second century, warns against speculations about such things as who the anti-Christ will be and what name is figured forth by the number 666. He says:

> But as for those who, for the sake of vainglory, lay it down for certain that names containing the spurious number are to be accepted, and affirm that this name, hit upon by themselves, is that of him who is to come; such persons shall not come forth without loss, because they have led into error both

themselves and those who confided in them. . . . It is therefore more certain, and less hazardous, to await the fulfillment of prophecy, than to be making surmises and casting about for any names that may present themselves, inasmuch as many names can be found possessing the number mentioned; and the same question will, after all, remain unsolved.[4]

There is room for dispute not only about the chronology and the *dramatis personae* of the end-time events, but also about the order of these events and a few of the elements in the schema presented above. We are really concerned with the overall pattern. There is more than sufficient clarity on that score to be able to say with some confidence that Jesus and Paul shared an eschatological framework, and both were closer to some of the Pharisaic visions of the future than to any other group in early Judaism about whom we have evidence in regard to their eschatological beliefs. But to what degree can modern persons affirm such an eschatological schema?

—25—

The Future
of a Future
in a Modern
World

When both scholars and laypersons have argued in the twentieth century that the eschatological framework of Jesus and Paul can no longer be affirmed in its original sense or in any sense, the argument has usually gone like this: "Since the end of the world did not arrive in the first century A.D. as Jesus and Paul predicted, we obviously can no longer believe in their teachings about such eschatological matters." I have shown in part one that it is very doubtful that either Jesus or Paul ever affirmed that the end *had to come* within their respective lifetimes. The perspective that they held was that of *possible*, not necessary, imminence. I also stressed that one must ask how that language of imminence was intended to function.

The objection that the eschatological teachings of Jesus and/or Paul no longer can be believed because they are bound up with inaccurate calculations about the end will not stand up when close scrutiny is given to the relevant New Testament data. Those conclusions are based on a false understanding of that data. Even if it could be shown that Jesus and Paul wrongly taught that the end would come in a generation, this in itself would not rule out that they might be right in the substance of their teaching. The scientist who predicts the coming of a great comet visible to the naked eye may well be wrong about the timing of the coming but right about the fact of its coming. The issue of timing and of the fact of the coming are related to each other, but inaccuracy about the former does not necessarily entail inaccuracy about the latter.

While eschatology is a concept that definitely involves the matter of time, it does not always involve the matter of timing or the calculation of time. It is striking, at least to this observer, that some who confidently reject New Testament eschatology as no longer valid often do so because they assume that the issues of time and timing are, if not one and the same, so interdependent as to be indistinguishable.

The problem with this sort of approach is that it does not sufficiently take into account what we have been learning from scientists in the twentieth century about the space-time continuum. Einstein had some remarkable things to say about time in his theory of relativity, but some biblical scholars and laypersons have apparently ignored this data and continue to operate with a pre-Einsteinian theory of time. I am suggesting that for some the real impediment to thinking that the New Testament eschatology can be affirmed in the twentieth century is not that the schema is too old and represents a discredited world view, but that a modern way of thinking about time and timing has not been incorporated into their world view.

Many scientists point out that "time is, in fact, elastic and can be stretched and shrunk by motion." Not only so, but "time really does run faster in space, where the Earth's gravity is weaker."[1] In short, time, space and gravity are interrelated and interdependent matters. P. Davies has stressed that in some eighty years of testing, not one experiment "has marred the flawless predictions of the theory of relativity."[2] Now this in itself ought to give us all pause. Our own *perception* of time lapse or the calculation of time is hardly a very firm or reliable basis to make a confident judgment about the validity of the eschatological concepts Jesus and Paul taught, whatever one may think about how they viewed the *timing* of such events.

Davies reminds us that our sensation of the passage of time "is so pronounced that it constitutes the most elementary aspect of our experience," and thus we have a great tendency to judge all things on the basis of our own internal perceptions of time.[3] Yet those perceptions often can be wrong. Most of us at one time or another have had the uncomfortable experience of crossing several time zones by airplane only to discover that our internal sense of time and timing has not immediately shifted. This should have alerted us to the fact that the judging of matters of time and timing on the basis of our own subjective perception of such things can indeed be very faulty. The theory of relativity tells us that "space-time is not 'flat,' obeying the usual rules of school geometry, but curved or warped, giving rise to both spacewarps and timewarps."[4] Precisely because it does not always comport with our commonsense perception of time, scientists have had to remind us repeatedly that "today time is seen to be *dynamical.* It can stretch and shrink, warp and even stop altogether at a singularity. Clock rates are not absolute, but relative to the state of motion or gravitational situation of the observer."[5]

Another related and equally complex matter is the relationship of time to eternity. What we have learned about time from the theory of relativity coupled with space exploration suggests that since time, space and gravity are interdependent, whatever else one can say, eternity or heaven must be very different from earth in regard to the whole matter of time. It may also indeed prove to be the case that the biblical author said more than he understood when he pointed out, "With the Lord a day is like a thousand years, and a thousand years are like a day" (2 Pet 3:8). As little as we understand about time, we understand even less about the relationship of time to eternity. Is eternity just time infinitely extended? Is there in fact time *in* eternity? The answer to this last question would presumably depend on whether there is gravity and space as we know it in eternity. Is God's perspective that of an eternal present?

Scientists who affirm the big bang theory have pointed out that it would be better to speak of the creation of space with, not *in,* time, and therefore one should talk about a space-time continuum. This means that time is something that exists only in connection with a material universe where there are motion, gravity and other related forces. I bring all of this up precisely because those who make confident assertions about the invalidity of New Testament eschatological ideas often seem to do so on the basis of presuppositions about such matters as the nature of time, timing and the relationship of time to eternity *without* taking into account the theory of relativity or how very little we know about the relationship of time and eternity. Enough has been said on this point to make clear that our perception of time lapse or timing is a dubious basis for making confident pronouncements about the validity or invalidity of New Testament eschatology for a modern world.

There is, however, another sort of objection to affirming the validity of the eschatological framework of Jesus and Paul, and it goes something like this: Since we live in a universe of natural cause and effect, it is now difficult if not impossible to believe in such things as miracles, the supernatural intervention of God in the space-time continuum, a three-story universe or a final renewal of the earth in a realm where the laws of entropy and thermodynamics apply.[6] This sort of post-Enlightenment objection does little justice either to modern science or to the world views of Jesus and/or Paul. This is one of the reasons that J. H. Yoder recently called for a retrieval of the "idiom of apostolic apocalyptic."[7]

In the first place, few modern scientists are so bold as to affirm with certainty that we live in a closed universe run only by natural cause and effect. We have only explored a minute part of the universe and are always learning new things, and a great deal of the new data has forced us to reconsider what were formerly considered scientific laws. The more science has explored "the quantum factor" the less dogmatic many have become about rigid chains of natural causation. "Uncertainty is the fundamental ingredient of the quantum theory. It leads directly to the consequence of *unpredictability*. . . . The quantum factor, however, apparently breaks the chain by allowing effects to occur that have no cause."[8] Quantum physics does not prove the reality of the supernatural or of miracles, but it does make unlikely the assumption that we live in a closed universe describable purely in terms of material and natural causation. In such a world one cannot confidently argue that there can be no such thing as miracles or divine intervention.

On this subject of divine intervention we must remember that it is we moderns who have insisted on a radical distinction between the natural and the supernatural, and it is not at all certain that the distinction is a viable one. Not only for the biblical writers but also for most of Western history a radical dichotomy between the natural and supernatural was not assumed. It was only as the effect of the Enlightenment critique of the miraculous began to be felt in full that clear distinctions were made between the natural and the supernatural. The language behind this distinction is also a relatively recent phenomenon.[9]

At least for those who believe in one almighty Creator God, it may fairly be asked what sense it makes to talk about a miracle or the intervention of the supernatural as a *violation* of natural law if God set up the so-called natural laws of the universe in the first place. It would be much better to speak of the supranatural and even the suprarational, that which goes *beyond* what we know and understand of natural causes, than to speak of that which goes *against* such causes. There is no scientific certainty at present that we live in a closed universe with only natural causation, nor is there likely to be such certainty in view of the size of the universe and how much more we need to learn about it. In such circumstances a belief in divine intervention and in particular in miraculous divine intervention cannot only *not* be ruled out, in many ways it better explains the nature of creation and the data of historical reality than do alternative explanations.

Yet another form of objection to a modern belief in the eschatological framework is the observation that eschatological and apocalyptic language was never meant to be taken literally, or if it was it now needs to be demythologized. Some scholars seem to suppose that what Jesus and Paul were really doing when they used eschatological or apocalyptic concepts was just inculcating faith and hope and moral resolve in their converts, not trying to say anything concrete about the realities that they believed would happen at the end of human history. I suspect that one of the main reasons some argue in this fashion is because, rightly or wrongly, some scholars assume that accepting a modern world view means we must treat eschatological language as purely figurative and thus as having no actual reference to the future of the real material world or the outcome of human history.

But is it really true that eschatological and apocalyptic language is inherently language without historical referents? This argument I think will not stand up to close scrutiny. For one thing, New Testament writers use eschatological language to describe historical events such as the death of Jesus or the fall of the temple that we know beyond reasonable doubt did happen. For another thing, this sort of reasoning seems to confuse figurative or metaphorical language with language that is not historically referential. The fact that eschatological language is often figurative or analogical in character neither rules in or out that it may have been intended to refer to actual historical events. Literal speech is by no means the only way to talk about historical events and realities.

One clue that lets us know that at least in Paul's case he takes his eschatological language to refer to real historical events is the link he makes between what he believed had already happened to Jesus in space and time, his death and resurrection, and what will yet happen to believers, their future deaths and resurrections. It is perhaps also worth noting that even in strictly apocalyptic literature we often find a "historical review" that culminates in future events painted in apocalyptic tones. That is, the apocalyptist sees eschatological events as part of a historical continuum with events he or she knew had already happened in space and time.

The program to demythologize apocalyptic and eschatological language is a useful exercise when it amounts to attempting to figure out what historical or future events or realities the author is using mythological language to describe, but when it becomes an exercise in deontologizing the language and in effect saying that the author did not intend for it to have any historical or space-time referents one has violated the intent of the language itself. Decoding symbolic language is one thing, denuding it of its intended referents is another.

Demythologizing also can be useful in making clear that we are not required to affirm the view of some ancients of a three-story material universe with heaven just beyond the earth's atmosphere and hell in the bowels of the earth. Yet nowhere in the eschatological material we have been investigating is there clear evidence that either Jesus or Paul ever *taught* a three-story universe. They may well have believed such a view, but even what they have to say about the coming of the Son of Man/Christ does not necessarily amount to *teaching* such a view of cosmology.

More telling is the way that both Jesus and Paul speak of heavenly realities as a matter of Spirit rather than of matter. Not only does Paul affirm that heavenly life is life without a body, but also both Jesus and Paul stress the discontinuity between this life and the life to come. Jesus compares it to the state of angels; Paul says bluntly, "Flesh and blood cannot inherit the Dominion." Eschatology is indeed meant to teach something about the conclusion of human history, not, at least directly, about cosmology. Even a belief in the renewal of the cosmos at the end of history can and should be differentiated from the three-story universe view. Paul believes in the renewal of the *earth;* he does not speak of the renewal of the eternal abode of God (not to be confused with the heavens, the heavenlies or the sky) or of hell, and this in itself at least implies that he does *not* think that either heaven or hell are part of the material universe!

We should heed the wise words of Andrew Lincoln on these matters:

It is not a question of whether modern people will interpret their lives by symbols or myths but rather the question is which symbols or myths they will accept or choose. Will it be rooted in the Biblical perspective or of those originating in some other world-view? If the vision involved in Pauline [or

Jesus'] eschatology is not dismissed simply because it employs symbolic language to speak of transcendent realities, it may be found to offer pointers to present-day concerns. . . . This involves a continuing dialogue where the reader questions the text about the function of its language and symbols and then expects a response as the text is allowed to interact with his or her imagination and intellectual constructs. In this way the gulf between ancient symbols and modern times can be bridged by what Gadamer calls a fusion of horizons.[10]

It is this sort of exercise that this chapter is attempting to urge the reader to undertake. If human salvation does indeed involve a cosmic and historical drama like the schema we have explored in this book, then it is as essential to ask if we are in need of remythologizing our modern concepts about salvation as it is to ask about the demythologizing of ancient eschatological symbols.

What I have sought to show to this point is that the usual presuppositions and bases in the twentieth century for abandoning the eschatological framework of Jesus and Paul are founded on faulty premises, either about what having a modern scientific world view requires of us, or of the character and meaning of the relevant New Testament data. I should now like to show why it is crucial for the Christian faith to maintain that eschatological framework.

In the first place, the lessons of Christian history teach us that the abandoning of eschatology has led to significant distortions in other areas of Christian teaching as well. In an earlier work I have argued in the following fashion:

As we have seen, the study of the post-NT, pre-Nicene evidence suggests an attenuation of the new element in Christianity that allowed women to assume new roles in the family of faith. I would submit that one major reason why this occurred was because the Church substituted one or another form of a realized eschatology for the balanced "already/not-yet" approach we find in Paul and to a lesser degree elsewhere in the NT. It is inadequate to talk about the Christianizing of the Roman Empire if one does not also talk about the acculturation of the Church. I submit that a main reason for that gradual acculturation was due to the acceptance of one form or another of realized eschatology that either made its peace with the world or assumed that worldly matters and material things were adiaphora. As a result, the Church gradually allowed the dominant culture to set the agenda in economic, political, and social matters (including the role of women).[11]

The effects of abandoning the eschatology of Jesus and Paul may also be seen in the realm of ethics. I have pointed out time and again in this study how eschatological ideas are used for parenetic purposes. Indeed, it appears at various points that Paul, and perhaps Jesus as well, thought there was *no* basis for parenesis without eschatology (see 1 Cor 15:17-19, 29-34, 58; Mk 13:32ff.). This point has been strongly brought home by O. O'Donovan, who stresses that

no account of the Christian moral life can be adequate unless it is allowed to point forward to the resurrection. The articulation of love into labour and reward in Jesus' teaching corresponds to the apostolic teaching that we must die with Christ so that at last we may rise with him. It is necessary to speak in this way . . . because the present hiddenness of God's new creation demands its fulfillment in public manifestation, the *parousia* or "presence" of the Son of man to the cosmos in which God is to be all in all. The suggestion that the believer already enjoys so complete a communion with God and his new creation, that no further manifestation is necessary or possible, conceals . . . a gnostic pretension to private redemption apart from, and dispensing with, the public redemption of the cosmos.[12]

Yoder has shown how our ethical thinking about such matters as nuclear war and nuclear disarmament reflects and is in part determined by our eschatology or lack thereof.[13] When present ethical responsibility for such matters is abandoned because of a particular form of eschatological thinking (such as, Why should we be concerned with such matters as nuclear disarmament or the ecology since God will one day destroy and renew the earth?) we have come a long way from St. Paul who sees future eschatology as the *basis* for ethical responsibility in the present.

We have noted how Beker makes much the same point in regard to the effect on one's view of history and ecology of abandoning the idea of future resurrection. A truly Christian concern for the environment can and should grow out of the conviction that God cares about the world as well as about believers and that redemption is something that must ultimately affect the former as well as the latter if it is to be complete.

A further reason why eschatology must not be jettisoned by modern Christianity is that God's character is at stake. The problem of theodicy has no final resolution without some sort of eschatological resolution to the dilemmas this world presents human beings. R. Bauckham rightly makes the following point:

The great merit of the apocalyptic approach to theodicy was that it refused to justify the present condition of the world by means of an abstract exoneration of God from responsibility for the evils of the present. Only the overcoming of present evil by eschatological righteousness could vindicate God as righteous, and only the hope of such a future triumph of righteousness could make the evils of the present bearable. . . . This universal challenge to the righteousness of God demanded a universal righting of wrongs, an elimination of evil on a universal, even cosmic, scale.[14]

We may also note that a proper faith in eschatological matters leads not to a fatalistic vision of a world that readily can be abandoned, but rather to a realistic vision that if the world is finally going to be one and truly a new creation then *God* must intervene to bring this about. That clearly is the vision both Paul and Jesus hold out to their followers. Their message is not just "in the beginning God" but also the triumphant message "in the end God."

On the one hand, this rules out certain purely human utopian programs, as if Christians can bring in the final form of the Dominion of God, without the return of God in Christ, by being a community that withdraws from the world. A healthy affirmation of New Testament eschatology should never lead to a sort of Qumranite world view or existence, for the eschatology we have been talking about is a world-transforming, not a world-negating, eschatology.

On the other hand, if one knows that it is God's plan ultimately to renew and redeem the material world, then blessed are they who participate in and foreshadow that by working to clean up the environment, feed the hungry, care for and heal the sick and so bear witness to God's perfect and final will for the world (see Mt 25:31ff.). This witness is all the more powerful in the context of a hedonistic and materialistic culture that is both selfish and self-centered in character. A proper belief in and understanding of eschatology rules out the gospel of conspicuous consumption and wealth, a distinctly North American gospel that bears no relationship to Jesus' or Paul's teachings.

A proper affirmation and appreciation of the eschatological framework of Jesus and Paul can indeed unsettle many cherished notions, such as the view that human beings can and should completely shape their own destiny, but it can also challenge deep-seated prejudices. For example, Romans 9—11 and Jesus' vision of participating in the messianic banquet with his Jewish forebears and those Jews who responded positively to his message make quite clear that there is no justification for anti-Semitism, least of all by Gentiles who have been grafted into the already existing people of God. If one really believes that God indeed will fulfill his promises to faithful Jews, that "all Israel" will indeed one day be saved, then anti-Semitism must be opposed for what it is, a sin, not only against God's people, but against God and his ultimate plan for those people. It is true that having said this does not mean that Jews and Christians will not have salient differences of opinion about many matters, including who the Messiah is, or about how Jews and Christians can be faithful to their own visions of particularistic monotheism without accusing each other of being guilty of a false faith. Nevertheless, when the implications of the eschatological teachings we reviewed in part four are allowed to have their effect, anti-Semitism is exposed for the ugly thing that it is.

Yet another possible result of a proper understanding and acceptance of the eschatological framework of Jesus and Paul is that certain modern forms of eschatological teaching, in particular Dispensational teaching, will be seen for what they are—distortions of the biblical data. In particular, the idea of a pre-tribulation rapture of the church out of this world provides us with yet another historical example of the attempt to convert the essentially horizontal eschatology of the New Testament into an otherworldly and vertical eschatology. The end result of this approach is not only an implicit denial of the cruciform shape of discipleship in this world, but a denial of the concern for the environment and cosmos that are proper New Testament concerns. As I have pointed out, a proper understanding of the language of imminence as used by Paul and Jesus should also forestall *all* theological weather-forecasting, whether by Dispensationalists or others.

The great tragedy about Dispensationalism is that while it has rightly attempted to focus our attention on the eschatological dimension of the New Testament, the manner in which it has done so has led to the very sort of distortions that Paul combatted in the New Testament era: (1) date setting of the end, over against which Paul holds out eschatological reserve; and (2) in reaction against Dispensationalism, the feeling in large portions of the church that eschatology should be rejected outright. Many of those today who say, "there is no (more) resurrection," do so in part because they do not wish to be associated with the ideas made famous by Hal Lindsey, J. Walvoord and others. All too often Dispensational authors, rather than clearly bringing to light the importance and true character of biblical prophecy, have had the effect of causing a whole host of people to reject biblical prophecy as false prophecy. This happens when a particular set of referents that are claimed to be what the Scripture was really foreshadowing turn out to be just another set of historical events that do not yet fulfill the biblical promises and oracles.[15] Spiritualizing tendencies now, as in first-century Corinth, seem frequently to be caused by an overreaction to false eschatological speculations.

"Spiritualizing" of the gospel can also result from ignoring the eschatological dimensions of the Christian faith. This has happened in large sections of the so-called mainline churches, evidenced by the fact that Easter sermons often celebrate either the natural life cycle of the seasons in general or spiritual redemption now to be followed by life in heaven later. In both cases the historical and horizontal eschatology of the New Testament has been abandoned and replaced with something else. North American culture, with its separation of church and state, has only exacerbated the tendency in the church to separate things spiritual and things material. In truth, the apolitical character of a good deal of the church and the spiritualizing of the social consequences of the gospel seems often to be caused by a faulty eschatology, whether of a purely otherworldly or of a more Dispensational character.

If there is even a small measure of justice in some of the above remarks, and no doubt one could find fault with one or another of them, they are sufficient to make clear that a church without a proper eschatological framework in which to live and believe is a church at odds not only with the world but with some of the crucial elements of the gospel. There is a major difference between redemption from and redemption in and of the world, and it is the latter that is proclaimed loud and clear in the teachings of Jesus and Paul. I hope that this study may in some small way further the recovery of New Testament eschatology in the church and elsewhere today. At stake is not only a teleological hope that history is going somewhere and will result in something good, but also a proper foundation for ethics, ecology, interfaith dialog between Christians and Jews and other dimensions of theology as well.

He who testifies to these things says,

"Yes, I am coming soon."

Amen. Come Lord Jesus.

The grace of the Lord Jesus be with God's people. Amen.

(Rev 22:20-21)

— Appendix —

Old Testament Prophecy: Its Historical Context and Character

In what follows I am attempting to provide an example of how biblical prophecy should be seen against the backdrop of its original historical context, and how such an effort makes a difference in how we understand such prophecy. I then will make some further remarks about the character of biblical prophecy.

Its Historical Context—A Sample

When we think of biblical prophecy we usually think of the Old Testament literary prophets whose oracles are found in the third division of the Old Testament (beginning with Isaiah and ending with Malachi). Their prophecies were given beginning in the eighth century B.C. and continuing on into the postexilic period (the late sixth century B.C. and afterwards). It is entirely possible and all too common to study these so-called latter Prophets as quarries for messianic proof texts and to take them totally out of their historical contexts. Doing this, however, is quite dangerous and can lead to distortion of what a given prophet was actually trying to say. For instance, an attempt to find a prophecy about

Christ under every prophetic rock in the Old Testament leads to a distortion of a lot of Old Testament prophecy, which is often not about Christ at all but rather about the immediate situation the prophet saw confronting his audience, Israel. Messianic prophecy can indeed be found in the Old Testament, but it is less prevalent than other sorts of prophetic material, and if we filter the prophets with a *purely* messianic grid it leads to a lopsided picture of them.

What we must strive to do is reconstruct the historical context in which these words of God were given and ask what they meant then and there, before we ask what they mean here and now. One of the most basic principles for interpreting biblical prophecy is that a prophecy cannot mean today something contrary to what it was intended to mean by the inspired author and would have been understood to mean in its original historical context. This is not to deny that sometimes Old Testament prophets spoke more than they or their original audiences fully understood, but it is to affirm that these prophecies first constituted God's Word to a much earlier group of believers than late-twentieth-century Christians. Since these oracles were first addressed to these earlier believers they must have been intended to say something meaningful that those believers could at least in part have understood. To deny this principle is to deny the essential historical character of biblical prophecy and the fact that these oracles were given in and to particular historical contexts long before the twentieth century. It was God's Word to and for these earlier believers long before it became God's Word to and for us.

A further point must be stressed. The majority of the material written in the classical or literary prophets' works was written during very dark days of Israel. All of it was written long after David and Solomon reigned and thus long after Israel's political heyday. Some of the material is from the period prior to the exile of the northern tribes in 722 B.C., some of it, such as Ezekiel, comes from the exile period itself, and some from the postexilic period.

Furthermore, since these prophets gave their oracles after the split between Israel and Judah, some are southern prophets (such as Isaiah), and some are northern (as Amos probably was). They are often only addressing part of the old united Israel when they speak. Unlike the books of the so-called former prophets (such as Samuel), these books are almost exclusively oracles, which give us few clues about the specific historical circumstances in which the prophet lived and to which he spoke. We must then rely on the historical books and extrabiblical sources to fill in the picture. At this point we will turn to providing a bit of historical background to aid in understanding the "latter prophets."

The very earliest of the literary prophets can have spoken no earlier than the eighth century B.C. (800-700 B.C.), and therefore we will begin our historical review at that point. After Solomon's time the country had split into two parts— the northern tribes called Israel, and the two southern tribes called Judah. If we back up to 869 B.C. we find the notorious Ahab and Jezebel ruling in the north. They were part of what the Assyrians called the House of Omri. The Omriide dynasty was noted for two sorts of actions that made prophets mad—political alliances with nearby neighbors such as Damascus, which led to an influx of foreign persons and culture, and worse still the deliberate bringing in of foreign gods and goddesses, along with the patronizing of some of the native pagan Canaanite deities such as Baal.

Various of the stories in the Elijah and Elisha cycle (see 1 Kings 17—2 Kings 13) tell of these prophets' condemnation of both the political and the religious compromise of God's people and land. Elijah and Elisha were not unique in such condemnation. As J. Bright points out, they stood in a line at least two hundred years old of prophets who criticized the rulers' compromises. We may remember Samuel during the age of Saul (1050-1010 B.C.), or Nathan during the age of David (1010-970 B.C.). Thus there was a long precedent for a prophet to be a critic of the powers that be. The classical prophets then were simply following in that tradition. They spoke for Yahweh to his people but especially to the leaders of that people. Their prophecy, like the lives of those whom they addressed, often was a mixture of political, religious, economic and social matters.

One thing that seems clear about these prophets is that they generally stood for what may be called old-fashioned Israel. They strongly disliked attempts to take matters out of God's hands by relying on big armies, entangling alliances and religious compromises. In particular they did not like rulers trying to establish a rite of primogeniture and a line of succession in a family. Rather, as the story of Samuel makes clear, they stood in the line of the charismatic judges, believing that God should raise up leaders and that he would raise up armies and fight for Israel. In short, they seem to have stood for the old tribal confederacy whose leadership was raised up by charismatic anointing by God, and they may even have endorsed a return to theocracy—where there would be only Yahweh as Israel's leader, not a human king.

There is a definite antiestablishment strain in the prophets, both former and latter. Though we may not be accustomed to such, the prophets believed politics and religion *did* go together, and they were deeply involved in political actions, including the raising up of kings. It is thus incorrect and inappropriate to try to derive a purely spiritual message from the prophets. Certainly they were deeply concerned about spiritual matters, but spiritual matters were intertwined with and provided direction and motivation for everyday economics, politics and social relationships.

The ideals of the prophets and the practices of the Omriides clashed directly and repeatedly in Israel (the north). Not only was Yahweh not relied on for security and in matters of war, but foreign gods were openly courted and imported. The policies of Ahab and the earlier Omriides were not only repulsive to the prophets, they were also repulsive to the people, and in fact to many of the soldiers as well, as evidenced by the revolt of the general Jehu who led a bloody purge of Israel in 843-842 B.C.

Yet Israel was not alone in being affected by Jehu's fury. In 2 Kings 8—9 we read that he slayed not only the northern ruler, Jehoram, but also his southern cousin, Ahaziah, who had just ascended to the Judahite throne. He then threw Jezebel out of a window, killing her, and slew the whole of Ahab's family. In addition he slew a delegation of peace from Jerusalem and invaded a temple of Baal in the capital, slaying all the local Baal worshipers there. He then razed that temple to the ground. The cult of Baal Melquart was wiped out temporarily. It is fair to say that Judah had never been as infected as the north was with the cult of Baal, it being more conservative and more removed from the influence of northern rulers and invaders.

After his purge Jehu was able to found a dynasty that was to last for about a hundred years, his own rule lasting until about 815, but he himself was not a strong ruler, and he did not escape various of the sins of his predecessors. In fact the practical effect of Jehu's policy left Israel vulnerable to attack and weak, due to a lack of allies. Jehu had cut Israel off from her only two dependable allies—Judah and Damascus. He had also executed all the natural leadership, and the judgment of him even a century later when Hosea prophesied (Hos 1:4) was that through his excesses he brought blood guilt on himself. Though Baal had been wiped out, it appears that Jehu was not so zealous for Yahweh in regard to other native deities, which he allowed to exist or even flourish (see 2 Kings 13:6).

What loomed on the horizon was real danger in the form of the Assyrians, for the great ruler Shalmaneser III was not taking the loss at Carcar in 853 B.C. lightly, and Israel had been one of the states, along with Damascus, who had defeated him there. This king was to rule until 825, and was to further destabilize the situation, invading again in 841 and laying seige to Damascus, and ravaging and pillaging the Phoenician coast, taking tribute from not only Tyre and Sidon but also from Jehu. After Shalmaneser there seems to have been a respite until the closing decades of the ninth century, because of trouble the Assyrians had with the Urartu and to internal strife. But the warning signal had been sent up—there was a large dangerous power in the east. The new ruler of Damascus was Hazael, a soldier who had taken the throne by force, and he attacked Jehu, which led to the loss of Transjordan all the way to the Arnon River. Jehoahaz the son of Jehu fared even worse. He was conquered, and retained as a client state of sorts. In this way Israel's weakness became apparent, and she was exploited by other neighboring states. Furthermore, Judah also avoided being taken by Hazael only by paying heavy tribute. The next ruler for Judah was Joash (837-800 B.C.), who came to the throne while very young and under the supervision of Jehoiada the chief priest. He acted in a godly manner, purifying the temple as long as the chief priest still lived, but once the priest died Joash allowed paganism to raise its ugly head again.

With this checkered history one might have expected steady decline in both Judah and Israel, but in fact during the eighth century both states achieved a certain stability and recovery of former glories. J. Bright is right to attribute this mainly to two stable rulers in both sections of the country, but also because Assyria rose up again in the person of Adad-nirari III (811-784 B.C.), who came and crushed Damascus and laid it under heavy tribute, thus freeing both Israel and Judah from being under Damascus's thumb. After Adad, at least until 746 or later, the Assyrians were not again a threat to the nations west and south of the Euphrates. It was just as the Assyrians crushed Damascus that Joash or Jehoash (802-786 B.C.), Jehu's grandson, came to the throne and recovered all the cities lost by his father to Damascus. Also, 2 Kings 14 suggests strongly that Judah was subjugated by Jehoash, with the ruler Amaziah (800-783 B.C.) being a virtual client of Jehoash, once the latter came and took Jerusalem by force.

In due course Amaziah's weakness was no longer tolerated—he was killed and his son Uzziah came to the throne (783-742 B.C.). He, along with Jereboam II in Israel (786-746 B.C.), provided prosperity and security for a generation for these states. There is little doubt that Jereboam was one of Israel's strongest military figures (see Amos 6:13), for he was even able to re-establish the Solomonic boundaries of Israel and also made several northern regions client states, called Aramean lands. The Moabites and Ammonites were ejected from Israel.

Uzziah, though he was younger than Jereboam, soon emerged as a full partner in this plan to recover the old glory of Israel. He repaired Jerusalem, refit the army, conquered Edom and appears to have re-established trade with the Arabian peninsula, as had Solomon. In addition he took various Philistine cities on the coast and controlled the Negev. Jereboam and Uzziah did so well that a class of the elite, who indulged in luxury, arose in both the north and the south, and Amos was not exaggerating when he criticized the ivory-inlaid houses and palaces.

Yet this brief period of economic prosperity was not a time of prosperity for all—indeed, it was a time of prosperity for the few rich elite, and oppression of the poor majority. Justice and righteousness were not being done, and all was not well in the religious sphere either. In fact, Israel at least, despite its apparent prosperity, was in an advanced stage of moral, religious and social decay.

It is this decay in the eighth century B.C. that, for example, Amos is attacking in his oracles, which may be some of the earliest oracles of the so-called literary prophets. He prophesies a judgment that will fall not only on Israel's neighbors but even on Israel itself (see Amos 3:1ff.) This judgment did in fact take place in about 722 B.C. when the Assyrians invaded and conquered the northern portion of the Holy Land. This raises the important point that what we have recorded in Amos, as in the other literary prophets, is by and large prophecy that has *already been fulfilled,* and it is doubtful we should look for a further fulfillment of it. It is recorded for our benefit so that we will learn from Israel's example and not suffer a like judgment (see 1 Cor 10:1-13). This character of already fulfilled prophecy is true not only of Amos but of all the literary prophets.

It is also well to bear in mind that early Christians, like the First Evangelist, believed that even most of the Old Testament messianic prophecies had already been fulfilled in the birth, life, death and resurrection of Jesus (for example, compare Is 7:14 to Mt 1:23). My point is that, looking at things from a historical (and Christian) perspective, in fact only a minority of prophecies in the books of the literary prophets refer to the final or eschatological future that is yet to transpire. Most prophecies have already been fulfilled long ago either in Israel or in the earthly career of Jesus. Even in the case of an apocalyptic book like Daniel a good argument can be made that the empires referred to in the material leading up to Daniel 7 are not late-twentieth-century empires but the empires that led up to the time of the first coming of the Son of Man. This would mean that the last of the beastly empires is the Roman Empire, and that with the *first* coming of the Son of Man the eschatological events had already begun. It seems likely that this is how the New Testament writers viewed these matters, and even the first-century Jewish historian Josephus assumed that the last of the beastly empires was the Roman Empire. Again, my point is that it is arguable that very *few* prophecies in the Old Testament have yet to be fulfilled. Bearing this in mind, I must now say a bit more about the character of biblical prophecy.

The Character of Old Testament Prophecy

In the past twenty years of Old Testament scholarship a considerable stress has been placed on seeing Old Testament prophecy as analogous to other forms of ancient Near Eastern prophecy, whether by a Balaam or by some other seer. There has been extensive study done trying to distinguish the ecstactic prophets, for instance, of Saul's day and the later classical prophets. It seems doubtful to me however that a *nābî'* (prophet) can really be categorically distinguished from a *ḥōzeh* (seer), or from some later figure such as Amos.

It does appear rather certain that various courts in the ancient Near East had seers and indeed magicians who were paid professionals and part of the court entourage. These figures can be distinguished from someone like Amos. Further, there seem to have been schools of the prophets—notice how Elijah seems to reflect this tendency. Thus we should be cautious about asserting that figures like Amos necessarily operated in a vacuum. Certainly another major stress in Old Testament scholarship in the recent past has been the attempt to analyze the kinds of experiences the prophets had that led to these oracles—were they purely ecstactic, or did the human figure have conscious control over what came forth? There has also been an interest in studying the personality or character of the prophet to give a context for studying his words. This last is often a difficult, if not impossible, task in view of the nonnarrative character of their work. Sometimes we have nothing more than a selection of their oracles.

Finally, as the literary study of prophecy has increased, there has been increasing stress on the character of prophecy as structured poetry, indeed in some cases carefully structured poetry. This may suggest a period of reflection by the poet before putting it in writing. It also means that we must be careful about pressing various poetic figures to give us more information than they intend to give. Also, a great deal of study has been done on ancient Near Eastern scribal techniques, and if it is true that these prophets gave their oracles orally, then later wrote them down, or even if someone else wrote them down (such as Baruch in Jeremiah's case), this suggests that we need to ask the question of what the relationship is between oral and written prophecy. Of what significance is it that we have this material only in the written, and in some cases edited, later form, not in the form it was originally given? These are the sort of issues that we must raise as we examine the prophetic material.

Perhaps of more interest to evangelicals is the old chestnut of whether we should see Old Testament prophecy as merely, or at least mainly, forth-telling, truth telling, soothsaying, or as mainly foretelling. It is quite clear to me that it is impossible to maintain that the prophets never engaged in foretelling events. Certainly we find this phenomena with great accuracy in the case of Amos, to the amazement of various Old Testament scholars, and therefore we cannot maintain that prophets spoke only of the present. This is simply untrue. It is however germane to note that they spoke of the future in a way that had some bearing on or interest for their present audiences. They did not engage in star-gazing about the remote future that had no relevance to the people of God to whom they spoke. It is quite unlikely, for instance, that Ezekiel had either Russia or China in mind when he prophesied about Gog and Magog—indeed, he would likely have been surprised to hear of such correspondences, since neither country existed in his time.

The reason so many *different* correlations have been suggested between these classical prophecies and later historical figures and events is precisely because these prophecies tend to be both *general* and often *figurative* or metaphorical in character. By this I mean we seldom find explicit particularistic predictions of the following sort in the Old Testament: "In the late twentieth century, an Iraqi ruler named Saddam will arise and combat the forces of the west on the plains of Kuwait." Such a prophecy, at least in that particularistic kind of form, would have had little meaning to an Amos or his audience since there were no nations called Iraq or Kuwait in that era, and Saddam Hussein would not be born for well over two thousand years.

What we *do* have in the prophets is the juxtaposition of their present, the near future, and in some cases eschatological matters, matters of the end of human history, not prognostications about distant history long after 800 B.C. but long prior to the eschaton. These facts become apparent when one takes the time to study Old Testament prophecy in its historical context. It has often been pointed out that the prophets saw events like mountain ranges—all bunched together, whether very near or more distant, and they usually do not give any indication of the valleys in between the near and the end. Usually they are not interested in precise chronology at all. Even in apocalyptic material the use of time language really does not seem to function in the way one might think—basically it serves to indicate that God has determined the amount of time left. Large numbers indicate a long time, small numbers indicate a shorter span. These numbers, which often are symbolic, cannot be taken literally, unless one wants to argue that the prophet made some major blunders. Figurative material must be interpreted accordingly, and some knowledge of apocalyptic literature is necessary to understand books like Daniel.

It may also be useful to point out that there is also a difference between conditional and unconditional prophecies. Some prophecies were given with provisos such as "this will happen unless you repent." If repentance happened, then the oracle of doom did not transpire. In such cases, God's mercy prevailed, and we should not talk about unfulfilled prophecy. Such prophecies would only come to pass if certain conditions were or were not met. This means that we have no business looking for fulfillment of various conditional Old Testament prophecies addressed to people in the era 800-400 B.C., addressed to Israel or some part of it and not to the church. Those prophecies either were or were not fulfilled, depending on conditions then, and it is debatable whether we should look for a second fulfillment later.

In other cases we simply do not have the necessary historical information to be sure whether a particular prophecy has or has not been fulfilled yet, and we cannot simply assume that they have not when we don't know. Here is another good reason why ancient prophecy always should be studied in conjunction with ancient history—to see the correspondence or connections between the two. We cannot pause here to address the hermeneutical question of the relevance of material addressed to Israel for the church today, and how we may use the material. At this point we must simply say that one cannot simply assume automatic applicability, although much in prophecy is applicable and it tells us much about what God is like and what we are like and what God expects of his people.

The word *prophet* in English comes from the Greek *prophētēs,* a word that means "to speak for" or "to speak beforehand." However, in our case we are dealing with Old Testament prophets and Hebrew, so what is more crucial is the Hebrew word *nābî'* and its plural *nᵉbî'îm.* W. F. Albright argued long ago, and his view still is held by most scholars, that *nābî'* is related to the Akkadian *nabû,* which means "appoint" or "call," which is in turn a statement about vocation. The noun form of the word refers to one who is called. In addition, we know that the verbal form of the word can mean "fall into ecstasy," and we should note that at Hosea 9:7 *nābi'* is taken as the equivalent of the pejorative term *mᶜšuggā'* ("fanatic, lunatic"). Another early Hebrew phrase for the prophet is "man of God"—which Samuel was called. Another common word used throughout the ancient Near East is *hōzeh* (seer).

A. Soggins and others have suggested that since the term *nābi'* can mean "seer" or "ecstatic" in certain contexts, this may explain why we find a reluctance among the eighth- to sixth-century classical prophets to call themselves *nᶜbi'im*. It is perhaps important to note that in the Hebrew version of the Old Testament, when the subject is falseness, the emphasis falls on the false prophecy, whereas in the Greek translation of the Old Testament the focus is on the false prophet.

So far as our analysis can take us it appears that Israelite prophets, even of the classical period, differed little in the form of their oracles, or in the nature in which they received these oracles, from other ancient Near Eastern prophets. We have abundant evidence from Mari and Ugarit and elsewhere indicating not only prophetic activity but prophecy that uses similar forms and idioms and metaphors to the classical Israelite prophets.

The chief difference is that the Israelite prophets drew their inspiration from a different source: Yahweh, the one true God. In the case of a figure like Balaam, God can use even a non-Israelite prophet to speak the truth; thus we cannot simply argue that the difference between Israelite and non-Israelite prophets is the difference between true and false prophets. For one thing, the Bible records some false Israelite prophets, mostly those who were the paid professionals of the courts of Israel or Judah. Sometimes too, as in the case of Ahab, non-Yahwistic prophets such as the prophets of Baal were deliberately employed by Israelite rulers.

It is not clear whether we can usefully make a distinction between ecstatic and nonecstatic prophets. In some cases it appears that Israelite prophets retained the full and conscious use of their faculties while receiving revelation, but, for instance, when revelation came by means of vision or dream, or some other form of ecstatic phenomena (see Ezekiel) this does not seem to be the case. The crucial factor is that all were convinced they were moved, even in some cases impelled, by God's Spirit to speak to Israel, or often to one particular segment of God's people, such as the rulers. Some prophets, such as Isaiah, seem to have accepted their call to such tasks willingly, while others like Jeremiah or Jonah obviously did not. All these prophets were convinced that what they said was Yahweh's words— "thus sayeth Yahweh" was their usual introductory phrase, and as such they assumed that their words had final authority, they were not just the opinion of a human prophet. Not surprisingly, we read little or nothing in the classical prophetic literature about testing such prophecy—it is simply to be received and believed. This seems to distinguish classical prophecy from what we read about in Deuteronomy, and also from New Testament prophecy as manifested at Corinth, which was to be weighed and judged.

It appears that the prevalence of prophets and prophecy waxed and waned during Israelite history. First Samuel 3:7-9 seems to hint that Samuel is a new sort of figure on the stage of local history. Apparently too, though prophecy did not totally disappear after Malachi, it had waned to a great extent by New Testament times, except perhaps in certain separatist groups such as at Qumran.

The form of the classical prophetic oracles suggests that they were originally given orally, and only later written down, perhaps for dissemination to a wider audience, or even a later audience. The writing down of the prophecy could have been done by scribes or the prophet himself, but the writing suggests that they thought the words were of value for more than just the immediate situation addressed. For a people so tied to a land, it is interesting to note that Israelite prophecy did not die out when Israel was carted off into exile.

Nonetheless, an adjustment of focus does come in exilic and postexilic prophecy whereby God is likewise seen as a God of the nations and not confined to one land. Ezekiel is surprised at this, but he admits it. Also, from the exilic period on, an increasing stress was placed on eschatological and apocalyptic elements in the prophecy, not surprisingly as it appeared less and less likely that the Davidic earthly "good old days" would ever return prior to the Day of Yahweh.

It was the basic task of the prophet to let God's people in on God's perspective on how things were going, what needed change and what was all right. Basically what we learn from prophecy is God's redemptive judgment for his people. Very few oracles are directed just to an individual, and none, it may safely be said, are given to satisfy mere pious curiosity about the future or how the world will end. W. Lasor has made quite clear too that we must treat this material as poetry—for metaphors, word plays, synthetic and antithetical and chain parallelism, repetition, merisms, word association and onomatapoeia, to name but a few features, are all used. Rhyme however is basically not a feature of such prophecy, and meter and rhythm varies, coming in clusters. Word pairs, that is, pairs of synonyms that are stock and were used elsewhere in the ancient Near East, are common.

Like some extrabiblical prophets, the classical prophets sometimes engaged in the use of signs or wonders as a way of legitimating their calling or the truth of their oracles. Some have sought to maintain that the prophets were essentially preachers, and there is some justice in this assessment, but sometimes they showed forth the future, and it is not the case that they usually do exegesis or exposition on some previous Word of God, written or oral. Rather, their task is to give a new Word of God. Whether it is about present, near future or the eschaton, it is relevant to their immediate audience. There seems to have been a connection of some Israelite prophets with sanctuaries, such as the temple in Jerusalem, or the one at Bethel.

Another feature of note is the fact that prophetic schools may have existed even long after Elijah. Some have thought that Isaiah 40—66 comes from a school whose original founder was Isaiah, at a much earlier period. It would be wrong, however, to assume that the classical prophets were bound to a cultic task, and it is not the case that they always appear as great supporters of the priestly tasks. For instance, in the case of Amos the cult comes in for heavy criticism. It appears that the major task of the classical prophet was to help in Israel's struggle against syncretism—they strove for a pure worship of the one true God, and the impression one gets is that their unwelcome oracles often were not well received.

It is perhaps because the prophets knew how the word would be received that we hear of them being impelled to go forth and speak God's word—these were not the words of people-pleasing preachers. Often, perhaps even in the vast majority of cases, we could call these men prophets of judgment, if not prophets of doom. We must stress that it is wrong to abstract the cheerful and hopeful oracles from the judgment oracles. Both come from the same God who is a God of redemptive-judgment, by which I mean that in the case of his own people, even when he wounds, he often does so to heal or cut out a cancer from the body politic. Soggins's summary about the relationship of prophets to the cult and establishment of Israel is useful: "The prophets then were critical of the cult but did not reject it in principle. This position is confirmed by the fact that . . . they were able to speak freely in the temple during the cult" (Introduction to the Old Testament, p. 228).

The prophets then were not mere functionaries of the cult, such as a hired preacher, but the oft-held Protestant judgment that the prophets justify an antisacramental religion is also untrue. Furthermore, the prophets were not *purely* interested in social or economic or political matters per se—what they were interested in is the underlying theological and spiritual causes and effects of certain behavior that was manifested in the political or economic or social realm.

For instance, the oppression of the poor by the rich indicated a serious spiritual problem, in regard to the treatment of fellow people of God and others of God's creatures fairly as God would wish. Or again the reliance on entangling alliances with non-Israelite nations bespoke a lack of faith in an all-powerful Yahweh and in his ability to save. The prophets looked for the underlying issues and causes of a moral, theological and spiritual nature. It is clear that God's people are not immune from judgment, indeed some prophets stress that God's people are more subject to it and in a more stringent manner. Judgment begins with the household of God.

Even in the most gloomy of the prophets there is usually a ray of hope, at least for a faithful remnant after the judgment falls. Quite clearly the prophets were not merely prophets of doom and would not have spoken if they did not feel that their words of warning might lead to a change of behavior and an improvement of circumstances. They were people who hoped for a better future, even if that required swallowing some bitter medicine in the present. Their messages should be studied carefully in light of the historical matrices in which they were given, and only after one has done that can one begin to ask the question, What does this prophecy have to say to us today in the late twentieth century?

I am quite convinced that all of God's Word, including already fulfilled biblical prophecy, has a message for us today, but often it is a message about the character of God, or God's people, or the interaction of the two, thus giving us clues about what sort of life and conduct God expects of us in the present, for we still have yet to come before the judgment seat for the deeds we have done in the body. The fulfilled prophecies of the Bible are in all likelihood not meant to be mysterious encoded messages about late-twentieth-century events and persons. As Paul suggests in 1 Corinthians 10:1-13, the message we may learn from God's past dealings with his people is either "go and do likewise" or equally frequently "go and do otherwise." We must heed this parenetic message regardless of our views of biblical prophecy, for the real question is not whether God in Christ will be faithful to his Word and conclude human history as promised, but rather "when the Son of Man comes, will he find faith on earth?" (Lk 18:8).

Notes

Introduction

[1]J. B. Lightfoot, *Notes on the Epistles of St. Paul* (Winona Lake: Alpha Pub. rpr.), p. 62.

Chapter One: Paul, Jesus and the Language of Imminence

[1]See J. Jeremias, "The Present Position in the Controversy Concerning the Problem of the Historical Jesus," *EvT* 69 (1958): 333-39; F. F. Bruce, *Paul and Jesus* (London: SCM, 1977); J. D. G. Dunn, *Unity and Diversity in the New Testament* (Philadelphia: Westminster, 1977).

[2]E. Käsemann, "Blind Alleys in the Jesus of History Controversy," in *New Testament Questions of Today* (London: SCM, 1969), pp. 23-65; R. Bultmann, "Jesus and Paul," in *Existence and Faith* (Cleveland: World, 1960), pp. 183-201.

[3]See the essays of A. J. M. Wedderburn in *Paul and Jesus: Collected Essays*, ed. A. J. M. Wedderburn (Sheffield: JSOT Press, 1989); and also S. G. Wilson's essay, "From Jesus to Paul: The Contours and Consequences of a Debate," in *From Jesus to Paul: Studies in Honour of F. W. Beare*, ed. P. Richardson and J. C. Hurd (Waterloo: W. Laurier Univ. Press, 1984), pp. 1-21.

[4]Wilson notes:

> Above all, it is their eschatological convictions which are considered to unite them. Jesus preached the imminent arrival of the kingdom and yet at the same time asserted that it had already arrived in connection with his ministry. Since a tension between the Already and the Not Yet is the dominant characteristic of Paul's teaching too, Jesus and Paul operate with the same underlying eschatological scheme ("From Jesus to Paul," p. 10).

[5]See especially J. C. Beker, *Paul the Apostle: The Triumph of God in Life and Thought* (Philadelphia: Fortress, 1980), and his *Paul's Apocalyptic Gospel: The Coming Triumph of God* (Philadelphia: Fortress, 1982).

[6]This remark requires some qualification depending on the degree to which one thinks Jesus spoke of the future coming Son of Man, and the degree to which one thinks the material collected in Mark 13 goes back to Jesus.

[7]C. K. Barrett, "New Testament Eschatology," *SJT* 6 (1953): 136-55, here p. 144 (also pp. 225-43).

[8]J. J. Collins, "Genre, Ideology, and Social Movements in the Domain of Jewish Apocalypticism," paper delivered at the SBL annual meeting, Nov. 1989.

[9]Note that Paul, at least in the undisputed Paulines, does not talk about the "age to come," and Jesus' discussion of such matters is couched in terms of the Dominion of God, which both has and will come.

[10]Experts in the area of apocalypticism generally distinguish between two sorts of apocalypses—historical and heavenly ascent. The former is horizontal in orientation, looking forward to the future and the culmination of history, while the latter is basically otherworldly in form, dealing with visions of, or journeys through, the heavens or heaven.

[11]J. J. Collins, *The Apocalyptic Imagination: An Introduction to the Jewish Matrix of Christianity* (New

York: Crossroad, 1984), p. 7.

[12]Again we may think of a few exceptions, such as the Markan account of Jesus' baptism (B. Withering-ton, *The Christology of Jesus* [Minneapolis: Fortress, 1990], pp. 148-55) or Paul's account of his ascent to the third heaven in 2 Corinthians 12.

[13]L. Keck, "Paul and Apocalyptic Theology," *Interpretation* 38 (1984): 229-41, here p. 240.

[14]One may also wish to consult the recent Festschrift, *Apocalyptic and the New Testament. Essays in Honor of J. L. Martyn* (Sheffield, JSOT Press, 1989), especially the essay by M. C. De Boer, "Paul and Jewish Apocalyptic Eschatology," pp. 169-89, as well as the essay Martyn himself wrote in support of Beker's approach, "Apocalyptic Antinomies in Paul's Letters to the Galatians," *NTS* 31 (1985): 410-24. For a critique of Beker that stresses that Paul also has elements of realized eschatology in regard to the condition of the believer in the present, and that therefore Paul's future eschatology cannot be seen as *the* key or center of his thought, see V. P. Branick, "Apocalyptic Paul?" *CBQ* 47 (1985): 664-75. I agree with Branick's basic critique, but here I am differing on the matter of proper termi-nology.

[15]Collins, *Apocalyptic Imagination*, p. 10.

[16]The book of Revelation, for example, provides an extensive list of seals and preliminary events that must precede the end while still using the language of imminence (see 22:20).

[17]Here and elsewhere I use the term *eschatological* in its technical sense of the discussion of the end things, the climactic events and happenings that bring human history as we know it to a climax and some sort of closure. Compare the remark of D. Gewalt, "1 Thess 4,15-17; 1 Kor 15,51 und Mk 9,1— zur Abgrenzung eines 'Herrenwortes,' " *Linguistica Biblica* 51 (1982): 105-13, here 110: "Paulus lasst in 1 Kor 15,51ff die apokalyptische Terminologie zurucktreten, ohne die Grundstruktur der Apoka-lypse aufheben."

[18]For a representative critique of the overuse and misuse of the term *apocalyptic* to describe what is actually eschatological in character, see C. Rowland's reply to J. D. G. Dunn's arguments in *The Open Heaven: A Study of Apocalyptic in Judaism and Early Christianity* (New York: Crossroad, 1982), p. 355: "What Dunn has indicated is the way in which eschatology dominated early Christianity as an eschatologically-orientated community, whose expectation about the future is distinguished, not so much by the so-called 'apocalyptic' elements but by the earnest conviction that the hopes of Judaism were already in process of being realized. They believed that the final climax of history was imminent, not because they had utilized a particular brand of eschatology, but because their beliefs about Jesus and their experience of the Spirit led them to understand their circumstances in this particular way." See Dunn's arguments in *Unity and Diversity in the New Testament*, pp. 309-40.

[19]W. D. Davies, *Paul and Rabbinic Judaism* (New York: Harper & Row, 1948), xiv. Cf. Albert Schweitzer, *The Mysticism of Paul the Apostle*, trans. W. Montgomery (New York: Holt and Co., 1931), and also *Paul and His Interpreters: A Critical History*, trans. W. Montgomery (London: A. & C. Black, 1912).

[20]Davies, *Paul*, xv.

[21]E. P. Sanders, *Paul and Palestinian Judaism* (London: SCM, 1977), 431ff., and S. Kim, *The Origin of Paul's Gospel* (Grand Rapids: Eerdmans, 1982), esp. 269ff.

[22]Sanders notes: "Schweitzer has been ignored in much of German Protestant scholarship . . ." *(Paul,* p. 434).

Chapter Two: Between Daybreak and Day: The Pauline Evidence

[1]A. Schweitzer, *The Mysticism of Paul the Apostle,* trans. W. Montgomery (New York: Holt and Co., 1931), p. 52. Note that he does not altogether deny any development but simply asserts: "It certainly did not consist in the slacking of his [Paul's] eschatological expectation as time went on."

[2]E. Best, *A Commentary on the First and Second Epistles to the Thessalonians* (London: A. & C. Black, 1972), p. 84.

[3]In other contexts *(Mysticism,* 91ff.), Schweitzer does refer to this material but not in order to address

the matter of the *timing* of the Second Coming.

[4]D. E. H. Whiteley, *The Theology of St. Paul* (Philadelphia: Fortress, 1972), p. 245.

[5]A. L. Moore, *The Parousia in the New Testament* (Leiden: Brill, 1966), 110 compares John 1:14 where the "we" also probably does not include the author. Paul may mean no more than "those Christians alive at the parousia" by "we."

[6]Moore, *Parousia,* pp. 118-19.

[7]H. Giesen, "Naherwartung des Paulus in Thess 4,13-18?" *Studien zum Neuen Testament und seiner Umwelt* 10 (1985): 123-50, esp. pp. 131-40.

[8]LSJ, 45; Abbott-Smith, p. 15.

[9]It is true, as Best *(Thessalonians,* p. 204) points out, that this phrase explains *how* Jesus will come, but it implies an uncertainty as to time, since the coming will be sudden, unexpected, surprising.

[10]For instance, Luke 12:39 = Matthew 24:43, a Q parable. There are differences in the two, one speaking of a person coming, the other of a day. It is not clear whether the two parables derive from Jesus or from the early church possibly by way of Paul, but see below.

[11]Schweitzer, *Mysticism,* p. 42.

[12]For instance, J. M. Court, "Paul and the Apocalyptic Pattern," in *Paul and Paulinism: Essays in Honor of C. K. Barrett,* ed. M. D. Hooker and S. G. Wilson (London: SPCK, 1982), pp. 57-66; A. F. J. Klijn, "1 Thessalonians 4:13-18 and its Background in Apocalyptic Literature," in *Paul and Paulinism,* pp. 67-73.

[13]W. G. Kümmel, *Introduction to the New Testament,* trans. H. C. Kee (London: SCM, 1975), pp. 265-66. The synoptic tradition witnesses this same dialectic between sudden and unexpected coming and events that precede (and delay?). Cf. Mark 13, Matthew 25.

[14]R. Jewett, *The Thessalonian Correspondence. Pauline Rhetoric and Millenarian Piety* (Philadelphia, Fortress, 1986), pp. 3-18.

[15]See Kümmel, *Introduction,* p. 265.

[16]Schweitzer, *Mysticism,* pp. 43-53.

[17]F. F. Bruce, *I & II Corinthians,* NCB (Greenwood, S.C.: Attic Press, 1971), 93; C. K. Barrett, *A Commentary on the First Epistle to the Corinthians* (N.Y.: Harper, 1968), pp. 227-28; H. Conzelmann, *1 Corinthians,* trans. James W. Leitch (Philadelphia: Fortress, 1975), p. 168, nn. 40, 41; Test. L. 14.1 in *APOT* 2:312.

[18]Schweitzer, *Mysticism,* p. 53.

[18a]Because my views have not changed in any significant way since the time when I previously discussed 1 Corinthians 7, in what follows in the next three pages I have adapted, with slight changes, my earlier discussion of this subject found in *Women in the Earliest Churches* (Cambridge: Cambridge Univ. Press, 1988), pp. 34-36, and notes on pp. 236-39.

[19]Pace Conzelmann, *1 Corinthians,* 132 and n. 19. Moore also points to 3 Maccabees 1:16 where "present distress" does not refer to some sort of messianic woes *(Parousia,* p. 116).

[20]*Synestalmenos* is taken from nautical usage where it means to shorten a sail. Its only other use in the New Testament is in Acts 5:6 where it has a somewhat transferred sense of wrapped up tight (shortened or contracted is what it likely means here). J. Weiss, *Der erste Korintherbrief,* in Meyer, *Kommentar über das Neue Testament* V (Göttingen, Vandenhoeck and Ruprecht, 1910), p. 196, stresses that Paul says "present distress," not "coming distress." In Romans 8:38 and 1 Corinthians 3:22 Paul contrasts the meaning of these two words (see also 3 Macc 1:16).

[21]"The outward form/pattern of this world is passing away." According to Barrett, "Paul's point is not the transiency of creation as such, but the fact that its outward pattern in social and mercantile institutions, for example, has no permanence" *(Corinthians,* p. 178). Cf. D. J. Doughty, "The Presence and Future of Salvation in Corinth," *ZNW* 66 (1975): 61-90, here 69. There is a possibility that *paragei* here means "is misleading (or deceiving)." Cf. Epictetus 2.7.14 (LCL), pp. 258-59, and 2.20.7 (LCL), p. 372, where *paragesthe* parallels *ezaratasthe* and means "leads astray." The point in 1 Corinthians 7 would be that the form of this world may seem to indicate a permanent order of things, but this

form is misleading.

[22]I could not disagree more with E. Käsemann, *New Testament Questions of Today*, p. 136, when he says, "Thus, what is described as the dialectic between the indicative and the imperative, between the state of having been redeemed and ultimate salvation which lies yet ahead, is nothing else but the projection into the human condition of the Christian of the relationship of the Lordship of Christ to the subjection of all cosmic principalities." Nor is Käsemann fully correct that Paul's fundamental response to the Corinthian problem is to set over against the Corinthians' overrealized eschatology, "eschatological reserve and apocalyptic" (p. 136). The fundamental issue in Paul's controversy with Corinth has to do not so much with the timing of salvation (though that is one facet of the difficulty), but with the nature of salvation. The "once . . . now" that determines Paul's view of Christian existence refers to the existence of those no longer under the dominion of sin, no longer enslaved to the powers and principalities, the form and plan of this world. Cf. Doughty, "Presence," pp. 60ff.

Paul's main concern as a task theologian has nothing to do with speculation about the future but with the existence of Christians now as a result of the work Christ has already performed. Paul's eschatology is not mainly a product of what he had learned and continued to accept of Jewish apocalyptic thinking. Rather, it is determined by his Christology, however much he may use language he imbibed from the Jewish thought-world within which he grew up. There is, of course, a future element in Paul's Christology, but his advice to the Corinthians is based not so much on the "not yet" but on the "already" of what Christ has done and the results of that action.

The problem in Corinth is that both the ascetics and the libertines misunderstand the nature of salvation in Christ in both its present and future aspects. The Corinthians continue to shape their lives with reference to the world and material existence as such. The libertines disdain the world, the ascetics renounce it, but in both cases their respective lifestyles are being determined more by what they reject than by real Christian principles. In neither case do they realize the importance of both the world and the human body (which is a part of this material existence).Thus, Paul counters by saying that the earth is the Lord's (10:26) and the body also is the Lord's (6:13, 19), both having a place in God's salvation plan (cf. 1 Cor 15).

In 1 Corinthians, Paul sets out to correct the fundamental misunderstandings the Corinthians have about the nature of salvation and in the process he corrects both their "already" and their "not yet." His advice in 1 Corinthians 7 is grounded primarily in what God has already done and is doing in Christ. The Christian existence he advocates and the imperatives he gives are determined not in reaction to a world gone wrong, nor are they determined by what is not yet true about Christians (a defensive posture), but as a result of what Christ has done and what is true about this eschatological "time," and about Christians in this time. To paraphrase Bultmann's idea, Paul is saying, "Be what you already are in Christ; recognize the time you already live in; see the scope and depth of what God's salvation plan involves even now."

Paul's view does not amount to an endorsement of the status quo; he is not suggesting any sort of endorsement for any ethnic group, social class, sex or economic situation no matter what it is. He does state his preference for the single life over the married state, but again his reasons for doing so have to do with his belief that in the Christian era a single person can better give his or her undivided attention to God. This is really a sort of religious pragmatism, not a sociological program that argues that singleness is inherently better than marriage, maleness better than femaleness, abstaining from sex better than having sexual relations, being circumcised better than not being circumcised (cf. v. 19).

[23]Cf. J. J. von Allmen, *Pauline Teaching on Marriage* (London: Faith, 1963), pp. 19-20. In 1 Corinthians 7:25-31 Paul is not digressing so much as revealing the basis of his advice and the nature of a Christian relationship to the world that determines all that he says in this chapter and explains why he continues to say "remain as you are."

[24]Doughty, "Presence," p. 67. It is quite unwarranted to import an "already" into the second half of each of these dialectical statements.

[25]Doughty, "Presence," p. 72, n. 50. Cf. H. J. Schoeps, *Paul—The Theology of the Apostle in Light of Jewish Religious History,* trans. H. Knight (Philadelphia: Westminster, 1961), p. 211; cf. Diogenes Laertius 6.29, LCL II, trans. R. D. Hicks (London, 1925), pp. 30-31.

[26]Doughty says the nuance between "to use" and "to take full advantage of" is slight but significant ("Presence," p. 71, n. 47).

[27]Cf. E. E. Ellis, *Paul and His Recent Interpreters* (Grand Rapids: Eerdmans, 1961), p. 35ff. Ellis argues that "it is probably a misconception to identify 'away from the body' (II Cor 5:8) with the intermediate state at all." Whether we are to see this intermediate condition as an altered or suspended time factor for the dead, or as an anticipated or partial fulfillment at death of the parousia consummation, Paul does not make clear, but it would seem that "at home with the Lord" refers to being in heaven, where the Lord's home is. Cf. O. Cullmann, *Immortality of the Soul or Resurrection of the Dead* (London: Epworth, 1958). In fact, Paul says our future home is in the heavens. This should not be seen as an alteration of his resurrection perspective any more than the parable about the rich man and Lazarus contradicts the teaching in the Jesus tradition about bodily resurrection. Both perspectives could be held at once, perhaps because Judaism in and before Jesus' and Paul's era had already considered such possibilities under the influence of Hellenistic ideas as well as of certain Old Testament texts (cf. Gen 5:24; 2 Kings 2:11-18).

[28]Cf. A. T. Robertson, *A Grammar of the Greek New Testament in the Light of Historical Research,* 2d ed. (New York: Hodder & Stoughton, 1915), p. 589; M. Zerwick, *Biblical Greek,* Eng. ed. adapted from the 4th Latin ed. by Joseph Smith (Rome: Scripta Pontificii Instituti Biblici, 1963), sec. 117, 39; G. Abbott-Smith, *A Manual Greek Lexicon of the New Testament,* 3d ed. (Edinburgh: T. & T. Clark, 1937), p. 441; MM, 627.

[29]C. K. Barrett, *A Commentary on the Epistle to the Romans* (New York: Harper & Row, 1957), p. 232.

[30]C. E. B. Cranfield, *The Epistle to the Romans,* Vol. 2 ICC (Edinburgh: T. & T. Clark, 1979), p. 682.

[31]Barrett, *Romans,* p. 253.

[32]W. R. Hutton, "The Kingdom of God Has Come," *ET* 64 (1952-53): 89-91.

[33]C. H. Dodd, *The Parables of the Kingdom* (N.Y.: Scribners, 1936).

[34]Cranfield, *Romans* 2:683. Ellis notes how Paul speaks of eschatological matters being past, present and future *(Paul,* p. 37).

[35]G. B. Caird, *Paul's Letters from Prison* (Oxford: Clarendon, 1976), p. 22.

[36]*Apostolic Fathers,* 1 (LCL), 46-47 and the context.

[37]J. B. Lightfoot, *St. Paul's Epistle to the Philippians* (London: Macmillan and Co., 1894), p. 160; Gerald F. Hawthorne, *Philippians* (Waco, Tex.: Word, 1983), p. 182.

[38]Cf. the conclusion of H. Ridderbos, *Paul: An Outline of His Theology* (Grand Rapids: Eerdmans, 1975), p. 492: "One will thus be allowed to conclude that living to see the parousia was for Paul indeed a real possibility, we may perhaps say the object of his hope and expectation, but that both for his own faith and for his parenesis this expectation was in no way a *conditio sine qua non.* The force of his expectation for the future and of his parenesis is to be sure dependent on the appearing of Christ in glory, and on its significance for the present, but not on still being alive to see this appearing."

[39]J. C. Beker, *Paul's Apocalyptic Gospel: The Coming Triumph of God* (Philadelphia: Fortress, 1982), pp. 48-49.

[40]L. E. Keck, "Paul and Apocalyptic Theology," *Interpretation* 38 (1984): 231.

[41]Schweitzer, *Mysticism,* p. 186.

Chapter Three: Dawn's First Light: The Evidence from Jesus' Teaching

[1]B. Witherington, *The Christology of Jesus* (Minneapolis: Fortress, 1990), pp. 228-33.

[2]I have argued in *Women in the Ministry of Jesus* (Cambridge: Cambridge Univ. Press, 1984), pp. 41-46, for the authenticity of this parable. The Jesus Seminar includes it among the gray parables, which means that the parable may not be authentic, but the ideas in it may well be close to his own. Cf.

262 JESUS, PAUL AND THE END OF THE WORLD ▪

R. W. Funk et al., *The Parables of Jesus. A Report of the Jesus Seminar* (Sonoma: Polebridge Press, 1988), p. 21. The majority of scholars in the Jesus Seminar ranked this parable in the pink or gray range (p. 63, cf. p. 103) while a minority placed it in the black range (i.e., definitely inauthentic, p. 37).

³E. Schweizer, "The Significance of Eschatology in the Teaching of Jesus," *Eschatology and the New Testament. Essays in Honor of G. R. Beasley-Murray* (Peabody, Mass.: Hendrikson, 1988), pp. 1-13, here p. 3.

⁴Moore, *The Parousia*, p. 127.

⁵Interpreting this verse as an allusion to the transfiguration has a long pedigree, going back at least to Origen. It became the most popular view among the early church fathers. I have argued in a forthcoming article, entitled "Transfigured Glory," that this is how Mark understood this particular saying of Jesus.

⁶W. G. Kümmel, *Promise and Fulfilment. The Eschatological Message of Jesus* (London: SCM Press, 1957), pp. 25-29. He thus takes this verse to be proof against Schweitzer that Jesus thought that the Dominion of God would come before Jesus' death. Cf. Schweitzer, *The Quest of the Historical Jesus* (London, 1954), pp. 357ff.

⁷Dodd, *Parables of the Kingdom*, p. 37ff.

⁸J. Y. Campbell, "The Kingdom of God Has Come," *ET* 48 (1936-37): 91-94; cf. G. R. Beasley-Murray, *Jesus and the Kingdom of God* (Grand Rapids: Eerdmans, 1986), pp. 188-89. B. D. Chilton, *God in Strength. Jesus' Announcement of the Kingdom* (Freistadt: Plochl, 1979), pp. 263-74 argues that this is likely an authentic saying of Jesus due to its Semitic elements and that *elēlythyian* has epiphanic rather than eschatological overtones, though it surely refers to something in the future. He also concludes that the use of 'seeing' here does not point to this being a parousia saying, in view of the epiphanic language.

⁹C. E. B. Cranfield, *The Gospel According to St. Mark* (Cambridge: Cambridge U. Press, 1972), pp. 287-88.

¹⁰This is all the more likely if one concludes that the original form of Mark's Gospel had no appearance narratives but rather ended at 16:8. I think this conclusion is unlikely, but the descriptive parallels between the transfiguration and the language about the coming of the Son of Man suggest an intended correspondence by Mark.

¹¹On this see Witherington, *Christology of Jesus*, pp. 186-89.

¹²I. H. Marshall, *The Gospel of Luke* (Grand Rapids: Eerdmans, 1978), pp. 378-79.

¹³Schweitzer, *Quest*, p. 358.

¹⁴Kümmel, *Promise and Fulfilment*, p. 61ff.

¹⁵But cf. H. Schürmann, "Zur Traditions—und Redaktionsgeschichte von Mt 10,23," *BZ* 3 (1959): 82-88; followed by R. Schnackenburg, *God's Rule and Kingdom* (Edinburgh: Nelson, 1963), p. 204.

¹⁶Cf. J. Riches, *Jesus and the Transformation of Judaism* (New York: Seabury, 1982); and esp. M. Borg, *Conflict, Holiness, and Politics in the Teaching of Jesus* (New York: Edwin Mellen, 1984).

¹⁷Moore, *Parousia*, pp. 143-45.

¹⁸Despite the insistence of Kümmel, *Promise and Fulfilment*, 61-2, who says it must mean before the Son of Man appears in glory.

¹⁹Witherington, *Christology of Jesus*, pp. 120-24, and E. Arens, *The ELTHON-Sayings in the Synoptic Tradition. A Historico-critical Investigation* (Göttingen, Vandenhoeck and Ruprecht, 1976), though Arens is more skeptical than I am about the authenticity of various *ELTHON* sayings.

²⁰I have argued for the authenticity of this saying in *Christology of Jesus*, pp. 49-53.

²¹S. McKnight, "Jesus and the Endtime: Matthew 10.23," *SBL Seminar Papers 1986* (Atlanta: Scholars Press, 1986), pp. 501-20, esp. pp. 516-17.

²²The attempt to structure the chapter on the basis of historical events vs. eschatological events (i.e., vv. 2, 5-6, 7-8, 9, 13 seen as historical, and vv. 15-27 seen as eschatological) will not work, not least because *all* these events are seen as eschatological in character and are described using stock eschat-

ological language. It is true that "this generation" (v. 30) must refer to the generation either of Jesus or of Mark's audience, but it is "all these things" that must transpire during that time frame, not the events *after* the tribulation in those days. Cf. S. J. Kidder, "This Generation in Mt. 24.34," *Andrews University Seminary Studies* 21 (1983): 203-9.

[23]I am not arguing that the phrase "in those days" is a technical one for the last days or those which ensue at the parousia. Mark also uses the same phrase in verses 17 and 19 to refer to happenings during the period of tribulation. Thus "in those days" by itself is also not a clue to the structure of Mark 13.

[24]W. L. Lane, *The Gospel of Mark* (Grand Rapids: Eerdmans, 1974), p. 478. On the notable parallels in the structure of Mark 13 to 2 Thessalonians 2 and 2 Peter 3, cf. Moore, *Parousia*, p. 152, n. 2. These parallels may suggest that Mark or his source has shaped his material according to some sort of early Christian eschatological schema involving: (1) warnings to take heed; (2) signs of the end; (3) proclamation of the gospel; (4) the final end; (5) imminence of the end; (6) ignorance of the date; and (7) exhortation to watch, in this order.

[25]As Moore points out *(Parousia,* p. 100 and n. 3), the phrase *hai hēmerai,* or *hai hēmera ekeinai,* is clearly used in the Jesus tradition for the end of time, often with direct connection to the *Yom Yahweh* (see Mt 10:15; 25:13; Mk 14:25; Lk 10:12; 17:26, 31). Kümmel finds it difficult to believe that Jesus could have spoken of preliminary events happening during this generation, and not also have at least implicitly commented on the nearness of the end (I agree, but what Jesus seems to have implied was that the end *could* or *might* be near, not that it definitely was, and he spoke an utterance like Mark 13:32 to make clear that he was not teaching a necessarily imminent end. In short, Kümmel's "flexible imminence" model is a good one, but unfortunately he did not always adhere to its implications faithfully.

[26]On the function of Mark 13, cf. M. D. Hooker, "Trial and Tribulation in Mark XIII," *Bulletin of John Rylands Library* 65 (1982): 78-99. Hooker draws an interesting comparison between the placement and function of Mark 13 and that of the farewell discourse in John. She notes the connection of preaching, persecution and parousia in several Gospel contexts.

[27]W. S. Vorster, "Literary Reflection on Mark 13.5-37: A Narrative Speech of Jesus," *Neotestamentica* 21 (1987): 203-24, here p. 219; cf. p. 217.

[28]See B. Reicke, "Synoptic Prophecies on the Destruction of Jerusalem," in *Studies in the New Testament and Early Christian Literature: Essays in Honor of Allen P. Wikgren,* Nov. Test. Sup. 33 (Leiden: Brill, 1972), pp. 121-34.

[29]See S. Laws, "Can Apocalyptic Be Relevant?" in *What about the New Testament? Essays in Honour of Christopher Evans,* ed. M. Hooker and C. Hickling (London, SCM Press, 1975), pp. 89-102, here 97ff. on Mark 13 and its relationship to apocalyptic literature. On the varied way *Yom Yahweh* language is used in the Old Testament, sometimes of God's present in-breaking judgment, rather than final judgment, cf. J. Gray, "The Day of Yahweh in Cultic Experience and Eschatological Prospect," *Svensk Exegetisk Arsbok* 39 (1974): 5-37; A. Knockaert, "A Fresh Look at Eschatological Discourse (Mt. 24-25)," *Lumen Vitae* 40 (1985): 167-79, here 172ff. It has often been ignored that in early Jewish literature, in particular some of the apocalyptic material in 4 Ezra, 2 Baruch, Apocalypse of Baruch and elsewhere, wrestles with the concept of the "flexible" imminence of God's day of vindicating justice. In many ways, the discussion of the so-called delay of the parousia is just a continuation of this early Jewish discussion. In texts like Apoc. Bar. 85:10 we already see the tension between already and not yet, between eschatological hope and the delay of final vindication. That other early Jews could continue to maintain a strong faith in the possible imminence of "the day" coupled with a discussion of its delay and possible reasons for it should warn us against the assumption that when someone like Jesus or Paul used the language of imminence it precluded any idea of flexibility about the timing or an interval before it happened. See esp. the fine study of R. J. Bauckham, "The Delay of the Parousia," *Tyndale Bulletin* (1980): 3-36.

[30]The attempt by A. Feuillet, "La Signification fondamentale de Marc XIII. Recherchés sur l'Eschatol-

ogie des Synoptiques," *Revue Thomiste* 80 (1980): 181-215, and others to suggest that Mark 13 describes some *purely* eschatological events (the coming of the Son of Man) and some *non*eschatological historical events that are nonetheless described in eschatological terms and prefigure eschatological events, seems artificial. Surely all the events described in Mark 13 are in some sense eschatological. They do not prefigure anything, but rather are the crucial eschatological events themselves. Feuillet's distinction between events that bring about the end of a world and events that bring about the end of *the* world is perhaps more apt. He is right that in apocalyptic as well as some late prophetic literature events are often juxtaposed without any clear indication of their temporal relationship or proximity to one another. When "all these things" are described as happening in this generation and the focus is on events affecting the center of early Jewish piety, one may rightly speak of the end of a particular world. Mark 13:24-27, however, is cosmic in scope.

[31]See Sanders, *Jesus and Judaism* (Philadelphia: Fortress Press, 1985), p. 61ff.

[32]Whether Jesus spoke of the fall of Jerusalem itself will depend on whether one thinks Luke 21:20-24 is purely Lukan redactional material, or whether it ultimately in some form goes back to Jesus. The attempt to make *genea* mean something like "race" is a ploy of desperation. Cf. Moore, *Parousia*, pp. 133-36.

[33]I am not arguing here for the authenticity of this whole discourse, only for some sort of word about the destruction of the temple (Mk 13:30, 32).

[34]See F. Mussner, "Wer ist 'dieses Geschlecht' in Mk 13,30 Parr.?" *Kairos* 29 (1987): 23-28. Mussner ends up suggesting that "this generation" means the whole of humanity that exists before the parousia, or at least all the blinded ones, or it refers to the Jewish people. In both cases he removes the natural temporal sense of the phrase. In his view Mark 13:30 is rather like the saying "the poor you always have with you," only in this case it is either humanity, blind humanity or the Jews.

[35]A majority of scholars in the Jesus Seminar think that the Q parable, at least in its Lukan form (14:16b-23), definitely or probably goes back to Jesus. Cf. Funk, *Parables of Jesus*, p. 98.

Chapter Four: The Origin of an Orientation

[1]I would not rule out the possibility that the connection between Luke 12:39 and 40 is original, since it is also manifest in the Matthean form of the saying and thus goes back before the Q collection. However, caution is in order here since Luke 12:40 is precisely the sort of explication one would expect from early Christian tradents who wanted to correct the incorrect assumption by some Christians that the parousia was necessarily imminent.

[2]I am not ruling out here that the material in 2 Peter may even reflect a use of this saying in the second century A.D.

[3]Since this motif derives ultimately from Jewish views about the *Yom Yahweh* it is hardly surprising that in some contexts the Day of the Lord seems to refer at least primarily to the coming of God Almighty (Rev 16:15; 2 Pet 3:10; cf. v. 12), and in some contexts to the coming of Christ (Rev 3:3; 1 Thess 5:2).

[4]J. Jeremias, *The Parables of Jesus* (New York: Scribners, 1963), pp. 48-49.

[5]I. H. Marshall, *The Gospel of Luke* (Grand Rapids: Eerdmans, 1978), p. 539. In the Old Testament prophetic literature watchfulness is regularly connected with the coming of the *Yom Yahweh* (Is 13:6; Joel 1:15; 2:1; Amos 5:18, passim).

[6]Ibid.

[7]J. Fitzmyer, *The Gospel According to Luke X-XXIV* (New York: Doubleday, 1985), p. 986.

[8]It is highly possible, in view of 2 Peter 3:14-16, that the author of 2 Peter assumes that his audience has read at least some of Paul's letters, and since the connection between 2 Peter 3:10-13 and what follows is close (note v. 14, "these things"), it may well be that this community received its teaching about the thief in the night from the Pauline corpus.

[9]R. P. Carroll, "Eschatological Delay in the Prophetic Tradition?" *ZAW*, no. 1 (1982): 47-58, here p. 55 n. 24., who finds no such eschatological delay motif in the late prophetic material.

Chapter Five: The Reign of the Regent: Paul and the *Basileia tou Theou*

[1]B. Witherington, *The Christology of Jesus* (Minneapolis: Fortress, 1990), p. 273.

[2]F. W. Beare, "Jesus and Paul," *CJT* 5 (1959): 79-86, here p. 84.

[3]What follows in this chapter was presented in a somewhat different form as a paper at the 1990 meeting of the SNTS in Milan, Italy.

[4]G. Johnston, "Kingdom of God Sayings in Paul's Letters," in *From Jesus to Paul. Studies in Honour of F. W. Beare*, ed. P. Richardson and J. C. Hurd (Waterloo, Wilfred Laurier U. Press, 1984), 143-56; G. Haufe, "Reich Gottes bei Paulus und in der Jesustradition," *NTS* 31 (1985): 467-72. After having completed this chapter, I discovered K. P. Donfried's helpful article entitled "The Kingdom of God in Paul" in *The Kingdom of God in 20th-Century Interpretation*, ed. W. Willis (Peabody, Mass.: Hendrickson, 1987), pp. 175-90. His conclusions are in fundamental agreement with what we have sought to argue here. He concludes, "Our study does show that Paul is dependent on the teaching of Jesus as reflected in the Synoptic tradition, particularly with regard to the kingdom of God . . . a fundamental unity and continuity between Jesus and Paul can be detected in the several themes which are common to both" (p. 189).

[5]So M. Stone, "The Concept of the Messiah in IV Ezra," in *Religions in Antiquity: Essays in Memory of E. R. Goodenough*, ed. J. Neusner (Leiden: Brill, 1968), pp. 295-312, here p. 298; L. J. Kreitzer, *Jesus and God in Paul's Eschatology* (Sheffield: JSOT Press, 1987), p. 60.

[6]Stone, "Concept," p. 298.

[7]It is another small point in favor of the authenticity of 2 Thessalonians that what Paul says here about the return of Jesus is basically just an amplification of what appears in 1 Thessalonians 1:10 and 3:13.

[8]See, for instance, J. W. Bailey, "The Temporary Messianic Reign in the Literature of Early Judaism," *JBL* 53 (1934): 170-87; S. R. Isenberg, "Millenarism in Greco-Roman Palestine," *Religion* 4 (1974): 26-46. However, since most of the evidence is based on 2 Baruch and 4 Ezra, documents that may have been produced as late as the end of the first century A.D., caution is in order. This is all the more needed if one uses the later Enochian literature.

[9]Kreitzer, *Jesus and God*, p. 32ff.

[10]Gordon D. Fee, *The First Epistle to the Corinthians* (Grand Rapids: Eerdmans, 1987), pp. 752-53.

[11]Colossians 1:13 may be the one place in the Pauline letters where Paul speaks of a present *realm* called the *basileia*, but on the other hand what he may mean is that the ones transferred have now come under the current ongoing reign of Christ. If so, *basileia* in Colossians 1:13 takes on the more generic sense of ongoing reign, rather than dynamic saving activity, which is what *basileia* in the present seems to mean normally in Paul. Since many scholars do not think Colossians was written by Paul, I have indicated this widely held opinion by using the phrase "if Colossians is by Paul." For my part, I think it very likely that Colossians is indeed written by Paul.

[12]Cf. C. H. Dodd, "Matthew and Paul," *ET* 58 (1946-47): 293-98.

[13]This remark requires some qualification since in the two passages about "not inheriting the *basileia*" (Gal 5; 1 Cor 6) Paul is speaking *about* those who are nonbelievers but *to* believers, warning that they may have a similar fate if they choose a similarly unethical lifestyle. One must ask how the material functions, not just whom it is about.

[14]Haufe, "Reich Gottes," pp. 467-68.

[15]Professor M. D. Goulder pointed out to me at the 1990 SNTS meeting that one should not overlook the polemical way in which Paul is using kingdom language here. He is striving to say what it is *not*, probably in response to certain misconceptions held by certain members of his audience. This is a valuable insight, but it does not follow from this that Paul felt uncomfortable with the concept of the future kingdom or had little positive to say about it. Either in the saying itself or in the larger context of these sayings Paul goes on to say of what the kingdom does consist.

[16]See below, pp. 59-72.

[17]Haufe, "Reiche Gottes," p. 468.

[18]A reasonable case can be made that Paul is not talking about an isolated sin when he uses the vice

catalogs to speak of those who are excluded, but about those who pursue an intentionally chosen ongoing course of behavior so that they may be *characterized* as idolators, adulterers, etc.

[19] I Corinthians 2:4 could be translated, "in demonstration of the Spirit and power."

[20] The phrase "reign of God" is probably not strong enough here to convey Paul's meaning because he is talking about an incursion of God's saving activity in history, not merely the ongoing reign of God in or from heaven. Cf. J. Marcus, "Entering into the Kingly Power of God," *JBL* 107 (1988): 663-75. I disagree with Marcus that the future sayings about entering the *baseleia* (either in the teaching of Jesus or of Paul) merely refer to entering into or participating in an event or activity of God that has already begun.

[21] A. J. M. Wedderburn, "Paul and Jesus: the Problem of Continuity," in *Paul and Jesus. Collected Essays,* ed. A. J. M. Wedderburn (Sheffield: JSOT Press, 1989), pp. 99-115, here p. 106.

Chapter Six: The Realm of Possibilities: Jesus and the *Basilei tou Theou*

[1] B. Witherington, *The Christology of Jesus* (Minneapolis: Fortress, 1990), pp. 192-98.

[2] J. Marcus, "Entering into the Kingly Power of God," *JBL* 107 (1988): 663-75.

[3] Ibid., p. 663.

[4] Ibid., p. 664, n. 9.

[5] So J. Fitzmyer, *The Gospel according to Luke X-XXIV* (New York: Doubleday, 1985), 1510-11; cf. I. H. Marshall, *The Gospel of Luke* (Grand Rapids: Eerdmans, 1978), p. 873.

[6] J. Jeremias, *"paradeisos,"* *TDNT,* 5:765-73.

[7] Marcus, "Entering," p. 670.

[8] Ibid.

[9] S. Aalen, "Reign and House in the Kingdom of God in the Gospels," *NTS* 8 (1961-62): 215-40.

[10] Witherington, *Christology of Jesus,* pp. 56-73, 107ff.

[11] Marcus, "Entering," p. 672.

[12] Aalen, "Reign and House," pp. 221ff.

[13] His view has been promulgated in several works, most recently in *Jesus and the End of the World* (Edinburgh: Saint Andrews Press, 1980), esp. 5ff.

[14] J. Riches, *Jesus and the Transformation of Judaism* (New York: Seabury, 1982), pp. 99-111.

[15] The phrase is George Ladd's in his fine work *The Presence of the Future* (Grand Rapids: Eerdmans, 1974), passim.

[16] D.C. Allison, *The End of the Ages Has Come* (Philadelphia: Fortress, 1985), p. 103.

[17] I. H. Marshall, "The Hope of a New Age: the Kingdom of God in the New Testament," *Themelios* 11 (1985): 5-15.

[18] This parable is given the highest rating of all parables by the Jesus Seminar in regard to its likely authenticity (Funk, *The Parables of Jesus,* pp. 98-99). This same group of one hundred Gospel scholars has rated all the others mentioned in the text as certainly or almost certainly authentic from a *Sitz im Leben Jesu.*

[19] Allison, *End of the Ages,* p. 105.

[20] Witherington, *Women in the Ministry of Jesus,* 15ff., pp. 140-41.

[21] Beasley-Murray, *Jesus and the Kingdom,* p. 177. The saying in Jn. 3.5 deserves further attention, but since it seems to be conveying the same sort of idea as we find in the synoptic saying, and may indeed be an alternate form of that saying we will not deal further with it here.

[22] Note how Luke has modified Mark's future *eiseleusontai* to a present indicative *eisporeuontai* (Fitzmyer, *Luke X-XXIV,* 1204).

[23] J. D. M. Derrett, *Studies in the New Testament* (Leiden: Brill, 1977), 1:4-31.

[24] I have discussed the tradition-history of the material in Mark 9:43-47 and parallels briefly in *Women in the Ministry of Jesus,* pp. 19-20 and notes.

[25] These two sayings, often regarded as reflecting the Matthean interests and thus being purely redactional, accordingly will not be treated here.

[26]R. Guelich, *The Sermon on the Mount: A Foundation for Understanding* (Waco, Tex.: Word, 1982), pp. 398-99.

[27]But cf. W. D. Davies and D. C. Allison, *The Gospel According to Saint Matthew* (Edinburgh: T & T Clark, 1988), 1:702ff.

[28]Cf. A. Polag's reconstruction of this Q saying in I. Havener, *Q. The Sayings of Jesus* (Wilmington: M. Glazier, 1987), p. 141. The Matthean order of the clauses seems to reflect the original better than does Luke's order.

[29]Marshall, *Luke*, pp. 567-68.

[30]D. E. Gowan, *Eschatology in the Old Testament* (Philadelphia: Fortress Press, 1986), pp. 52, 92.

[31]J. Jeremias, *Jesus' Promise to the Nations* (London: SCM, 1959), p. 55, n. 185; cf. A. Polag, *Die Christologie der Logienquelle* (Neukirchen-Vluyn: Neukirchen Verlag, 1977), p. 92.

[32]O. Kaiser, *Isaiah 13-39* (Philadelphia: Westminster Press, 1974), p. 199 cf. J. N. Oswalt, *The Book of Isaiah Chapters 1-39* (Grand Rapids: Eerdmans, 1986), p. 463ff. As Oswalt says, this prophecy combines particularity with universality. The banquet comes through the Jews and their cultic center but it is for everyone.

[33] Beasley-Murray, *Jesus and the Kingdom of God*, pp. 172-73.

[34]We will examine Paul's and Jesus' views of the future of Israel in part four.

[35]See, for instance, E. Schweizer, "The Significance of Eschatology in the Teaching of Jesus," p. 3.

[36]We must exercise caution at this point. Some of the extracanonical early Jewish literature mentions God's activity in both the present and future, as Allison *(End of the Ages*, 105ff.) shows, but not in terms of the *basileia tou theou*, and not in the manner Jesus talks about it, as one who personally brings in that activity through his ministry.

[37]Beasley-Murray, *Jesus and the Kingdom of God*, pp. 71-143.

[38]Witherington, *Christology of Jesus*, p. 198ff.

[39]Schnackenburg, *God's Rule and Kingdom*, p. 124.

[40]Marshall, "Hope," pp. 10-11.

[41]On the authenticity of this material, cf. Witherington, *Christology of Jesus*, pp. 42-53, 165-66.

[42]G. Theissen, *The Miracle Stories of the Early Christian Tradition*, trans. F. McDonagh (Philadelphia: Fortress Press, 1983), pp. 278-80.

[43]If this is the drift of Paul's argument, then Paul is not trying to argue that the *basileia* is a matter of purely spiritual qualities. Indeed it is a matter of proper human relationships and acting in a Christlike (not self-serving) manner in such relationships. This entails tangible deeds, not merely attitudes or inner qualities. Nevertheless, it is not hard to see how Romans 14:17 taken out of the context of the larger argument has led to a "spiritualizing" of the present *basileia* in subsequent church history.

[44]R. Bultmann, *History of the Synoptic Tradition* (Oxford: Blackwell, 1968), p. 25.

[45]The Greek version of the saying preserved in Oxyrhynchus Papyrus 654.9-16 varies only slightly from the Coptic. D. Mueller, "Kingdom of Heaven or Kingdom of God?" *VChr* 27 (1973): 266-76.

[46]Cf. R. Schnackenburg, "Der eschatologische Abschnitt Lk 17,20-37," reprinted in his *Schriften zum Neuen Testament* (Munich: Kosel-Verlag, 1971), pp. 220-43.

[47]So Marshall, *Luke*, pp. 652-53; Fitzmyer, *Luke X-XXIV*, pp. 1158-59; Kümmel, *Promise and Fulfilment*, p. 32.

[48]Mark 13:21 is *not* referring to the parousia, which is described later in 13:24-27, 32ff. This verse is *not* about a figure that comes from heaven, but about false messianic figures that arise *(egerthēsontai* refers to arising on the human scene, not to resurrection) and try to perform wonders to substantiate their claims.

[49]Even so it is hardly a Lukan trait to add the Pharisees into his narratives. Contrast Matthew 3:7 to Luke 3:7, where Luke seems to have edited them out (or possibly the First Evangelist added them).

[50]H. Riesenfeld, *TDNT*, 8:148-49.

[51]Aalen, "Reign and House," pp. 223-25. As we shall see, it is the *Yom Yahweh* in Jesus' and Paul's

teaching that is spoken of in the language of theophany, not the present coming of the *basileia*.
[52]On Jesus' relationship with the Pharisees, see Witherington, *Christology of Jesus*, pp. 56-80.
[53]Cf. the evidence in Fitzmyer, *Luke X-XXIV*, p. 1161.
[54]Ibid., p. 1161.
[55]Marshall, *Luke*, p. 655.
[56]See R. J. Sneed, "The Kingdom of God Is within You (Lk. 17.21)," *CBQ* 24 (1962): 363-82.
[57]Cf. the analysis of these texts in Kümmel, *Promise and Fulfilment*, p. 33, n. 50.
[58]See C. H. Roberts, "The Kingdom of Heaven (Lk.xvii.21)," *HTR* 41 (1948): 1-8; H. J. Cadbury, "The Kingdom of God and Ourselves," *Christian Century* 67 (1950): 172-73.
[59]Cf. H. Riesenfeld, *"Emboleuein-Entos,"* *Nuntius* 2 (1949): 11-12; A. Wikgren, *"Entos,"* *Nuntius* 4 (1950): 27-28.

Chapter Seven: Conclusions
[1]The influence seems to be going in this direction rather than their views about the present *basileia* shaping their views of salvation in the present. It is thus not surprising that their views about the future *basileia* are more in line with what we find elsewhere in early Judaism.

Chapter Eight: Introduction
[1]Cf., for instance, A. Loisy's famous dictum, "Jesus proclaimed the kingdom, but it was the Church which came."
[2]Cf. R. E. Brown et al., eds., *Peter in the New Testament* (Minneapolis: Augsburg Press, 1973), p. 92: "The theology of the Qumran . . . group was marked by apocalypticism. Its members expected the end soon; but still they developed a structured community with rules for admitting and disciplining members." This point cannot be totally vitiated by the argument either that some of the organizational volumes found at Qumran were purely dealing with the future ideal community of God's elect, or that some of the eschatological material is simply archival. Both of these claims are in part true, but the evidence is so plentiful for both eschatological expectation and community organization as a part of the living hope and daily life at Qumran that our point stands regardless of the merits of the argument about a particular document or portion thereof (e.g., The Manual of Discipline).

Chapter Nine: Paul and the Body of Christ
[1]For a good deal of what follows I am indebted to R. Banks's fine study *Paul's Idea of Community: The Early House Churches in their Historical Setting* (Grand Rapids: Eerdmans, 1980).
[2]See ibid., pp. 37ff.
[3]Ibid., p. 41.
[4]See W. A. Meeks, *The First Urban Christians. The Social World of the Apostle Paul* (New Haven: Yale U. Press, 1983), pp. 74-139.
[5]See B. Witherington, *Women in the Earliest Churches* (Cambridge: Cambridge Univ. Press, 1988), pp. 42-61 on the so-called household tables.
[6]They do use the term household, but always "household of truth," or "holiness."
[7]B. Witherington, *Women in the Ministry of Jesus* (Cambridge: Cambridge Univ. Press, 1984), pp. 11ff.
[8]I can find no Pauline sentences where the two terms are used together or in a parallel sense.

Chapter Ten: Jesus and the Foundation Stones
[1]B. Witherington, *Women in the Ministry of Jesus* (Cambridge: Cambridge Univ. Press, 1984), pp. 11ff.
[2]Note the Lukan attempt to ameliorate the offensiveness of this saying at Luke 8:21.
[3]Also to be considered in this connection are the sayings in Q that speak of Jesus realigning family allegiances or requiring the abandonment of such allegiance to the physical family in order to be a disciple (Lk 12:51-53 and parallels; 14:26-27 and parallels).
[4]I use the term *fact* as E. P. Sanders does in "Jesus and the Kingdom: The Restoration of Israel and

the New People of God," in *Jesus, the Gospels and the Church* (Macon: Mercer U. Press, 1987), pp. 225-39, here p. 232.

[5]B. Witherington, *The Christology of Jesus* (Minneapolis: Fortress, 1990), pp. 120ff.

[6]Ibid., passim.

[7]See O. Cullmann, *Peter—Disciple, Apostle, Martyr* (London: SCM Press, 1953), p. 189.

[8]G. Lohfink, *Jesus and Community* (Philadelphia: Fortress Press/Paulist Press, 1984), p. 71.

[9]Witherington, *Christology of Jesus*, p. 56ff.

[10]F. W. Beare, *The Gospel according to Matthew* (Peabody: Hendrickson, 1981), p. 353.

[11]See B. P. Robinson, "Peter and his Successors: Tradition and Redaction in Matthew 16.17-19," *JSNT* 21 (1981): 85-104. Our concern is with the authenticity of verses 18-19 in particular. Several other scholars have argued for the authenticity of this saying basically in the form in which we find it. Cf. J. M. Van Cangh and M. Van Esbroeck, "La primauté de Pierre (Mt 16,16-19) et son context judaique," *Rev. Theol. Louv.* 11 (1980): 310-24; J. Galot, "La prima professione di fede cristiana," *Civilta Cattolica* 132 (1981): 27-40.

[12]D. C. Duling, "Binding and Loosing: Matthew 16:19; 18:18; John 20:23," *Forum* 3 (1987): 3-31, has recently urged that source, form, language and Jewish environmental criteria favor the authenticity of this saying, while the criteria of dissimiliarity, coherence, multiple forms and early church environment count against it.

[13]G. Bornkamm, "The Authority to Bind and Loose in the Church in Matthew's Gospel," in *The Interpretation of Matthew*, ed. G. N. Stanton (Philadelphia: Fortress Press, 1983), pp. 85-97, here p. 94. Bornkamm goes on to argue for the inauthenticity of Matthew 16:17ff. on basically the same grounds as does F. W. Beare.

[14]See van Cangh and van Esbroeck, "La Primauté," pp. 323-24.

[15]See B. F. Meyer, *The Aims of Jesus* (London, SCM Press, 1979), p. 192.

[16]See Robinson, "Peter and His Successors," p. 89.

[17]See the evidence in J. R. Mantey, "Distorted Translations in John 20.23; Matthew 16:18-19 and 18:18," *Review and Expositor* 78 (1981): 409-16, here pp. 412-13. Mantey claims to have surveyed every usage of *petros* and *petra* in the Septuagint, New Testament, Xenophon, Diodorus Siculus, Josephus, Philo, Strabo and Plutarch.

[18] Brown, *Peter in the New Testament*, pp. 83-101, esp. p. 89.

[19]For this reason especially, the attempt to make Matthew 17:1 the clue to the setting and timing of the saying in Matthew 16:16-19 must be considered an uncertain hypothesis. Cf. van Cangh and van Esbroeck, "La Primaute," pp. 310-11.

[20]See Meyer, *Aims of Jesus*, p. 302. n. 28, and the Aramaic reconstruction in C. F. Burney, *The Poetry of our Lord* (Oxford: Clarendon Press, 1925), p. 117; also J. Jeremias, *"kleis,"* *TDNT,* 3:744-53, here p. 749.

[21]See E. Schweizer, *The Good News according to Matthew* (Atlanta: John Knox Press, 1975), pp. 341-42.

[22]The attempt to suggest that Jesus used the term *kēpha* as a sort of play on the name of the high priest Caiaphas (compare the orthography in Jn 11:49; *kēphas* in p[45] and p[75] as well as several other witnesses; Jn 1:42 on Peter), so as to suggest that Peter would be the high priest of the new community is intriguing, but if this were the intent, none of the Gospel writers writing in Greek picked up the hint, and so it is wiser to follow their lead. But cf. van Canagh and van Esbroeck, "La Primauté," p. 315.

[23]Witherington, *Christology of Jesus*, p. 107ff.

[24]But cf. M. A. Chevallier, " 'Tu es Pierre, Tu es le Nouvel Abraham' (Mt 16/18)," *Étude Theol. Rel.* 57 (1982): 375-87, esp. 377ff. Isaiah 51:1-2 speaks not only of Abraham but also of Sarah and the statement is not about a foundation rock but a quarry that one has been taken out of, or a rock from which one has been carved out. In short, these verses are about a question of one's source, not one's foundation, nor about the building of a new community.

[25]I would not rule this out as a meaning of the text at the level of Matthean redaction, but even this is uncertain.

[26]See J. Marcus, "The Gates of Hades and the Keys of the Kingdom (Matt 16:18-19)," *CBQ* 50 (1988): 443-55.

[27]See, for example, Robinson, "Peter and His Successors," pp. 94-95; Brown, *Peter*, pp. 98-100.

[28]See G. W. E. Nickelsburg, "Enoch, Levi, and Peter: Recipients of Revelation in Upper Galilee," *JBL* 100 (1981): 575-600, here 594. This would make Matthew 16:19 mean much the same as what Matthew 18:18 means, and I suspect this is a mistake as the latter saying is much more likely to reflect a later development than what we find in Matthew 16. The suggestion of R. H. Hiers, "Binding and Loosing: The Matthean Authorizations," *JBL* 104 (1985): 233-50 that what is referred to in Matthew 16:19 is exorcism is possible, but then it becomes more difficult to make sense of the future perfects "will have been bound/loosed in heaven," and it requires that one see the demons as bound on the one hand but the human beings as loosed on the other. See rightly Marcus, "Gates of Hades," pp. 450-51.

[29]See the interesting comparison of the parallels between this material and what we find in Paul by Dodd, "Matthew and Paul," pp. 293-98.

[30]Hiers, " 'Binding and Loosing,' " pp. 233-50.

[31]Meyer, *Aims of Jesus*, 196. Yet is it totally inconceivable that Jesus could have spoken of "my people" or in this case "my assembled people" and mean by it the gathered eschatological Israel (cf. Mt 13), especially if Jesus did refer in this saying to the *future* final gathered community of God's people?

[32]D. Juel, *Messiah and Temple* (Missoula: Scholar's Press, 1977), p. 204.

[33]See the discussion in ibid., pp. 159-68.

Chapter Twelve: Introduction

[1]See, for instance, W. D. Davies, *The Gospel and the Land. Early Christianity and Jewish Territorial Doctrine* (Berkeley and Los Angeles: Univ. of California Press, 1974).

[2]See B. Witherington, *The Christology of Jesus*, pp. 73ff.

Chapter Thirteen: Paul and the Plight of His People

[1]I am assuming with M. Barth that it is probable that Paul at least stands behind Ephesians even if he did not write the final form. Cf. M. Barth, *The People of God* (Sheffield: JSOT, 1983), and the introductory material in his earlier commentary on Ephesians 1—3.

[2]See "Paul and the People of Israel," in W. D. Davies, *Jewish and Pauline Studies* (Philadelphia: Fortress, 1984), pp. 123-52.

[3]I think Galatians is Paul's earliest letter, followed by 1 Thessalonians, but since I do not think that holding to a particular chronological order of these two letters is crucial to the discussion at this point, I will proceed on the basis of the majority view on these matters.

[4]Perhaps the strongest case for interpolation has been made by B. A. Pierson, "1 Thessalonians 2:13-16: A Deutero-Pauline Interpolation," *HTR* 64 (1971): 79-94. Pierson also urges some literary reasons for interpolation here, e.g., that if one omits vv. 13-16, the text flows naturally from v. 12 to v. 17. One problem with this observation is that most scholars see only vv. 15-16 or possibly vv. 14-16 as the interpolation whereas Pierson must urge a larger section to suit his literary arguments.

[5]For 1 Corinthians 14:34-35, however, there is only evidence for displacement, not omission; B. Witherington, *Women in the Earliest Churches* (Cambridge: Cambridge Univ. Press, 1988), pp. 90-104.

[6]D. Wenham, "Paul and the Synoptic Apocalypse," in *Gospel Perspectives. Studies of History and Tradition in the Four Gospels* (Sheffield: JSOT, 1981), 2:345-75, here pp. 361-62.

[7]Davies, *Jewish and Pauline Studies*, p. 125ff.

[8]In this study I use the term *salvation-historical* not because I endorse all of what O. Cullmann meant by *Heilsgeschichte*, but because it is the most convenient term to describe a perspective that focuses on God's saving acts in human history.

[9]On the growing martyrological traditions in regard to the prophets, cf. O. H. Steck, *Israel und das*

gewaltsame Geschick der Propheten (Neukirchen: Neukirchen Verlag, 1967), p. 243ff.; cf. Mart Isa 5:1-14.

[10]Steck, *Israel,* pp. 274-76.

[11]Ibid., p. 136.

[12]See J. Coppens, "Miscellanees bibliques. LXXX. Une diatribe antijuive dans 1 Thess. II,13-16," *ETL* 80 (1976): 90-85.

[13]W. Marxsen, *Der erste Brief an die Thessalonicher,* Zuricher Bibelkommentare (Zurich: Theologischer Verlag, 1979), pp. 47ff.

[14]K. P. Donfried, "Paul and Judaism. 1 Thessalonians 2:13-16 as a Test Case," *Interpretation* 38 (1984): 242-53, here p. 246.

[15]A text like Galatians 2:13-15 provides a partial exception, but in v. 15 Paul makes clear that he is talking about those who are Jews by birth.

[16]I concur with Donfried that in 1 Thessalonians 2:14 Paul likely includes some Jews in the "country-men," in which case the analogy with the persecution of the Judean church makes good sense. Acts 17:1-11 should not be dismissed as unreliable on this score; cf. Donfried, "Paul and Judaism," pp. 246-48.

[17]G. E. Okeke's attempt to pit 1 Thessalonians 2 against Romans 9—11 will not work. Paul in Romans 9—11 still speaks of non-Christian Jews as broken off from the people of God, or partially hardened. Okeke is right, however, to stress that it is unlikely that Paul's pre-Christian period of persecuting the church was a case of an isolated vendetta by an eccentric Jew. He is also right that it is difficult to believe that Diaspora Jews had more zeal for persecuting Christians than did Judean Jews. The idea of the Judean churches enjoying peaceful coexistence with other sects of early Judaism during Paul's day is likely a myth. It may well be that the Judaizers Paul confronts in Galatia and elsewhere are a Christian response to such persecution, i.e., they were people who hoped to forestall such persecution by requiring Gentile believers to submit to the Jewish requirements for proselytes. I suspect that Jewett and others may well be right that this lies in the background and in part explains 1 Thessalonians 2:14-16. See G. E. Okeke, "1 Thessalonians 2:13-16: The Fate of the Unbelieving Jews," *NTS* 27 (1980): 127-36, esp. p. 129.

[18]See, e.g., F. F. Bruce, *1 and 2 Thessalonians* (Waco, Tex.: Word, 1982), pp. 48-49; the expulsion of the Jews from Rome (Suetonius, *Claudius* 25.4) or the massacre in the temple courts in A.D. 49 (Josephus, *Bell* 2.224-27) *might* be in view. Best, *Thessalonians,* pp. 119-20.

[19]C. F. D. Moule, *An Idiom Book of the New Testament* (Cambridge: Cambridge U. Press, 1953), p. 70.

[20]Wenham, "Paul and the Synoptic Apocalypse," p. 362.

[21]P. R. Ackroyd, *"NTSH—eis telos,"* *ET* 80 (1969): 126. Ackroyd, however, allows that the meaning "utterly" and "end" is possible for *NTSH.*

[22]See H. C. Kee's comments on his translation of this testament in *OTP,* 1:777.

[23]Best, *Thessalonians,* p. 122.

[24]See I. H. Marshall, *First and Second Thessalonians,* NCBC (Grand Rapids: Eerdmans, 1978), p. 81.

[25]J. Munck, *Christ and Israel. An Interpretation of Romans 9—11* (Philadelphia: Fortress, 1967), 63-65; so also Donfried, "Paul and Judaism," pp. 249-52.

[26]C. K. Barrett, "The Allegory of Abraham, Sarah, and Hagar in the Argument of Galatians," in *Essays on Paul* (Philadelphia: Westminster Press, 1982) pp. 154-70, here p. 161.

[27]Cf. F. F. Bruce, *The Epistle to the Galatians* (Grand Rapids: Eerdmans, 1982), p. 181ff.

[28]What we have in 4:21ff. is much more nearly a typological argument than an allegory as it involves a historical analogy; cf. Bruce, *Galatians,* pp. 216-17.

[29]R. Y. K. Fung, *The Epistle to the Galatians* (Grand Rapids: Eerdmans, 1988), p. 213 and n. 47.

[30]H. D. Betz, *Galatians* (Philadelphia: Fortress, 1979), p. 245. Contrast Fung, *Galatians,* p. 213, for whom the bottom line reads legalists vs. Christians. Cf. W. D. Davies, *Jewish and Pauline Studies,* pp. 172-88. I am mainly in agreement with Davies' detailed critique of Betz's Galatians commentary.

[31]Davies, *Jewish and Pauline Studies*, p. 136. Davies goes on to point out that the real separation of Christians from non-Christian Jews came after Paul's day, and was a "forced withdrawal at that" (p. 137).

[32]Betz, *Galatians*, p. 323.

[33]This blessing is a closer parallel than the closing ascription of the Eighteenth Benediction as Bruce cites it, "Blessed art thou O Lord, who dost bless thy people Israel with peace" (Bruce, *Galatians*, pp. 273-74).

[34]See Fung, *Galatians*, p. 310.

[35]M. Zerwick, *Biblical Greek* (Rome, Pontifical Institute Press, 1963), p. 154.

[36]See Fung, *Galatians*, pp. 310-11.

[37]See Betz, *Galatians*, pp. 322-23, and esp. N. A. Dahl's arguments against G. Schrenk in "Der Name Israel: Zur Auslegung von Gal 6,16," *Judaica* 6 (1950): 161-70, esp. pp. 168-69.

[38]On this whole matter, cf. Dahl, "Der Name Israel," pp. 161-70.

[39]Pace Barth, *People of God*, p. 45; cf. also Davies, *Jewish and Pauline Studies*, pp. 127-29. Beker, *Paul the Apostle*, passim, is right to stress that to a real extent the situation Paul is addressing controls how Paul shapes and presents his argument. As Beker urges, allowance thus must be made for each of Paul's letters for the contextuality of the argument and also its ad hoc nature.

[40]It is not certain whether 2 Corinthians was written before or after Galatians, though I would suggest the latter. It is also less certain whether Paul's opponents in Corinth were Judaizers. Cf. C. K. Barrett, *The Second Epistle to the Corinthians* (New York: Harper and Row, 1973), p. 28ff.

[41]Not, we should note, an Old *Testament*. Paul's argument is not about the Scripture, nor is it about two ways of interpreting that Scripture—a legalistic vs. a spiritual one. The term *diatheke*, which is here the natural rendering for the Hebrew term *berith*, is clearly associated with the act of covenanting on Sinai that resulted in letters written on stone, and glory on Moses' face. Cf. V. P. Furnish, *II Corinthians* (Garden City, N.J.: Doubleday, 1984), p. 208; R. Martin, *2 Corinthians* (Waco, Tex.: Word, 1986), p. 69.

[42]See S. J. Hafemann, *Suffering and Ministry in the Spirit: Paul's Defense of his Ministry in II Corinthians 2:14—3:3* (Grand Rapids: Eerdmans, 1990), pp. 180-225.

[43]The verb *epōrōthē* in v. 14, which is in the aorist tense, is probably ingressive, denoting the inception of an ongoing condition. It probably should be translated "hardened" here. Cf. Barrett, *Second Corinthians*, p. 14; Furnish, *II Corinthians*, pp. 207-8.

[44]Not withstanding the arguments of Davies, *Jewish and Pauline Studies*, pp. 129-30; and of Barrett, *Second Corinthians*, pp. 114-16. It is not just the law as letter, but the law as law that is inadequate and is being annulled.

[45]See Furnish, *II Corinthians*, p. 203; BAG, p. 418.

[46]The argument of A. T. Hanson, "The Midrash in II Corinthians 3: a Reconsideration," *JSNT* 9 (1980): 2-28, that Moses was veiling the pre-existent Christ from the Israelites has not won many adherents, not least because it is hardly likely that Paul would argue that Christ had a splendor that was fading away!

[47]It is not, for instance, a matter of the proper hermeneutical approach to the law—a "spiritual" approach as opposed to a legalistic or literal one. Paul says nothing about spiritual hermeneutics or exegesis here; he speaks of the transforming power of the Holy Spirit on human lives. Furnish is quite right that "the description Paul gives of the *new covenant* does not so much reflect his hermeneutical perspective on the law or scripture in general as it does his eschatological perspective on God's redemptive work in history" *(II Corinthians*, p. 200). Why then go on to conclude that Paul is merely rejecting a way of using the law? Here as in Galatians 3:21 Paul is quite clear—the law itself, no matter how it is handled or used, is unable to give life, and in fact it conveys just the opposite to fallen people.

[48]Furnish, *II Corinthians*, p. 205.

[49]Hanson, "Midrash in II Corinthians 3," p. 18.

[50]Beker, *Paul's Apocalyptic Gospel*, and esp. his *Paul the Apostle*, pp. 328-47.

[51]But cf. Munck, *Christ and Israel*, pp. 119-20, on *plērōma*.

[52]The distinction between apocalyptic visions and the literary form in which their contents are conveyed is an important one. Romans 9—11 is not simply a record of a vision, but a reflection on Scripture on the basis of such a vision, among other things. That Paul had such apocalyptic visions or revelations seems certain on the basis of 2 Corinthians 12:1-4.

[53]R. B. Hays, *Echoes of Scripture in the Letters of Paul* (New Haven: Yale Univ. Press, 1989), pp. 34-35.

[54]J. D. G. Dunn, *Romans 9—16* (Waco, Tex.: Word, 1988), p. 520. Interestingly, A. Segal, *Paul the Convert: The Apostolate and Apostasy of Saul the Pharisee* (New Haven: Yale Univ. Press, 1990), sees Paul's manner of handling texts here as rabbinic rather than apocalyptic; see pp. 276ff.

[55]Cf. the detailed analysis of the literary structure in J. W. Aageson, "Scripture and Structure in the Development of the Argument in Romans 9—11," *CBQ* 48 (1986): 265-89, esp. pp. 286-87.

[56]See G. Wagner, "The Future of Israel: Reflections on Romans 9—11," in *Eschatology and the New Testament*, ed. W. H. Gloer (Peabody: Hendrickson, 1988), pp. 77-112.

[57]Hays, *Echoes*, p. 40.

[58]Dahl, *Studies in Paul*, p. 139.

[59]Barth, *People of God*, pp. 29-30.

[60]For a somewhat helpful overview of Romans 9—11, see J. L. de Villiers, "The Salvation of Israel according to Romans 9—11," *Neotestamentica* 15 (1981): 199-221.

[61]E. Käsemann, *Commentary on Romans* (Grand Rapids: Eerdmans, 1980), 253ff.; cf. C. A. Evans, "Paul and the Hermeneutics of 'True Prophecy': a Study of Romans 9—11," *Biblica* 65 (1984): 560-70, here p. 562.

[62]Hays, *Echoes*, p. 64; R. Badenas, *Christ the End of the Law: Romans 10:4 in Pauline Perspective*, JSOT Sup. 10 (Sheffield: JSOT, 1985), pp. 94-96.

[63]So Hays, *Echoes*, p. 64.

[64]Rightly E. J. Epp, "Jewish-Gentile Continuity in Paul: Torah and/or Faith? (Romans 9:1-5)," *HTR* 79 (1986): 80-90, here p. 87.

[65]E. P. Sanders is quite right to stress, against K. Stendahl, that in terms of soteriology Paul does not here change his view of things. For Paul salvation is still a matter of faith in Christ, even for Jews. This is precisely why he is so anxious for those Jews who have not accepted Christ. They are at least temporarily cut off from the salvation God provides for his people. Paul does not relinquish his soteriological exclusivism in these chapters. For him, saving faith always means faith in Jesus Christ, as 10:9 and 11:23 make clear. See E. P. Sanders, "Paul's Attitude toward the Jewish People," *Union Seminary Quarterly Review* 33 (1978): 175-87.

[66]Barrett, *Romans*, p. 178.

[67]The plural "covenants" is probably preferable here as the more difficult reading; cf. Metzger, *TC*, p. 519.

[68]Wagner, "Future of Israel," p. 82ff.

[69]For a helpful and interesting discussion of predestination in Romans 9—11, see G. B. Caird, "Expository Problems: Predestination—Romans ix-xi," *ET* 68 (1956-57): 324-27.

> Indeed Paul is not here at all concerned with the eternal destiny of individuals. . . . He is concerned with the use God makes of [people] and nations in the working out of His historic purpose. Election and rejection, wrath and mercy are alike prompted by the one Divine purpose of salvation, which faith can not hurry nor unbelief delay. [Humankind's] freedom, exercised in obedience or in rebellion, is no limitation on God's omnipotence (p. 326).

Even in the case of the quoting of the text "Jacob I loved but Esau I hated" (Mal 1:2-3) the context in Malachi clearly shows that the subject of discussion is nations, Israel and Edom, not individuals. About predestination it would seem Paul agreed with Akiba, who is reputed to have said, "All is foreseen, but freedom of choice is given; and the world is judged by grace . . ." (M Aboth 3:16).

[70]As we shall see Paul also does not suggest that there are two true peoples of God at any given time

in human history, but only one that individual Jews and Gentiles may be grafted into or broken off from. See J. Radermakers and J. P. Sonnet, "Israel et l'Église," *Nouvelle Revue Theologique* 107 (1985): 675-97.

[71] Dunn, *Romans 9—16*, p. 646.

[72] See Dunn, *Romans 9—16*, p. 646; F. Mussner, " 'Ganz Israel wird gerettet werden' (Rom 11,26)," *Kairos* 18 (1976): 241-55, here p. 244.

[73] *BAG*, p. 763.

[74] So Barrett, *Romans*, p. 223.

[75] So Käsemann, *Romans*, p. 313, contrast Cranfield, *Romans*, 2:575.

[76] Dunn, *Romans 9—16*, p. 589.

[77] Rightly ibid., p. 590.

[78] F. Refoule, "Romains X,4. Encore une Fois," *Revue Biblique* 91 (1984): 321-50, points out the various deficiencies of all views of this verse. The problem is in part that in some places in the Pauline corpus Paul faults the law itself for being unable to provide life or the Spirit or power needed to obey it, while in other places he seems to fault the way the Jews have used the law—as a means to establish their own righteousness. Here it seems the latter is primarily in view, though it is possible that the salvation-historical argument lies in the background, i.e., the age of the law is at an end now that Christ has come (see Gal 3-4).

[79] Here Hays, *Echoes*, pp. 75-76, fails to convince. So also Cranfield, *Romans*, 2:516-20; Badenas, *Christ the End of the Law*, 112-16. F. Refoule, "Notes sur Romains IX,30-33," *Revue Biblique* 92 (1985): 161-86, is on the right track in seeing 9:30-33 and 10:1-10 as of one piece and essentially arguing that Christ is the end of the law as a means of salvation. The essential mistake is for Israel to keep on looking for justification through the law after Christ has come.

[80] C. K. Barrett, "Romans 9:30—10:21. The Fall and Responsibility of Israel," in *Essays on Paul*, pp. 132-53, here p. 152.

[81] Davies, "Paul and the Gentiles: A Suggestion Concerning Romans 11:13-24," in *Jewish and Pauline Studies*, pp. 153-63, here p. 160.

[82] Ibid., pp. 154-55.

[83] Dunn, *Romans 9—16*, p. 659; cf. Cranfield, *Romans*, 2:563-64.

[84] See Dahl, "The Future of Israel," in *Studies in Paul*, p. 151.

[85] Cf. Cranfield, *Romans*, p. 575: "But it seems more likely that a), b) and c) should be understood as indicating three successive stages in the divine plan of salvation."

[86] See below, pp. 210-11.

[87] Cf. Wagner, "Future of Israel," p. 93.

[88] See D. C. Allison, "Romans 11:11-15: A Suggestion," *Perspectives in Religious Studies* 12 (1985): 23-30.

[89] As Dunn, *Romans 9—16*, p. 658, says, a purely spiritual sense would be anticlimactic after the reference to "the reconciliation of the world."

[90] F. Mussner, " 'Ganz Israel'," *Kairos* 18 (1976): 253.

[91] For a review of the relevant Old Testament texts see W. R. Osborne, "The Old Testament Background of Paul's 'All Israel' in Romans 11:26a," *Asia Journal of Theology* 2 (1988): 282-93. He concludes that "all Israel" in the Old Testament most often refers to the leadership of Israel, or Israel that is loyal to its ruler.

[92] "All Israel" parallels the *plērōma* of Gentiles. This could suggest that we should not contrast "all Israel" with the part of Israel that is now already Christian—the so-called righteous remnant (11:5), or the "some" that Paul hopes yet to save as a result of his ministry (11:14). Against this, however, is the fact that Israel in v. 25 is hardened Israel. Cf. A. Feuillet, "Les Privilèges et l'Incrédulité d'Israel d'après les Chapitres 9-11 de l'Épître aux Romans," *Esprit et Vie* 92 (1982): 481-93, 497-506, here p. 502.

[93] Mussner, " 'Ganz Israel,' " pp. 245-48. This makes sense in light of the fact that Paul also connects the salvation of Israel with the resurrection of the dead believers. However, in Romans 10:9-13 and

also in Philippians 2:10 Paul connects salvation with confession of Jesus as Lord, and so we should not envision here the salvation of Israel *apart* from faith in Christ. The eschatological miracle Paul celebrates in Romans 11:33-36 is a miracle of Israel finally finding faith in Christ.

[94]The term *laology* is taken from Barth, *People of God*, p. 49.

[95]Ibid., p. 33.

[96]Beker, *Paul the Apostle*, pp. 335, 337. Segal, *Paul the Convert*, p. 281, is strikingly frank in rejecting the efforts of Stendahl, Gaston and Gagner in their attempts to interpret Paul in a less particularistic way so that modern Judaism may find the apostle less scandalous. He is quite right in saying that for Paul "faith in Mosaic legislation is not the equal of faith in Christ, as Stendahl, Gager, and Gaston think. Paul only equates the faithful in Christ who observe Torah with the faithful in Christ who do not observe Torah" (p. 279). Precisely because this is Paul's view he must take pains to make clear in Romans 9—11 that God has *not* forsaken non-Christian Jews. A good deal of his argument could have been omitted (esp. in chap. 11) had he held the views attributed to him by Stendahl and others.

[97]Barth, *Ephesians 1—3* (Garden City, N.J.: Doubleday, 1974), p. 337.

[98]Cf. Barth, *Ephesians 1—3*, pp. 286-87; J. A. Robinson, *St. Paul's Epistle to the Ephesians* (London: Macmillan, 1904), p. 64.

[99]A. T. Lincoln, "The Church and Israel in Ephesians 2," *CBQ* 49 (1987): 605-24, here p. 612. Notice how he translates the crucial phrase "having abolished the law consisting of commandments which are expressed in regulations" (p. 611).

[100]Pace Lincoln, "Church and Israel," p. 614, the meaning of *hagioi* here, which is after all not a technical term for Christians or Jews, must be determined by the immediate context, in particular what is said in vv. 11-12 and 3:6. It is quite beside the point that all Christians are called *hagioi* elsewhere in this document (1:1, 15, 18; 4:12; 5:3; 6:18). The context must determine the content of *hagioi* in each case.

[101]*Akrogōniaios* was originally an adjective and etymologically means "the one high on the corner" (Zech 4:7-9 may stand in the background here). The context, which stresses that Christ is above, favors either "head of the corner" or "capstone." Would the author really have wanted to say that Christ was merely one stone among many in the foundation (cf. 1 Cor 3:11)? Cf. J. Jeremias, "*Kephalē gonias-Akrogōniaios,*" *ZNW* 29 (1930): 264-80; and his "Eckstein-Schlusstein," *ZNW* 36 (1937): 154-57. Also Barth, *Ephesians 1—3*, pp. 317-19.

Chapter Fourteen: Jesus and the Jews' Just Due

[1]See above, pp. 86-92.

[2]See the extended discussion on Jesus' relationship to his disciples in B. Witherington, *The Christology of Jesus* (Minneapolis: Fortress, 1990), pp. 118-44.

[3]E. P. Sanders, "Jesus and the Kingdom: The Restoration of Israel and the New People of God," in *Jesus, the Gospels, and the Church: Essays in Honor of William R. Farmer,* ed. E. P. Sanders (Macon, Ga.: Mercer Univ. Press, 1987), p. 226.

[4]G. Bornkamm, *Jesus of Nazareth,* trans. I. and F. McLuskey with J. M. Robinson (New York: Harper & Row, 1960), p. 78 (not p. 66 as Sanders has it).

[5]J. Jeremias, *Jesus' Promise to the Nations* (London: SCM, 1959), passim.

[6]Ibid., p. 71; cf. p. 73.

[7]G. B. Caird, *Jesus and the Jewish Nation* (London: Athlone Press, 1965), pp. 16-17.

[8]W. D. Davies, *The Gospel and the Land* (Berkeley: Univ. of California Press, 1974), p. 349.

[9]See E. P. Sanders, *Jesus and Judaism* (Philadelphia: Fortress, 1985), passim.

[10]See Witherington, *Christology of Jesus*, pp. 56-73.

[11]M. Borg, *Conflict, Holiness* (New York: Edwin Mellen, 1984), passim; J. Riches, *Jesus and the Transformation* (New York: Seabury, 1982), passim.

[12]A. Segal, "The Cost of Proselytism and Conversion," *SBL Seminar Papers 1988* (Atlanta: Scholars Press, 1988), pp. 336-69, here pp. 347-48, has pointed out, following Shaye Cohen, that Jewish identity in Israel before A.D. 70 resembles citizenship in that it was usually determined by birth, and not easily

obtainable otherwise. Further, the Greek term *Ioudaios* still basically meant "Judean," retaining more geographical and national connotations than the term *Jew* today. On the other hand, some early Jews believed one could become a Jew by conversion or adherence, and this view seems especially to have existed in the Diaspora (see Philo), but was not absent in *eretz Israel* as well. The point I am making here is that Jesus was not one who affirmed exclusive ethnic claims and in this he was at odds with the opinion of many early Jews (see Lk 3:8 and parallels; Jn 8:31-41).

[13]J. Fitzmyer, *The Gospel according to Luke X-XXIV* (New York: Doubleday, 1985), p. 1419.

[14]Davies, *Gospel and the Land*, p. 364.

[15]See B. Witherington, *Women in the Ministry of Jesus* (Cambridge: Cambridge Univ. Press, 1984), pp. 44-45 on the authenticity of at least the Queen of the South saying.

[16]Marshall, *Luke*, p. 299; cf. Fitzmyer, *Luke I-IX*, p. 679: "Used of the Palestinian contemporaries of John and Jesus."

[17]At the very least the twelve Jews who followed Jesus are given a positive role. But even Matthew 25 does not suggest that all Israel will be treated as foolish virgins or goats at the eschaton. Thus it is likely that Jesus envisioned at least a righteous remnant of Israel remaining after the final judgment.

[18]See Davies, *Gospel and the Land*, p. 360 and notes.

[19]B. Metzger, *A Textual Commentary on the New Testament* (New York: United Bible Societies, 1971), p. 12.

[20]Davies and Allison, *Matthew*, 1:434-36.

[21]Metzger, *TC*, p. 12.

[22]But cf. Guelich, *The Sermon on the Mount*, pp. 81-82.

[23]Cf. R. A. Horsley's protest against overspiritualizing some of the beatitudes in *The Liberation of Christmas* (New York: Crossroad, 1989), p. 70.

[24]*Gēn* can also be translated "earth," but this would mean severing Matthew 5:5 from its Old Testament background in Psalm 37, where the psalmist is talking about dwelling in a particular piece of land where there would be security, prosperity, divine blessing and permanence. Cf. Davies, *Gospel and Land*, p. 362.

[25]Guelich, *Sermon on the Mount*, p. 82.

[26] Schweizer, *Matthew*, pp. 89-90.

[27]Davies and Allison, *Matthew*, 1:449.

[28]One should perhaps compare the promise of homes and fields in Mark 10:29-30 to those who have given up all and followed Jesus, though there it is said they will receive such in this age.

[29]Pace the impression left by Jeremias, *Jesus' Promise*, pp. 40-41. Sanders is right to object to such an insinuation. See Sanders, "Jesus and the Kingdom," p. 230.

[30]A. Segal, "Cost of Proselytism and Conversion," pp. 336-69.

[31]Ibid., p. 346.

[32]Ibid., 341.

[33]See Jeremias, *Jesus' Promise*, p. 60ff.

[34]Cf. the reconstruction by I. Polag in Havener, *Q*, p. 141. For a meticulous reconstruction of the *Vorlage* of this saying, see M. E. Boring, "A Proposed Reconstruction of Q 13:28-9," *SBL Seminar Papers 1989* (Atlanta: Scholars, 1989), pp. 1-22. Boring concludes that the Lukan form of the saying, with the exception of the reference to "north and south" and "all the prophets," is closer to the original than the Matthean form of the saying. I concur.

[35]R. Bultmann, *History of the Synoptic Tradition*, p. 116.

[36]See Jeremias, *Jesus' Promise*, p. 55, n. 5; Marshall, *Luke*, pp. 567-68.

[37]The Lukan form generally is regarded as more primitive and likely authentic by a majority of the Jesus Seminar. See Funk et al., *The Parables of Jesus*, pp. 74, 101.

[38]The displacement motif is not unlike the theme of reversal (the first become last and vice versa) except that the reversal motif does not always suggest exclusion of the demoted ones. The theme of reversal, for example, is found in Luke 4:18-19 and 25-27. Bultmann, *History*, p. 32, has plausibly suggested that

Luke derived at least these verses from an Aramaic tradition. If so, whatever the character of the rest of Luke 4:16-30, much of which is often thought to derive from Mark 6:1-6, vv. 25-27 may go back to Jesus. In this saying we find Jesus in effect arguing for a precedent for Jewish prophets helping out Gentiles and being accepted by them. The context (v. 24) contrasts this with Jesus' rejection by his hometown folk. At most, however, this saying would only provide evidence that Jesus believed that Gentiles could receive the benefit from Jewish prophets, perhaps even at the expense of Jews. This, however, is not different in theme from what we find in Matthew 19:28-29 and parallels. Jeremias's exegesis of Luke 4:22 as being negative in thrust is far-fetched, as Sanders points out, but Sanders's failure to note the final negative response to Jesus' words (vv. 28ff.) is equally inadequate. Cf. Jeremias, *Jesus' Promise*, pp. 44-45; Sanders, "Jesus and the Kingdom," pp. 230-31. I would not rule out that Jesus may indeed have read Isaiah 61 and commented on its fulfillment at some synagogue service. The influence of this text is clear in some of the authentic beatitudes. If the reading here does represent a historical occasion it is noticeable that the words about vengeance in Isaiah 61.2b are omitted.

[39]Gentiles could eat with Jews in a Jewish home if they followed the ritual prescriptions to become ritually clean, i.e., if they were converts or God-fearers. But Jesus says nothing about these Gentiles being in a state of ritual cleanness.

[40]Cf. R. T. France, *Matthew* (Grand Rapids: Eerdmans, 1985), p. 156; and Witherington, *Christology of Jesus*, p. 59ff.

[41]The vast majority of scholars take this to be an authentic parable in some form, with the Markan and Thomas forms being thought nearest the original; see Jeremias, *The Parables of Jesus*, pp. 34, 74.

[42]The conclusion that Gentiles are meant is not completely certain but is highly probable. See Dodd, *Parables of the Kingdom*, p. 154; Jeremias, *Parables of Jesus*, p. 147. The evidence from 1 Enoch 90:30-37 points in this direction. If one accepts that Matthew 8:11-12 and parallels goes back to Jesus in some form, then a reference to Gentiles here seems highly likely.

[43]Jeremias, *Jesus' Promise*, p. 11ff.

[44]On this story and its authenticity, cf. Witherington, *Women in the Ministry of Jesus*, pp. 63-66. This story does attest to the fact that Jesus believed that Jews had precedence at the table, and that non-Jews would be sharing in Jewish bounty when they did so at all.

[45]Cf. Taylor, *Mark*, p. 509.

[46]R. Bultmann, *Die Geschichte*, pp. 36, 58-59, urged that John 2:16 may have been the original text and Mark replaced it with the exact quote from the Septuagint.

[47]C. K. Barrett, "The Gentile Mission as an Eschatological Phenomenon," in *Eschatology and the New Testament* (Peabody: Hendrickson, 1988), p. 68.

[48]Jeremias, *Jesus' Promise*, pp. 22-24; also Barrett, "Gentile Mission," pp. 67-68.

Chapter Fifteen: Conclusions

[1]On the authenticity in some form of the Q pericope about Jerusalem, see B. Witherington, *Women in the Ministry of Jesus* (Cambridge: Cambridge Univ. Press, 1984), pp. 46-47.

[2]It is interesting that in 1990 the Supreme Court in Israel ruled that messianic Jews (Jewish Christians) were not really Jews, therefore establishing that a Jew would be defined religiously and not because he or she was born of a Jewish mother. Ironically enough, both Paul and Jesus would likely have agreed with this decision in so far as it bases Jewishness on the basis of what one believes.

[3]A. Segal, "The Cost of Proselytism," *SBL Seminar Papers 1988* (Atlanta: Scholars Press, 1988), p. 363.

[4]See B. Witherington, *The Christology of Jesus* (Minneapolis: Fortress, 1990), p. 71ff.

[5]W. D. Davies, *Jewish and Pauline Studies* (Philadelphia: Fortress, 1984), p. 137.

[6]In many ways the assessment that best encapsulates Jesus' view of his people is that of C. H. Dodd who in his last work, *The Founder of Christianity* (New York: Collins, 1970), pp. 91-107, suggests that Jesus was about the business of rebuilding the epicenter of God's people. He says: "The call to repentance was addressed to individuals, certainly, but individuals as members of a nation which was

intended to be a "people of God" but had lost its way. If we ask what overt result Jesus may have hoped for, the answer is not easy, because he issued no programme of religious or political reform. . . . Hereditary membership of the chosen people is no passport to membership of the true people of God. To bring the "new" Israel out of the existing system a fresh start must be made, and it must be by a creative act of God. That was John's view; it is unlikely that Jesus was less radical than he. Indeed only a like radicalism can explain some of his words and actions reported in the gospels" (pp. 96-97).

Chapter Sixteen: Introduction

[1]The literature on this subject is incredibly vast and detailed. The following are some of the more helpful treatments on the subject: J. Gray, "The Day of Yahweh," pp. 5-37; J. Gray, *The Biblical Doctrine of the Reign of God* (Edinburgh: T&T Clark, 1979), pp. 182-273; S. Mowinckel, *He That Cometh*, trans. G. W. Anderson (Nashville: Abingdon, 1954); Y. Hoffmann, "The Day of the Lord as a Concept and a Term in the Prophetic Literature," *ZAW* 93 (1981): 37-50; F. C. Fensham, "A Possible Origin of the Concept of the Day of the Lord," *Ou Testamentiese Werkgemeenskap Suider Afrika* 9 (1966): 90-97; G. von Rad, *Old Testament Theology*, vol. 2 (New York: Harper and Row, 1965), pp. 119-25; Carroll, "Eschatological Delay," pp. 47-58.
[2]Fensham, "Possible Origin," p. 90.
[3]See Hoffmann's critique of Mowinckel, "Day of the Lord," pp. 41-43.
[4]Following E. Issac's translation in the *OTP*, 1:81.
[5]Cf. H. C. Kee's comment in *OTP* 1:788, n. 1a.
[6]Flinders Petrie Papyrus II,39e; cf. A. Deissmann, *Light from the Ancient East* (reprint, Grand Rapids: Baker, 1978), p. 369.
[7]Ibid.
[8]G. Braumann, *"parousia,"* *DNTT*, 2:898.
[9]G. D. Kilpatrick, "Acts 7.52 *ELEUSIS,"* *JTS* 46 (1945): 136-45. He perhaps pressed the evidence too far when he suggested that *eleusis* was the technical term used for the coming of Messiah, while "parousia" always was used for a divine theophany.
[10]Deissmann, *Light*, p. 370, n. 4.
[11]Best, *Thessalonians*, p. 353; cf. A. Oepke, *"παρουσία, παρειμι,"* *TDNT*, 5:859-65.

Chapter Seventeen: Perusing the Parousia: The Pauline Evidence

[1]This depends on how one dates the book of James; see James 5:7-8. It also depends on whether one takes "Lord" in James 5 to refer to Christ rather than to God. James 1:1 probably indicates it is a reference to Christ, but cf. 5:4. See P. Ware, "The Coming of the Lord: Eschatology and 1 Thessalonians," *Restoration Quarterly* 22 (1979): 109-20, here p. 110.
[2]See R. W. Funk, "The Apostolic *Parousia:* Form and Significance," in *Christian History and Interpretation: Studies Presented to John Knox*, ed. W. R. Farmer et al. (Cambridge: Cambridge Univ. Press, 1967), pp. 249-68.
[3]Some have suggested that Paul used a variety of images to describe the eschaton, and that he replaced the earlier imagery by later more adequate metaphorical speech. The use of judicial, organic, military and royal or familial imagery of the eschaton is all in evidence in Paul's letters, but it is doubtful we can speak of one set of images replacing another. Rather, as P. Mackey has recently urged, we should see these images as four different ways of viewing and expressing the same reality. See his "Paul's Four Windows on the Eschaton," a paper presented at the Midwest regional meeting of the SBL in Pittsburgh, Spring 1990.
[4]W. Baird, "Pauline Eschatology in Hermeneutic Perspective," *NTS* 17 (1970-71): 314-27, esp. pp. 324-27.
[5]Ibid., p. 323.
[6]C. L. Mearns, "Early Eschatological Development in Paul: the Evidence of I and II Thessalonians,"

NTS 27 (1981): 137-58.

[7]See G. Vos, *The Pauline Eschatology* (reprint, Grand Rapids, Eerdmans, 1972), pp. 172-205 for a lengthy review of alleged development in Paul's eschatological thinking.

[8]Kreitzer, *Jesus and God*, p. 102, urges that any major difference between Paul's view of the Day of the Lord and that found in Jewish pseudepigrapha is caused by Paul's belief in a two-stage Christ event, not because Paul held to a fundamentally different view of Messiah's relationship to God than was held by other early Jewish writers. He is right in what he asserts but wrong in what he denies. Paul's Christology not only leads to a bifurcation of the Christ and resurrection event, but also leads to a substantive re-evaluation of the relationship of Christ to God.

[9]I have modified the conclusion of Davies, *Paul and Rabbinic Judaism*, xxix-xxxviii, who is followed by R. N. Longenecker, "The Nature of Paul's Early Eschatology," *NTS* 31 (1985): 85-95, here 94. While I find much of Beker's attempt to re-emphasize the thoroughly eschatological character of Paul's thought as salutary, his attempt to make the eschatological or apocalyptic framework the most crucial and formative element in Paul's thought at the expense of Christology in the end does not work—not least because it does not explain why, for instance, Paul even has a doctrine of a *return* of Christ. Furthermore, the attempt to see Christology as fully replaced by theology at the eschaton on the basis of a certain interpretation of 1 Corinthians 15, at the expense of various earlier and later Pauline texts, also must be pronounced a failure. Beker fails to reckon with the fact that, in various regards, for Paul Christology is a form of theology, or at least the two overlap, and though Paul is happy to speak of the functional subordination of the Son to the Father in 1 Corinthians 15 he is equally happy to quote a christological hymn that stresses that the Son has by right the status of "the being equal with God" (Phil 2:6). Cf. Beker, *Paul's Apocalyptic Gospel*, passim.

[10]Bruce, *1 and 2 Thessalonians*, p. 57.

[11]So Baird, "Pauline Eschatology," p. 321.

[12]Longenecker, "Paul's Early Eschatology," pp. 92-93.

[13]See Marshall, *Thessalonians*, pp. 102-3; Best, *Thessalonians*, p. 153; Vos, *Pauline Eschatology*, pp. 137-38. We may also compare the Jesus traditions in Mark 8:38, 13:27 and parallels, which Paul may have known about (see below). Here, however, it would seem Zechariah 14 lies in the background.

[14]On the parenetic, not doctrinal, focus and function of this material see Klijn, "1 Thessalonians 4:13-18," 68. Cf. R. H. E. Uprichard, "Exposition of 1 Thessalonians 4:13-18," *Irish Biblical Studies* 1 (1979): 150-56.

[15]D. Gewalt, "1 Thess 4,15-17," pp. 105-13, argues that here, as in 1 Corinthians 15:51-52, Paul is drawing on traditional material also found in Mark 9:1. This is likely but the parallels are not exact (see his chart on p. 109).

[16]See Klijn, "1 Thess 4:13-18," p. 71.

[17]See B. Rigaux, *Les Épîtres aux Thessaloniciens* (Paris: Gabalda, 1956), pp. 394-95.

[18]From the Jesus tradition one may compare Luke 16:22; cf. 1 Enoch 41:2.

[19]Vos, *Pauline Eschatology*, pp. 137-39.

[20]Bruce, *1 and 2 Thessalonians*, 100-101.

[21]Ibid., p. 103.

[22]For detailed critiques of modern Dispensational theology see G. E. Ladd, *The Blessed Hope* (Grand Rapids: Eerdmans, 1956), and R. H. Gundry, *The Church and the Tribulation: A Biblical Examination of Post-tribulationism* (Grand Rapids: Zondervan, 1973).

[23]E. Lohse, *Colossians and Philemon*, trans. W. R. Poehlmann and R. J. Karris (Philadelphia: Fortress, 1971), p. 71; see also Allison, *End of the Ages*, pp. 62-69, on all of this.

[24]J. J. Collins, "The Date and Provenance of the Testament of Moses," in *Studies on the Testament of Moses: Seminar Papers*, ed. G. W. Nickelsburg (Cambridge: SBL Literature, 1973), p. 20.

[25]Allison, *End of the Ages*, pp. 19-20.

[26]Its authenticity is beyond reasonable doubt; see J. Plevnik, "1 Thess. 5.1-11: Its Authenticity, Intention, and Message," *Biblica* 60 (1979): 71-90, esp. pp. 72-74.

[27]See Best, *Thessalonians*, pp. 189-92; Bruce, *Thessalonians*, pp. 98-99; Marshall, *Thessalonians*, pp. 125-27.

[28]N. Walter, "Paul and the Early Christian Jesus-Tradition," in *Paul and Jesus. Collected Essays*, ed. A. J. M. Wedderburn (Sheffield: JSOT Press, 1989), pp. 51-80, here pp. 66-67, suggests that the phrase *legomen en logō kyriou* indicates by whose authority and commission Paul himself is speaking. But we would have expected some other word than *logō* here if that were the case. This is especially dubious in view of the parallel in Matthew 24:43.

[29]G. R. Beasley-Murray, *Jesus and the Future: An Examination of the Criticism of the Eschatological Discourse, Mark 13, with Special Reference to the Little Apocalypse Theory* (London: Macmillan, 1954), pp. 226-30; and J. C. Hurd, "The Jesus whom Paul Preaches (Acts 19.13)," in *From Jesus to Paul. Studies in Honour of F. W. Beare*, ed. P. Richardson and J. C. Hurd (Waterloo: W. Laurier Press, 1984), pp. 73-89, here p. 83.

[30]D. Wenham, *The Rediscovery of Jesus' Eschatological Discourse* (Sheffield: JSOT, 1984); on the use of it by Paul see Wenham, "Paul and the Synoptic Apocalypse," in *Gospel Perspectives. Studies of History and Tradition in the Four Gospels* (Sheffield: JSOT, 1981), 2:345-75.

[31]It is possible that the First Evangelist has drawn not only on Mark in Matthew 24 but also on the Q apocalypse. Note that Paul's eschatological material is at various points closer to the Matthean (and perhaps behind that the Q) material than he is to Mark. Compare Matthew 24:43 to Mark 13:35 and 1 Thessalonians 5:1-11. This may well suggest that Paul had access to some version of Q.

[32]Beasley-Murray, "Second Thoughts on the Composition of Mk. 13," *NTS* 29 (1983): 414-20.

[33]See Wenham, *Rediscovery*, pp. 366-67, for his conclusions about the points at which Paul is drawing on an eschatological discourse.

[34]The aorist verb here could mean a once-for-all action by God for the believer at the point of the parousia, but in view of 3:13 it is more likely that Paul means an action by God completed by the time the parousia happens. See Marshall, *Thessalonians*, pp. 161-62; Bruce, *Thessalonians*, p. 129.

[35]Cf. the Epiphany coin struck by Actium-Nicopolis for Hadrian with the inscription "Epiphany of Augustus"; see A. Deissmann, *Light from the Ancient East* (reprint; Grand Rapids: Baker, 1978), p. 373, and W. M. Ramsay, "The Manifest God," *ET* 10 (1899): 208 on inscriptions about the appearing of a god.

[36]Besides the commentaries, compare the labored attempt of H. K. La Rondelle to decipher this material in "Paul's Prophetic Outline in 2 Thessalonians," *Andrews University Seminary Studies*, 21 (1983): 61-69.

[37]Here the perfect *enestēken* must surely be given its natural sense of "is present" as in Romans 8:38 and 1 Corinthians 3:22; see Bruce, *1 and 2 Thessalonians*, p. 165.

[38]See the arguments in Fee, *First Corinthians*, pp. 753-54, and contrast W. B. Wallis, "The Problem of an Intermediate Kingdom in 1 Corinthians 15.20-28," *JETS* 18 (1975): 229-42.

[39]See Kreitzer, *Jesus and God*, pp. 112-13.

[40]Ibid., pp. 128-29.

[41]J. D. G. Dunn, *Romans 1—8*, pp. 84-85.

[42]The phrase is Dunn's (ibid., p. 84).

[43]Dunn, *Romans 1—8*, p. 84. On the whole matter of Paul's view of final judgment and its connection to the parousia see Kreitzer, *Jesus and God*, pp. 99-112. "Paul continues the Old Testament concept of the Day of the Lord, especially with reference to God's wrath or judgment as being made manifest in that Day. . . . This Day of the Lord has an obvious Christological connection so that Paul can speak of the Old Testament idea and the coming of the Day of the Lord Jesus Christ interchangeably" (p. 99).

[44]Barrett, *First Corinthians*, pp. 126-27.

[45]Fee, *First Corinthians*, pp. 211-12.

[46]Hawthorne, *Philippians*, p. 104.

[47]Caird, *Paul's Letters*, pp. 126-27.

[48]I do not mean to deny that there is a sense in which there is already a "new creation." But for Paul

this consists of individuals who have been spiritually transformed by Christ (see 2 Cor 4:7-18; 5:16-21). They have a new spiritual condition and a new set of relationships with both God and other human beings, especially with Christians. Thus far, however, Paul is aware that this new world order has not changed anyone's body, including those of Christians, or the basic economic and political structures of the world though they are living on borrowed time (see 1 Cor 7) or the condition of the earth itself. When Paul talks about the Dominion of God being present he speaks of the spiritual condition of Christians (peace, joy and so forth in the Holy Spirit), and the changed relationships that should exist in the *ekklesia*—not of new world structures *outside* the community of believers.

[49]It may be debated whether Paul means that God's work must be completed in the believer by the time of the parousia or that it will be completed on that day. Hawthorne, *Philippians*, 21, takes *achri* here to mean "at" but its normal sense is "until," "to" or "as far as." Thus Paul is affirming that the process of God's work in the believer must be complete before the "Day" arrives. Cf. J. B. Lightfoot, *Philippians*, 84: "so that you may be prepared [in advance] to meet the day of trial."

[50]Caird, *Paul's Letters*, p. 107.

[51]The term *aproskopoi* may be either intransitive ("without stumbling," "blameless") or transitive ("not causing offense," "harmless"). Here, unlike in 1 Corinthians 10:32, it probably has the former sense. But cf. Hawthorne, *Philippians*, p. 28; Lightfoot, *Philippians*, p. 87; Caird, *Paul's Letters*, pp. 108-9; R. Martin, *Philippians*, p. 69.

[52]Compare *en tē apokalypsei tou kyriou Iēsou ap ouranou* (2 Thess 1:7) to *tēn apokalypsin tou kyriou hēmon Iēsou Christou* (1 Cor 1:7).

[53]Martin, *2 Corinthians*, p. 114.

[54]Barrett, *Second Corinthians*, p. 161.

[55]Furnish, *II Corinthians*, pp. 275-76.

[56]Martin, *2 Corinthians*, p. 115. Martin stresses that habitual action not simply an individual act is the basis for judgment. The text does not make this clear, even if it is a reasonable inference.

[57]So Furnish, *II Corinthians*, pp. 275-76. This being the case it may be significant that Paul uses the word *phaulos* instead of *kakos*. The former term may be translated "worthless," perhaps referring to an evil intention. Note that this judgment is apparently not about salvation and damnation, unlike Romans 2:5-6, but about the judicial review of Christians' deeds and whether or not they have been pleasing to the Lord. Notice that nothing is said about rewards or punishments; the focus is on one's future accountability for one's present actions, words, intentions. See L. Mattern, *Das Verständnis des Gerichtes bei Paulus*, ATANT 47 (Zürich/Stuttgart: Zwingli Verlag, 1966), pp. 157-58. Paul, however, believed in both future rewards and punishments for the deeds Christians performed during this life (Rom 14:10; Phil 4:17; 1 Cor 3:5ff.; 4:4-6). Thus once again we see how future eschatology is linked to living life in an ethical and responsible manner now (cf. Mattern, p. 158). Texts such as Romans 2:5-10 clearly show that Paul is no universalist insofar as salvation is concerned. Nor unlike others in early Judaism does he merely talk about the vindication of the righteous when the subject of final judgment comes up. Even Christians' deeds will be subject to the judgment of God/Christ (see 2 Cor 5:10). I agree with Mattern's conclusions (pp. 212-15) that Paul has not simply adopted the views on judgment found in early Jewish literature. He has modified what he has taken over in light of his Christology and his theology of grace and justification. Paul's views can be compared profitably to some of the Jesus material dealing with judgment, such as Matthew 25:31-46 where again judgment is according to deeds. Some evidence also exists that Jesus spoke of eternal rewards, or rewards in the kingdom for those who followed his example or teaching (see Mt 5:11-12; 6:3-4, 19-21 and parallels; Mk 10:29-31). Cf. A. Feuillet, "Le caractère universel du jugement et la charité sans frontière en Mt 25.31-46," *Nouvelle Revue Theologique* 102 (1980): 179-96.

[58]Barrett, *Second Corinthians*, p. 161.

Chapter Eighteen: Future Shock: Jesus on the Coming Son of Man

[1]B. Witherington, *The Christology of Jesus* (Minneapolis: Fortress, 1990), p. 233ff.

[2]The material in Revelation 1:13, 14:14 is no exception to this rule since in both cases we have a simple use of analogy, as is the case in Daniel 7. Acts 7:56 stands as the only real non-Gospel use of the phrase.

[3]On the authenticity of this saying see Witherington, *Christology of Jesus*, pp. 248-50.

[4]So rightly I. H. Marshall, "The Synoptic Son of Man Sayings in Recent Discussion," *NTS* 12 (1965-66): 327-51.

[5]Pace D. Wenham, *The Rediscovery of Jesus' Eschatological Discourse* (Sheffield: JSOT Press, 1984), p. 153ff., who wants to argue that the Lukan phrase "Day of the Son of Man" is a correction of an original parousia phrase. The problem with this view is not only that we have clear evidence that Paul used "parousia" to describe the future Day of the Lord, but also the redactional change of Mark 13:4 in Matthew 24:3. I am of course assuming the usual scholarly approach which holds Mark to be the earliest Gospel, and argues that the First Evangelist used Mark. If these assumptions are valid then the parousia language in Mt 24 is surely redactional. This, however, is basically a matter of terminology. I am not suggesting that the First Evangelist is inventing the *idea* of a parousia here, only that he has substituted parousia language for the earlier Markan language about the Son of Man's coming.

[6]See A. J. B. Higgins, *The Son of Man in the Sayings of Jesus* (Cambridge: Cambridge Univ. Press, 1980), p. 60ff. E. Schweizer, *The Good News According to Mark* (Atlanta: John Knox Press, 1970), p. 262: "In the mother tongue of Jesus and the early church there is no word for 'return' or 'come again.' "

[7]See T. F. Glasson, *Jesus and the End of the World* (Edinburgh: St. Andrews, 1980), pp. 94-106.

[8]N. Perrin, *Rediscovering the Teaching of Jesus* (New York: Harper & Row, 1967), p. 173ff.

[9]Witherington, *Christology of Jesus*, p. 256ff.

[10]Moore, *The Parousia*, p. 139.

[11]See pp. 39-41 above.

[12]See Havener, *Q*, p. 144.

[13]See Metzger, *TC*, p. 167.

[14]See Higgins, *Son of Man*, p. 61; Fitzmyer, *Luke X-XXIV*, p. 1170.

[15]See Bultmann, *History of the Synoptic Tradition*, p. 116ff.

[16]On this saying see Witherington, *Christology of Jesus*, p. 165ff.

[17]Jeremias, *Theology*, p. 276.

[18]See Fitzmyer, *Luke X-XXIV*, p. 1167; I. H. Marshall, *Luke*, p. 661.

[19]Note that sometimes in these examples the focus is on the notable piety of the few in the midst of wickedness.

[20]See Marshall, *Luke*, pp. 662-63; Higgins, *Son of Man*, p. 60ff.; and the series of articles by R. Leaney, E. Ashby and W. Powell, "The Days of the Son of Man (Luke xvii.22)," *ET* 67 (1955-56): 28-29 (Leaney); pp. 124-25 (Ashby), and p. 219 (Powell).

[21]Kümmel, *Promise and Fulfilment*, p. 38 and n. 61.

[22]Ibid. The next most plausible view is that "the days of the Son of Man" refers to the dark days that lead up to the darkest day of judgment; cf. Ashby, "Days of the Son of Man," p. 124.

[23]Higgins, *Son of Man*, pp. 63-64.

[24]Ibid., p. 67.

[25]Witherington, *Christology of Jesus*, pp. 243-48.

[26]Higgins, *Son of Man*, p. 66.

[27]S. Mowinckel, *He That Cometh*, trans. G. W. Anderson (Nashville: Abingdon, 1954), p. 392.

[28]Witherington, *Christology of Jesus*, p. 238ff. I think Maurice Casey may well be right that even in Daniel the site of the judgment spoken of in chapter 7 is not in heaven but on earth, in which case the Son of Man was descending, not ascending, to the throne. See Casey, *Son of Man. The Interpretation and Influence of Daniel 7* (London: SPCK, 1979), p. 18ff. A few commentators have urged the argument that not only in Daniel 7 but also in Jesus' use of it, "coming on a cloud" refers to ascension to the Ancient of Days rather than descension to earth. Cf. W. K. Lowther Clarke, "The

Clouds of Heaven: an Eschatological Study," *Theology,* 31 (1935): 63-72, 128-41. The case for this being Jesus' view is weak, not least because the idea of the ascension is only found in the writings of the Third Evangelist (Lk 24; Acts 1). It also requires exegetical gymnastics, especially in regard to a text like Mark 13:26-27.

[29]Beasley-Murray, "Second Thoughts," p. 415.

[30]Ibid., p. 417.

[31]Compare R. Pesch, *Das Markusevangelium,* vol. 2 (Freiburg: Herder, 1977), pp. 266-67 to J. Lambrecht, *Die Redaktion der Markus-Apokalypse* (Rome: Pontifical Institute Press, 1967), p. 259.

[32]Marshall, *Luke,* p. 777.

[33]Beasley-Murray, *Jesus and the Kingdom,* p. 331.

[34]Ibid., p. 332.

[35]Perrin, *Rediscovering,* pp. 173-85.

[36]Lane, *Mark,* p. 475.

Chapter Nineteen: Conclusions

[1]L. Hurtado, *One God, One Lord. Early Christian Devotion and Ancient Jewish Monotheism* (Philadelphia: Fortress, 1988), passim.

[2]Mark 13:14 has often been thought to go back to a Jewish apocalyptic source rather than to the early church (see W. G. Kümmel, *Promise and Fulfilment* (London: SCM, 1957), p. 102). It seems clear that Mark 13:14 circulated very early since Paul seems to reflect clear knowledge of this verse in 2 Thessalonians 2:4 (note that in both Mk 13:14 and in 2 Thess 2:4 it is a person who causes this sacrilege—*erēmōseōs* in Mk 13:14 is a masculine participle; see G. R. Beasley-Murray, *Jesus and the Kingdom of God* (Grand Rapids: Eerdmans, 1986), p. 329.

Furthermore, we should not argue that Mark 13:14 is a *vaticinium ex eventu,* since, as was long ago pointed out, it is a simple adaptation of previous Jewish prophecy in Daniel 11:31, perhaps with some help from its later development in 1 Maccabees 1:54-59, 6:7 where the prophecy is specifically related to the act of Antiochus Epiphanes in 168 B.C. The prophecy as we have it does not reflect hindsight about the specific conditions involved in what happened in Jerusalem during and after the final seige and destruction of the temple, the ruins of which were later toured by Titus. See Josephus, *Wars* 7.112-15; B. Reicke, "Synoptic Prophecies," pp. 121-34.

It is then not impossible that this prophecy does go back to Jesus, especially since many scholars think Jesus may have in fact predicted the destruction of the temple (see, e.g., Schweizer, *Good News according to Mark,* p. 262, and pp. 43-44 above). What is impossible to determine, especially in view of the present structure of Mark 13, is what Jesus may have thought the relationship of an event like this might be to the Coming of the Son of Man insofar as timing or cause and effect is concerned. In 2 Thessalonians 2 the "abomination" seems to be the event that triggers, or at least immediately precedes, the return of Christ. This is not so clear in Mark 13 where we are told that at some unspecified and unknowable time (v. 32) *after* the final tribulation the cosmic events and the Son of Man's return will happen.

[3]Note the distinction made in Mark 13 between "these things" *(tauta),* which refer to the events leading up to and including the destruction of Jerusalem and the temple, and what will happen "in those days" as described in verses 24ff. *(en ekeinais tais hēmerais,* however, clearly is not a technical term for the events accompanying the coming since it can also be used to describe some of the preliminary events in vv. 17, 19), which is seen as at some unspecified time *after* "all these things" have been accomplished, even after the final tribulation. In short, it appears that only Mark 13:24-25, 32-36 speaks of any events immediately connected with the coming of the Son of Man. Verses 28-31 would then perhaps refer to the preliminary events again, with *engys estin* in verse 29 being neuter rather than masculine: "it is near" not "he is near." Then verses 32-36 make a final reference again to the event of the return of the Son of Man at an unknown time and coming in a sudden or abrupt fashion. This ABAB structure to Mark 13 may be Mark's own contribution to the discussion. In any case, we cannot be

sure that Jesus necessarily spoke of any historical events as *immediate* antecedents to, much less causes of, the coming of the Son of Man.

[4]Allison, *Ends of the Ages*, p. 101ff. I think that the imagery is meant to allude to something very real happening to the cosmos. We cannot be sure about this since in the Old Testament the theophanic language of hills skipping like rams and the like is probably not meant to be taken literally, but rather suggests the reaction of the creation to the coming of its Maker.

Chapter Twenty-One: Body Language: Paul and the Resurrection

[1]J. C. Beker, *Paul the Apostle* (Philadelphia: Fortress, 1980), pp. 152, 155-56.

[2]Ibid., p. 152.

[3]W. D. Davies, *Paul and Rabbinic Judaism* (New York: Harper & Row, 1948), p. 290.

[4]On all this, see ibid., pp. 300-301.

[5]Note that where the Greek idea of the immortality of the soul had penetrated early Judaism, early Jews did not call this idea resurrection, but rather immortality. Thus the substitution of immortality for resurrection as a form of eternal life in some early Jewish texts is no proof that even Hellenized early Jews meant something purely spiritual by the term *resurrection*.

[6]G. W. E. Nickelsburg, *Resurrection, Immortality, and Eternal Life in Intertestamental Judaism* (Cambridge: Harvard Univ. Press, 1972), p. 180.

[7]Ibid., pp. 93ff. esp. 124, 142-43.

[8]See Best, *Thessalonians*, pp. 85-86; Marshall, *Thessalonians*, p. 57.

[9]See Bruce, *Thessalonians*, pp. 18-19.

[10]A very few manuscripts omit *tōn* before *nekrōn*, e.g., A, C, K. This is surely a later oversight.

[11]It is possible that Paul is reflecting the idea of the dead sleeping in Sheol until they are summoned from that realm. See B. Rigaux, *Thessaloniciens*, p. 395. Paul says that Jesus was raised out of the midst of the dead persons, but when he speaks of believers in 1 Thessalonians 4:14-16 he says they are "in Christ." Since, according to Paul, Christ is no longer in Sheol this probably implies that Paul believes that deceased believers are with Christ in heaven. This is surely his later view (see 2 Cor 5:8; Phil 1:23). It is thus probable that for Paul the condition of the believing dead is different since Christ's resurrection than it was prior to Christ's resurrection. When Jesus died he went to Sheol and was raised *ek tōn nekrōn*. Believers are now with the Lord. Yet Paul can use the same phrase to refer to their resurrection. See Philippians 3:11 *ek nekrōn* and especially 1 Corinthians 15:12 where Paul speaks of both Christ's and believers' resurrection in the same breath. It is thus best not to overpress the phrase *ek tōn nekrōn* here or elsewhere. Conzelmann, *1 Corinthians*, p. 264, n. 13: "The *nekroi* are the totality of the dead, not merely as a number but also as a realm: the world of the dead."

[12]Bruce, *1 and 2 Thessalonians*, p. 19.

[13]Vos, *Pauline Eschatology*, p. 147, n. 6.

[14]See C. A. Wanamaker, "Apocalypticism at Thessalonica," *Neotestamentica* 21 (1987): 1-10.

[15]J. Becker, *Auferstehung der Toten im Urchristentum* (Stuttgart: KBW Verlag, 1976), p. 46ff., seems to think that Paul in his initial missionary preaching had failed fundamentally to connect that preaching with the theme of the resurrection of Christ. This is hard to believe, especially in view of 1 Thessalonians 1:10. He may, however, be right that in 4:15-17 Paul has added a phrase to a traditional formula, namely "and so we will always be with the Lord" (see p. 51).

[16]Vos, *Pauline Eschatology*, p. 156; p. 155, n. 10.

[17]Resurrection is mentioned in passing in Galatians 1:10. This text adds nothing new to the discussion. As in 1 Thessalonians we read that God raised Christ from the dead.

[18]Metzger, *TC*, 552. The future reading is supported by Aleph, C, K, L, and one corrector of p^{46}.

[19]Fee, *First Corinthians*, p. 257.

[20]See A. J. M. Wedderburn, "The Problem of the Denial of the Resurrection in 1 Corinthians XV," *Novum Testamentum* 23 (1981): 229-41, here p. 231.

[21] Ibid., p. 236.

[22] Ibid., p. 238.

[23] Ibid., p. 238, points to the fact that Paul seems to assume that the Corinthians accept various other elements of early Christian eschatology—the coming end of the ages, judgment to come, the return of Christ, the basic elements of the gospel (see 11:2; 15:1-2, 11). It is striking that in 1 Corinthians 15 Paul does not simply accuse the Corinthians of abandoning all belief in the idea of resurrection, or abandoning the Christian faith per se.

[24] See K. A. Plank, "Resurrection Theology: the Corinthian Controversy Reexamined," *Perspectives in Religious Studies* 8 (1981): 41-54, here pp. 41-42.

[25] On the general problems in Corinth vis-à-vis eschatology see A. C. Thiselton, "Realized Eschatology at Corinth," *NTS* 24 (1977-78): 510-26.

[26] Plank, "Resurrection Theology," p. 45, quoting a phrase of Käsemann's in the last sentence.

[27] See R. H. Fuller, *The Formation of the Resurrection Narratives* (New York: Macmillan, 1971), p. 10ff.

[28] See Court, "Paul and the Apocalyptic Pattern," 57-66. He points especially to the use of the terms *telos* and *tagma* to structure a pattern of eschatological events (see Mk 13:7, 13; Sib Or. 8.311).

[29] Davies, *Paul and Rabbinic Judaism*, p. 305.

[30] A. J. Malherbe, "The Beasts of Ephesus," *JBL* 37 (1968): 71-80.

[31] See M. E. Dahl, *The Resurrection of the Body: A Study of 1 Corinthians 15*, SBT (London: SCM, 1962), p. 18.

[32] J. Jeremias, " Ἀδάμ" *TDNT*, 1:142.

[33] K. W. Trim, "Paul: Life after Death. An Analysis of 1 Corinthians 15," *Crux* 14 (1978): 129-50, here p. 133.

[34] While it may be that Paul refers to Christ's pre-existence when he uses the phrase "the man from heaven," that is certainly not the focus here. The focus here is on what is true of Christ since the resurrection. Contrast A. T. Hanson, "The Midrash in II Corinthians 3: a Reconsideration," *JSNT* 9 (1980): 9-10 and J. D. G. Dunn, "1 Corinthians 15.45. Last Adam. Life-Giving Spirit," in *Christ and Spirit in the New Testament*, ed. B. Lindars and S. Smalley (Cambridge: Cambridge Univ. Press, 1973), pp. 127-41. I tend to agree with Dunn that Paul is focusing on the Last Adam, not the *Urmensch*, and this means that he is concerned with what is true about Christ since the resurrection. He is also right that Paul is concerned to point out how we will be totally conformed to the Son's image, and this process is only completed by resurrection.

[35] On the Christ/Adam typology, cf. C. K. Barrett, *From First Adam to Last* (London: A. & C. Black, 1962).

[36] M. J. Harris, *Raised Immortal: Resurrection and Immortality in the New Testament* (Grand Rapids: Eerdmans, 1985), p. 111.

[37] Ibid., p. 110.

[38] Barrett, *First Corinthians*, p. 350, says, "The first instalment of the crop which foreshadows and pledges the ultimate offering of the whole."

[39] Moore, *The Parousia*, p. 172.

[40] It is at this sort of juncture that the argument by E. E. Ellis for both a monistic and a corporate view of *sōma* in Paul fails. Paul is arguing that each one will have his or her own new body given by God, just as each plant gets a separate one. Furthermore, just as the seed can be distinguished from the plant body that is given to it, so also believers in their present state can be distinguished from their future resurrection bodies, as well as their present bodies. See Ellis, "*SŌMA* in First Corinthians," *Interpretation* 44/2 (1990): 132-44.

[41] Hering, *First Corinthians*, p. 174.

[42] This is the distinction Dahl, *Resurrection*, pp. 10, 94-95, seeks to make.

[43] R. J. Sider, "The Pauline Conception of the Resurrection Body in 1 Corinthians XV.35-54," *NTS* 21 (1974-75): 428-39, is so intent on insisting on bodily continuity between this body and the resurrection body that he fails to see the logical outcome of his very proper critique of Bultmann. One can reject

Bultmann's view of *sōma* without insisting on "somatical identity."

[44]R. Bultmann, *Theology of the New Testament*, vol. I (New York: Scribner's, 1951), pp. 192-95.

[45]Ibid., p. 198.

[46]Nickelsburg, *Resurrection*, pp. 177-80; J. W. Cooper, *Body, Soul, and Life Everlasting: Biblical Anthropology and the Monism-Dualism Debate* (Grand Rapid: Eerdmans, 1989), pp. 81-103.

[47]R. H. Gundry, *SŌMA in Biblical Theology (with emphasis on Pauline anthropology)*, SNTS Monograph 29 (Cambridge: Cambridge Univ. Press, 1976), pp. 79-80, 156. See the critique by Fee, *First Corinthians*, p. 776, n. 4.

[48]As Dahl, *Resurrection*, p. 32, admits, this is the basic distinction one finds in nonbiblical Greek. However, he wishes to argue that Paul's usage is controlled by the idea of "Semitic totality."

[49]See Dahl, *Resurrection*, p. 25ff. Dahl is right that Paul uses *psuche* basically in a neutral sense to mean natural life principle, that which makes a human body alive (see 1 Cor 15:45; Rom 13:1; 2:9; 2 Cor 12:15). I might add that Paul uses *psychikos* to mean something inferior, especially to that which is *pneumatikos* (cf. Dahl, pp. 15, 56).

[50]See Harris, *Raised Immortal*, pp. 118-21; H. Clavier, "Brèves Remarques sur la Notion de *SŌMA PNEUMATIKON*," in *The Background of the New Testament and its Eschatology*, ed. W. D. Davies and D. Daube (Cambridge: Cambridge Univ. Press, 1964), pp. 342-62. Clavier stresses that the pneumatic body is to be distinguished from the psychical body in its very constitution (p. 348). Clavier, however, wrongly goes on to see a continuity between the pneumatic body and the inner person referred to in 2 Corinthians 4.

[51]Cooper, *Body, Soul, and Life Everlasting*, pp. 152ff.

[52]C. F. D. Moule, "St. Paul and Dualism: The Pauline Conception of Resurrection," *NTS* 13 (1965-66): 106-23.

[53]Since for Dahl, *Resurrection*, pp. 81-95, *Sōma* means human personality, and in the end he argues for the resurrection of *sōma* in *that* sense, while conceding there may not be material identity between the old body and the new, the end result of his views are little different from what I have been arguing for.

[54]J. Jeremias, "Flesh and Blood cannot inherit the Kingdom of God," *NTS* 2 (1955-56): 151-59; followed by Barrett, *First Corinthians*, p. 379.

[55]See J. Gillman, "Transformation in 1 Cor 15.50-53," *Ephemerides Theologicae Lovanienses* 58 (1982): 309-33, here p. 314, n. 21.

[56]So ibid., p. 318.

[57]Fee, *First Corinthians*, p. 754.

[58]So Gillman, "Transformation," pp. 319-20; Fee, *First Corinthians*, p. 802, n. 27.

[59]Beker, *Paul the Apostle*, p. 180.

[60]See Barrett, *Second Corinthians*, p. 65; Martin, *2 Corinthians*, p. 15.

[61]Furnish, *II Corinthians*, p. 114.

[62]Martin, *2 Corinthians*, p. 90.

[63]Furnish, *II Corinthians*, p. 286.

[64]See Davies, *Paul and Rabbinic Judaism*, pp. 314-17. That various early Jews often thought of the realities of the world to come already existing in heaven must also be borne in mind, for it would seem that such texts as Galatians 4:26 suggest that Paul does as well. Thus we should not be surprised at the idea of future resurrection bodies already being present or formed in heaven.

[65]Furnish, *II Corinthians*, p. 291ff.

[66]Pace Ellis, "*Sōma*," 138ff, following the older work by J. A. T. Robinson, *The Body: A Study in Pauline Theology* (London: SCM, 1952).

[67]A. T. Lincoln, *Paradise Now and Not Yet: Studies in the Role of the Heavenly Dimension in Paul's Thought with Special Reference to His Eschatology* (Cambridge: Cambridge Univ. Press, 1981), p. 62.

[68]See J. F. Collange, *Énigmes de la Deuxième Épitre de Paul aux Corinthiens. Études Exégetique de*

2 Cor. 2,14-7,4 (Cambridge: Cambridge Univ. Press, 1972), p. 183ff.

[69]Moule, "St. Paul and Dualism," pp. 106-23.

[70]Lincoln, *Paradise Now*, p. 69.

[71]J. N. Sevenster, "Some Remarks on the *GUMNOS* in II Cor. v. 3," in *Studia Paulina in Honorem Johannis de Zwann* (Haarlem: Bohn, 1953), pp. 202-14, here p. 208. Sevenster also rightly points out that for Paul it is the inner person (cf. 2 Cor 4:16) or human spirit, not the "soul," that will be found naked at death.

[72]See Metzger, *TC*, pp. 579-80.

[73]See Martin, *2 Corinthians*, p. 96. *Ei ge kai* is probably to be preferred to *eiper*, and expresses assurance rather than "a spasm of doubt" as Moule argued. Cf. Lincoln, *Paradise Now*, p. 212, n. 50.

[74]Lincoln, *Paradise Now*, p. 66.

[74]See *BAG*, 284. Note that the noun form *ependytes* means an outer coat. Cf. Josephus, *Ant.* 3.159.

[76]Barrett, *Second Corinthians*, p. 159. For a very helpful overview of the development of the idea that Paul's thought about resurrection developed from a Jewish and Pharisaic one to a more Greek idea of afterlife, see B. F. Meyer, "Did Paul's View of the Resurrection of the Dead Undergo Development?" *Theological Studies* 47 (1986): 363-87. Meyer concludes that "there is a total lack of persuasive evidence that Paul's teaching on the resurrection of the dead underwent significant development either between 1 Thess. 4 and 1 Cor. 15, or between 1 Cor. 15 and 2 Cor 5. Allusion to the "intermediate state" occurs at least in 2 Cor. 5 and Phil. 1, apparently without entailing any change in Paul's conception of resurrection of the dead and transformation of the living at the Parousia" (p. 382). I quite agree, and thus must reject the sort of arguments we find offered by G. M. M. Pelser, "Resurrection and Eschatology in Paul's Letters," *Neotestamentica* 20 (1986): 37-46 that Paul couldn't have possibly conceived of the notion of an intermediate state, and therefore his thought about resurrection must have undergone a radical shift over the course of time.

[77]Ellis, "*SŌMA*," p. 143.

[78]Becker, *Auferstehung*, p. 24, concludes that the *Vorlage* ended with the phrase "on the ground of the resurrection from the dead" to which Paul has added "Jesus Christ our Lord." He is right to note that general resurrection of the dead is not envisioned in this traditional formula, but rather the specifically Christian view of Jesus' resurrection (see p. 30).

[79]See Cranfield, *Romans*, 1:61; Dunn, *Romans 1—8*, p. 13.

[80]See Dunn, *Romans 1—8*, pp. 16-17.

[81]On the meaning of *dikaiōsin* here see Dunn, *Romans 1—8*, p. 225; on *dia* see W. Sanday and A. C. Headlam, *Romans* (Edinburgh: T. & T. Clark, 1902), p. 116.

[82]See Beker, *Paul's Apocalyptic Gospel*, passim. Even the attempt to suggest that Christology is in the end resolved or dissolved into theology because Paul ultimately places Christ under God is not a fully adequate assessment of how Paul's thought flows. For one thing, this is a matter of functional subordination once Christ has completed certain roles as 1 Corinthians 15 suggests. For another, it is not merely a matter of the One who has come to us in Christ (p. 90), but also a matter of the One who has come to us *as* Christ. Though he has no developed doctrine of the Trinity, Paul does believe that Jesus may be called by the Old Testament name for God *(kyrios)* precisely because he had and has divine prerogatives (see Phil 2), not just because he acts like or for God. One who is worshiped as God by Paul, is prayed to as divine and who shares the very nature of God *(morphē theou)*, must have been considered by Paul as in some sense truly divine.

[83]What is not clear is whether or not Paul is talking about logical consequences (in which case we would have a sort of if . . . then relationship of the protasis to the apodosis). I incline to the view that *esometha* refers to eschatological fulfillment, not merely to logical consequences in the present of dying with Christ; so Cranfield, *Romans*, 1:308; cf. Dunn, *Romans 1—8*, p. 318.

[84]*Zōopoiesei*, which is in the future tense, surely refers to the final resurrection; cf. Dunn, *Romans 1—8*, p. 432; Cranfield, *Romans*, 1:391.

[85]Barrett, *Romans*, p. 201.

[86]Sanday and Headlam, *Romans*, p. 388.

[87]See Caird, *Letters from Prison*, p. 139.

[88]The authorship of Colossians is much debated, and I have not treated it as Pauline in this chapter since my focus has been on the undisputed Paulines. I think Colossians is likely to be a late Pauline letter that manifests some of the same sort of ideas about resurrection as those in Philippians.

[89]See Hawthorne, *Philippians*, p. 140.

[90]Ibid., p. 143, following Goodspeed and Moffatt.

[91]See Hawthorne, *Philippians*, pp. 146-47; Lightfoot, *Philippians*, p. 151.

[92]Martin, *Philippians*, p. 150.

[93]See J. Becker, "Erwagungen zu Phil. 3,20-21," *Theologische Zeitschrift* 27 (1971): 16-29, who concludes that Paul is definitely drawing on traditional material here.

[94]Hawthorne, *Philippians*, p. 174.

[95]See O. O'Donovan, *Resurrection and Moral Order: An Outline for Evangelical Ethics* (Grand Rapids: Eerdmans, 1986), passim.

Chapter Twenty-Two: Before and Afterlife: Jesus and the Resurrection

[1]See B. Witherington, *Women in the Ministry of Jesus* (Cambridge: Cambridge Univ. Press, 1984), pp. 32-35.

[2]G. E. Ladd, *A Theology of the New Testament* (Grand Rapids: Eerdmans, 1974), p. 69, is representative of many in saying, "Here is a truly inconceivable order of existence. There are no human analogies to describe existence without the physiological and sociological bonds of sex and family."

[3]Here we may also want to compare the apparently primitive logion in John 5:28-29, which, while speaking of a general resurrection in which the dead are called from the tombs, nonetheless distinguishes between a resurrection of life and a resurrection of judgment. In view of the lack of any discussion of the future resurrection of the dead (other than Jesus') in the Fourth Gospel, this material is not likely to be redactional in character. What may be redactional is the paralleling of the spiritually dead hearing the voice of the Son (vv. 25-26) with the physically dead hearing his voice, as well as the suggestion that it is Jesus' voice that raises the dead.

[4]See J. Fitzmyer, *The Gospel according to Luke X-XXIV* (New York: Doubleday, 1985), 1305.

[5]Luke 22:16 may well be secondary, but in any case it is notable that Luke treats it independently of the saying he has in Luke 22:18.

[6]See pp. 136-38.

[7]R. E. Brown has rightly urged that this saying's original referent is to Jesus' participation in the final eschatological meal. See his book review of P. Lebeau's full-length study of this verse, *La Vin Nouveau du Royaume* (Paris/Bruges: Desclee de Brouwer, 1966) in *Theological Studies* 29 (1968): 765-66.

[8]See Taylor, *Mark*, pp. 546-47 and Pesch, *Markusevangelium*, 2.354-61.

[9]On the possibility of its being an independent logion, see B. Balembo, "Le produit de la vigne et la vin nouveau. Analyse èxegetique de Mc 14,25," *Rev. African Theol.* 8 (1984): 5-16.

[10]See Taylor, *Mark*, p. 436 for the chart. On church embellishment, see J. Jeremias, *New Testament Theology* (N.Y.: Scribner's, 1971), p. 276ff.

[11]So A. Perez Gordo, "Notas Sobre los Annucios de la Pasion," *Burgenese* 17 (1976): 251-70 (available to me only in *NTA* 21 [1977]: 23).

[12]See G. Strecker, "The Passion and Resurrection Predictions in Mark's Gospel. (Mark 8:31; 9:31; 10:32-34)," *Interpretation* 22 (1968): 421-42, esp. 429ff. Strecker concludes, however, that the saying only goes back to the early church before Mark, not to Jesus. One must ask, then, how it is that this saying has avoided being cast in the language of the early Passion narrative and creedal formulations that are pre-Markan.

[13]See Fitzmyer, *Luke I-IX*, p. 781.

[14]See J. B. Bauer, "Drei Tage," *Biblical* 39 (1958): 354-58.

Chapter Twenty-Four: The Eschatological Schema

[1]A. Schweitzer, *The Mysticism of Paul the Apostle* (New York: Holt and Co., 1931), p. 113.

[2]G. B. Caird, *Paul's Letters from Prison* (Oxford: Clarendon, 1976), p. 40. This is not to deny or minimize the otherworldly aspect to either Jesus' or Paul's thought, but the point is that it takes a decidedly secondary place in emphasis and importance in the teaching of both Jesus and Paul. The purpose of this book was not to focus on the heavenly dimension in either of these early Jews' teachings. Paul's reflections on heaven, the heavens and the heavenly condition have been brilliantly set forth by Lincoln in his *Paradise Now and Not Yet*, passim.

[3]Quite clearly, Mark indicates that this composite discourse is directed to Jesus' disciples (Mk 13:1-4), and therefore we must conclude that Mark's audience would have understood the reference to the elect as a reference to themselves, not to non-Christian Jews. Notice how in Mark 13:21-22 the disciples are clearly addressed ("you") and then are called the elect in verse 22. Elsewhere I have dealt with Luke 17:34-35 and parallels, which is most unlikely to provide any warrant for the supposition of a pretribulation exit of the church from this world *(Women in the Ministry of Jesus*, pp. 45-46). Indeed this saying may suggest that those "taken" are the ones who face the judgment, not those left, since that is the normal juridical procedure. In any case, the saying says nothing about being taken away into heaven.

[4]See the translation in *The Ante-Nicene Fathers*, vol. 1, ed. A. Roberts and J. Donaldson (reprint, Grand Rapids: Eerdmans, 1975), p. 559.

Chapter Twenty-Five: The Future of a Future in a Modern World

[1]See P. Davies, *God and the New Physics* (New York: Simon and Schuster, 1983), pp. 120, 122.

[2]Ibid., p. 119.

[3]Ibid., p. 125.

[4]Ibid., p. 121.

[5]Ibid., p. 123.

[6]I am thinking of the famous statement by R. Bultmann, "We no longer believe in the three-storied universe which the creeds take for granted. . . . No one who is old enough to think for himself supposes that God lives in a local heaven. There is no longer any heaven in the traditional sense of the word. . . . And if this is so . . . we can no longer look for the return of the Son of Man on the clouds of heaven or hope that the faithful will meet him in the air" (1 Thess 4:15ff), in his famous essay, "The New Testament and Mythology," in *Kerygma and Myth*, ed. H. W. Bartsch (New York: Harper & Row, 1961), p. 4.

[7]J. H. Yoder, "Armaments and Eschatology," in *Studies in Christian Ethics: Ethics and Ecumenism*, vol. 1.1 (1988), pp. 43-61, esp. 47ff.

[8]Davies, *God and the New Physics*, p. 102. This element of unpredictability coupled with apparent lack of causation has led some to reopen the question of whether or not divine intervention as a viable but invisible cause might be a reality.

[9]It is instructive to explore the origin and early use of the term *supernatural* in the relevant dictionaries, especially the Oxford English Dictionary.

[10]A. T. Lincoln, *Paradise Now and Not Yet* (Cambridge: Cambridge Univ. Press, 1981), pp. 4-5.

[11]B. Witherington, *Women in the Earliest Churches* (Cambridge: Cambridge Univ. Press, 1988), p. 219. I also pointed out that the two sorts of vertical eschatology that developed in the early church, which supplanted the essentially horizontal eschatology of Paul and Jesus, had the effect they did because of the nature of their views about realized eschatology, not because of their views about the *timing* of the end (pp. 216-17).

[12]O. O'Donovan, *Resurrection and Moral Order* (Grand Rapids: Eerdmans, 1986), p. 249.

[13]See J. H. Yoder, "Armament and Eschatology," *Studies in Christian Ethics: Ethics and Ecumenism* 1.1 (1984): 44-46.

[14]R. Bauckham, "Delay of the Parousia," *Tyndale Bulletin* (1980): 8.

[15]For a helpful guide to understanding biblical prophecy in its historical context and character from an evangelical but non-Dispensational perspective, see C. E. Armerding and W. W. Gasque, eds., *A Guide to Biblical Prophecy* (Peabody: Hendrikson, 1989). Though this present book has been about New Testament eschatological teaching of Jesus and Paul, the reader may find helpful the appendix on the character of Old Testament prophecy that concludes this study.

Bibliography

A. Commentaries

Barrett, C. K. *A Commentary on the Epistle to the Romans.* New York: Harper & Row, 1957.

_____ . *A Commentary on the First epistle to the Corinthians.* New York: Harper & Row, 1968.

_____ . *The Second Epistle to the Corinthians.* New York: Harper & Row, 1973.

Barth, M. *Ephesians 1—3.* Garden City: Doubleday, 1974.

Beare, F. W. *The Gospel according to Matthew* Peabody: Hendrickson, 1981.

Best, E. *A Commentary on the First and Second Epistles to the Thessalonians.* London: A. & C. Black, 1972.

Betz, H. D. *Galatians.* Philadelphia: Fortress, 1979.

Bruce, F. F. *I & II Corinthians.* Greenwood, S.C.: Attic Press, 1971.

_____ . *I and 2 Thessalonians.* Waco, Tex.: Word, 1982.

_____ . *The Epistle to the Galatians.* Grand Rapids: Eerdmans, 1982.

Caird, G. B. *Paul's Letters from Prison.* Oxford: Clarendon, 1976.

Conzelmann, H. *I Corinthians.* Trans. James W. Leitch. Philadelphia: Fortress, 1975.

Cranfield, C. E. B. *The Epistle to the Romans.* Vol. 2. Edinburgh: T. & T. Clark, 1979.

_____ . *The Gospel according to St. Mark.* Cambridge: Cambridge Univ. Press, 1972.

Davies, W. D., and D. C. Allison, *The Gospel according to Saint Matthew.* Vol. 1. Edinburgh: T. & T. Clark, 1988.

Dunn, J. D. G. *Romans 1—8.* Waco, Tex.: Word, 1988.

_____ . *Romans 9—16.* Waco, Tex.: Word, 1988.

Fee, G. D. *The First Epistle to the Corinthians.* Grand Rapids: Eerdmans, 1987.

Fitzmyer, J. A. *The Gospel according to Luke X-XXIV.* New York, Doubleday, 1985.

France, R. T. *Matthew.* Grand Rapids: Eerdmans, 1985.

Fung, R. Y. K. *The Epistle to the Galatians.* Grand Rapids: Eerdmans, 1988.

Furnish, V. P. *II Corinthians.* Garden City: Doubleday, 1984.

Hawthorne, G. F. *Philippians.* Waco, Tex.: Word, 1983.

Kaiser, O. *Isaiah 13—39.* Philadelphia: Westminster Press, 1974.

Käsemann, E. *Commentary on Romans.* Grand Rapids: Eerdmans, 1980.

Lane, W. L. *The Gospel of Mark.* Grand Rapids: Eerdmans, 1974.

Lightfoot, J. B. *St. Paul's Epistle to the Philippians.* London: Macmillan and Co., 1894.

_____ . *Notes on the Epistles of St. Paul.* Winona Lake: Alpha Lake Pub. rpr.

Lohse, E. *Colossians and Philemon.* Trans. W. R. Poehlmann and R. J. Karris. Philadelphia: Fortress, 1971.

Marshall, I. H. *First and Second Thessalonians.* Grand Rapids: Eerdmans, 1978.

_____ . *The Gospel of Luke.* Grand Rapids: Eerdmans, 1978.

Martin, R. P. *2 Corinthians.* Waco, Tex.: Word, 1986.

Marxsen, W. *Der erste Brief an die Thessalonicher*. Zürich: Theologischer Verlag, 1979.

Oswalt, J. N. *The Book of Isaiah Chapters 1—39*. Grand Rapids: Eerdmans, 1986.

Pesch, R. *Das Markusevangelium*. vol. 2 Freiburg: Herder, 1977.

Rigaux, B. *Les Épîtres aux Thessaloniciens*. Paris: Gabalda, 1956.

Robinson, J. A. *St. Paul's Epistle to the Ephesians*. London: Macmillan, 1904.

Sanday, W., and A. C. Headlam, *Romans*. Edinburgh: T. & T. Clark, 1902.

Schweizer, E. *The Good News according to Mark*. Atlanta: John Knox Press, 1970.

——————. *The Good News according to Matthew*. Atlanta: John Knox Press, 1975.

Weiss, J. *Der erste Korintherbrief*. Göttingen: Vandhoeckt Ruprecht, 1910.

B. Monographs and Articles

Aageson, J. W. "Scripture and Structure in the Development of the Argument in Romans 9—11." *CBQ* 48 (1986): 265-89.

Aalen, S. "Reign and House in the Kingdom of God in the Gospels." *NTS* 8 (1961-62): 215-40.

Ackroyd, P. R. "*NTSH—eis telos.*" *ET* 80 (1969): 126.

Allison, D. C. *The End of the Ages Has Come*. Philadelphia: Fortress, 1985.

——————. "Romans 11:11-15: A Suggestion." *Perspectives in Religious Studies* 12 (1985): 23-30.

Allmen, J. J. von. *Pauline Teaching on Marriage*. London: Faith, 1963.

Arens, E. *The ELTHON-Sayings in the Synoptic Tradition. A Historico-critical Investigation*. Göttingen: Vandenhoeck and Ruprecht, 1976.

Armerding, C. E., and W. W. Gasque, eds. *A Guide to Biblical Prophecy*. Peabody: Hendrikson, 1989.

Badenas, R. *Christ the End of the Law: Romans 10:4 in Pauline Perspective*. JSOT Sup. 10. Sheffield: JSOT, 1985.

Bailey, J. W. "The Temporary Messianic Reign in the Literature of Early Judaism." *JBL* 53 (1934): 170-87.

Baird, W. "Pauline Eschatology in Hermeneutic Perspective." *NTS* 17 (1970-71): 314-27.

Balembo, B. "Le produit de la vigne et le vin nouveau. Analyse èxegetique de Mc 14,25." *Rev. African Theol.* 8 (1984): 5-16.

Banks, R. *Paul's Idea of Community: The Early House Churches in Their Historical Setting*. Grand Rapids: Eerdmans, 1980.

Barrett, C. K. *From First Adam to Last*. London: A. & C. Black, 1962.

——————. "New Testament Eschatology." *SJT* 6 (1953): 136-55, 225-43.

——————. "Romans 9:30—10:21. The Fall and Responsibility of Israel." In *Essays on Paul*, pp. 132-53. Philadelphia: Westminster Press, 1982.

——————. "The Allegory of Abraham, Sarah, and Hagar in the Argument of Galatians." In *Essays on Paul*, pp. 154-70. Philadelphia: Westminster Press, 1982.

——————. "The Gentile Mission as an Eschatological Phenomenon." In *Eschatology and the New Testament*, pp. 65-75. Peabody: Hendrickson, 1988.

Barth, M. *The People of God*. Sheffield: JSOT, 1983.

Bauckham, R. J. "The Delay of the Parousia." *Tyndale Bulletin* (1980): 3-36.

Bauer, J. B. "Drei Tage." *Biblical* 39 (1958): 354-58.

Beare, F. W. "Jesus and Paul." *CJT* 5 (1959): 79-86.

Beasley-Murray, G. R. *Jesus and the Future: An Examination of the Criticism of the Eschatological Discourse, Mark 13, with Special Reference to the Little Apocalypse Theory*. London: Macmillan, 1954.

——————. *Jesus and the Kingdom of God*. Grand Rapids: Eerdmans, 1986.

——————. "*Second Thoughts on the Composition of Mk. 13.*" *NTS* 29 (1983): 414-20.

Becker, J. *Auferstehung der Toten im Urchristentum*. Stuttgart: KBW Verlag, 1976.

——————. "Erwägungen zu Phil. 3,20-21." *Theologische Zeitschrift* 27 (1971): 16-29.

Beker, J. C. *Paul the Apostle: The Triumph of God in Life and Thought*. Philadelphia: Fortress, 1980.

_____. *Paul's Apocalyptic Gospel: The Coming Triumph of God*. Philadelphia: Fortress, 1982.

Borg, M. *Conflict, Holiness, and Politics in the Teaching of Jesus*. New York: Edwin Mellen, 1984.

Boring, M. E. "A Proposed Reconstruction of Q 13:28-9." In *SBL Seminar Papers 1989*, pp. 1-22. Atlanta: Scholars Press, 1989.

Bornkamm, G. *Jesus of Nazareth*. Trans. I. and F. McLuskey with J. M. Robinson. New York: Harper & Row, 1960.

_____. "The Authority to Bind and Loose in the Church in Matthew's Gospel." In *The Interpretation of Matthew*, ed. G. N. Stanton, pp. 85-97. Philadelphia: Fortress Press, 1983.

Branick, V. P. "Apocalyptic Paul?" *CBQ* 47 (1985): 664-75.

Braumann, G. "*parousia.*" *DNTT*, 2:898.

Brown, R. E. Book review of P. Lebeau's *La Vin Nouveau du Royaume* (Paris/Bruges: Desclee de Brouwer, 1966) in *Theological Studies* 29 (1968): 765-66.

Brown, R. E., et al., eds. *Peter in the New Testament*. Minneapolis: Augsburg Press, 1973.

Bruce, F. F. *Paul and Jesus*. London: SCM Press, 1977.

Bultmann, R. *History of the Synoptic Tradition*. Oxford: Blackwell, 1968.

_____. "Jesus and Paul." In *Existence and Faith*, pp. 183-201. Cleveland: World, 1960.

_____. *Theology of the New Testament*. Vol. 1. New York: Scribner's, 1951.

Burney, C. F. *The Poetry of our Lord*. Oxford: Clarendon Press, 1925.

Cadbury, H. J. "The Kingdom of God and Ourselves," *Christian Century* 67 (1950): 172-73.

Caird, G. B. "Expository Problems: Predestination—Romans ix-xi." *ET* 68 (1956-57): 324-27.

_____. *Jesus and the Jewish Nation*. London: Athlone Press, 1965.

Campbell, J. Y. "The Kingdom of God Has Come." *ET* 48 (1936-37): 91-94.

Cangh, J. M. Van, and M. Van Esbroeck. "La primauté de Pierre (Mt 16,16-19) et son context judaique." *Rev. Theol. Louv.* 11 (1980): 310-24.

Carroll, R. P. "Eschatological Delay in the Prophetic Tradition?" *ZAW*, no. 1 (1982): 47-58.

Casey, M. *Son of Man. The Interpretation and Influence of Daniel 7*. London: SPCK, 1979.

Chevallier, M. A. " 'Tu es Pierre, Tu es le Nouvel Abraham' (Mt 16/18)." *Étude Theol. Rel.* 57 (1982): 375-87.

Chilton, B. D. *God in Strength. Jesus' Announcement of the Kingdom*. Freistadt: Plochl, 1979.

Clarke W. K. Lowther, "The Clouds of Heaven: An Eschatological Study." *Theology* 31 (1935): 63-72, 128-41.

Clavier, H. "Brèves Remarques sur la Notion de *SOMA PNEUMATIKON.*" In *The Background of the New Testament and Its Eschatology*, ed. W. D. Davies and D. Daube, pp. 342-62. Cambridge: Cambridge Univ. Press, 1964.

Collange, J. F. *Énigmes de la Deuxième Épître de Paul aux Corinthiens. Études Exegetique de 2 Cor. 2,14-7,4*. Cambridge: Cambridge Univ. Press, 1972.

Collins, J. J. "Genre, Ideology, and Social Movements in the Domain of Jewish Apocalypticism." Paper delivered at the SBL annual meeting, Nov. 1989.

_____. *The Apocalyptic Imagination: An Introduction to the Jewish Matrix of Christianity*. New York: Crossroad, 1984.

_____. "The Date and Provenance of the Testament of Moses." In *Studies on the Testament of Moses: Seminar Papers*, ed. G. W. Nickelsburg, pp. 15-32. Missoula: Scholars Press, 1973.

Cooper, J. W. *Body, Soul, and Life Everlasting: Biblical Anthropology and the Monism-Dualism Debate*. Grand Rapid: Eerdmans, 1989.

Coppens, J. "Miscellanees bibliques. LXXX. Une diatribe antijuive dans 1 Thess. II,13-16." *ETL* 80 (1976): 90-85.

Court, J. M. "Paul and the Apocalyptic Pattern." In *Paul and Paulinism: Essays in Honor of C. K. Barrett*, ed. M. D. Hooker and S. G. Wilson, pp. 57-66. London: SPCK, 1982.

Cullmann, O. *Immortality of the Soul or Resurrection of the Dead*. London: The Epworth Press, 1958.

_____. *Peter—Disciple, Apostle, Martyr*. London: SCM Press, 1953.

Dahl, M. E. *The Resurrection of the Body: A Study of 1 Corinthians 15*. London: SCM, 1962.

Dahl, N. A. "Der Name Israel: Zur Auslegung von Gal 6,16." *Judaica* 6 (1950): 161-70.

Davies, P. *God and the New Physics*. New York: Simon and Schuster, 1983.

Davies, W. D. *The Gospel and the Land. Early Christianity and Jewish Territorial Doctrine*. Berkeley and Los Angeles: Univ. of California Press, 1974.

————. *Jewish and Pauline Studies*. Philadelphia: Fortress, 1984.

————. *Paul and Rabbinic Judaism*. New York: Harper & Row, 1948.

De Boer, M. C. "Paul and Jewish Apocalyptic Eschatology." In *Apocalyptic and the New Testament: Essays in Honor of J. L Martyn*, pp. 169-89. Sheffield: JSOT, 1989.

Deissmann, A. *Light from the Ancient East*. Reprint. Grand Rapids: Baker, 1978.

Derrett, J. D. M. *Studies in the New Testament*. Vol. 1. Leiden: Brill, 1977.

Dodd, C. H. *The Founder of Christianity*. New York: Collins, 1970.

————. "Matthew and Paul." *ET* 58 (1946-47): 293-98.

————. *The Parables of the Kingdom*. New York: Scribners, 1936.

Donfried, K. P. "Paul and Judaism. 1 Thessalonians 2:13-16 as a Test Case." *Interpretation* 38 (1984): 242-53.

————. "The Kingdom of God in Paul." In *The Kingdom of God in 20th-Century Interpretation*, ed. W. Willis, pp. 175-90. Peabody, Mass.: Hendrickson, 1987.

Doughty, D. J. "The Presence and Future of Salvation in Corinth." *ZNW* 66 (1975): 61-90.

Duling, D. C. "Binding and Loosing: Matthew 16:19; 18:18; John 20:23." *Forum* 3 (1987): 3-31.

Dunn, J. D. G. "I Corinthians 15.45. Last Adam. Life-Giving Spirit." In *Christ and Spirit in the New Testament*, ed. B. Lindars and S. Smalley, pp. 127-41. Cambridge: Cambridge Univ. Press, 1973.

————. *Unity and Diversity in the New Testament*. Philadelphia: Westminster, 1977.

Ellis, E. E. *Paul and His Recent Interpreters*. Grand Rapids: Eerdmans, 1961.

————. "*SŌMA* in First Corinthians." *Interpretation* 44/2 (1990): 132-44.

Epp, E. J. "Jewish-Gentile Continuity in Paul: Torah and/or Faith? (Romans 9:1-5)." *HTR* 79 (1986): 80-90.

Evans, C. A. "Paul and the Hermeneutics of 'True Prophecy': A Study of Romans 9—11." *Biblica* 65 (1984): 560-70.

Fensham, F. C. "A Possible Origin of the Concept of the Day of the Lord." *Ou Testamentiese Werkgemeenskap Suider Afrika* 9 (1966): 90-97.

Feuillet, A. "Le caractère universel du jugement et la charité sans frontière en Mt 25.31-46." *Nouvelle Revue Theologique* 102 (1980): 179-96.

————. "La Signification fondamentale de Marc XIII. Recherches sur l'Eschatologie des Synoptiques." *Revue Thomiste* 80 (1980): 181-215.

————. "Les Privilèges et l'Incredulité d'Israel d'après les Chapitres 9-11 de l'Épître aux Romans." *Esprit et Vie* 92 (1982): 481-93, 497-506.

Fuller, R. H. *The Formation of the Resurrection Narratives*. New York: Macmillan, 1971.

Funk, R. W. "The Apostolic *Parousia*: Form and Significance." *Christian History and Interpretation: Studies Presented to John Knox*, ed. W. R. Farmer et al., pp. 249-68. Cambridge: Cambridge Univ. Press, 1967.

Funk, R. W., et al. *The Parables of Jesus. A Report of the Jesus Seminar*. Sonoma: Polebridge Press, 1988.

Galot, J. "La prima professione di fede cristiana." *Civilta Cattolica* 132 (1981): 27-40.

Gewalt, D. "1 Thess 4,15-17; 1 Kor 15,51 und Mk 9,1—zur Abgrenzung eines 'Herrenwortes.' " *Linguistica Biblica* 51 (1982): 105-13.

Giesen, H. "Naherwartung des Paulus in Thess 4,13-18?" *Studien zum Neuen Testament und seiner Umwelt* 10 (1985): 123-50.

Gillman, J. "Transformation in 1 Cor 15.50-53." *Ephemerides Theologicae Lovanienses* 58 (1982): 309-33.

Glasson, T. F. *Jesus and the End of the World*. Edinburgh: St. Andrews, 1980.

Gowan, D. E. *Eschatology in the Old Testament*. Philadelphia: Fortress Press, 1986.

Gray, J. *The Biblical Doctrine of the Reign of God*. Edinburgh: T. & T. Clark, 1979.

————. "The Day of Yahweh in Cultic Experience and Eschatological Prospect." *Svensk Exegetisk Arsbok* 39 (1974): 5-37.

Guelich, R. A. *The Sermon on the Mount: A Foundation for Understanding*. Waco, Tex.: Word, 1982.

Gundry, R. H. *The Church and the Tribulation. A Biblical Examination of Post-tribulationism*. Grand Rapids: Zondervan, 1973.

————. *SŌMA in Biblical Theology (with emphasis on Pauline anthropology)*. SNTS Monograph 29. Cambridge: Cambridge Univ. Press, 1976.

Hafemann, S. J. *Suffering and Ministry in the Spirit: Paul's Defense of his Ministry in II Corinthians 2:14—3:3*. Grand Rapids: Eerdmans, 1990.

Hanson, A. T. "The Midrash in II Corinthians 3: A Reconsideration," *JSNT* 9 (1980): 2-28.

Harris, M. J. *Raised Immortal: Resurrection and Immortality in the New Testament*. Grand Rapids: Eerdmans, 1985.

Haufe, G. "Reich Gottes bei Paulus und in der Jesustradition." *NTS* 31 (1985): 467-72.

Havener, I. Q. *The Sayings of Jesus*. Wilmington: M. Glazier, 1987.

Hays, R. B. *Echoes of Scripture in the Letters of Paul*. New Haven: Yale Univ. Press, 1989.

Hiers, R. H. "Binding and Loosing: The Matthean Authorizations." *JBL* 104 (1985): 233-50.

Higgins, A. J. B. *The Son of Man in the Sayings of Jesus*. Cambridge: Cambridge Univ. Press, 1980.

Hoffmann, Y. "The Day of the Lord as a Concept and a Term in the Prophetic Literature." *ZAW* 93 (1981): 37-50.

Hooker, M. D. "Trial and Tribulation in Mark XIII." *Bulletin of John Rylands Library* 65 (1982): 78-99.

Horsley, R. A. *The Liberation of Christmas*. New York: Crossroad, 1989.

Hurd, J. C. "The Jesus whom Paul Preaches (Acts 19.13)," in *From Jesus to Paul. Studies in Honour of F. W. Beare*, ed. P. Richardson and J. C. Hurd, pp. 73-89. Waterloo: W. Laurier Press, 1984.

Hurtado, L. *One God, One Lord. Early Christian Devotion and Ancient Jewish Monotheism*. Philadelphia: Fortress, 1988.

Hutton, W. R. "The Kingdom of God Has Come." *ET* 64 (1952-53): 89-91.

Isenberg, S. R. "Millenarism in Greco-Roman Palestine." *Religion* 4 (1974): 26-46.

Jeremias, J. "Ἀδάμ." *TDNT*, 1:141-43.

————. "Eckstein-Schlusstein." *ZNW* 36 (1937): 154-57.

————. "Flesh and Blood Cannot Inherit the Kingdom of God." *NTS* 2 (1955-56): 151-59.

————. *Jesus' Promise to the Nations*. London: SCM Press, 1959.

————. "*Kephalē gonias-Akrogoniaios.*" *ZNW* 29 (1930): 264-80.

————. "κλείς." *TDNT* 3:744-53.

————. *New Testament Theology. The Proclamation of Jesus*. New York: Scribners, 1971.

————. *The Parables of Jesus*. New York: Scribners, 1963.

————. "παράδεισος." *TDNT* 5:765-73.

————. "*The Present Position in the Controversy Concerning the Problem of the Historical Jesus.*" *EvT* 69 (1958): 333-39.

Jewett, R. *The Thessalonian Correspondence. Pauline Rhetoric and Millenarian Piety*. Philadelphia: Fortress Press, 1986.

Johnston, G. "Kingdom of God Sayings in Paul's Letters," in *From Jesus to Paul. Studies in Honour of F. W. Beare*, ed. P. Richardson and J. C. Hurd, pp. 143-56. Waterloo: Wilfred Laurier Univ. Press, 1984.

Juel, D. *Messiah and Temple*. Missoula: Scholars Press, 1977.

Käsemann, E. "Blind Alleys in the Jesus of History Controversy." In *New Testament Questions of Today*, pp. 23-65. London: SCM Press, 1969.

Keck, L. E. "Paul and Apocalyptic Theology." *Int* 38 (1984): 229-41.

Kidder, S. J. "This Generation in Mt. 24.34." *Andrews University Seminary Studies* 21 (1983): 203-9.

Kilpatrick, G. D. "Acts 7.52 *ELEUSIS.*" *JTS* 46 (1945): 136-45.

Kim, S. *The Origin of Paul's Gospel.* Grand Rapids: Eerdmans, 1982.

Klijn, A. F. J. "I Thessalonians 4:13-18 and Its Background in Apocalyptic Literature." In *Paul and Paulinism: Essays in Honor of C. K. Barrett,* ed. M. D. Hooker and S. G. Wilson, pp. 67-73. London: SPCK, 1982.

Knockaert, A. "A Fresh Look at Eschatological Discourse (Mt. 24-25)" *Lumen Vitae* 40 (1985): 167-79.

Kreitzer, L. J. *Jesus and God in Paul's Eschatology.* Sheffield: JSOT Press, 1987.

Kümmel, W. G. *Introduction to the New Testament.* Trans. H. C. Kee. London: SCM, 1975.

_____ . *Promise and Fulfilment. The Eschatological Message of Jesus.* London: SCM Press, 1957.

La Rondelle H. K. "Paul's Prophetic Outline in 2 Thessalonians." *Andrews University Seminary Studies* 21 (1983): 61-69.

Ladd, G. E. *The Blessed Hope.* Grand Rapids: Eerdmans, 1956.

_____ . *The Presence of the Future.* Grand Rapids: Eerdmans, 1974.

_____ . *A Theology of the New Testament.* Grand Rapids: Eerdmans, 1974.

Lambrecht, J. *Die Redaktion der Markus-Apokalypse.* Rome: Pontifical Institute Press, 1967.

Laws, S. "Can Apocalyptic Be Relevant?" In *What About the New Testament? Essays in Honour of Christopher Evans,* ed. M. Hooker and C. Hickling, pp. 89-102. London: SCM Press, 1975.

Leaney, R., E. Ashby and W. Powell. "The Days of the Son of Man (Luke xvii.22)." *ET* 67 (1955-56): 28-29, 124-25, 219.

Lincoln, A. T. "The Church and Israel in Ephesians 2," *CBQ* 49 (1987): 605-24.

_____ . *Paradise Now and Not Yet: Studies in the Role of the Heavenly Dimension in Paul's Thought with Special Reference to His Eschatology.* Cambridge: Cambridge Univ. Press, 1981.

Lohfink, G. *Jesus and Community.* Philadelphia: Fortress Press/Paulist Press, 1984.

Longenecker, R. N. "The Nature of Paul's Early Eschatology." *NTS* 31 (1985): 85-95.

Mackey P. "Paul's Four Windows on the Eschaton." A paper presented at the Midwest regional meeting of the SBL in Pittsburgh. Spring 1990.

McKnight, S. "Jesus and the Endtime: Matthew 10.23." In *SBL Seminar Papers 1986,* pp. 501-20. Atlanta: Scholars Press, 1986.

Malherbe, A. J. "The Beasts of Ephesus," *JBL* 37 (1968): 71-80.

Mantey, J. R. "Distorted Translations in John 20.23; Matthew 16:18-19 and 18:18." *Review and Expositor* 78 (1981): 409-16.

Marcus, J. "Entering into the Kingly Power of God." *JBL* 107 (1988): 663-75.

_____ . "The Gates of Hades and the Keys of the Kingdom (Matt 16:18-19)." *CBQ* 50 (1988): 443-55.

Marshall, I. H. "The Hope of a New Age: the Kingdom of God in the New Testament." *Themelios* 11 (1985): 5-15.

_____ . "The Synoptic Son of Man Sayings in Recent Discussion." *NTS* 12 (1965-66): 327-51.

Martyn J. L. "Apocalyptic Antinomies in Paul's Letters to the Galatians." *NTS* 31 (1985): 410-24.

Mattern, L. *Das Verständnis des Gerichtes bei Paulus.* Zürich/Stuttgart: Zwingli Verlag, 1966.

Mearns, C. L. "Early Eschatological Development in Paul: The Evidence of I and II Thessalonians." *NTS* 27 (1981): 137-58.

Meeks, W. A. *The First Urban Christians. The Social World of the Apostle Paul.* New Haven: Yale Univ. Press, 1983.

Meyer, B. F. *The Aims of Jesus.* London: SCM Press, 1979.

_____ . "Did Paul's View of the Resurrection of the Dead Undergo Development?" *Theological Studies* 47 (1986): 363-87.

Moore, A. L. *The Parousia in the New Testament.* Leiden: Brill, 1966.

Moule, C. F. D. "St. Paul and Dualism: The Pauline Conception of Resurrection." *NTS* 13 (1965-66):

106-23.

Mowinckel, S. *He That Cometh*. Trans. G. W. Anderson. Nashville: Abingdon, 1954.

Mueller, D. "Kingdom of Heaven or Kingdom of God?" *VChr* 27 (1973): 266-76.

Munck, J. *Christ and Israel. An Interpretation of Romans 9—11.* Philadelphia: Fortress, 1967.

Mussner, F. " 'Ganz Israel wird gerettet werden' (Rom 11,26)." *Kairos* 18 (1976): 241-55.

──────. "Wer ist 'dieses Geschlecht' in Mk 13,30 Parr.?" *Kairos* 29 (1987): 23-28.

Nickelsburg, G. W. E. "Enoch, Levi, and Peter: Recipients of Revelation in Upper Galilee." *JBL* 100 (1981): 575-600

──────. *Resurrection, Immortality, and Eternal Life in Intertestamental Judaism.* Cambridge: Harvard Univ. Press, 1972.

Oepke, A. "παρουσία, πάρειμι." *TDNT,* 5:859-65.

O'Donovan, O. *Resurrection and Moral Order: An Outline for Evangelical Ethics.* Grand Rapids: Eerdmans, 1986.

Okeke, G. E. "1 Thessalonians 2:13-16: The Fate of the Unbelieving Jews." *NTS* 27 (1980): 127-36.

Osborne, W. R. "The Old Testament Background of Paul's 'All Israel' in Romans 11:26a." *Asia Journal of Theology* 2 (1988): 282-93.

Pelser G. M. M. "Resurrection and Eschatology in Paul's Letters." *Neotestamentica* 20 (1986): 37-46.

Perrin, N. *Rediscovering the Teaching of Jesus.* New York: Harper & Row, 1967.

Pierson, B. A. "1 Thessalonians 2:13-16: A Deutero-Pauline Interpolation." *HTR* 64 (1971): 79-94.

Plank, K. A. "Resurrection Theology: the Corinthian Controversy Reexamined." *Perpsectives in Religious Studies* 8 (1981): 41-54.

Plevnik, J. "1 Thess. 5.1-11: Its Authenticity, Intention, and Message." *Biblica* 60 (1979): 71-90.

Polag, A. *Die Christologie der Logienquelle.* Neukirchen-Vluyn: Neukirchen Verlag, 1977.

Rad, G. Von. *Old Testament Theology.* Vol. 2. New York: Harper and Row, 1965.

Radermakers, J., and J. P. Sonnet. "Israel et l'Église." *Nouvelle Revue Theologique* 107 (1985): 675-97.

Ramsay, W. M. "The Manifest God." *ET* 10 (1899): 208.

Refoule, F. "Romains X,4. Encore une Fois." *Revue Biblique* 91 (1984): 321-50.

──────. "Notes sur Romains IX,30-33" *Revue Biblique* 92 (1985): 161-86.

Reicke, B. "Synoptic Prophecies on the Destruction of Jerusalem." In *Studies in the New Testament and Early Christian Literature: Essays in Honor of Allen P. Wikgren,* pp. 121-34. Nov. Test. Sup. 33. Leiden: Brill, 1972.

Riches, J. *Jesus and the Transformation of Judaism.* New York: Seabury, 1982.

Ridderbos, H. *Paul: An Outline of His Theology.* Grand Rapids: Eerdmans, 1975.

Riesenfeld, H. *"Emboleuein-Entos."* *Nuntius* 2 (1949): 11-12.

Roberts, C. H. "The Kingdom of Heaven (Lk.xvii.21)." *HTR* 41 (1948): 1-8.

Robinson, B. P. "Peter and His Successors: Tradition and Redaction in Matthew 16.17-19." *JSNT* 21 (1981): 85-104.

Robinson, J. A. T. *The Body: A Study in Pauline Theology.* London: SCM Press, 1952.

Rowland, C. *The Open Heaven: A Study of Apocalyptic in Judaism and Early Christianity.* New York: Crossroad, 1982.

Sanders, E. P. *Jesus and Judaism.* Philadelphia: Fortress Press, 1985.

──────. *Paul and Palestinian Judaism.* London: SCM Press, 1977.

──────. "Paul's Attitude toward the Jewish People." *Union Seminary Quarterly Review* 33 (1978): 175-87.

──────. "Jesus and the Kingdom: The Restoration of Israel and the New People of God." In *Jesus, the Gospels and the Church,* pp. 225-39. Macon: Mercer Univ. Press, 1987.

Schnackenburg, R. "Der eschatologische Abschnitt Lk 17,20-37." Reprinted in his *Schriften zum Neuen Testament.* Munich: Kosel-Verlag, 1971: 220-43.

──────. *God's Rule and Kingdom.* Edinburgh: Nelson, 1963.

Schoeps, H. J. *Paul—The Theology of the Apostle in Light of Jewish Religious History.* Trans. H. Knight. Philadelphia:Westminster Press, 1961.

Schürmann, H. "Zur Traditions—und Redaktionsgeschichte von Mt 10,23." *BZ* 3 (1959): 82-88.

Schweitzer, A. *The Mysticism of Paul the Apostle.* Trans. W. Montgomery. New York: Holt and Co., 1931.

————. *Paul and His Interpreters: A Critical History.* Trans. W. Montgomery. London: A. & C. Black, 1912.

————. *The Quest of the Historical Jesus.* Trans. W. Montgomery. New York: Macmillan, 1961.

Schweizer, E. "The Significance of Eschatology in the Teaching of Jesus," *Eschatology and the New Testament: Essays in Honor of G. R. Beasley-Murray,* pp. 1-13. Peabody, Mass.: Hendrikson, 1988.

Segal, A. "The Cost of Proselytism and Conversion," *SBL Seminar Papers 1988,* pp. 336-69. Atlanta: Scholars Press, 1988.

————. *Paul the Convert: The Apostolate and Apostasy of Saul the Pharisee.* New Haven: Yale Univ. Press, 1990.

Sevenster, J. N. "Some Remarks on the *GUMNOS* in II Cor. v. 3." *Studia Paulina in Honorem Johannis de Zwann.* Haarlem: Bohn, 1953: 202-14.

Sider, R. J. "The Pauline Conception of the Resurrection Body in I Corinthians XV.35-54." *NTS* 21 (1974-75): 428-39.

Sneed, R. J. "The Kingdom of God Is within You (Lk. 17.21)." *CBQ* 24 (1962): 363-82.

Steck, O. H. *Israel und das gewaltsame Geschick der Propheten.* Neukirchen: Neukirchen Verlag, 1967.

Stone, M. "The Concept of the Messiah in IV Ezra." In *Religions in Antiquity: Essays in Memory of E. R. Goodenough,* ed. J. Neusner, pp. 295-312. Leiden: Brill, 1968.

Strecker, G. "The Passion and Resurrection Predictions in Mark's Gospel (Mark 8:31; 9:31; 10:32-34)." *Interpretation* 22 (1968): 421-42.

Theissen, G. *The Miracle Stories of the Early Christian Tradition.* Trans. F. McDonagh. Philadelphia: Fortress Press, 1983.

Thiselton, A. C. "Realized Eschatology at Corinth." *NTS* 24 (1977-78): 510-26.

Trim, K. W. "Paul: Life after Death. An Analysis of I Corinthians 15." *Crux* 14 (1978): 129-50.

Uprichard, R. H. E. "Exposition of I Thessalonians 4:13-18." *Irish Biblical Studies* 1 (1979): 150-56.

Villiers, J. L. de. "The Salvation of Israel according to Romans 9—11." *Neotestamentica* 15 (1981): 199-221.

Vorster, W. S. "Literary Reflection on Mark 13.5-37: A Narrative Speech of Jesus." *Neotestamentica* 21 (1987): 203-24.

Vos, G. *The Pauline Eschatology.* Grand Rapids: Eerdmans, 1972 rpr.

Wagner, G. "The Future of Israel: Reflections on Romans 9—11." In *Eschatology and the New Testament,* ed. W. H. Gloer, pp. 77-112. Peabody: Hendrickson, 1988.

Wallis, W. B. "The Problem of an Intermediate Kingdom in I Corinthians 15.20-28." *JETS* 18 (1975): 229-42.

Walter, N. "Paul and the Early Christian Jesus-Tradition." In *Paul and Jesus: Collected Essays,* ed. A. J.M. Wedderburn, pp. 51-80. Sheffield: JSOT Press, 1989.

Wanamaker, C. A. "Apocalypticism at Thessalonica." *Neotestamentica* 21 (1987): 1-10.

Ware, P. "The Coming of the Lord: Eschatology and I Thessalonians." *Restoration Quarterly* 22 (1979): 109-20.

Wedderburn, A. J. M. "Paul and Jesus: the Problem of Continuity." In *Paul and Jesus: Collected Essays,* ed. A. J. M. Wedderburn, pp. 99-115. Sheffield: JSOT Press, 1989.

————. "The Problem of the Denial of the Resurrection in I Corinthians XV." *Novum Testamentum* 23 (1981): 229-41.

Wenham, D. "Paul and the Synoptic Apocalypse." In *Gospel Perspectives: Studies of History and Tradition in the Four Gospels,* 2:345-75. Sheffield: JSOT, 1981.

————. *The Rediscovery of Jesus' Eschatological Discourse.* Sheffield: JSOT Press, 1984.

Whiteley, D. E. H. *The Theology of St. Paul.* Philadelphia: Fortress, 1972.

Wikgren, A. *"Entos." Nuntius* 4 (1950): 27-28.

Wilson, S. G. "From Jesus to Paul: The Contours and Consequences of a Debate." In *From Jesus to Paul: Studies in Honour of F. W. Beare,* ed. P. Richardson and J. C. Hurd, pp. 1-21. Waterloo: W. Laurier U. Press, 1984.

Witherington, B. *The Christology of Jesus.* Minneapolis: 1990.

————. *Women in the Earliest Churches.* Cambridge: Cambridge Univ. Press, 1988.

————. *Women in the Ministry of Jesus.* Cambridge: Cambridge Univ. Press, 1984.

Yoder, J. H. "Armaments and Eschatology." *Studies in Christian Ethics: Ethics and Ecumenism.* 1.1 (1988): 43-61.

Index of Scripture and Other Ancient Literature